American
Frontier Activities
in Asia

American Frontier Activities in Asia

U.S.–Asian Relations in the Twentieth Century

YOUNG HUM KIM, Professor

History and International Relations
U.S. International University

Nelson-Hall nh Chicago

To Susan

Library of Congress Cataloging in Publication Data

Kim, Young Hum.
American frontier activities in Asia.

    Bibliography: p.
    Includes index.
    1. Asia—Foreign relations—United States.
2. United States—Foreign relations—Asia.
3. Asia—History—20th century.   I. Title.
DS33.4.U6K5   327.7305   81–3989
ISBN 0–88229–707–4 (cloth)   AACR2
ISBN 0–88229–789–9 (paper)

Manufactured in the United States of America

10 9 8 7 6 5 4 3 2 1

Contents

Preface

In 1976 the United States of America celebrated the two-hundredth anniversary of her independence. This is a nation which, conceived in Laws of Nature, delivered in Liberty, dedicated to Equality and Justice, and matured in the pursuit of Happiness, has grown to be the wealthiest and the mightiest commonwealth on earth.

America's bicentennial history is characterized by its ever-expanding frontier from the eastern seaboard, across the vast untamed continent westward, to the shores of the Pacific and beyond. Included in the frontier activities were: governmental and private exploration; Indian-pioneer contacts including missions and trade; mining, fur trade, and the gold rush; wars with Indians and Mexicans; lacing the nation with railroads; farming, ranching, and homestead settlements. Thus, the frontier experience is the principal theme of American national life. Americans came to identify their liberty with their free movement to new and uncharted frontiers. They came to believe that their freedom coincided with their new acquisition of *free* land—notwithstanding whoever happened to occupy it.

After the completion of the Westward Movement in North America and after the continental consolidation within the Union, the American frontier was pushed across the Pacific to Asia. The United States sought and received trading privileges in China, opened up Japan from its feudal isolation, and then, in 1898, acquired the Philippines as her colony at the end of the Spanish-American War.

Beginning with the territorial acquisition of the Philippines, this book examines America's frontier activities in Asia during the past fourscore years.

At the time when the United States first set her footing in Asian soil as an Asian power, the Asians themselves were in the midst of political, social, economic, and ideological changes. These changes, described as Westernization and Modernization, undoubtedly brought about by the penetrating influence of the West, constituted the balancing force for and against America's frontier spirit and action in Asia. The American dream and desire to *Christianize* the pagans, to implant the cherished concepts of liberty and democracy in the minds of Asians, and to enable them to pursue happiness in their lives by trade and *commerce* ran frequently into stubborn resistance. And whenever resistance was presented, the United States attempted either to elicit *cooperation* where possible or to use *coercion* if necessary to overcome it. In this way, Christianity, commerce, cooperation and coercion became the four pillars of the United States Asian policy. They were the guiding principles for governmental as well as private activities in Asian frontiers.

Eighty years in the history of a nation is ephemeral by any standard. Yet, those eighty years of United States-Asian relations are filled with bittersweet experiences of conflict and cooperation, success and failure, war and peace, glory and disaster, hope and frustration. Specifically, some of the highlights of American frontier activities in Asia include: the enunciation of the Open Door policy; the participation in quelling the Boxer Rebellion and in the making of the Boxer protocol; the exercise of gunboat diplomacy, dollar diplomacy, and railroad diplomacy; conclusion of disarmament agreements in the Pacific region; the declaration of the Stimson Doctrine; the defeat and occupation of Japan; the Korean and Vietnam wars.

Unfortunately, more often than not, American failure and frustration were construed to be success and satisfaction to those Asians involved; and vice versa. Now is the time for both American and

Asian peoples to come to realize the importance of accentuating the positive in their relations and to find more common grounds—common frontiers—in search for, and in fulfillment of, their common interests. In this respect, it is hoped that this book will serve to provide some basic background knowledge for the future.

The lay reader as well as the non-Asian student interested in the study of Asia is often confused and lost in the maze of strange names of persons and places, seemingly unrelated historical facts and events, and fragmentary occurrences and phenomena. This book, therefore, is written in a simple, lucid style to help readers better understand the history of American-Asian relations since the beginning of this century. Oriental personal names are given with the family name first.

This book will be found useful as a classroom or supplementary text for such college courses as Modern East Asian History, Contemporary United States-Asian Diplomacy, United States Foreign Policy in Asia, and Contemporary International Relations in East and Southeast Asia.

A few words of acknowledgment are in order. I owe so much to my wife, Susan, who assisted me in every way conceivable. To elaborate further on her help would be redundant. I am indebted to many of my academic colleagues and to scholars whose works on East Asia and American foreign policy have provided me with a challenge and inspiration. I regret that I cannot acknowledge them here individually. I am grateful to my secretary, Mrs. Elizabeth Krauss, who typed the draft, to Teresa Evert for her unselfish services in the final preparation of the manuscript, and to Sherry Beyersdorf and Linda Ladislaus whose assistance proved valuable.

CHAPTER ONE

Manifest Destiny Across the Pacific

Acquisition of the Philippines

The McKinley Decision

The year 1898 signaled the introduction of the United States as a bona fide Asian power by virtue of America's acquisition of the Philippines. It heralded the opening of a brave new chapter in the history of American involvement in Asia. In terms of political importance and historic significance, this event surpassed the signing of the Treaty of Wanghia with China in 1844 (the first U.S.-China treaty for commerce and trade) and the opening of Japan by Commodore Perry in 1853.

When the Paris conference was launched on October 1, 1898, to settle the Spanish-American War, there were two items of prime importance on the agenda: the Cuban problems and the Philippine issue. As to the former, after a month of negotiation the Spanish government agreed to relinquish its sovereignty over Cuba and assume responsibility for the Cuban debt of about $400 million, whereas the United States government agreed to occupy the island until the Cubans could establish a self-government.

As for the question of the Philippines, the peace negotiators found the issue thornier and larger than they could handle because

1

the United States initially did not know what it wanted to do with the islands, and a policy thereon would have to be made by the highest authority in Washington.

President McKinley was confronted with the task of making a decision on the fate of the Philippines. Heeding the mood of the nation, he had to steer the ship of presidential leadership through a delicate course between the Scylla of the isolationist argument to give the Filipinos the right to self-government, and the Charybdis of imperialist demands to shoulder the "White Man's Burden" of a "Civilizing Mission" in the Philippines. He is reported to have said that "if old Dewey had just sailed away when he smashed that Spanish fleet, what a lot of trouble he would have saved us." What he considered "a lot of trouble" were the numerous presidential alternatives the situation initially yielded. At first he was thinking only of a coaling station in the Philippines. Then, he decided to take at least the island of Luzon which includes Manila. But, if the United States occupied only one island, the greedy rival powers might seize the rest, rendering the American possession strategically impotent. To McKinley, returning the Filipinos to Spanish rule was unthinkable, and granting the islanders immediate independence was unwise. The choice, therefore, was between taking all or taking none. There were no acceptable, middle ground alternatives.

McKinley later dramatized the process of how he reached the final decision in the following words:

> The truth is I didn't want the Philippines and when they came to us a gift from the gods, I did not know what to do about them. . . . I sought counsel from all sides—Democrats as well as Republicans—but got little help. I thought first we would take only Manila; then Luzon; then other islands, perhaps, also. I walked the floor of the White House night after night until midnight; and I am not ashamed to tell you, gentlemen, that I went down on my knees and prayed Almighty God for light and guidance more than one night. And one night late it came to me this way—I don't know how it was, but it came: (1) that we could not give them back to Spain—that would be cowardly and dishonorable; (2) that we could not turn

them over to France or Germany—our *commercial* rivals in the Orient—that would be bad business and discreditable; (3) that we could not leave them to themselves—they were unfit for self-government—and they would soon have anarchy and misrule over there worse than Spain's was; and (4) that there was nothing left for us to do but to take them all, and to educate the Filipinos, and uplift and civilize and *Christianize* them, and by God's grace do the very best we could by them as our fellow-men for whom Christ also died. And then I went to bed, and went to sleep soundly.[1] (author's italics)

Divine guidance or not, in the realm of practical politics President McKinley must have listened to the voice of the people. His eventful decision was made on the basis of three vital considerations: (1) the politico-military milieu in Asia, (2) economic-commercial motives, and (3) the moral-religious impetus. These were the three pillars of United States Asian policy, each of which is briefly analyzed as follows:

The United States could have given the Filipinos their right to self-government and independence. But the assumption was that through the centuries of Spanish control, they were neither trained nor given the opportunity to practice the art of self-rule. Immediate independence, therefore, would degenerate into social disorder and political chaos, which certainly would invite external intervention by major imperialist powers. Well-intentioned but ill-conceived policy might plunge the islands into the center of gunboat diplomacy, imperial rivalry, colonial expansion, and world power politics. In May 1898, when Dewey's naval victory in Manila Bay rang out, Senator Henry Cabot Lodge, one of the most staunch advocates of American imperialism, had written Henry White that "we must on no account let the islands go, . . . they must be ours under the treaty of peace, . . . the American flag is up and it must stay. . . . We hold the other side of the Pacific and the value to this country is almost beyond imagination."[2] The question, then, was no longer between Philippine independence or American imperialism, but whether ruthless colonial powers or the "humanitarian" United States should take possession of the islands.

The imperialist powers were scrambling for concessions in China, and American business circles became apprehensive that they might be excluded from the potentially vast market. The annexation of the Philippines by the United States would not only constitute an effective counterweight against advantages gained by the aggressive powers, but also should prove a valuable staging area for American businessmen in their commercial activities in Asia. "Memorials poured in upon the State Department from business groups and chambers of commerce all over the country, urging the value of the archipelago to the United States, especially as the key to the markets of Eastern Asia."[3] They also emphasized the value of the islands' natural resources, especially tobacco, hemp, wood, coffee, sugarcane, and cheap labor, all of which would unquestionably benefit American commerce. Senator Mark Hanna, a close personal friend of President McKinley, said, "If it is commercialism to want the possession of a strategic point giving the American people an opportunity to maintain a foothold in the markets of that great Eastern country, for God's sake let us have commercialism."[4]

In the same vein, Albert J. Beveridge, a gifted orator who was later elected to the United States Senate, roared, "We must find new markets for our produce, new occupation for our capital, new work for our labor. And so, while we did not need the territory taken during the past century at the time it was acquired, we do need what we have taken in 1898, and we need it now."[5]

The church element in the United States was likewise inspired. During the Spanish rule the Roman Catholic missionaries had enjoyed their success in the Philippines, but to American Protestants, who had long been active in China, Korea, and Japan, an annexation of the islands would open a new mission field to spread the gospel to the "little brown brother." Churches of all denominations without exception came out fervently in favor of Philippine annexation. "Manila stretches out her torn and bleeding hands," appealed a clergyman, "and we must clasp them and accept our work of redemption, not as a piece of political ambition, but as a mission we have from God." "Every American missionary in Asia from whom I have heard in recent months," wrote another, "has thanked God that the American flag has entered the Far East." And the First Lady was reported to have been deeply concerned about "converting the Igorots." It was in this climate that the Philippines became American territory and the United States achieved a partial fulfillment of the American idea of "Manifest Destiny." Over half a century earlier, in 1845, at the height of American expansion in the North American continent, in the *New York Morning News,* John L. O'Sullivan declared "the right of our manifest destiny to overspread and to possess the whole of the continent which Providence has given us for the development of the great experiment in liberty and federative self-government entrusted to us." He further asserted that United States territorial expansion should not be confined to the continent of North America: "Its floor be as a hemisphere—its roof the firmament of the star-studded heavens, and its congregation a Union of happy millions ... governed by God's natural law and moral law of equality."[6] Thus, America's westward movement, or its *rendezvous* with destiny, outstretched beyond the edge of the West Coast and reached over the horizon of the Pacific to seize Hawaii, Midway, Guam, and the Philippines.

Opposition Forces

It should be pointed out that the road of American imperialism to Manila was not so smooth and easy as it appeared to be. There were formidable anti-imperialist forces in Congress and in the country. They waged a losing battle against American annexation of the Philippines. Senator George F. Hoar of Massachusetts, a leading opponent of the treaty, had declared that McKinley's Philippine policy was repugnant to the American ideals of liberty, equality, and justice, and contrary to the principles of the Declaration of Independence. Joining him were such other prominent leaders as senators Hale of Maine, Pettigrew of South Dakota, and Thomas B. Reed, Speaker of the House. They warned that the colonial possession in Asia would engulf the United States in the throes of never-ending Far Eastern power politics, that it would necessitate an establishment of a strong armed force which would place a heavy burden of taxation on the people and at the same time stimulate the rise of militarism, and that exploitation and tyranny abroad would return home to rest, breeding the same kind of oppression and tyranny in the United States.

The anti-imperialists argued further that the imperialist course of American policy would ignore Washington's farewell warning against foreign entanglement, would violate the nonintervention principle embedded in the Monroe Doctrine, and would make a mockery out of the Emancipation Proclamation. Pointing to the fallacies of the imperialists, Professor William G. Sumner of Yale stated:

There is not a civilized nation which does not talk about its civilizing mission just as grandly as we do. . . . We assume that what we think better, must come as a welcome blessing to Spanish-Americans and Filipinos. This is grossly and obviously untrue. They hate our ways. They are hostile to our ideas. Our religion, language, institutions, and manners offend them. They like their own ways, and if we appear amongst them as rulers, there will be social discord in all the great departments of social interest. . . . If we believe in liberty, as an American principle, why do we not stand by it? Why are we going to throw it away to enter upon a Spanish policy of dominion and regulation?[7]

Many Americans who were opposed to annexation conducted a series of great debates on American foreign policy and formed a number of anti-imperialist leagues in major cities of the nation. Spearheading this movement were such distinguished and influential leaders of industry, labor, intellectual and literary communities as Andrew Carnegie, Samuel Gompers, Charles W. Eliot (Harvard president), David Starr Jordan (Stanford president), William James, Mark Twain, and Hamlin Garland.

Their gallant efforts were in the end drowned in the newly rising sentiment of America's glory and greatness, courage and confidence. The national psyche of imperialistic aspirations and ambitions had launched the United States into the turbulent waters of the Far Pacific, from which neither destiny nor design seemed capable of extricating it for generations to come.

The United States, a full-fledged Asian power with the Philippines in its dominion, was immediately confronted with three critical issues—the Philippine insurrection, power rivalries in China, and the Boxer Rebellion.

The Philippine Insurrection

In the last days of Spanish colonial rule, the Philippines produced a number of indigenous revolutionary patriots such as Andrés Bonifacio, José Rizal, and Emilio Aguinaldo. In July 1892, a secret society known as the Katipunan was founded in Manila with two specific objectives: to unite all Filipinos and to win national independence. In July 1896, for the purpose of discussing a plan for a revolution, the leaders of the Katipunan, including Bonifacio, got in contact with Rizal, a young, brilliant nationalist with recognized ability as a poet, writer, sculptor, and physician. Rizal thought a revolution was premature. But events took an unexpected course. The Spanish authorities discovered the existence of the Katipunan and its revolutionary plan and, as they attempted to apprehend its leaders, fighting broke out. Soon a nationwide rebellion against the Spaniards flared up. A reign of terror ensued. Bonifacio took refuge in the hills of northern Luzon, but José Rizal was arrested, tried on charges of rebellion, sedition, and illicit association, and in December 1896 was executed before a firing squad. His death added fury to the revolution. But in the face of ruthless suppression and the continued reinforcement of government forces, the rebellion began to collapse. The main insurrection in the Cavite region led by Emilio Aguinaldo was likewise weakened. He, nevertheless, carried on his fight, and, in March 1897, a revolutionary assembly elected him president of the Philippine Republic. His revolutionaries were, however, unable to defeat the better-equipped Spanish forces, nor could they dislodge their colonial rulers. Skirmishes continued until December 1897, when the so-called Pact of Biacnabato was reached, whereby the revolution was to cease and its leaders were to go into voluntary exile in Hong Kong. Thus Aguinaldo landed on Hong Kong.

When Commodore George Dewey smashed the feeble Spanish fleet in Manila Bay on May 1, 1898, he was unable to land adequate forces to capture the city. Dewey then made contact with Aguinaldo in Hong Kong and brought the exiled leader home to head another nationalist revolution against the Spaniards. The reward for such cooperation with the United States was the promise of independence for the Philippines.[8] Within a few weeks, all of Luzon, except Manila, fell into the hands of Aguinaldo's forces, and on June 12, 1898, Filipino independence was solemnly declared. Aguinaldo was once again named president of the revolutionary government. Manila fell on August 13, 1898, as the Spanish governor-general surrendered to the United States high command by a prearranged ruse that kept Aguinaldo's army out of the city. This was the first of a series of events which led to American annexation of the islands and to the denial of Filipino independence. The fate of the Filipinos and their independence were to be determined by Spaniards and Americans. Even Aguinaldo's envoy was denied entrance to the Paris Conference.

As the Filipinos came to realize that they were merely going to exchange Spanish for American overlords, they rose in rebellion on February 4, 1899. The leader of this revolt was Aguinaldo, who felt betrayed by the Americans. He had at times as many as seventy thousand men under his command, and the United States sent about the same number of troops to crush the revolt. By the end of the year, large-scale organized battle engagements dissipated, but a more deadly guerrilla warfare continued. Both sides resorted to means and tactics intolerable to a civilized mind. The frustrated American soldiers expressed their sentiment toward their foes in an Army song:

> Damn, damn the Filippines
> Pock-marked Khakiac ladrone:
> Underneath the starry flag
> Civilize him with a Krag,
> And return us to our beloved home.

The national mood in 1899 was depicted by the *New York World*:

> We've taken up the white man's burden
> Of ebony and brown;
> Now will you kindly tell us, Rudyard,
> How we may put it down?

The war divided the nation into bitter factions. On the one hand, there were those who condemned American repression for "bringing disgrace upon the American name and civilization," and on the other hand, there were those who insisted that the United States should press on to victory in the name of national prestige and honor, claiming that protestations in the country were giving "aid and comfort" to the enemy and prolonging the war.

The military struggle in the Philippine jungles turned in America's favor in March 1901, when Aguinaldo was captured by General Frederick Funston, who successfully lured him into a trap by the use of his native enemies and forged documents.[9] With their leader made a prisoner, the guerrillas became disheartened and their operations became less effective, and in the summer of 1902 the guerrilla warfare was ended.

Entering the Door of China

Power Rivalries in China

The defeat of China in the Sino-Japanese War, 1894–95, proved beyond a doubt that China had been a "paper tiger" rather than a "sleeping dragon" as had been widely believed. In 1896 Russia acquired the rights to build the Chinese Eastern Railway across Manchuria as a shortcut for the Trans-Siberian route to Vladivostok. Two years later the so-called scramble for concessions by the European powers began in China. The empress dowager lamented, "the various powers cast upon us looks of tiger-like voracity, hustling each other in their endeavors to be the first to seize upon our innermost territories."

Germany was deeply concerned with developments in East Asia, especially Russia's growing interests in Korea, and in early 1897 expressed her plan to establish a naval base in China. In November of that year two German missionary priests were murdered in Shantung. In this incident Germany found a justifiable reason to land her troops, and they seized the port of Tsingtao. Sino-German negotiations which followed brought about the signing of the Kiaochow Convention in March 1898.[10] Germany thus acquired by lease the Kiaochow Bay for a term of ninety-nine years as well as railway and mining concessions in Shantung.

The occupation of Kiaochow by Germany offered a favorable occasion for Russia to seize one of the Chinese ports, notably Port Arthur and the adjacent Dairen Bay. Russia immediately dispatched war vessels to that area and demanded that China cede not only the port and bay but also the Liaotung Peninsula.[11] At first the Chinese government was reluctant to comply with the Russian demands, but in March 1898 it signed two conventions, at Peking and at St. Petersburg, granting Russia by lease the two ports and their adjacent waters and islands for a period of twenty-five years.

Two weeks after the Russian occupation of Port Arthur and Dairen Bay, the French Minister at Peking informed his government that China had agreed to lease to France for ninety-nine years Kwangchow Bay with its dependencies. At the same time, France was given both the right to build railroads in Yunan Province and the assurance that China would not cede to any other power all or part of the provinces bordering on Tongking. A year earlier France had demanded that China not "alienate or cede the island of Hainan to any other foreign power, either as final or temporary cession, or as a naval station or coaling depot"; with this demand China had complied.

British policy from the time of the Treaty of Nanking in 1842 had been one of equal opportunities for all. Britain was opposed both to the disintegration of the Chinese Empire and to any dominant position of a single power in that country. In view of the increasing ascendancy of Russia, therefore, the British government had to obtain in July 1898 a lease of Weihaiwei and the adjacent waters "for as long a period as Port Arthur shall remain in the occupation of Russia."[12] In addition, Britain secured from China (1) an assurance of nonalienation to any power of the provinces adjoining the Yangtze River, (2) a promise to place a British subject in the post of inspector-general of Customs and Posts so long as British trade enjoyed predominancy, and (3) a lease for ninety-nine years of the whole of the Kowloon Peninsula together with other islands nearby.

Finally, Japan established her sphere of interest in Fukien Province across from Formosa. Only Italy's demand for a sphere was refused.

The Open Door Policy

Against this background, President McKinley, influenced by the military branch of his government, was initially prepared to share in the partition of China in case the dismemberment of the Manchu Empire was actually to take place. In his annual message to Congress in December 1898, President McKinley declared:

> The United States has not been an indifferent spectator of the extraordinary events transpiring in the Chinese Empire, whereby portions of its maritime provinces are passing under the control of various European powers; but the prospect that the vast commerce which the energy of our citizens and the necessity of our staple productions for Chinese uses has built up in those regions may not be prejudiced through any exclusive treatment by the new occupants has obviated the need of our country becoming an actor in the scene. Our position among nations, having a large Pacific coast and a constantly expanding direct trade with the farther Orient, gives us the *equitable claim* to consideration and friendly treatment in this regard, and it will be my aim to subserve our large interests in that quarter by *all means* appropriate to the constant policy of our Government.[13]

But the appointment of John Hay, an able, experienced diplomat, as secretary of state restored the ascendancy of diplomacy over military intervention. The president also came around to endorse Hay's handling of foreign affairs. One of the more widely known foreign policies John Hay pursued was that of the Open Door in China.

The enunciation of the Open Door was influenced by two principal factors. First, as the result of the scramble for concessions in which the British acquired a lion's share, Britain felt that her interests in the Far East in general, and those in China in particular, were threatened by political rivals and economic competitors. Her position became untenable in upholding the integrity of China as a means to prevent further deterioration of the situation. Since the 1840s, especially after the Opium War, Britain played the leading part in the economic exploitation of China. By 1894, 65 percent of China's total foreign trade was transacted with Britain. In an effort to protect her lucrative China trade from the encroachment of other powers, Britain had to formulate a new and more effective method of safeguarding the territorial integrity of China. The British hoped that rival powers might be persuaded to open their spheres of influence and leaseholds to British commerce on the most-favored-nation clause, or an open door principle. Britain extended to Russia the first feeler for an alliance. When this overture was spurned, she turned to the United States.

At this juncture, the choice before the United States was either independent action or cooperation with Britain. Independent action, regardless of its intent and purpose, might prove to be abrasive to other powers and cause them to clam up their spheres to the total exclusion of American commercial participation. Or, to reject an alliance without offering any alternatives would be a purely negative policy which would contribute nothing constructive to the existing problems. Yet twice in 1898–99, the United States eschewed the British proposal of a cooperative arrangement to insure equal commercial opportunity in China. Such an alliance was believed to be contrary to American traditions of nonalignment. But the United States seemed to have undergone a change of heart. She came to realize that political reality and national interest made it imperative for the United States to cooperate with Britain to keep China open.

Second, perhaps more important, the United States had to devise a most efficacious policy to safeguard American commercial interests in China. Since the signing of the Wanghia Treaty of 1844, the United States had been enjoying the same commercial and extraterritorial privileges which were granted to other powers. Now with the annexation of the Philippines, American interests in China trade as well as strategic concern in the Western Pacific vastly accelerated. The "vivisection" of China into protectorates, spheres of influence, and the foreign concessions seemed to jeopardize American trade and commerce with China. Although relatively small—about 2 percent of the nation's total—America's China trade was rapidly growing in volume. American businessmen were concerned and worried that their hopes and prospects might be dashed if the other selfish powers should impose prohibitively high tariffs or create other forms of restrictions and barriers within their respective spheres of influence. They pressed Secretary Hay to act.

In formulating a new China policy, Secretary Hay solicited the advice and recommendations of William W. Rockhill, an explorer-writer-diplomat, who was regarded as one of the best-informed authorities on China in his generation. Rockhill, in turn, consulted his lifelong friend, Alfred E. Hippisley, for ideas and suggestions. Hippisley was a British subject, a fellow resident in China, an expert on Chinese affairs, and a former commissioner of the Chinese Imperial Maritime Customs Service.[14] Through the late summer of 1899, Rockhill and Hippisley, working with Secretary Hay, hammered out a memorandum which eventually became United States official policy. The Open Door was born—conceived by the British and delivered by the Americans.

The first Open Door note, as sent out on September 6, 1899, to Germany, England, and Russia, and later to Japan, Italy, and France, contained the following key points:

1. That it will in no way interfere with any treaty port of any vested interest within any so-called sphere of interest or leased territory it may have in China.

2. That the Chinese treaty tariff of the time being shall apply to all merchandise landed or shipped to all such ports as are within said "sphere of interest" (unless they be "free ports") no matter to what nationality it may belong, and that duties so leviable shall be collected by the Chinese government.

3. That it will levy no higher harbor dues on vessels of another nationality frequenting any such port in such "sphere" than shall be levied on vessels of its own nationality, and no higher railroad charges over lines built, controlled, or operated within its "sphere" than shall be levied on similar merchandise belonging to its own nationals transported over equal distances.[15]

The initial Open Door policy, in essence, was designed to preserve and strengthen American commercial interests in China by restraining the powers from rigid compartmentalization of their respective spheres of interest and influence. It attempted neither to safeguard the territorial integrity of China nor to abolish the spheres of interest. It was not a new policy, but only a restatement of the most-favored-nation principle; it sought to establish within the spheres nondiscriminatory commercial treatment, noninterference with the treaty ports, and nonimpediment of the collection of Chinese customs duties. The Open Door was then a manifestation of America's demand for equal opportunity for commerce rather than a recognition of China's claim for the total sovereign right of independence.

As applied to China, it was the Monroe Doctrine in reverse. To the Chinese it was difficult to understand that the country which had passed the Dingley Tariff Act would proclaim the pious principle of the Open Door, that the government which had enacted the Chinese exclusion legislation would preach the brotherhood of man and equal opportunity for all, and that the nation which had rejected European intervention in the western hemisphere would actively carry on "dollar diplomacy" in the Far East.

The powers received the Open Door note with mixed feelings and responded to it with little enthusiasm. Only Italy, who had no sphere in China, fully accepted Hay's principles. Neither Russia, Germany, nor France expressed any intention of relinquishing the exclusive privileges in exploitation and development demanded of their subjects in their spheres of interest. Russia, maintaining that the question of customs duties should be settled by the Chinese themselves, evasively replied that she had never claimed any special privileges in China to the exclusion of interests of other powers; Germany declared that she had been, in fact, carrying out absolute equality of treatment of all nations regarding trade, commerce, and navigation; and France declared that she had advocated equal treatment of all nationals, especially with respect to customs duties, navigation dues, and transportation tariffs on railroads. Japan's response was evasive with a lukewarm approval, but she agreed to accede to Hay's suggestions if the other powers did likewise. Great Britain readily assented, but with reservations regarding the leased territory of Kowloon.

What did the Open Door policy accomplish at this stage? Perhaps it did serve to avert the immediate partition of China since the powers gave their assent, no matter how reluctantly, to the general principle of the Hay notes. On March 20, 1900, Secretary Hay had announced that the assent of all the powers was "final and definitive" in maintaining the Open Door.

The Boxer Rebellion and Protocol

The incipient Open Door policy, with its precarious "final and definitive" assent of the powers, was to undergo a second phase of metamorphosis. The occasion was presented in June 1900, with the outbreak of the Boxer Rebellion in China.

The Boxers,[16] initially not without antigovernment sentiment because of the Manchu inability to protect the country, began to react violently to what they considered to be the main source of national woes—foreigners. The rebellion took the form of mounting hatred against foreigners who had been infringing upon Chinese sovereignty and against what the Boxers called "the secondary devils"—the Chinese converts who were believed to be "tainted with foreign poison." According to Li Hung-chang, a prominent Chinese soldier-diplomat, it "was due to the deep-seated hatred of the Chinese people towards foreigners. China had been oppressed, trampled upon, coerced, cajoled, her territory taken, and her usages flouted."[17]

The Chinese, especially the Boxers, believed that the foreigners came to China with strange customs, habits, and religions, subverted the age-old Chinese beliefs, disparaged Confucianism, and derided Buddhism. They carved off ports, harbors, bays, territories, established spheres of interests, and seized mining and railway rights at the expense of China's autonomy and sovereignty. The Chinese had long been subject to their constant aggression and unceasing insults.

The Boxers rampaged in the destruction of railroads, churches, communications, and lives. On June 20, 1900, the German envoy, Baron von Ketteler, was murdered on his way to the Chinese foreign office by a Manchu bannerman. This murder horrified diplomatic circles and the foreign communities in Peking. Barricaded in their legations for protection and convinced of the unreliability of the imperial authorities, the foreigners had no thought of leaving Peking under any form of Chinese escort. From this time the safety of nearly one thousand foreign civilians and legation guards, and several thousands of Chinese converts, was constantly threatened, not only by the Boxers but also by Chinese Imperial troops.

Alarmed by the critical situation, the Western powers, along with Japan, organized the international expeditionary forces which landed in Tientsin and fought their way through to Peking. The United States dispatched some twenty-five hundred troops from the Philippines. The purposes of the joint expedition were to protect the lives and property of their nationals and to punish the Chinese government.

It was quite apparent to Secretary Hay from the outset that the uprising had provided the powers with certain "opportune" pretexts for expanding and consolidating their spheres of influence in China. The imperialist powers might brush the Open Door into the dustbin. Hay sensed an urgent need to redefine American policy. On July 3, 1900, with presidential approval, he dispatched to the powers another circular note.

Reaffirming the right of the United States to protect "lives and property of our citizens by all means guaranteed under extraterritorial treaty rights," Hay in his circular set forth the purpose of his government to "act concurrently with the other powers" in restoring order and guarding "all legitimate American interests." Perhaps the most significant aspect of this circular was the addition of a new momentous objective:

> The policy of the government of the United States is to seek a solution which may bring about permanent safety and peace to China, preserve *Chinese territorial and administrative entity,* protect all rights guaranteed to friendly powers by treaty and international law, and safeguard for the world the principle of equal and impartial trade with all parts of the Chinese Empire.[18] (Author's italics)

Secretary Hay seemed to have concluded that the Open Door principle could not be effectively maintained unless China herself could exercise her complete sovereignty over all her territories. It should be recalled that the original Open Door note sought to safeguard equal opportunity for commerce within the spheres of influence and foreign leaseholds. Now, in this July circular containing what might be called an "Open Door corollary," Hay stepped farther into the Open Door and proclaimed that the United States would preserve the Chinese territorial and administrative entity. Thus, he implicitly suggested to other powers that they follow America's lead. It could be regarded as a warning shot to the powers against what eventual fate might fall upon China after the rebellion, namely, a complete partition of China by the predatory powers. The Hay circular was a unilateral declaration of American policy and did not solicit any "assurance" from the powers, as did the September note of 1899. The powers proceeded in a business-as-usual manner with their independent designs for obtaining maximum advantages from China. Russia, for instance, continued to pour troops into Manchuria to consolidate her position. Britain, having no faith in the Hay policy, moved to protect her interests through a series of bilateral agreements with her rivals. Indeed, China escaped mortal dismemberment, not because of Hay's Open Door notes, but because of a political stalemate among the powers.

With the suppression of the Boxers and the fall of Peking into the hands of the international army, the powers embarked upon the task of drawing up the terms of peace and punitive measures. The United States policy was, as expressed by Secretary Hay,

> ... to limit as far as possible our military operations in China, to withdraw our troops at the earliest day consistent with our obligations and in the final adjustment to do everything we can for the integrity and reform of China, and to hold on like grim death to the Open Door.[19]

The United States, supported by Russia, was opposed to the German proposal that the Western powers should have the sole right to designate, as well as execute, the guilty. The American-

Russian stand prevailed, and the execution of penalties was carried out by the Chinese government. But the American opposition to further punitive expeditions after the fall of Peking was not successful. Some of the European powers exhibited to the Chinese the worst phases of their characters. "The soldiers have committed atrocities beyond description, and the Ministers of their nationals are all engaged in looting. . . . Right and reason disappear, and we return to the ethics of the Dark Ages. To an outsider it is all very sad and shows utter demoralization."[20]

The United States proposal regarding the assessment of the indemnity likewise failed, although it had a modifying effect upon the excessive demands presented by some powers. Jealousy, greed, distrust, and self-interest were the rule during the negotiations among the powers. The United States was no exception. Under pressure from the military, Secretary Hay on this late date tried to join the rank of imperialist powers by gaining a territorial concession from China. The professed champion for the preservation of Chinese territorial and administrative integrity, Hay, still outwardly loyal to his Open Door policy, dispatched the following telegram to American minister Alfred E. Buck in Tokyo on December 7, 1900:[21]

> The Navy greatly desires a coaling station at Samsah Inlet north of Fuchow. Ascertain informally and discreetly whether Japanese Government would see any objection to our negotiating for this with China.

Japan had to be consulted, for Samsah Bay was located in Fukien Province which had already been preempted as the Japanese sphere of influence. Japan gently and diplomatically admonished Secretary Hay by stating that the declared end of the United States "to preserve the territorial entity" of China would be "best attained by those Powers which entertain similar views refraining from accepting any advantages which might give other Powers a pretext for territorial demands."[22] It must have been both embarrassing and disappointing for Hay to read the Japanese reply.

America's territorial design for Samsah Bay was a behind-the-scenes sideshow, so to speak. The Boxer negotiations were being conducted in Peking in the midst of continued discord and dissension. Finally, however, on September 7, 1901, the Boxer protocol was signed. It stipulated, among other provisions: (1) indemnity payment by China of 450 million haikwan taels ($300 million) and a 5 percent effective tariff, (2) reservation of the Foreign legation quarters at Peking under the exclusive control of the legations, (3) the occupation by the foreigners of a number of key areas as a security for open communications to Peking, (4) an agreement by China to the revision of commercial treaties with the powers, (5) prohibition by China of the importation of arms and materials to be used in their manufacture, (6) punishment of Chinese officials responsible for the rebellion, and (7) erection of expiatory monuments in foreign cemeteries.

By this time it became abundantly clear that the powers had no intention of observing the principle of Chinese territorial or administrative integrity in any form of cooperative joint endeavor. They stood together only in common defense of their nationals and interests, or in concerted military expeditions to crush antiforeign revolts, but never in common cause for Chinese sovereignty or equal opportunity. Lacking in means or will to enforce the doctrine of the territorial integrity of China, the United States forsook the theme to all intents and purposes. Thus the Open Door policy was born in the cradle of American commercial interests, draped by the high ideals of equality and justice, swaddled by the rapacity of powers, and stripped of its garb of altruism. It was yet to be reared by the hands of the expanding power of American presence in Asia in the twentieth century.

CHAPTER TWO

The Ray of the "Rising Sun": From Amity to Enmity

American-Japanese Amity

The Anglo-Japanese Alliance

During the Boxer Rebellion, Russia was quick to seize upon the opportunity to tighten her grip on Manchuria. In February 1901, the Japanese government sought a clarification of the American position toward Russian encroachments in Manchuria. Secretary Hay responded that the United States was "not at present prepared to attempt singly or in concert with other Powers, to enforce these views (regarding China's territorial integrity) by any demonstration which could present a character of hostility to any other power."[1] This meant, in short, that the Open Door was not a shield to blunt Russian entrenchment. Russia continued to penetrate into Manchuria and Korea, occupying the former militarily and constantly demanding more concessions from the Korean government. Russia's unbridled imperialism in East Asia was on a collision course with Japan. On her part, Japan was assiduously strengthening her position in Korea by means of political, economic, and cultural penetration.

At this time there were two rival factions in the Japanese government: (1) a group of advocates for a Russo-Japanese alliance

21

led by Prince Ito who believed that Japanese interests in Korea could be preserved by an entente with Russia; and (2) a group of proponents of an Anglo-Japanese alliance led by General Katsura who was strongly anti-Russian. When the latter group came into power, they were determined to keep Russia out of Korea even at the risk of war. Russia was allied with France, and the crucial question was how to restrain France from aiding her ally in the event of a war between Japan and Russia. The Katsura group decided, therefore, to explore the possibility of an Anglo-Japanese alliance.

The British considered the Russian ascendancy in China a constant threat to their interests not only in China but also, unavoidably, in India. Moreover, a Russo-Japanese alliance would certainly enhance that threat; such a move had to be thwarted. Count Hayashi, the Japanese envoy in London, observed:

The pro-Japanese sentiment in England extended from the highest to the lowest and humblest citizen. On the other hand, Russia was planning to occupy the Manchurian Provinces as a setoff to and as an indemnity for the Boxer outrages. Then began the infamous campaign of bloodshed along the Amur River. England could not but feel rather resentful towards Russia. She realized the necessity of joint action with Japan in the Far East.[2]

Against these backgrounds, the Anglo-Japanese Alliance was signed on January 30, 1902. This alliance, the first East-West military pact of its kind, recognized each nation's respective interests in China and Japan's special interests in Korea "politically, as well as commercially and industrially." It stipulated further:

If either Great Britain or Japan, in the defense of their respective interests ... should become involved in war with another power, the other high contracting party will maintain a strict neutrality, and use its efforts to prevent other powers from joining in hostilities against its ally. If in the above event any other power or powers should join in hostilities against that ally, the other high contracting party will come to its assistance and will conduct the war in common, and make peace in mutual agreement with it.[3]

As British foreign secretary Landsdowne saw it, the alliance treaty "contains no provisions which can be regarded as an indication of aggressive or self-seeking tendencies in the regions to which it applies. It had been concluded purely as a measure of precaution, to be invoked, should occasion arise, in the defense of important British interests. It in no way threatens the present position or the legitimate interests of other Powers."[4] In brief, Britain had abandoned Korea to Japan in return for a Japanese guarantee of British interests in China. At the same time, Britain was also assured of the diminution of Russia's thrust on the Indian frontier.

The alliance treaty came as a surprise to Secretary Hay, who had been poorly informed and given no advance notice of its signing. The negotiations which culminated in the treaty "were absolutely unknown to the Government of the United States until the day when the terms of that treaty were made public."[5]

Russia and France reacted with a declaration that they found in the treaty "the affirmation of the essential principles" of "assuring status quo and general peace in the Far East as well as of maintaining the independence of China and Korea"; but they would reserve to themselves the right to devise "suitable means" to protect their interests. Secretary Hay, on his part, expressed his gratification at seeing in this Franco-Russian declaration as well as in the Anglo-Japanese treaty a "renewed confirmation of the assurances" of those essential principles of the Open Door policy; but he too would reserve to himself "entire liberty of action" should American interests in China and Korea be disturbed or impaired.[6]

Russo-Japanese Conflicts

Japan, with her international position strengthened, was determined to settle, one way or another, her outstanding difficulties with Russia. In April 1902, Russia signed a convention with China, whereby Russia agreed to withdraw all her troops from Manchuria in three stages: (1) within the first six months, from South Manchuria, (2) within the second six months, from Central Manchuria and Kirin Province, and (3) within the third six months, from the Province of Heilung-chiang. Russia, however, did not carry out her part of the bargain with China, and during 1902–1903 she was sending her troops over into the Yalu River region disguised as woodcutters. Several years before this Russia had exacted timber concessions from Korea along the Yalu.

Alarmed by the seriousness of the Russian thrust into Korea, Japan attempted to reach some kind of an agreement with Russia that would define their interests in Korea. Accordingly, the Japanese minister in the Russian capital was instructed to enter into conversations with Russia. The negotiations that followed between the two countries revolved largely around a plan aiming at the establishment of a neutral zone dividing Korea into two distinctive spheres of interests:

> Russia presented to Japan her counter-proposal. . . . In it Japan was asked to declare Manchuria and its littoral as entirely outside her sphere of interests and to make the stipulation applicable exclusively to Korea, the Chinese Empire being left entirely untouched. Moreover, Russia proposed to make the territory of Korea lying in the north of the thirty-ninth parallel a neutral zone into which neither of the contracting powers should introduce troops. . . .
> The Imperial Government (of Japan) agreed to the establishment of a neutral zone in the northern part of Korea provided that a similar zone of equal extent be created in Manchuria along the Korea-Manchuria frontier. They also proposed, respectively, to declare Manchuria and Korea as outside of their special interests.[7]

For a few months neither side would retreat in any way from its fundamental position. The only way out of the impasse was to resort to war. Japanese public opinion was in favor of this position. The memory of the Triple Intervention was still in the minds of the Japanese people.[8]

The Russo-Japanese hostilities broke out with naval engagements on the Yellow Sea and in Port Arthur, followed by the Japanese declaration of war on Russia on February 10, 1904.

Both Germany and France were compelled to remain neutral for obvious reasons. Initially, on the suggestion of Germany, the United States immediately dispatched a circular to Japan and Russia calling upon them "to respect the neutrality of China and in all practical ways her administrative entity, (and) to localize and limit as much as possible the area of hostilities."[9] Copies of the circular were sent to all the signatory powers of the Boxer protocol, urging them to take a similar stand with respect to the belligerents.

Japan accepted the "principle" of China's neutrality provided Russia would do likewise. But Russia did not accede to the neutralization of Manchuria. The responses of the other powers were: Germany, cooperative; Britain, cautious; and France, reluctant. The circular had little effect either upon the manner in which the war was fought or upon the ultimate outcome of the hostilities. The real significance of the circular lay in reviving the principle that Manchuria was an integral part of Chinese territory where the Chinese alone should exercise their sovereign power. The powers reassured this moral principle by their acceptance of the circular. It was especially meaningful in the light of the fact that Manchuria, which the United States had once considered as being under Russia's sole hegemony, now became the actual arena of the Russo-Japanese military contest and could easily be lost permanently to China.

Another interesting feature of the circular was an omission, intentional or unintentional, of any reference to Korea. Customarily both Russia and Japan had long considered Manchuria and Korea in the same category. Logically speaking, therefore, when the question of the integrity of Manchuria was raised, simultaneously the question of Korea's sovereignty and integrity should have been raised. The fact of the matter was that the Anglo-Japanese Alliance had already paved the way for the Japanese annexation of Korea. The United States, the first Western power to open the "Hermit Kingdom" and a consistent champion for its independence, was now prepared to follow Britain's lead and abandon that country to be subsequently absorbed by the Japanese Empire. President Theodore Roosevelt, in August 1904, proposed to Germany that they should unite at the end of the Russo-Japanese

War in sanctioning a Japanese protectorate over Korea.[10] About a year later in the renewed Anglo-Japanese Alliance Treaty, Britain recognized Japan's "paramount political, military, and economic interests" in Korea and her right to establish a protectorate over that country. Thus, in retrospect, the seed of the Korean War in the 1950s had been sown some half a century earlier.

Turning to the military aspects of the war, Japan enjoyed geographic proximity; the scene of hostility was on foreign soil—Korea and Manchuria—yet near enough to maintain comfortable supply lines for men and matériel. From the standpoint of the national morale, the people as a whole were firmly united behind the war objectives and efforts.

Russia, on the other hand, was unable to deploy her full military forces against Japan because she was compelled to keep the greater portion of her armed power in Europe, ready to meet a possible German invasion. Russo-German relations, after the downfall of Chancellor Bismarck, had deteriorated steadily and were fraught with the danger of war. An even more crucial factor which impeded Russian military operations was that the Trans-Siberian Railroad had not been completed. The problem of logistics across the immense distances to the battlefields was itself a formidable enemy. Worst of all, Russia lacked national unity and was in a ferment of internal discontent.

Within three months the Russian troops had been driven out of Korea and the decisive battle of Mukden ended in a Japanese victory in March 1905. The defeat of the Russian land forces in Manchuria was followed by an overwhelming Japanese naval victory in May over the Russian Baltic Fleet which had been sent around the world to the Sea of Japan.

The Roosevelt Stratagem

At this juncture there were two forces which, seemingly unrelated and yet affecting each other, began to emerge to shape the outcome of the war and the peace: one, President Roosevelt's stratagem; the other, Britain's alliance policy.

When the Russo-Japanese War broke out, the American people, in the tradition of their quixotic sympathy for the "underdog," cheered the Japanese. President Roosevelt, sharing the mood of his compatriots, took the course of neutrality and benevolence toward Japan. His objective was to rid Manchuria of the overwhelming Russian influence and to bring it under an Open Door protection. Diplomatic negotiations to that effect had been unrewarding. Now the president came to believe that Japan might just as well clip the Russian claws and dislodge her tight grip on Manchuria so that American business could move in. American financiers made loans generously to Japan for her war chest. But the Japanese *blitzkrieg,* the swift and decisive military victories over the Russian forces, was an astonishing turn of events which the president, along with most of the world, had never anticipated. It appeared to the president that Russia was about to be totally and completely eliminated from Manchuria, only to be replaced by an equally ambitious militaristic power—Japan. Roosevelt feared that a powerful, expansionistic Japan might pose an even greater threat to China's integrity and to the Open Door than the avaricious, imperialistic Russia. An equitable balance of power between Russia and Japan was thought to be a better scheme to keep Manchuria open than the control of it singularly by either of the two nations. Such reasoning brought about changes in Roosevelt's stratagem in two ways: from the elimination of Russian influence in Manchuria to the establishment of a Russo-Japanese balance of power on the one hand, and from the friendly encouragement of Japan's growth as a modern power to the prevention of her territorial expansion on the other. With these goals in mind, President Roosevelt embarked upon a policy of enlisting the support of two rival European powers—Germany and Britain—in his grand design to bring the war to a close through his mediation, eventually in favor of Russia. Germany rendered her cooperation, but Britain did not.

Behind Britain's noncooperative attitude lay her alliance policy with Japan, the subtleties of which President Roosevelt had failed to grasp. Impressed by the series of military victories won by the Japanese imperial forces, Britain in early 1905 proposed to Japan the renewal of the Anglo-Japanese Alliance. The negotiations to this end were well under way by the time of the Mukden campaign. What benefits would Japan draw from the renewal? The extension and broadening of the alliance would unmistakably strengthen the status of Japan as a first-rate world power and would unquestionably solidify her position in Korea as the sole overseer. The British objectives, on the other hand, were to bring India under the protective cover of the alliance and to prevent a possible Russo-Japanese rapprochement under German auspices at the end of the war. The renewal negotiations happened to run parallel, from June to August 1905, with the preparatory setting for the Russo-Japanese peace negotiations to be held under Roosevelt's mediation. Yet President Roosevelt was not informed of the Anglo-Japanese parley until the last days of their talks; the treaty was signed August 12 and published September 27, 1905.

These sensitive diplomatic maneuvers kept Great Britain from assisting Roosevelt in his efforts to achieve the scheme described above. Britain wanted no part in constraining Japan or helping Russia by exerting her influence upon her alliance partner in East Asia.

Some added features of the renewed alliance were: (1) Britain's recognition, as pointed out before, of Japan's "paramount political, military, and economic interests" in Korea and her right to place Korea under her protectorate, (2) Japan's recognition of Britain's "special interest in all that concerns the security of the Indian frontier" and "her right to take such measures in the proximity of that frontier as she may find necessary for safeguarding her Indian possessions," (3) the other to render immediate assistance in case of an attack by a third power upon either signatory, and (4) the applicability of the treaty to any attack or threat to their interests originating not only in the Far East but "wherever arising."

Despite the dazzling military victories on land and sea, Japan realized that she was incapable of carrying on a protracted war of attrition because of her limited economic resources and manpower. War debts mounted; loans ran out. Prolonged hostilities would have bled the nation white and resulted in a catastrophic economic collapse. The Imperial armies occupied Korea, Sakhalin, and strategic points of Manchuria. Continued military operations would have meant further dispersion of troops over the vast regions of Manchuria or even over Siberia. Moreover, the czarist armies were far from being annihilated. Under these circumstances, Japan preferred a negotiated termination of the war. As early as February 1905, Japan had put forth peace feelers to Russia and received a responsive signal. Encouraged, Japan turned to President Roosevelt for his good offices. While Japan formally requested Roosevelt to act as mediator, the kaiser of Germany urged the czar of Russia to accept American mediation.[11] Before the president would consent to take up the role of mediator, however, he demanded and received Japanese assurance that she would "adhere to the position of maintaining the Open Door in Manchuria and of restoring that province to China."[12]

On June 8, 1905, the president extended his invitations to Russia and Japan for a peace conference, which subsequently opened at Portsmouth, New Hampshire, on August 10. Taking a victor's attitude, Japan demanded that her supreme position in Korea be recognized. She was prepared to restore Manchuria to China, while the principle of equal opportunity would be honored in the province. Additional Japanese demands were: (1) the transfer to Japan of Russia's leases and rights in the Liaotung Peninsula and of the South Manchurian Railway, (2) the cession of full sovereignty of the entire island of Sakhalin, and (3) the payment by Russia of an indemnity for the costs of the war.

The Russian delegates headed by Count Witte balked at the second and third Japanese demands. Japan would not yield, yet she could not afford a resumption of hostilities either. The Russians knew too well the predicament of Japan and they were adamantly opposed to what they considered to be excessive demands. In addition, Russia began to enjoy world public opinion in her favor, including the American press. After two weeks, the negotiations had reached an impasse. The Russian delegation threatened a walkout. At this point, President Roosevelt once more intervened. He devised a compromise formula: no indemnity by Russia, half of Sakhalin to Japan. Soliciting the kaiser's cooperation in persuading the czar to accept the compromise, Roosevelt personally advised Japan to settle for this formula. Both sides finally accepted the compromise agreement and the Treaty of Portsmouth was signed on September 5, 1905.[13]

The peace settlement was regarded as a Russian victory. This implied that Russia could have lost more and Japan could have gained more. The Japanese public was bitterly disappointed by the terms of peace. They felt that the indemnity clause should have been included, that all of Sakhalin should have been ceded to Japan, and that even a portion, if not all, of the maritime provinces in Siberia should have been taken. They demanded a resignation of the Katsura cabinet. They were resentful over President Roosevelt's role in the peace settlement. Riots broke out in Tokyo and martial law was proclaimed. Uninformed and emotionally charged, the Japanese populace did not know of their country's genuine incapability to sustain a prolonged war with Russia. Had the war been continued, Japan's initial military victory might have been turned into an irrevocable national disaster. Responsible leaders in the government as well as in the military were well aware of this fact. In a sense, it was fortunate for the Japanese leaders to have Roosevelt for a scapegoat.

President Roosevelt earned the Nobel Peace Prize for his role as the mediator in bringing about the successful conclusion of the Portsmouth Treaty terminating the Russo-Japanese War. Ironically, for the same role, he also earned the resentment of considerable segments of the Japanese populace. Personally Roosevelt admired the Japanese, but at the same time he feared them. The powerful nation of the "Rising Sun" cast ominous shadows over East Asia as well as the Philippines. Within a decade of their acquisition, the Philippines had become more of an American hostage in Asian power politics. In 1906 Roosevelt was reported to have said that "he would be glad to be rid of them." The "ransom" the United States had to pay for the "hostage" was the acceptance of Japanese imperialism in Korea and Manchuria.

The specter of a Japanese invasion of the Philippines nagged many Americans, including the president. The Taft-Katsura "agreed memorandum" was a calculated product of this fear. In July 1905, Secretary of War Taft, on a mission to Manila, visited Tokyo and negotiated an agreement with Prime Minister Katsura whereby the United States recognized Japan's "suzerainty" over Korea in return for a Japanese disavowal of any aggressive designs toward the Philippines. President Roosevelt wholeheartedly endorsed this formal understanding and accepted it as insurance against a Japanese conquest of the islands. Japan interpreted it as

America's entry into the Anglo-Japanese Alliance through a back door:

> The Anglo-Japanese Alliance is in fact a Japanese-Anglo-American Alliance. We may be sure that when once England became our ally America also became a party to the agreement. Owing to peculiar national conditions America cannot make any open alliance, but we should bear in mind that America is our ally though bound by no formal treaty.[14]

This view is valid in the sense that the United States, as had Great Britain, yielded to Japanese imperialism in order to protect and secure its own colonial possessions in Asia.

The United States kept its part of the bargain with respect to Korea. In November 1905, Ambassador Takahira informed Secretary of State Root that Japan would hereafter control and direct the foreign relations of Korea. The following day, Secretary Root notified Takahira that he had "directed by telegraph the withdrawal of the American mission to Korea and had given instructions that the representation of the United States in diplomatic matters in relation to Korea hereafter be conducted directly with your legation, or through the American legation at Tokyo."[15]

The Taft-Katsura agreement and the subsequent American recognition of Japan's paramount position in Korea had some sweetening effects upon the bitterness resulting from the Portsmouth Treaty. The period of goodwill, however, was short-lived. The immigration controversy on the West Coast of the United States and conflicting interests in Manchuria began to plague Japanese-American relations.

American-Japanese Enmity

Oriental Immigrants and Racial Controversies

It should be pointed out that the United States policy on Oriental immigration had a long history of confusion, contradiction, and conflict. The Chinese were the first to be lured to California by the gold rush of 1848. The construction of the transcontinental railroad further spurred a steady stream of contract laborers and coolies who provided major sources of cheap labor. In 1868 Anson Burlingame, former American minister to Peking, but then serving as a special envoy of the Chinese government, had negotiated a treaty with Secretary of State Seward. That treaty recognized the right of free immigration of Chinese subjects "for purposes of curiosity, or trade, or as permanent residents." But the fast-growing Chinese population in the United States accentuated its cultural and ethnic peculiarities, infusing economic competition with racial antipathy and discrimination. After more than a generation of trepidation involving the Chinese immigration issue, the United States Congress enacted a law permanently excluding Chinese laborers from the United States. No Chinese could become a citizen of the United States by naturalization. Thus the American immigration policy on the Chinese swung from the Burlingame-Seward ideals of total freedom to the anti-Chinese chauvinistic policy of total exclusion.

The anti-Chinese sentiment was, in fact, only one aspect of the overall anti-Orientalism in America. Hence, the prejudice against Oriental immigrants quite naturally brewed the anti-Japanese movement just as vehemently as it had against the Chinese.

Japanese immigration to the United States began after 1900. Japanese contract laborers were first brought to Hawaii and later to the West Coast of the United States. Despite the fact that the number of Japanese immigrants in California constituted less than 1 percent of the total population there, a strong anti-Japanese agitation began to emerge. Demagogues, agitators, segregationists, racists, and their followers held mass meetings demanding outright expulsion and exclusion of the Japanese. The Japanese government, concerned over the injurious racial discrimination against their nationals, voluntarily suspended the emigration of laborers to the United States. This move, however, had little effect in curbing the anti-Japanese agitation.

On May 6, 1905, the San Francisco board of education adopted a resolution "to effect the establishment of separate schools for Chinese and Japanese pupils, not only for relieving the congestion at present prevailing in our schools, but also for the higher end that our children should not be placed in any position where their youthful impression may be affected by association with pupils of the Mongolian race."[16]

Condemning the anti-Japanese activities in California and emphasizing the need for a naval build-up, President Roosevelt wrote in his letter to Senator Henry Cabot Lodge:

> The feeling on the Pacific slope, taking it from several different standpoints, is as foolish as if conceived by the mind of a Hottentot. These Pacific Coast people wish grossly to insult the Japanese and to keep out the Japanese immigrants on the ground that they are an immoral, degraded, and worthless race; and at the same time that they desire to do this for the Japanese, and are already doing it for the Chinese, they expect to be given advantages in Oriental Markets; and with besotted folly are indifferent to building up the navy while provoking this formidable new power—a power jealous, sensitive, and warlike, and which if irritated could at once take both the Philippines and Hawaii from us if she obtained the upper hand on the seas.[17]

The president's admonition had no influence upon the determined segregationists in California, nor did the magnanimity of the Japanese people during the San Francisco earthquake in 1906. The Japanese Red Cross contributed more to the victims of the calamity than all other countries of the world combined. Yet Japanese restaurants were boycotted, visiting Japanese scientists were stoned in the streets, and other instances of anti-Japanese agitation and violence continued.

The Root-Takahira Agreement

The climax to this racial discrimination appeared to have been reached in October 1906, when the San Francisco school board passed its fateful resolution excluding all children of Oriental extraction from the city's public schools. In an attempt to justify the board's action, it was alleged that the Japanese pupils were vicious, immoral, overcrowding the schools, and too old for safe association with the younger American children.[18] The Japanese government promptly lodged a protest with the United States government:

The Imperial Government is not aware whether the special schools, which the authorities of San Francisco propose to provide for the accommodation of Japanese children of school age, are equally good as the schools established and maintained for the instruction of the children generally of that city; but even if they were equally good, the fact that Japanese children, because of their nationality, are segregated in special schools and not permitted to attend the ordinary public schools, constitutes an act of discrimination carrying with it a stigma and odium which it is impossible to overlook.[19]

President Roosevelt thereupon assured the Japanese government that he would take appropriate action within his power. In his message to Congress in December 1906, he termed the discrimination a "wicked absurdity" and called for legislation lifting the naturalization ban against the Japanese. He bluntly warned the Californians that he would use federal troops, if necessary, to protect the Japanese from further injuries and violence. The president's stern warning, however, once again fell on deaf ears. The *San Francisco Chronicle* responded: "Our feeling is not against Japan, but against an unpatriotic President who united with aliens to break down the civilization of his own countrymen."

President Roosevelt was fully aware of the moral and strategic contradictions in his nation's immigration policy toward Asians. While opening Asia to the Americans on the basis of equality and opportunity, the United States had made no provisions for the possibility of Asians seeking reciprocity of equal opportunity in America. Moreover, the Open Door in China and the security of the Philippines were largely dependent upon the goodwill of Japan, whose nationals in California were now subjected to unwarranted discrimination, segregation, and humiliation.

The situation engendered what the president considered the gravest diplomatic crisis of his presidency. One of the leading newspapers in Tokyo, the *Mainichi Shinbun* (daily), had carried the following sabre-rattling statement:

The whole world knows that the poorly equipped army and navy of the United States are no match for our efficient army and navy. . . . Our countrymen have been humiliated on the other side of the Pacific. Our poor boys and girls have been expelled from the public schools by the rascals of the United States, cruel and merciless like demons. At this time we would be ready to give a blow to the United States.[20]

The president's decision to send the American battle fleet on a world cruise was intended to demonstrate American naval prowess and to dampen Japanese bellicosity. In the meantime he had to find a satisfactory solution to the racial crisis in California. His "big-stick" approach to domestic issues proved ineffective; he decided to "walk softly." He invited to the White House the entire board of education of San Francisco and Mayor Schmitz, who was then under indictment for graft. There a compromise was reached. He was able to have the San Francisco school board rescind the segregation resolution in return for his promise to halt immigration of Japanese laborers both directly from Japan and indirectly from Hawaii.

As for indirect immigration from Hawaii and elsewhere, the president persuaded Congress to pass an amendment to the Immigration Law of 1907 making such entry unlawful. As for direct immigration from Japan, he was equally successful in persuading the Japanese government to impose upon the Japanese people those restrictions desired by the United States: Japan agreed to deny passports for unskilled laborers other than members of the families of Japanese residents and settled agriculturalists already residing in the United States. This action was documented in a series of exchanges of diplomatic notes, subsequently known as the Gentlemen's Agreement. Thereafter immigration directly from Japan decreased rapidly, but many so-called picture brides—who married *in absentia* Japanese laborers already residing in the United States—were issued passports. Although the emotions engendered by racial segregation, discrimination, and prejudice could not be solved by a mere diplomatic agreement, the immigration issue and the crisis precipitated in California thus found a temporary respite.

An additional safeguard against Japanese-American irritation was the understanding reached between Ambassador Takahira and Secretary of State Root. The Root-Takahira Agreement of November 30, 1908, provided that the governments of the United States and Japan were:

1. To encourage the free and peaceful development of their commerce in the region of the Pacific Ocean.
2. To maintain the existing status quo in that region and to defend the principle of equal opportunity for commerce and industry in China.
3. To respect each other's territorial possessions in the said region.
4. To preserve the common interest of all powers in China by supporting the independence and integrity of China as well as the principle of the Open Door.
5. To communicate with each other in order to arrive at an understanding as to what measures they may take in the event that the status quo and the principle of equal opportunity are threatened.

This agreement was born out of the subsisting enmity between the two nations. They attempted to clarify their fundamental positions regarding their respective interests in the Pacific region. But the terms used were extremely broad and general, and what was implicit in the notes seemed as important as what was explicit. By inference, the United States was assured of the safety and security of the Philippines, Hawaii, the Aleutian Islands, and Alaska in exchange for an American pledge to respect Japan's interests as embedded in the "existing status quo."

What constituted those Japanese interests which were included in the "existing status quo"? First, the Treaty of Portsmouth, it should be recalled, provided for the transfer to Japan of the Russian leasehold in South Manchuria, including the railway and mining rights. Since China had not been a party to the treaty, her consent was required to make the transfer legal. Japan secured this consent by a treaty with China in late 1905. In addition, Japan exacted from China more economic concessions. The most significant of all was China's pledge not to construct any railway parallel to the South Manchurian Railway, which became an indispensable agency for Japanese imperialism in Manchuria. Second, the Franco-Japanese *démarche* brought about the signing of a treaty between the two powers. In this Franco-Japanese treaty of June 10, 1907, they agreed "to respect the independence and integrity of China as well as the principle of equal treatment in that country for the commerce and subjects or citizens of all nations." They declared that the preservation of peace and order was their special interest, "especially in the regions of the Chinese Empire adjoining the territories where they possess rights of sovereignty, protection, or occupation." They further agreed to support each other in maintaining "peace and security in those regions, with a view to maintaining the respective situation and the territorial rights of (the signatories) in the continent of Asia."

It was implicitly understood by the two powers that the areas affected by their influence in China were, for Japan, the province of Fukien and "the regions of Manchuria and Mongolia," and, for France, the provinces of Kwangtung, Kwangsi, and Yunnan. Third, the Franco-Japanese entente paved the way for Russo-Japanese rapprochement. Japan and Russia concluded a treaty of commerce and navigation, a fisheries convention, and two political conventions—one open, the other secret. The open convention upheld, as always, the principles of the Open Door and pledged to maintain the status quo by all means. The secret convention clarified their respective positions with regard to Korea, Manchuria, and Mongolia. Russia could neither interfere with nor place any obstacles in the way of Japan's political development in Korea. Japan, on the other hand, would recognize the special interests of Russia in Outer Mongolia. Manchuria was to be divided into two distinct spheres of influence: the north for Russia and the south for Japan. Finally, the renewed Anglo-Japanese Alliance had firmly established the principle that geographic propinquity creates special interests. In specific terms, the United States had recognized this principle and accepted Japan's "suzerainty" over Korea in the Taft-Katsura agreement. The United States had at that time assented to Japan's free hand in Korea and now acquiesced to her "special interests" in Manchuria.

The Dollar Diplomacy

An executive agreement in American foreign relations is not a formal treaty which has to meet the constitutional requirement of "advise and consent" of the Senate. Such a pact binds only the executive branch of the government which has negotiated it with a foreign power. Hence, it could be argued that the Root-Takahira Agreement bound only the Roosevelt regime but not the Taft administration which succeeded it. Realizing this legal finesse, the Japanese government had cause for apprehension as Taft took office. Their apprehension became a reality. President Taft and Secretary of State Knox, both constitutional lawyers, pursued the policy of reviving the doctrine of China's territorial integrity which their predecessors had virtually abandoned insofar as Manchuria was concerned. In a policy characterized "as substituting dollars for bullets," the president and the secretary of state carried what was called "the dollar diplomacy" into the far corners of East Asia —Manchuria—in an attempt to stem the steady ascendancy therein of Japan and Russia at the expense of China.

The new administration set forth a China policy aiming at "the general extension of American influence in China so that the commercial interests and exporters of the United States turn their attention more vigorously toward securing the markets of the Orient."[21] The administration went on to observe, "The one great drawback to the really successful development of such intercourse is the attitude of our own manufacturers and exporters who are not sufficiently alive to the importance of sending their own representatives to China to report to them directly the needs of the Chinese people. Our bankers show the same spirit although they are undoubtedly anxious to provide some of the great loans which China is now placing in England, Germany, and France."[22]

The State Department designated a group of American businesses—J. P. Morgan and Company, the First National Bank and the National City Bank, Harriman and Kuhn, and Loeb and Company—as the official agents of American railway financing in China. The Chinese government was then duly requested to accord this group the same status as similar representatives of other powers. Such combination of business and diplomacy signified the eloquent manifestation of President Taft's political belief that governmental policy should be "directed to the increase of American trade upon the axiomatic principle that the Government of the United States shall extend all proper support to every legitimate and beneficial American enterprise abroad."[23]

In 1909, the American "dollar offensive" took dual routes: (1) a challenge to Japanese financial supremacy in Manchuria, and (2) a contest over the British-Franco-German consortium in China proper. As discussed below, these routes led the United States to a blind alley and eventually to abysmal defeats.

By the time Secretary Knox launched his Far Eastern policy, Japan had made her position in Manchuria well-nigh impregnable. The recognition of the "existing status quo" in the Root-Takahira Agreement had endorsed and confirmed the Japanese claim, but Knox either ignored it or interpreted it otherwise. He set out to dislodge Japan by pouring American dollars into Manchuria to wage a "railway warfare."

In the summer of 1909, E. H. Harriman, the railroad magnate, initiated conversations with the Russians for the sale of the Chinese Eastern Railway. But his real aim was the purchase of the South Manchurian Railway from the Japanese, who did not show the slightest inclination to sell. Failing in his effort, Harriman obtained from China the right to build a railroad from Chinchow in the south to Aigun on the Siberian border through the heart of Manchuria, parallel to the South Manchurian Railway. The projected line was designed to create such severe competition that it would compel Japan either to sell out or to suffer a loss in operation. The death of Harriman in September, 1909, however, changed the course of this moribund scheme. At this juncture Secretary Knox intervened. On November 6, he made two proposals to the British government:

First, perhaps the most effective way to preserve the undisturbed enjoyment by China of all political rights in Manchuria and to promote the development of those Provinces under a practical application of the policy of the open door and equal commercial opportunity would be to bring the Manchurian highways and the railroad under an economic and scientific and impartial administration by some plan vesting in China the ownership of the railroads through funds furnished for that purpose by the interested powers willing to participate. . . . The execution of such a plan would naturally require the cooperation of China and of Japan and Russia, the reversionary and the concessionaries, respectively, of the existing Manchurian railroads, as well as that of Great Britain and the United States, whose special interests rest upon the existing contract relative to the Chin Chou-Aigun Railroad. . . . Secondly, should this suggestion not be found feasible in its entirety, then the desired end would be approximated if not attained by Great Britain and the United States diplomatically supporting the Chin Chou-Aigun arrangement and inviting interested powers friendly to the complete commercial neutrality of Manchuria to participate in the financing and construction of that line and of such additional lines as future commercial development may demand, and at the same time to supply funds for the purchase by China of such of the existing lines as might be offered for inclusion in this system.[24]

The first proposal called for a plan for total neutralization of all railways in Manchuria; and the second suggested that, in the event the first proved not feasible, the two nations together with other interested powers should support the Chinchow-Aigun project.

The British response was cordial and cautious, but unmistakably negative:

Until the pending negotiations for the Hukuang loan [a British-Franco-German consortium for a railway system in Central and Southern China] have been completed it would seem undesirable to consider the question of another international loan for China's railway undertakings. And . . . it would be wiser to postpone consideration of the first scheme. As regards the alternative proposal . . . the two Governments should unite in endeavoring to admit the Japanese to participation in the Chinchow-Aigun line, as being the parties most interested. The question of supplying funds for the purchase by China of existing lines to be connected with the Chinchow-Aigun line could be considered subsequently.[25]

Secretary Knox, however, interpreted this reply as positive and favorable. He presented his two-point plan to Japan, Russia, France, Germany, and China for a similarly "favorable consideration." Both Japan and Russia rejected the first without hesitation and refused the second with regret. In fact, alarmed by the Knox scheme, Japan and Russia then concluded a new treaty in July 1910 designed to strengthen their rights and privileges in their respective spheres of influence in Manchuria. As the British government endorsed the new Russo-Japanese pact, the two countries expressed their public appreciation to Britain for her stand against the United States intrusion.

The results of the Knox "dollar offensive" in Manchuria may be summarized as follows: (1) the United States turned out to be the sole diplomatic casualty, (2) the American attempt to loosen the Japanese and the Russian grips had the reverse effect of tightening them up to a greater extent, (3) the Russo-Japanese rivalry was converted into their solidarity, (4) the Open Door through which American financial enterprise was to be introduced in Manchuria was shut tight in America's face, and (5) China's territorial integrity in Manchuria was weakened.

As to the American contest over the European three-power consortium in China proper, the dollar offensive likewise fizzled. When in June 1909 the Chinese government was prepared to sign an agreement with the British-Franco-German banking groups for the Hukuang railway loan, the United States lodged a protest with the three European powers. Then the following month the American banking group presented in London its demand for equal participation in the loan. Here again the British rejection was cordial and firm. The United States thereupon turned to the weak hostess —China—pressing the issue of equal participation of American capital in the railway loan. In an unprecedented diplomatic maneuver, on behalf of *private* American financial interests, President Taft sent a telegram to Prince Chun, the regent of the Manchu throne:

I have an intense personal interest in making the use of American capital in the development of China an instrument for the promotion of the welfare of China, and an increase in her material prosperity without entanglements or creating embarrassments affecting the growth of her independent political power and the preservation of her territorial integrity.[26]

Secretary Knox at the same time sent to the Chinese foreign office unsolicited advice:

> If the objections of bankers of other countries to equal American participation are so insistent as not to be overcome by the wishes of China and of their own governments, the time has arrived when China should exercise its right to determine the matter by confining her dealings to those who are willing to respect her highest interests.[27]

The financial skirmishes among the powers involving the Hukuang loan continued until May 1910, when the four Western powers, the United States, Great Britain, France, and Germany, finally forced China to sign the loan agreement, which many Chinese regarded as another form of foreign imperialism.

The Chinese revolution of October 1911, overthrowing the Manchu Dynasty, prevented actual construction of the railway, but it provided opportunities for further exploitation of China by the powers. As had been the case in the past, the powers hardly united in preserving China's integrity; instead each sought to maximize its gains by fishing in the troubled waters. The old pattern of power rivalries emerged in the midst of factional strife and political chaos in China. Adhering to a "strict neutrality," Great Britain quickly seized upon the turmoil and detached Tibet from China to place it under her control. Russia severed Outer Mongolia from China to embrace it in her protection, while acknowledging Britain's free hand in Tibet. Japan declared her intention to support the crumbling Manchu government, probably with a Japanese-controlled "independent" Manchuria as *quid pro quo* in mind. The United States, in the spirit of the Open Door, attempted to bring a semblance of united action among the powers to preserve China's territorial integrity. Secretary Knox came out in support of Yüan Shih-k'ai. A month after the outbreak of the revolution, Yüan Shih-k'ai, the soldier-statesman and a leading political figure in China, had appealed to the consortium powers for a loan to be used in paying his troops, maintaining law and order, and recognizing the government of his infant republic. With the outcome of the revolution being far from certain, most of the consortium members were unwilling to comply with Yüan's request because granting a loan officially would be tantamount to a formal recognition of his regime. No major loan was made, only a few cash advances.

In a surprise move, Secretary Knox also argued for the admission of Japan and Russia into the four-power consortium. Knox reasoned, and the powers concurred, that these two nations would be restrained better inside the organization than outside it. They were admitted to the consortium in June 1912. Their admission was conditioned upon the further international recognition of their special interests in Manchuria and Mongolia. It should be readily recognized that American acceptance of this condition was totally incompatible with and contradictory to the earlier neutralization scheme as well as the Chinchow-Aigun project. The following month Japan and Russia concluded a third secret treaty to consolidate their respective holdings in those two regions. Thus Japan and Russia pushed the Open Door out of Manchuria by the first treaty of 1907, closed it by the second in 1910, and now locked it by the third. As the dollar diplomacy began to lose its impetus, American banking groups became disenchanted and demanded explicit government support.

Meanwhile, the republican government of China, pressed as it was by financial difficulties, initiated the negotiations for a comprehensive loan with the six-power consortium, which at once insisted on stringent conditions including provisions for control of the revenues as security. When President Wilson took office in March 1913, he refused to support American bankers in the matter and withdrew from the international consortium. The president stated that "the conditions of the loan seem to us to touch very nearly the administrative independence of China itself, and this administration does not feel that it ought, even by implication, to be a party to these conditions."[28]

The Knox strategy of the two-front dollar offensive fizzled and faded away. It left the battle marks of having lost Manchuria to American investment, having impaired China's territorial and administrative integrity, and having demonstrated the utter inadequacies of American Far East policy.

CHAPTER THREE

United States Vigilance in East Asia

On the Two Shores of the Pacific

Wilson's Home Front with the Japanese

President Wilson's withdrawal of American participation from the six-power consortium was predicated not so much upon his knowledge of China or of United States interests in the Far East as on his aversion to "undemocratic" features of foreign financial monopolies meddling in Chinese domestic affairs. His decision was a reflection, in part, of his basic postulates that a worldwide democratic order of rationality and justice should replace the aggressive and tyrannical use of power. To his chagrin, he was soon to discover that this idealistic approach to the problems of the world in general, and to those of the Far East in particular, could hardly make headway in the face of the realities of international power politics.

In the Far East, President Wilson assumed willy-nilly the unrewarding burden of resisting Japanese expansionist policies. Wilson's predecessors, it should be recalled, had been challenging Japanese imperialism in China for nearly two decades with questionable results. Japan had been keeping a steady pace on the path to hegemony over China. The Wilson policy of "resisting Japan" was carried out mainly during and after World War I, fostering a Japanese-American antagonism. It was unfortunate that his administration at the outset was beset by the enmity between the two nations generated by the resurgent anti-Japanese racial discrimination on the Pacific Coast.

The Gentlemen's Agreement under the Roosevelt administration had been a palliative measure adopted to cushion the intensity of prejudice of the Californians toward the Japanese immigrants. The simmering antagonism and discriminatory practices continued to persist and the California legislature had frequently discussed proposals against the Japanese. Then, in March 1913, a legislative bill was introduced designed to bar the Japanese from owning land. This action was both in response to and the cause of heightened anti-Japanese agitation in California. In Tokyo the Japanese held mass protest meetings against the proposed law, demanding war with the United States. Alarmed by the undesirable developments on both sides of the Pacific, President Wilson appealed by telegrams to the California lawmakers for restraint. At the same time he also sent Secretary of State William Jennings Bryan to California to plead with the governor and the legislators for moderation and modification. Neither Wilson's prestige nor Bryan's eloquence prevailed. On May 3, 1913, California passed its Alien Land Bill forbidding aliens "ineligible to citizenship" to own agricultural land.[1] For all intents and purposes the law with its ingenious wording was directed against the Japanese without mentioning them. Governor Hiram Johnson was rather frank when he declared after the passage of the law: "We have prevented the Japanese from driving the root of their civilization deep into California soil."[2] The state attorney-general, one of the framers of the law, was even more specific when he said, "The fundamental basis of all legislation upon this subject . . . has been, and is, race desirability." One of the means to reduce the number of Japanese in California, he believed, was to deny the "privileges which they may enjoy here; for they will not come in large numbers and long abide with us if they may not acquire land."[3]

Convinced that the discriminatory law was a malicious affront to their national pride and honor, the Japanese government lodged strong protests with the United States. In both countries tempers heightened, tensions mounted, and war preparations were has-tened. The American military drew up a plan to dispatch several warships to the Philippines, only to be vetoed by the president. Wilson assured the Japanese and his own countrymen that talk of war was irresponsible and that the crisis would be overcome by peaceful means. He made it clear that the California law was a "state" action, not a national policy. Wilson's conciliatory policy sufficiently soothed the Japanese government, which acknowledged in June 1914 that "the said enactment which was intended to have international effect is also in excess of the authority of the state of California for the reason that the separate states of the United States are, internationally speaking, wholly unknown and entirely without responsibility." Japan thus responded to the Wilson ap-proach with the same conciliatory attitude, adding: "The Imperial government [is] confident that such action as complained of stands without historical parallel, and [it is] happy to believe that the legis-lation in question forms no part of the general policy of the federal government, but is the outcome of unfortunate local conditions."[4]

Japanese Design in China

With the outbreak of World War I, Japan became more en-grossed in her plans of continental expansion than in the racial dis-crimination controversies. Japan was determined to take advantage of the colossal development. She reasoned that the extension of the hostilities in Europe to China, where the interests of many bellig-erent powers lay crisscross, would so aggravate China's political stability and intensify its economic disruption as to make it an easy prey for her territorial aggrandizement. Precisely for the same reason China desired to stay neutral and to keep the war from spreading into her territory. With this in mind, on August 3, 1914, China proposed that the United States should "endeavor to obtain the consent of the belligerent European nations to an undertaking not to engage in hostilities either in Chinese territory and marginal waters or in adjacent leased territories."[5] The United States re-sponded by suggesting to the powers, including Germany, that they should observe the neutrality of the Pacific Ocean as well as the status quo of the entire Far East.[6] No general agreement was reached, and the spark of war began to threaten the Far East.

Fearful of Japanese ambitious designs for China, Great Britain wished to keep her Asian alliance partner out of the war altogether. If necessary, Japan could be allowed to conduct only a limited naval operation against German shipping in the China Sea, but no major military action on the German leasehold of Kiaochow in Shantung or on the German islands in the Pacific should be permitted. Japan insisted, however, on the necessity of attacking Kiaochow. After a momentary policy disagreement, Great Britain was compelled to consent to a Japanese strategy, obtaining from Japan a pledge that Kiaochow would eventually be restored to China. The Chinese government turned once again to the United States with a plea that she should "undertake to bring about the immediate retrocession of the leased territory." Specifically, China suggested that the United States should take over the German rights in Shantung and then hand them over to her. In his reply the secretary of state was noncommittal: "The Department feels sure that such a course would do more to provoke than to avert war."[7]

The fact was that war had come to the threshold of the Far East. Japan sent to Germany an ultimatum demanding that Germany turn over to Japan her leasehold interests in Shantung and withdraw all her armed vessels from Japanese and Chinese waters. When this ultimatum was ignored, Japan declared war on Germany, landed her troops in Shantung, and carried out military operations far beyond the bounds of the German leasehold. Hopeless in obtaining the belligerents' respect for her territorial integrity and helpless in resisting Japanese encroachments, China for the third time requested the United States to intervene on her behalf. The United States answer was terse and clear: "It would be quixotic in the extreme to allow the question of China's territorial integrity to entangle the United States in international difficulties."[8]

By the end of 1914, Japan occupied the entire province of Shantung and most of the German islands in the Pacific north of the equator. Thus, Japan succeeded in removing one of the powerful European rivals—Germany—from the Far East and in so doing took revenge on Germany for its part in the Triple Intervention nearly two decades earlier.

Japan's military occupation of Shantung was but a prelude to her all-out political and diplomatic offensive toward what she hoped would be the unrivaled dominance of all China. When President Yüan Shih-k'ai notified the Japanese of the termination of the "war zone"[9] and China's extension of neutrality to cover the Shantung Province outside of the leased territory, the Japanese lodged a strong protest and countered with far-reaching demands —the Twenty-One Demands.

The demands were presented to President Yüan in person by the Japanese minister Hioki in a private interview held on the night of January 18, 1915. The method of presentation itself was unorthodox; the documents should have been submitted first to the foreign minister, not to the head of state, in accordance with diplomatic practice. Minister Hioki further requested President Yüan to keep the whole matter in absolute secrecy. Four days later, however, American minister Paul Reinsch learned of the essence of the demands and within a few days thereafter the foreign diplomatic circles in Peking became fully acquainted with them. Although the daily press in China took up and discussed the matter, the British and American press did not report on the issue for two weeks because the Japanese embassy in Washington had denied the truth of the reports coming from China. Finally, on February 14, the Japanese government admitted that it had made eleven, not twenty-one, demands upon the Chinese government. But this was the altered version of the original demands.

The original demands, in five groups with twenty-one articles, may be summarized as follows:[10]

Group One: Shantung

China was required to give full assent to all matters upon which Japan and Germany might agree in relation to Shantung, not to cede to a third power the Shantung Province under any pretext, to consent to Japan's building a railroad from Chefoo to join the Kiaochow-Chinanfu line, and to open certain cities in Shantung by joint decision of Japan and China.

Group Two: South Manchuria and Eastern Inner Mongolia

The Japanese subjects in South Manchuria and Eastern Inner Mongolia would have the right to reside and travel and to lease or own land for trade, manufacture, farming, and mining; China was required to secure Japan's consent in making a loan with a third power or in granting to a third power the right to build a railway in these areas; China would employ political, financial, or military advisors in the same areas; and China would agree to hand over to Japan the control and management of the Kirin-Changchun Railway for a period of ninety-nine years.

Group Three: The Hanyehping Company[11]

The Hanyehping Company would be made a joint concern of the two countries; and China was not allowed, without the consent of Japan, to dispose of the company's rights and property or to permit any other party to work on the mines in the neighborhood of those owned by the company.

Group Four: Nonalienation of Territory

China was required not to cede or lease to a third power any harbor or bay or island along the coast of China.

Group Five: Japan's Desires

China would employ influential Japanese as advisors in political, financial, and military affairs; China would grant to Japanese hospitals, temples, and schools the right to own land in the interior of China; the police department of the important places in China would be administered jointly by Japan and China; China would purchase from Japan a fixed quantity of arms or establish a Sino-Japanese joint arsenal; China would first consult Japan with respect to any foreign capital needed for development work in Fukien; and Japanese subjects would have the right to propagate Buddhism in China.

In May 1915, China, reportedly under duress, accepted the demands with the exception of Group Five. Among the powers only the United States was paying close attention to these developments, for the European powers were involved in a life-or-death struggle themselves. What the United States did, however, was to send identical notes to the governments of China and Japan, clarifying her position not to recognize any change in the status quo brought about as the result of any agreement impairing the treaty rights of the United States and violating the principles of the Open Door. This policy clarification was intended to stiffen the American position relative to the earlier one[12] "so that any agreement forced upon China ... would properly become the subject of discussion in the future when the conditions are more propitious."[13]

Japanese Diplomacy in World War I

During World War I, the primary objective of Japanese foreign policy was to consolidate and to safeguard her gains in the Far East by obtaining international sanction for their legitimacy. First, in October 1915, Japan adhered to the Anglo-Franco-Russo Declaration of London of September 5, 1914, in which each had pledged not to seek separate peace nor to discuss peace terms except in unanimous agreement. This move assured Japan of her membership and participation in the peace conference. Second, on July 3, 1916, Japan concluded with Russia a secret treaty which not only delimited their respective interests in East Asia but also provided for a military alliance. By this treaty Japan recognized the Russian position in Outer Mongolia as an established fact; Russia in return recognized the Japanese special interests in China derived from the Twenty-One Demands; and the two signatories agreed to assure "that China should not fall under the political domination of any third Power hostile to Russia or Japan."

Third, in late January 1917, Japan's skillful diplomacy induced Great Britain into negotiations for an agreement whereby Britain would promise to support at the peace conference Japan's claims for the transfer of German rights in Shantung and the German islands in the Pacific, north of the equator. Japan in return would support British claims to the German islands south of the equator. The agreement, or the bargain, was reached on February 6, 1917, and was kept secret until the Bolsheviks disclosed it after the revolution.

Fourth, in late February and early March 1917, Japan obtained similar agreements from France, Russia, and Italy. The Japanese *quid pro quo* was her promise to remain in the Allied camp and to use her influence in persuading China to enter the war on the side of the associated powers.

Finally, Japan embarked upon the task of establishing a Japanese-American entente so as to complete the chain of diplomatic fencing to protect her newly gained interests in East Asia. The ambiguities, and at the time outright contradictions, in America's Asian policy were the cause for Japanese apprehension. The American entry into the war placed the United States and Japan on the same side, fighting common enemies, but the former appeared to be challenging the latter's dominant position in East Asia. Japan desired to resolve the subsisting irritation and to enlist United States assent to her war claims, which she had had other allies committed to recognize.

In September 1917, the Japanese government sent Viscount Ishii Kikujiro to Washington as the head of a special mission for the express purpose of expediting military and political cooperation with the United States. Such missions had already been sent by France and Great Britain. In the case of the Ishii mission, however, the primary objective was to open negotiations with the Department of State to iron out the conflicting Japanese and American policies in China. From September through early November special envoy Ishii and Secretary of State Lansing carried out difficult and delicate discussions on the policy differences of their two countries. Ishii insisted on Lansing's recognition of the Japanese "paramount interest" in China in the same sense of the phrase as that used in the Anglo-Japanese Alliance treaty of 1905 to define Japan's position over Korea, or as that applied to American interests in Mexico. Lansing refused to consent. Instead, he countered with the proposal of a joint declaration of respect for the Open Door and the territorial integrity of China. Ishii maintained that such a declaration would be superfluous.

Secretary Lansing then made a compromise proposal, whereby he would recognize Japan's "special interests" growing out of geographical propinquity in return for Japan's acceptance of the following stipulation:

The Governments of the United States and Japan . . . will not take advantage of present conditions to seek special rights or privileges in China which would abridge the rights of the citizens or subjects of other friendly states.[14]

Ambassador Ishii was hesitant and reluctant. The fact was that Japan had already obtained "special rights or privileges in China" by the consent of Kiaochow, the Twenty-One Demands, and a series of secret treaties with the Allies. Finally, on October 31, 1917, the two negotiators agreed to a *secret* protocol incorporating the Lansing proposal. Two days later they signed the public agreement which, bearing their names, provided:

> The Governments of the United States and Japan recognized that territorial propinquity creates special relations between countries, and consequently, the Government of the United States recognizes that Japan has special interests in China, particularly in the part to which her possessions are contiguous. . . . [They] deny that they have any purpose to infringe in any way the independence or territorial integrity of China and they declare, furthermore, that they always adhere to the principle of the so-called "open-door" or equal opportunity for commerce and industry in China.[15]

Each country claimed that the Lansing-Ishii agreement was its own diplomatic victory. Equating the "special interests" with the "paramount interests," Japan hailed the agreement as America's endorsement of her gains in China. The United States, on the other hand, was content with the notion that Japan had pledged to respect the Open Door and China's territorial integrity. The truth was that due to the ambiguous character of the agreement, each signatory construed it to suit its own purposes.

The agreement was primarily concerned with Japanese-American relations in China. Yet, China was neither contacted nor consulted. When informed of the agreement, the Chinese government responded with a declaration that it "will not allow itself to be bound by any agreement entered into by other nations."[16]

A few months prior to the signing of this agreement, China had declared war on the Central Powers and joined the Allies. What part did the United States play in this event? On February 3, 1917,

President Wilson severed diplomatic relations with Germany and suggested to all other neutral powers that they follow his lead if they could in order to "make for the peace of the world." Interpreting Wilson's message as "more than a pious wish," the American minister Paul Reinsch in Peking considered it his "plain duty to prevail upon China to associate herself with the American action." After a week of discussions between Reinsch and the Chinese authorities, the Chinese foreign office dispatched a carefully worded note to the German government protesting the unlimited submarine warfare and threatening to break off diplomatic relations. At this juncture, Secretary Lansing was so fearful that Reinsch might be overcommitting his country that he instructed the latter to "avoid giving any promises or assurances" to China. On February 26, Lansing reiterated that, should America declare war on Germany, the United States would not urge China to do likewise because his government "would not be able to give China the assistance." On March 14, China broke off diplomatic relations with Germany, for which Lansing expressed his appreciation.

Now that China had taken the first step, what would be her next move toward entry into the war—the declaration of war itself? This issue divided the country. The proponents, led by Prime Minister Tuan Ch'i-jui, saw in joining the Allies the opportunities for China to obtain immediate financial aid from them, hopefully to exercise the right of administrative independence and integrity, to revise, if not eliminate, unequal treaties which had been forced upon her, to secure her place in the peace conference with much weight and voice, and to assume an equal and respectful station among the powers. The opponents, on the other hand, argued that China had no basic causes for antagonism to Germany, who might even win the war, that the entente powers had shown no less predatory propensities upon China than Germany, that it was more important to solve internal problems than to seek external war, and that war would strengthen the military faction in China and weaken the forces of representative government.

Against this background, in June 1917 Secretary Lansing declared that "the entry of China into the war with Germany, or the continuance of the status quo of her relations with that Government, are matters of secondary consideration." Stressing that the

United States was deeply interested in a "central, united, and responsible Government" of China, Lansing further expressed the hope that:

> China in her own interest and in that of the world will immediately set aside her factional political disputes, and that all parties and persons will work for the reestablishment of a coordinate government . . . but the full attainment of which is impossible in the midst of internal strife and discord.[17]

Lansing's policy enunciation had little effect in China although it was as a whole favorably received. Japan interpreted it as an act of interference in the domestic affairs of China. Rejecting Lansing's proposal that "an identic representation be made by the Governments of the United States, France, Great Britain, and Japan to the Chinese Government," Japanese ambassador Sato delivered to the secretary of state a memorandum containing the following remarkable statement:

> Japan possesses paramount interests both political and economic in China and she would no doubt suffer more than any other country should the turn of events there present a grave aspect, but the Japanese government holding to their avowed policy of noninterference in the essentially domestic affairs of China have scrupulously refrained from making any representation to the Chinese government touching the present crises. They . . . do not find themselves justified in joining in the proposed representation to the Chinese government.[18]

On August 14, 1917, with the United States already in the struggle, China, after a long period of hesitancy, indecision, and domestic squabbles, formally declared war on the Central Powers, accusing them of gross violations of "international law" by the continued operation of "submarine attacks." As the *quid pro quo* for China's entry into the war, it was understood that the Allied powers would make several concessions to China. Among them were the cancellation of the German-Austrian portion of Boxer indemnities due to the Allies, a limited entry of Chinese troops into

Tientsin, a revision of the conventional tariffs upward, and an assurance to China of the right to a seat at the peace conference on terms of complete equality with Japan. Militarily, Chinese participation had little weight on the scale of the war, but it made a considerable contribution to the Allied war efforts through the supply of labor forces, foodstuffs, and raw materials.

Unsettled Settlements

Dollar Offensive and the Siberian Expedition

China's entry into the war frustrated the United States' desire for China to set her own house in order rather than take to the warpath. It also meant a diplomatic defeat for the United States vis-a-vis Japan because the latter had earnestly supported the Chinese declaration of war on Germany. President Wilson was now determined to challenge and contain the Japanese ascendancy in East Asia by two unrelated means: economic warfare through a revived version of dollar diplomacy; and U.S. military participation in the Allied intervention in Siberia.

When President Wilson withdrew from the six-power consortium in 1913, he had not, in fact, given up the principles of the Open Door or of protecting China from the rapacity of the foreign powers. The war had forced the Western powers to remove their capital from China, leaving that country no choice but to borrow from Japan. With British and French urging, President Wilson decided to reverse his previous policy and reenter the consortium, and to enlist, as did his predecessor in the days of dollar diplomacy, the bankers as agents of American diplomacy.

In November 1917 Secretary Lansing made a proposal for the formation of a new four-power consortium composed of the United States, Great Britain, France, and Japan. In the summer of the following year the American bankers were invited to Washington and urged by the government to participate in the consortium. They were less than willing to do so. But they set forth two conditions under which they might consider loans to China: the aid had to be broadly international in character, including the bankers of the other three powers, and the American government would let it be known that the loans were being made at its suggestion. The Wilson administration accepted these conditions. It then sent the plan to Great Britain, France, and Japan, inviting them to join the new consortium. The key principles of the American plan called for: (1) each member government to render positive support to its own national group, (2) the member banks to pool their preferences and options in China, and (3) the member nations to respect the administrative integrity and independence of China.

These principles had been carefully designed to thwart the Japanese expansionist policy and program in China. To the Japanese the Lansing-sponsored four-power consortium was unmistakably a ghost of the Knox neutralization scheme a decade earlier. One could not help being amazed by the striking historic parallel between Knox's abortive "dollar offensive" in the form of neutralization of railways in Manchuria and Lansing's economic warfare against Japan in the form of the four-power consortium in China. Japan was fully cognizant of the United States' intent, and negotiations between the two countries became protracted. Finally Japan agreed to join only after the United States yielded to the proposition that the South Manchurian Railway zone and other specified projects and their related industrial and mining privileges in Manchuria and Inner Mongolia were to be excluded from the application of the consortium. Discussions among the powers on the specific rules and structure of the consortium continued throughout the Versailles Peace Conference after World War I and lasted until October 1920, when the final agreement was signed. The new consortium was looked upon by the Chinese as another instrument of international financial imperialism in their country. This fear gradually dissipated, but the consortium remained inactive partly because China sought loans in the world market where she could obtain the best terms available and largely because some of its members were not really interested in the joint international undertaking.

If the United States policy to curb Japanese dominance in China in the form of an international banking system was to be called a "failure," the American attempt to check the Japanese expansion in Siberia in the form of a military intervention should be termed a "fiasco."

The Bolshevik Revolution in Russia in October 1917 not only created a new situation in Europe, but it also caused the breakdown of Russian control in northern Manchuria. In this situation China saw an opportunity to regain her sovereignty over the region and in December sent troops to cooperate with the local White Russians against the Bolsheviks. The Allies, however, had no special desire to have China dragged into the Russian civil war or to see Russian rights reverted to China. The United States, for instance, warned China against her intervention, while recognizing that "China is entirely within her right in employing means to protect her sovereignty and territorial integrity."

Following Chinese troop withdrawal in January 1918, the Manchurian-Siberian border region rapidly turned into a staging area for plots and counterplots, attacks and counterattacks, financed and instigated by the British, the French, and the Japanese against the Bolsheviks. The confusion and chaos had provided Japan with a convenient opportunity for her expansionist action. She dispatched two warships to Vladivostok to protect Allied personnel and property, and in April landed marines there to maintain peace and order. The following month two Sino-Japanese treaties were signed providing for joint planning and cooperation in the defense of their interests and joint use of the Chinese Eastern Railway in the event that their territories or "the general peace and tranquility in the extreme Orient" should be threatened by the enemy.

The crushing defeat of Semënov, an Allied-supported cossack chief who had been fighting the Bolsheviks, furnished the occasion for Japan to invoke her military pact with China. In July, Japan ordered her troops into northern Manchuria. She was determined to carry out the policy of expansion on the continent at the expense of Russia whose power in the Far East had never been weaker. In doing so Japan ignored America's expressed concern that a military occupation of Manchuria would not only "arouse deep resentment in Russia" but also "defeat the desire of the United States and Japan to aid in the rehabilitation of Russia and to reenlist her people in war" against their common enemy.[19] This was the situation which compelled the United States to agree to the Siberian expedition and take steps to "impose greater restraint on Japan."

The United States had initially been opposed to intervention. Now she decided to take part in the expedition for the primary purpose of constraining unilateral Japanese action in Siberia. There were, to be sure, a number of other professed objectives of the Allied Siberian intervention. They were: (1) to restore the eastern front in the wake of the collapse of the czarist and Kerensky regimes in World War I, (2) to nip the Bolshevik government in the bud, (3) to prevent Austro-German prisoners of war from being released and armed by the Bolsheviks on behalf of the Central Powers, (4) to safeguard Allied interests in Siberia, (5) to prevent a quantity of arms and war supplies, which had been sent to Russia before her collapse, from falling into the wrong hands, and (6) to provide assistance to the Czechs who were fighting their way through Siberia eastward in an effort to reach the European western front on the Allied side.

The problem of the Czechs in Siberia played no small part in the Allied decision to intervene. During the war the czarist government allowed the Czechs who had deserted from the Austrian army, as well as those found among Austrian prisoners of war, to organize a Czech legion to fight with the Allies for the establishment of an independent state of Czechoslovakia. When Lenin's Bolshevik regime concluded the separate Treaty of Brest-Litovsk with Germany in March 1918, terminating the Russo-German hostilities, the Czechs were stranded in western Siberia. The only way for them to extricate themselves from Russia was toward the east across Siberia. Despite a negotiated agreement between the Czechs and the Bolsheviks, on the former's retreat along the Trans-Siberian Railway clashes took place between them as the Czechs made their way toward Vladivostok.

The Allied troops began landing at Vladivostok. On August 3, 1918, a British contingent arrived. A week later a battalion of the French colonial army from Indochina disembarked, followed by additional Japanese forces. On August 15-16, two United States infantry regiments from the Philippines moved in, augmented two weeks later by additional detachments from San Francisco commanded by General William Graves.

Japan and the United States came to an understanding that they would not let the intervention lead to interference in the domestic affairs of Russia or the violation of her territorial integrity. It was also understood that upon fulfillment of the avowed objectives they would immediately withdraw their troops. At the outset the two countries agreed to dispatch approximately 7,500 troops each, but in the end the total strength of the expeditionary forces of the United States and that of Japan exceeded 9,000 and 72,000, respectively.

Once in Siberia, each of the Allied forces carried out the policy of its own home government. There was no workable coordinated policy nor a unified military command among the Allies. France, failing in an attempt to reconstitute the eastern front, vainly tried to salvage her investments in Siberian railways. Great Britain, disregarding the stated principle of noninterference in Russia's domestic affairs, fought the Bolsheviks with cash, cannon, and conspiracy. Japan, playing one White Russian faction against another, hoped to absorb the maritime provinces. The United States, interjecting herself in the path of Japanese ambition, endeavored in vain to stem the tide of Japanese reinforcements.

By early 1920 the Western Allies had become extremely weary of the whole Siberian adventure. In January the United States government announced its intention to withdraw its troops and suggested that Japan should follow suit. While Japan refused to heed the American suggestion, the last United States contingent pulled out of Vladivostok on April 1, 1920.[20] Great Britain and France also withdrew their troops, leaving Siberia to the Russians and the Japanese who continued to pursue their own aims.

America's Siberian expedition was an unrewarding adventure. It was another unsuccessful American policy designed to resist Japanese imperialism-expansionism. In a sense it was a bold, perhaps vain, attempt to apply the principles of the Open Door to Siberia by military means. President Wilson, in his personally drafted *aide-mémoire,* had requested that the intervening Allies not contemplate "any interference of any kind with the political sovereignty of Russia, any intervention in her internal affairs, or *any impairment of her territorial integrity* either now or hereafter"[21] (author's italics).

Wilson's Battle at Versailles

The United States policy to blunt the tide of Japanese expansion in East Asia had manifested itself not only in the dispatch of

American troops into the Siberian steppe, but also in the diplomatic struggle of American delegates at the Versailles Peace Conference. Both proved ineffective.

When the peace conference was convened, January 12, 1919, Japanese prime objectives were centered around two important issues. One was to seek and establish racial equality among nations in principle as well as in practice. The other was to have Japanese possessions in Shantung permanently recognized by the powers and legalized by the peace treaty.

The question of racial equality had special significance to the Japanese people and to their delegates at the peace conference in view of the fact that their nationals had been subjected to invidious racial discrimination on the West Coast of the United States and in Australia. Now that Japan had become an undisputed world power, she desired to present the case at the world conference table. In doing so she assumed the leadership of the nonwhite peoples of the world in their fight against the "act of discrimination carrying with it a stigma and odium." Japan sought to establish the principle that all peoples were created equal and that they deserved equal opportunities wherever they might be on the basis of the equality of man. It was a racial Open Door and a challenge to the theory of white supremacy.

As the presentation of this delicate question to the conference appeared inevitable, President Wilson assigned his trusted advisor, Edward M. House, to secure preliminary agreement among the key participants on the general principle of racial equality, which would eventually be inserted in the covenant of the League of Nations. In his conversations with Lord Robert Cecil of Great Britain and Prime Minister William M. Hughes of Australia, House found the former noncommittal and the latter unequivocally opposed.

In the middle of February 1919, the issue was formally brought to a meeting of the commission drafting the League covenant. Here Baron Makino of Japan proposed what the covenant should provide:

The equality of nations being a basic principle of the League of Nations, the High Contracting Parties agree to accord, as soon as possible, to all alien nationals of the States members of the League equal and just treatment in every respect, making no distinction, either in law or in fact, on account of their race or nationality.[22]

The members of the commission, however, decided to delete the Makino amendment from the covenant with the reservation that the issue could be brought up again. Although Japan had consented to the deletion, the initial defeat had invariably cast doubts in the minds of the Japanese as to Wilson's sincerity respecting the League as a means to secure justice and equality among all nations and all people. In addition, the Japanese could clearly perceive that the American Asian policy contained within it obvious contradictions and obstructionist tactics. The United States sought to dislodge Japan from China, while demanding Japan's assurances of nonaggression toward the Philippines; she advocated equal opportunities for all peoples in Asia, while discriminating against the Orientals in her own domain; she endeavored to restore Shantung to China, while óbtaining for herself the strategic island of Yap in the Southwest Pacific; she attempted to prevent Japan from acquiring portions of Siberia, while dispatching troops there to counteract Japan's move; and she decided to thwart Japanese financial hegemony in China by instituting the new four-power international consortium.

The United States officials, including the president and his advisors, were not unaware of these contradictions. A State Department memorandum dated March 19, 1919, for instance, recognized the advisability of supporting the racial equality amendment and suggested that "if . . . [we] grant Japan our approval of the proposed amendment, a concession to her pride of race which she will highly appreciate, we are entitled to ask Japan to be equally conciliatory and to do justice to China in Shantung." Nevertheless, the American delegates at the peace conference did not follow their better judgment.

For the second time, at another session of the commission, Japan proposed to include a clause of racial equality and nondiscriminatory treatment in the text of the preamble to the covenant. To Japan the issue had become a matter of national prestige and pride. She let it be known that she would join the League only on terms of equality with other member nations and the rejection of her proposal might result in a Japanese boycott of the organization. The French and the Italian delegations favored the proposal. Prime Minister Hughes of Australia was vehemently opposed. Lord Robert Cecil of Great Britain had to make the choice between the friendship of the Anglo-Japanese Alliance partner and the solidarity of the British Empire; he chose the latter. Not unlike Lord Cecil, President Wilson was also faced with a difficult and delicate dilemma. He personally favored the adoption of the Japanese proposal. But the practical and real questions haunting the president were numerous. Would the United States Senate readily give its consent to a treaty embodying the principle of racial equality? Which was more important, the continued enhancement of the Anglo-American friendship or the temporary mitigation of Japanese-American enmity? The most crucial question of all was how to reconcile international recognition of the doctrine of racial equality with internal condonation of the practice of racial discrimination.

President Wilson answered these questions with his action. On April 11, 1919, the commission voted on the Japanese proposal, with the result of eleven to six in its favor. Wilson, who, together with his advisor Colonel House, had abstained from voting and who was chairman of the meeting on that day, ruled that the motion was defeated on account of the lack of unanimity. Without a doubt, political realities outweighed the political idealism of the president. To the Japanese the rejection was a bitter reality. Baron Makino insisted that he would raise the issue again in the plenary session of the conference, but to all intents and purposes the fight was unmistakably lost. The first demand of Japan was denied.

But the denial placed Japan in a strong bargaining position to press for the second demand—the Shantung claims. Shantung was actually the most important proposition on which Japan could accept neither defeat nor retreat.

Before the opening of the conference, Japan had assumed that the various secret treaties of 1917 with the European powers had guaranteed her claims in Shantung. After the opening of the conference, however, Japan soon discovered that some of the Allied powers, especially the United States, questioned Japan's claims. When the Shantung issue was first presented to a meeting of the

Council of Ten in January 1919, Baron Makino protested the presence of the Chinese representatives on the grounds that China had no right to participate in any of these discussions relating to Shantung. He was overruled and the Chinese delegates attended the meetings.

The Japanese delegation contended that Japan had captured Kiaochow from Germany in the beginning of the hostilities and continued to occupy the Shantung Province, that by the Sino-Japanese agreement of 1915 (the Twenty-One Demands) China had consented to the direct transfer of German rights to Japan, and that by the Sino-Japanese agreement of 1918 China had further recognized the validity of Japan's rights and privileges in Shantung.

Against these contentions the Chinese delegation, headed by Wellington Koo, argued that Japanese occupation of Kiaochow constituted a constant threat to the capital city of Peking, that the 1915 agreement was illegal and void because it had been signed under duress, and that China had formally entered the war against the Central Powers, declaring "all treaties, agreements, conventions, concluded between China and Germany and between China and Austria-Hungary are, in conformity with the law of nations and international practice, all abrogated."[23]

China's position won support from almost all delegates, whereas Japan's position became increasingly unpopular. But Japan's defense for her argument was augmented by the secret treaties with the Allies who had committed themselves to support Japan. President Wilson also came to realize the detrimental consequence of the Lansing-Ishii agreement. In vain he proposed that all spheres of influence of the powers in China be abolished.

The deadlock appeared insurmountable; Japan was determined not to give in or to compromise, threatening to walk out of the conference if her demands were again rejected. President Wilson's position proved untenable; he could not save the conference and reject the Japanese demands at the same time. Seemingly, the means to surmount this impasse and to save the conference was for the Allied powers to concede to Japan. Lloyd George had announced that Britain considered the secret treaties binding and therefore would support Japan's demands. Wilson reluctantly yielded to Japan against the strong protest of China. On April 30 the Council of Three (Wilson, George, Clemenceau) approved the transfer of Germany's rights in Shantung to Japan. Specifically, the terms as incorporated in the Versailles treaty were as follows:

> The policy of Japan is to hand back the Shantung Peninsula in full sovereignty to China, retaining only the economic privileges granted to Germany and the right to establish a settlement under the usual conditions at Tsingtao. . . . The owners of the railway will use special police only to ensure security for traffic. They will be used for no other purpose. The police force will be composed of Chinese, and such Japanese instructors as the directors of the railway may select will be appointed by the Chinese Government.[24]

The stipulation in the international treaty was intended to be a substitute for the provisions of the Sino-Japanese bilateral treaties of 1915 and 1918. President Wilson, while refusing to recognize the validity of the latter, hoped to see the controversies between China and Japan resolved through the mediation of the Council of the League of Nations. From the standpoint of Japan, however, the 1915 and 1918 agreements were internationalized, without affecting Japan's right to invoke them should China fail to carry out the agreements. Thus Japan had lost the fight for the intangible principle of racial equality but won the battle for her tangible privileges in Shantung.

Chinese Reaction to the Treaty of Versailles

When the news of the Shantung decision at Paris reached China, public anger, resentment, and disappointment took the form of numerous protest rallies and anti-Japanese boycotts spearheaded by students. Especially on May 4, 1919, thousands of students marched through the streets of Peking, accusing the Tuan Ch'i-jui regime of traitorous effeminacy and denouncing the Western powers for their ever-treacherous chicanery. The May Fourth Movement, as it became subsequently known, clearly represented a resurgence of Chinese nationalism directed internally against the enfeebled national leadership and externally against vigorous international imperialism. The political consciousness of the Chinese people as manifested in public opinion, street demonstrations, and mass rallies had emerged as new forces in Chinese politics. The May Fourth Movement indeed signaled the end of an era and heralded the dawning of a new one. China refused to sign the Treaty of Versailles, stating, "Dissatisfied with the conditions embodied in three clauses relating to Shantung, this country refuses to sign the Treaty."[25] China felt betrayed by the Versailles peacemakers. The Allied promises, explicit or implicit, made to China at the time of her entry into the war were forgotten or ignored. Once victory was won, the Allied leaders reassessed China's role and what she deserved. Lord Balfour of Britain tersely concluded that "by the efforts of Japan and her allies, China, without the expenditure of a single life, had restored to her rights which she could never have recovered for herself."[26] Clemenceau of France bluntly told the unhappy Chinese delegates that "they must sign the Treaty with the intention of abiding by it or not sign."[27] President Wilson's prime concern was "to keep the world together, get the League of Nations with Japan in it and then try to secure justice for the Chinese not only as regarding Japan but England, France, Russia, all of whom had concessions in China."[28]

In the tradition of the Open Door, Wilson aspired for the preservation and maintenance of the territorial integrity of China. But Japan's adamant claims on Shantung negated that aspiration. To deny the Japanese demand would have caused Japan to wreck the conference and to torpedo the League. In an effort to save the conference and the League, therefore, President Wilson was compelled to give in to the Shantung issue in the manner Secretary of State Lansing termed "a complete surrender to Japan . . . a calamity and an abandonment of principles."[29] He was fully aware of the repercussions of his decision, which would infuriate the Chinese, jubilate the Japanese, and disappoint the Americans. He anticipated that he would be accused of violating his own principles, but he had to work for the greater aim of international order more than for that of his own personal credibility. He seemed to have believed that those inconsistencies inherent in his decisions could be eradicated or forgotten in due time by maintenance of world security through the League of Nations.

Later, in August 1919, President Wilson answered some of the questions put to him by the members of the United States Senate Committee on Foreign Relations:

Q. You would have preferred, as I think most of us would, that there had been a different conclusion of the Shantung provision, or the Shantung difficulty or controversy, at the Paris Peace Conference?

A. Yes; I frankly intimated that.

Q. Did it require the unanimous consent of the members of the peace conference to reach a decision like the Shantung decision?

A. Every decision; yes, sir . . .

Q. Do you mind stating, or would you prefer not, what it was that was demanded by Japan?

A. Only the conclusion that I thought it was the best that could be got under the circumstances. . . .

Q. You could not have got the signature of Japan if you had not given Shantung?

A. That is my judgment.

Q. You say you were notified to that effect?

A. Yes, sir.

Q. As I understand, you were notified that they had instructions not to sign unless this was included?

A. Yes.

Q. And it was your judgment that after the treaty had been ratified, China's rights would be protected and Japan would surrender to China what she said she would?

A. Yes.

Q. As I understand it, you consider this verbal agreement effective as relating to Shantung and you understood that this conveyance would be followed by a conveyance to China?

A. Not to supersede it, but the action by Japan is to follow.[30]

The post-Versailles, Wilson-Lansing strategy vis-a-vis Japan centered on how to make her honor her "commitment" to restore Shantung to China. The United States assumed the role of self-appointed guardian for China's political and territorial integrity.

Such a policy was easily interpreted by the Japanese public, if not by the officials, as having ultimate designs in China, such as America's desires to obtain the former German settlement in Tientsin. Japan likewise claimed to be the "protector" of China against Western imperialism and aggression. Expressing the typical viewpoint of the average Japanese, the *Herald of Asia* observed:

> It is unfortunate that all Japan's efforts in trying to discourage Western aggression in China should be interpreted in that country as aiming at aggression on the part of Japan herself. ... If China wants to test Japan's sincerity let her refuse all further concessions to Occidental nations and secure for all time the inalienation of her territory, and Japan's task in regard to China will be finished. It is a question, however, whether China is yet able to do without the assistance of Japan in keeping foreign nations at bay; and this help, strange to say, is what China does not want. Is it that China would rather be a slave of the white races than the equal of Japan? ..."[31]

Herein lay the point of conflict between the United States and Japan. Beneath the veneer of the rhetoric of "safeguarding" or "protecting" China's integrity, was the truth that the United States and Japan were in each other's way in the pursuit of their respective national interests.

Japan, therefore, looked upon the United States as the principal opponent in East Asia and the Pacific region. Viewed from Tokyo, the United States policies were less than candid, if not obnoxious. America's expeditionary forces in Siberia posed more of a hindrance than cooperation. The United States was reportedly aligning herself with the Bolsheviks and had developed ambitions in Siberia at variance with other powers. The State Department manipulated the international consortium groups against independent Japanese loans. The touchy issue of immigration was allowed to deteriorate to the point of constant irritation. The island of Yap was staked out for special use, strategic as well as commercial, in the midst of the Pacific islands to be mandated to

Japan. The menacing and undesirable race in naval armaments was about to begin.

There had been other unofficial sources of irritation which aggravated U.S.-Japanese relations. With respect to the Shantung decision at Paris, the American Chamber of Commerce of China sent a statement to the president, declaring in part, "unless those pledges [to return Shantung to China] are accompanied with guarantees which make it [patent] to all that they will be made effective within reasonable time, otherwise all pledges regarding the maintenance of the Open Door, of equal opportunity, will become mere scraps of paper . . ." The American University Club of China expressed its apprehension that "their helpful work may be destroyed unless some sort of confidence in the Western nations can be restored." In the same vein, the Anglo-American Association of Peking adopted a resolution, stating in part: "The evil consequences of conditions which are not only subversive of the principle of national self-determination, but also of equality of opportunity, will be greatly accentuated, if Japan, a near neighbor, be now substituted for Germany, . . ."³² Those protests against the Japanese in Shantung prompted the Japanese government to dispatch a memorandum to the Department of State, emphasizing that "the agitation . . . has ceased to be a mere demonstration against Japan and is fast becoming a menace to the general peace and order in China."³³ The State Department, in response, undertoned the Japanese apprehension by replying that "the agitation will of itself subside in due course without the ill consequences now so much feared by the Japanese government," adding that "these minor incidents can in no way impair the cordial and friendly feelings which have so long existed between the two governments."³⁴

These words were a diplomatic nicety which camouflaged the basic, unresolved problems regarding Shantung. The United States had never recognized the 1915 and 1918 agreements and looked upon the Versailles treaty as superseding them. Japan, on the other hand, doggedly maintained the validity and sanctity of the agreements. In August 1919, the Japanese foreign minister, Uchida, attempted to clarify his government's policy respecting the Shantung question which he believed was "little understood or appreciated abroad." He announced:

> Abiding faithfully by pledge which she [Japan] gave China in 1915 she is quite willing to restore to China whole territory in question and enter upon negotiations with Peking government regarding necessary arrangements to give effect to pledge as soon as possible after Versailles Treaty shall have been ratified by Japan. . . . Japanese government has moreover under contemplation proposals for establishment at Tsingtao of general foreign settlement instead of exclusive Japanese settlement which by agreement of 1915 with China they are entitled to claim.[35]

Japan thus rejected the persistent United States presumption that these agreements had questionable validity. The references in the above announcement to the 1915 treaty proved not only irritating to the United States but also contrary to President Wilson's expressed view that "negotiations on basis of agreements of 1915 and 1918 would not be tolerated." Secretary Lansing in his rebuttal asserted that the United States government had given assent to Articles 156, 157, and 158 of the Versailles treaty with the understanding that Japan should agree that "the Sino-Japanese Agreements of 1915 and 1918 should not be relied upon or referred to in the negotiations for the return [of Shantung] to China, . . . unless the latter refused to negotiate" under the same articles of the Versailles treaty.[36]

Since China had refused to sign the Versailles treaty at all, the United States had found little basis for insisting that Sino-Japanese negotiations should be conducted under these specified articles of the treaty. Conversely, Japan had all the rights and justification to invoke the 1915 and 1918 agreements in initiating negotiations with China for a settlement of the Shantung issue.

The Peking regime, however, was in no mood or position to enter into bilateral negotiations with Japan. The government itself was plagued with factional strife. Popular resentment toward Japan was prevalent throughout the country as manifested in strikes and boycotts of Japanese goods. Most major powers, except the United

States, were either committed by treaties to support Japan or openly sympathetic to her. Hence, any direct negotiations which the Peking government might undertake with Japan would invite most vehement protest by the Chinese people and the outcome might result in the strengthening of Japan's hold on Shantung. Japan, repeatedly professing her readiness, pressed for negotiations, but China stalled, demanding the withdrawal of Japanese troops as a prerequisite for negotiation. But Japan was determined to station her troops not only in Shantung, but in Manchuria, Siberia, and Sakhalin. These and other issues remained unsolved until the opening of the Washington conference in 1921–1922.

President Wilson's vision of a harmonious world order which was to be founded on twin pillars—the Versailles treaty and the League of Nations—was shattered as the United States Senate on March 19, 1920, voted against the treaty. It was disheartening for Wilson. The following year he appealed to his countrymen in the presidential election for a "solemn referendum" on American membership in the world organization which the Senate had rejected. The confused voters delivered a verdict by electing the Republican Warren G. Harding. The League was once again rejected. The great majority of the American people seemed to have believed that the United States should revive the policy of neutrality, uphold the Monroe Doctrine, and take the path of noninvolvement in foreign policy. Mindful of the great sacrifices incurred by their participation in World War I, they wanted little or no involvement in the affairs of Europe if possible. The impulse in Washington was to disengage from the Old World. President Harding set the tone and direction of his foreign policy by proclaiming in his inaugural address that the United States would have "no part in directing the destinies of the Old World" and could "enter into no political commitments, nor assume any economic obligations or subject our decisions to any other than our own authority." Contained in this speech was the unmistakable signal of isolationism which sought to pursue nonentanglement in international politics.

CHAPTER FOUR

The Simmering Decade
1921—1931

Naval Limitations and After

Isolation or Participation

American isolationism at this time, however, was not a universally applied policy. It purported, for certain, to keep the United States out of trouble spots in Europe, but it did not mean a complete end of American participation in other regions of the world. On the contrary, the United States continued to be actively involved in East Asian affairs. This was readily understandable. Generally speaking, isolationism in its application was indistinguishable from the Monroe Doctrine, which was originally designed to prevent European powers from intervening in the western hemisphere.[1] As the American frontiers extended from Alaska through the Aleutians, Hawaii, Midway, Guam, and Yap to the Philippines, so was the concept of the Monroe Doctrine expanded to bring these territories as well as their adjacent areas under its cover. The United States could not exclude East Asia from the scope of "isolationism" any more than she could exclude Canada or Latin America from the domain of the Monroe Doctrine. Thus seen, isolationism was an expression of the national temper that desired nonengulfment in continental affairs across the Atlantic, but not across the Pacific.

Indeed, the Harding administration from the very beginning was compelled to deal with an enormous volume of unfinished business in East Asia. Among the most pressing unresolved problems were the naval armament race between Japan and the United States, the Shantung issue, the Allied Siberian intervention, the mandate territories in the Pacific, and the immigration controversy.

Having emerged from World War I unscathed, Japan and the United States were at odds with each other and demonstrated every symptom of power rivalry in the Far East. The United States came to realize the inherent danger of increasing Japanese power and influence, which was manifested in Japanese militarism, expansionism, and imperialism. America's deepest concern was the rapid rise of Japanese naval power.

There were a number of ways for the United States to meet this challenge. First, the United States could resort to the time-honored "gunboat diplomacy"—coercion—at the risk of waging a war with Japan. But as times changed, so did the situation. Japan was no longer the feudal society which had been frightened by the sight of "black ships." She had become a formidable world power imbued with a sense of national destiny to make "Asia for the Asians." Japan could not be easily intimidated nor cajoled into submission.

Second, the United States could plunge into the naval armament race with Japan so as either to neutralize or to surpass the latter's naval force. Such a course of action would certainly alarm the British whose policy had been to maintain absolute naval supremacy over the Seven Seas. Consequently, it could result in a three-way armaments race, without assurance of bringing about stability or security in East Asia. Moreover, the Anglo-Japanese Alliance was still in effect and if the United States program of naval construction should "drive these two powers to make common cause against the United States before the program could be completed, or should it merely conduce Anglo-Japanese political solidarity in the Far East, it would be defeating its purpose."[2] Third, the United States could devise diplomatic means to lessen the U.S.-Japanese rivalry, to restrain Japan, to promote general reduction of naval armaments, and to minimize the chances for armed conflict. Furthermore, the United States could try to replace the obnoxious Anglo-Japanese Alliance with a more general multilateral agreement with a view to relieving Great Britain of the legal obligation of having to come to aid Japan should Japan be at war with the United States.

The Harding administration chose the third alternative. Earlier, in December 1920, Senator Borah of Idaho had introduced a resolution calling on the president to invite Japan and Great Britain to a three-power conference to discuss reduction in the naval building programs. President Harding adopted the Borah plan and declared in his inaugural address:

> We are ready to associate ourselves with the nations of the world, great and small, for conference, for counsel, to seek the expressed views of world opinion, to recommend a way to approximate disarmament and relieve the crushing burden of military and naval establishment.... America is ready to encourage, eager to initiate, anxious to participate in any seemly program likely to lessen the probability of war....[3]

When Harding's intentions were known, Great Britain responded favorably for several reasons. First, exhausted by the war in terms of national resources and manpower coupled with heavy war debts, Great Britain could ill afford any form of costly armament race with major powers. Second, the British came to realize the inevitable fact that they were no longer able to maintain the traditional two-power standard (superior to any two nations combined) and were prepared to concede to the United States a naval parity. A disarmament conference would provide the British with an opportunity to formalize naval equality on a more realistic basis without critically upsetting the balance of power. Third, they hoped that the United States, accepting the parity, would concentrate her navy in the Pacific and leave the Atlantic to Britain's dominance, thus removing the chances of British-American rivalry.

Through formal as well as informal channels of communications, the United States and Great Britain by June 1921 came to understand and appreciate each other's position: both favored an international disarmament conference and both were deeply concerned with the fate of the Anglo-Japanese Alliance which was due for renewal in July 1921.

As for the latter, the United States viewed it with a contemptuous apprehension. Originally designed as a measure of mutual assistance and cooperation in view of the threat of Russia and Germany in the Far East, the continuance of the alliance after all dangers from those sources had been eliminated could rightly be regarded as prejudicial to the United States. In the light of a new state of international tension arising from the Japanese-American rivalry, the recurring question was: The original source of danger having been removed, against whom and for what purpose is the Alliance maintained?

As Anglo-Japanese negotiations for its renewal were rumored, the United States let it be known that she hoped to see it terminated; or should it be renewed, it should contain the provisions affirming "the principle of equal opportunity in China" and indicating clearly "that the Alliance is not aimed at the United States."[4]

Great Britain, meanwhile, was initially determined to renew the alliance for at least a year with an inclusion of the specific legal exemption from military obligations for the United States. However, in one of the Imperial conferences held in June 1921, the British government, persuaded by Canadian prime minister Arthur Meighen's forceful argument, reversed its earlier position and accepted the idea of replacing the alliance with a general agreement reached among the major nations concerned at a conference on Far Eastern and Pacific affairs. A crucial question at this juncture for the British government was what reasonable explanations for the termination of the alliance could be given to Japan without offending her pride and sensitivity. For nearly two decades the alliance had been regarded by many Japanese as a status symbol of great power and as a guarantee for national security by virtue of being allied with the then mightiest Western power. Lloyd George had to come up with a satisfactory and attractive substitute for the alliance. He decided to capitalize on the American desire for a disarmament conference in which he hoped some form of international agreements in lieu of the alliance could be arranged.

Both the United States and Great Britain were now moving in the same direction with common objectives. After the flurry of exchanges of diplomatic dispatches among Washington, London,

Tokyo, Paris, Rome, and Peking for the purpose of arranging the time, place, and agenda of the conference, on August 21 the United States extended formal invitations to the major powers to a conference on the limitation of armaments and problems of the Pacific and the Far East, to convene in Washington on November 11 (Armistice Day), 1921.[5]

The Washington Conference

The Washington Conference, from November 12, 1921, to February 6, 1922, produced seven treaties and twelve resolutions. Among them were the Four-Power Treaty, the Five-Power Treaty, and the Nine-Power Treaty.

At the opening session Secretary of State Hughes bluntly proposed a plan for reduction of naval armaments of the three powers —the United States, Great Britain, and Japan. Specifically he urged an immediate stoppage in the construction of battleships, the scrapping of those already in service, the limitation by treaty of dreadnought replacement on the basis of prescribed ratios, and the application of the same principle to aircraft carriers, destroyers, cruisers, and submarines.

The Hughes plan constituted the foundation for subsequent Four-Power and Five-Power treaties. The Four-Power Treaty,[6] agreed to on December 10 and signed three days later, bound the signatories (the United States, Great Britain, Japan, and France) "to respect their rights in relation to their insular possessions and insular dominions in the region of the Pacific Ocean."[7] Should a controversy arise between any of the signatories "out of any Pacific question and involving their said rights," which could not be settled by diplomacy, then they would invite other parties "to a joint conference to which the whole subject will be referred for consideration and adjustment."

The second article of the treaty, reminiscent of the Root-Takahira Agreement of 1908, stipulated:

If the said rights are threatened by the aggressive action of any other power, the High Contracting Parties shall communicate with one another fully and frankly in order to arrive at an understanding as to the most efficient measures to be taken, jointly or separately, to meet the exigencies of the particular situation.

The treaty would remain in force for ten years. After that period it would continue to be in effect unless terminated by any of the signatories with twelve months' notice. The treaty replaced the Anglo-Japanese Alliance. In essence it substituted a multilateral diplomatic consultation for a bilateral military obligation. The treaty was neither a quadripartite mutual defense pact nor a collective self-defense measure. But it was a regional nonaggression pact designed to settle international disputes by peaceful means.

The powers proceeded a step further to translate their nonaggression, self-restrained, well-meaning pledges into specifics. War was fought by nations with will and weapons. They succeeded in controlling their "will" by the Four-Power Treaty; now they desired to regulate the instruments and installations of war—warships and fortifications. The Five-Power Treaty was the culmination of these desires and their efforts to limit naval armaments, and at the same time it was an inseparable companion of the Four-Power Treaty.

Signed on February 6, 1922, by the United States, Great Britain, Japan, France, and Italy, the Five-Power Treaty had two principal components: (1) the limitations on naval armaments and (2) the nonfortification of insular possessions. As for the naval limitations, capital ships constituted the prime concern. Hence, the five powers agreed: (1) to abandon current capital ship programs, (2) to accept prescribed tonnage quotas which might require the scrapping of specific ships, built or being built, (3) to enforce a ten-year moratorium in capital ship construction, and (4) to set the maximum size of capital ships to 35,000 tons with guns no larger than sixteen-inch caliber. The tonnage quotas, when finalized, would be 525,000 each for the United States and Great Britain; 315,000 for Japan; and 175,000 each for France and Italy—a ratio of 5 : 5 : 3 : 1.67 : 1.67. The limitations on quotas, size, tonnage, and gun caliber were also placed on aircraft carriers. No cruiser could weigh more than 10,000 tons or mount guns of more than eight inches. No restrictions were placed on destroyers or submarines. As for the question of nonfortification, Article XIX of the treaty provided for the maintenance of the status quo in the specified territories. In brief, those specified territories were: (1) for the United States—the insular possessions in the Pacific Ocean and the Aleutian Islands, but not those adjacent to the coast of the United States, Alaska, the Panama Canal Zone, and the Hawaiian Islands; (2) for Great Britain—Hong Kong and the insular possessions in the Pacific Ocean (east of the meridian of 110° east longitude), but not those adjacent to the coasts of Canada, Australia, and New Zealand; and (3) for Japan —the Kuril Islands, the Bonin Islands, Amami-Oshima, the Ryu-kyu Islands, Formosa and Pescadores, and the mandate territories in the Pacific Ocean, but not, of course, the Japanese home islands. On the above specified areas, "no new fortifications or naval bases," no measures "to increase the existing naval facilities for the repair and maintenance of naval forces," or no increase "in the coast defense" were permitted.

The Five-Power Treaty was to remain in force until the end of 1936 and thereafter it could be terminated, with two years' notice, by any one of the signatories. The treaty was regarded as beneficial by each member in its own way.

Secretary of State Hughes appeared to have conceded more than he received in return, but what he had given away were a few warships under construction which would have remained unfinished for lack of funds. Congress had been reluctant to appropriate enough funds either for building a strong navy or for fortification of Guam and the Philippines. None of the capital ships which were subsequently scrapped would ever have proved battleworthy. The fact that the Senate promptly approved the treaty in March 1922 by a vote of 74 to 1 reflected unmistakably the prevailing national mood for less military expenditure. Having correctly assessed the reality and having given away nothing substantial, Secretary Hughes skillfully managed to achieve the foreign policy goal set forth by President Harding in his inaugural address a year earlier.

Japan, on the other hand, had strengthened her security by the treaty. The 5 : 5 : 3 ratio for capital ships appeared to be disadvantageous to her, but it would not create any disastrous naval inferiority in view of the fact that the United States, Japan's fore-most potential adversary, had to defend the two oceans and Great Britain had to deploy her fleet thinly throughout the seven seas. Moreover, Japan could continue to build naval armaments by concentrating on smaller vessels such as cruisers, destroyers, and submarines. In addition, the nonfortification of the Aleutians, Guam, and the Philippines meant that the United States, in the event of hostilities with Japan, would be compelled to conduct military operations from the home bases in Hawaii, some four thousand miles away from Japan. Likewise, Britain's operational naval bases nearest to Japan were located in Singapore, some two thousand miles away from the southernmost territory of Formosa.

Great Britain was equally benefitted by the treaty. The brightest jewel on the British crown was India. The treaty did not prohibit Britain from fortifying the first line of defense against possible Japanese attack running from Burma through Malaya, Singapore, and Australia to New Zealand. Viewed from Singapore, Britain's Asian fortress, the nearest Japanese offensive bases were nearly thirty-five hundred miles away. Thus the security of India as well as other of Britain's Asian dominions was considerably enhanced.

The Nine-Power Treaty, also signed on February 6, 1922, was exclusively dedicated to China problems. The powers attempted to stabilize their relations in China by an international agreement lest China would become a "Balkan" of East Asia. The initial idea came from Lord Balfour, who presented to Hughes a draft design to formulate a five-power (the United States, Great Britain, China, Japan, and France) treaty on China. The draft sought to establish four key principles: (1) the general peace in Asia, (2) preservation of the territorial integrity and independence of China, (3) equal commercial opportunity in China, and (4) international cooperation with respect to China.[8] Balfour then passed the baton to Hughes, who was determined to make the Open Door "a matter of binding international obligation among all the powers concerned."

During the course of debate and discussions in the conferences on Pacific and East Asian questions, the Chinese representatives presented a series of demands which the Versailles conference had failed to effectuate; namely, the abrogation of the unequal treaties, the restoration of Shantung, cancellation of the Twenty-One Demands together with "all special rights, privileges, immunities, or commitments . . . claimed by any of the powers in or relating to China."[9] The ensuing negotiations resulted in the treaty which incorporated some, not all, of these demands.

Article One, the nucleus of the Nine-Power Treaty, stipulated that the contracting powers, other than China, agreed:

1. To respect the sovereignty, the independence, and the territorial and administrative integrity of China;
2. To provide the fullest and most unembarrassed opportunity to China to develop and maintain for herself an effective and stable government;
3. To use their influence for the purpose of effectually establishing and maintaining the principle of equal opportunity for the commerce and industry of all nations throughout the territory of China;
4. To refrain from taking advantage of conditions in China in order to seek special rights of subjects or citizens of friendly States, and from countenancing action inimical to the security of such States.[10]

Article Two was devoted to the strict preservation of the status quo in China and forbade the powers to "infringe upon or impair the principles stated in Article One."

The words "Open Door" were explicitly mentioned in Article Three. Thus the Open Door policy of the United States was written into international law. This article also bound the powers not to seek special privileges or interests in China, nor frustrate "the practical application of the principle of equal opportunity."

The remainder of the treaty provided for: nonsupport of their nationals in seeking spheres of influence (Article Four), China's obligation not to exercise or permit unfair discrimination of any kind (Article Five), China's neutrality in time of war (Article Six), full and frank communication among the signatories whenever a situation was deemed to necessitate the application of the treaty (Article Seven), and an invitation to nonsignatories to adhere to the treaty (Article Eight). The treaty contained no provisions for a terminal date or procedure.

The Nine-Power Treaty, like the Four-Power Treaty and the Five-Power Treaty, was not a mutual defense pact or a collective self-defense agreement. The preservation of China's integrity, political and territorial, depended upon the *integrity* and good faith of the powers to keep their promises made in behalf of China. Should China be attacked, none of the signatories was obliged to come to her aid. All they could do was to "communicate" and "discuss" the application of the treaty.[11] The United States was not ready to use force to back up her Asian policy. Lacking in any form of military commitment, the Nine-Power Treaty was favorably received in the United States as shown by the senatorial consent of a 66 to 0 vote.

The Nine-Power Treaty was another disappointment to China because it failed to meet the full range of China's demands and aspirations. Tariff autonomy was not restored; territorial integrity in Manchuria and Shantung was not reestablished; and foreign powers' extraterritorial rights in China were not rescinded. The conference, however, produced some compensatory agreements and resolutions on behalf of China. The nine powers signed a customs convention providing for an immediate 5 percent increase in import duties. A commission was created to study the problems of extraterritorial jurisdiction in China and to make recommendations for improving the situation. The conference adopted a resolution calling for the withdrawal of foreign troops from China. Great Britain offered to restore Weihaiwei in due time. A bilateral Sino-Japanese treaty was signed, whereby Japan would return the Kiaochow leasehold while retaining the Tsinan-Tsingtao Railway for another fifteen years. All in all China reaped lean crops in Washington. Nevertheless, China was better treated at Washington than at Paris.

The Washington Conference also brought an end to the episode of the Siberian intervention. It should be recalled that the United States withdrew her Siberian expeditionary forces in April 1920. Great Britain and France likewise pulled out their troops. But the Japanese troops remained in occupation of the huge circular area stretching from Vladivostok to Chita. Japan hoped to establish a buffer state in this region separate from and independent of the Bolshevik regime in Moscow. This hope materialized momentarily

when the Far Eastern Republic of Siberia was formed as a buffer
state in eastern Siberia against Japan. Working closely with Moscow, Kransnoshchekov, head of "Far Eastern Republic" in Siberia,
paved the way for Japan to terminate her Siberian intervention,
which had become more and more costly and unpopular at home
and abroad.

Against this background, in January 1922 Baron Shidehara,
the Japanese delegate to the conference, made the following
statement:

> The military expedition of Japan to Siberia was originally
> undertaken in common accord and in cooperation with the
> United States in 1918. It was primarily intended to render
> assistance to the Czechoslovak troops who in their homeward
> journey across Siberia from European Russia, found them-
> selves in grave and pressing danger at the hands of hostile
> forces under German command.... The Japanese govern-
> ment [is] now seriously considering plans which would justify
> them in carrying out their decision of the complete withdrawal
> of Japanese troops from the Maritime Province, with
> reasonable precaution for the security of Japanese residents
> and of the Korean frontier regions. It is for this purpose that
> negotiations were opened some time ago at Dairen between
> the Japanese representatives and the agents of the Chinese
> Government.... The military occupation of the Russian
> Province of Sakhalin is only a temporary measure, and will
> naturally come to an end as soon as a satisfactory settlement
> of the question shall have been arranged with an orderly
> Russian Government.[12]

Subsequently, Japan withdrew her troops from Siberia in October 1922 and from northern Sakhalin in January 1925.

Immigration Conflagration

The Washington Conference as a whole did not solve basic
problems, it simply "froze" the status quo. This was followed by
a general climate of "thaw"—the atmosphere of international
amity among the powers. Yet beneath the surface irreconcilable

enmity persisted. Both in the United States and in Japan a small group of critics, powerful and influential, attacked the Washington arrangements with stinging impact. William Randolph Hearst, for instance, blasted the Washington Conference in a chauvinistic tone:

> Great Britain and Japan are the ones who gain in this Conference, the ones who are going home satisfied. . . . We have surrendered the naval supremacy that lay within our grasp, and which would always have protected us from any attack by overseas nations. . . . But worst of all is the fact that Japan, by the recognition formally accorded it in this Conference, has been made the dominant nation among the yellow nations of the world, the militaristic leader of a thousand million racial enemies of the white peoples.[13]

On the other side of the Pacific, the Tokyo newspaper *Kokumin* deplored the same conference in a caustic mood:

> Under the circumstances, no Japanese, however optimistic, will have the heart to be optimistic of Japan's future. No one will be able to deny that Japan has [had] her hands and feet cut off in Washington. . . . American public opinion make[s] it believe that benefits have been conferred upon Japan. Japan was in a position wherein she was obliged to abandon the Anglo-Japanese Alliance. In place of the Alliance, a quadruple agreement was given to Japan. Thus America has saved Japan's face, American public opinion claims. . . . By virtue of the quadruple entente, Japan decided not to make an issue out of race discrimination in America. Our government and delegates are so magnanimous that they would not raise an issue out of the race discrimination which is insulting to the Japanese race. . . . They have never been magnanimous to our countrymen. They are magnanimous to Western peoples. Because they are afraid of Western peoples, they feign to be magnanimous. . . .[14]

Voices such as these tended to have special appeal to ready ears and to incense potent racism and xenophobia. A new wave of ill-feeling toward each other surged so high as to place an added strain on Japanese-American relations. This was the situation when in 1924 the United States Congress enacted the discriminatory, anti-Japanese immigration law.

It should be recalled that in 1913 the California legislature, in defiance of President Wilson's advice, had passed the law prohibiting Japanese from owning land. In 1920, by another law, California denied Japanese nationals in the state all privileges to lease land, to act as guardians for *nisei* children, and to invest in landowning companies. In the following years, some fourteen other states, from Oregon to Delaware, joined California in enacting similar alien land laws. In a series of litigations[15] the Supreme Court of the United States ruled that Japanese were ineligible for naturalization and that the state land laws were valid and constitutional without violating the U.S.-Japanese treaty of 1911.

At the federal level Congress passed discriminatory laws establishing quotas for aliens of any particular nationality to be granted admission to the United States. This quota system, outrageously unfair to Orientals, however, did not exclude them completely. The volatile question of Oriental exclusion became critical again in December 1923, when the United States Congress began debating a new immigration bill designed to bar persons ineligible for citizenship (meaning Japanese without naming them) from entering the United States. Both Japanese Ambassador Masanao Hanihara and Secretary of State Hughes were concerned and alarmed. Secretary Hughes was strongly opposed to the proposed legislation and in February 1924 advised Congress not to pass it because "the Japanese are a sensitive people, and unquestionably would regard such a legislative enactment as fixing a stigma upon them." He believed "such legislative action would largely undo the work of the Washington Conference on Limitation of Armaments, which so greatly improved our relations with Japan."[16] In his opinion the measure was ill-conceived and inconsistent with the treaty of 1911. The singling out of Japanese immigrants for exclusion would be unnecessary because the rigid application of the quota system as well as the rigorous enforcement of the Gentlemen's Agreement would have reduced the inflow to a trickle—less than 250 a year. Hughes' advice and warnings were ignored and Congress was prepared to pass the bill. At this critical moment Ambassador Hanihara, expressing his profound concern about the pending legislation, sent a memorandum to Secretary Hughes. While making it clear that his government had no intention of questioning "the sovereign right of any country to regulate immigration to its own territories," the ambassador went on to emphasize:

> The important question is whether Japan as a nation is or is not entitled to the proper respect and consideration of other nations. . . . It is indeed difficult to believe that it can be the intention of the people of your great country, who always stand for high principles of justice and fair play in the intercourse of nations, to resort . . . to a measure which could not only seriously offend the just pride of a friendly nation, . . . but would also seem to involve the question of the good faith and therefore of the honor of their government, . . . Relying upon the confidence you have been good enough to show me at all times, I have stated, or rather repeated, all this to you very cordially and in a most friendly spirit, for I realize, as I believe you do, the grave consequences which the enactment of the measure retaining that particular provision would inevitably bring upon the otherwise happy and mutually advantageous relations between our two countries.[17]

Secretary Hughes concurred with the expressed view of the Japanese ambassador. Believing that Hanihara's letter would strengthen the position of the opponents of the bill, Hughes sent it to the Congress. But it proved counterproductive. Some members of the Congress, especially Senator Lodge, interpreted the term "grave consequences" as a "veiled threat" and implicit intimidation of the United States. They even considered the administration's eleventh-hour efforts to dissuade the legislation as an encroachment upon their legislative prerogatives:

> To pass the control of our immigration policy to the treaty-making power [i.e. the president] will completely silence the voice of the House of Representatives therein. It would sur-

render a sovereign right and give to foreign countries a power which the country has never conceded.[18]

The members of Congress were now caught in the whirlwind of regional self-interests, political opportunism, the false alarm of the "veiled threat," blatant demagoguery, xenophobic racism, and the fear of Executive "impudence." On May 15, 1924, both the Senate and the House, by an overwhelming majority in each chamber, passed the bill with the exclusion clause intact. Such principles as "equal opportunities for all peoples" and "the universal brotherhood of men," which constituted the cornerstone of the American nation, were now denied to the Japanese. Irate citizens of Tokyo held protest demonstrations in front of the United States embassy. Cries for boycotts of American goods reverberated throughout the country. Ambassador Hanihara sent his final memorandum to Secretary Hughes, stating, "The Japanese Government consider it their duty to maintain and to place on record their solemn protest against the discriminatory clause . . . of the Immigration Act of 1924, and to request the American Government to take all possible and suitable measures for the removal of such discrimination,"[19] and then he resigned in shame.

Japan had never questioned the sovereign right of the United States to enact an exclusion law. What did hurt her national pride, dignity, honor, and integrity was the singling out of Japanese immigrants for discriminatory exclusion. It soon became apparent that the injustice inherent in the law against Japan would remain a source of irritation and friction between American-Japanese relations. The Department of State continued to influence the forces for revision of the 1924 law. By 1931, on the eve of the Manchurian Incident, discernible progress was made, enabling Secretary Stimson to express his hope to "be able to take up for successful solution the long standing source of irritation arising out of our immigration laws of nearly ten years before, and to put them upon a basis which . . . might not be offensive to the sensibilities of the Japanese people."[20] In September 1931, a dynamic explosion near Mukden, which ripped a portion of the tracks of the South Manchurian Railway, dashed his hopes.

Manchurian Crisis

Japanese Moves in Manchuria

The Manchurian Incident of September 18, 1931, was the harbinger of overt Japanese aggression in China. It was to lead East Asia on the road to Pearl Harbor—only a decade away.

The incident itself was a focal point of three major forces, which, emerging in the 1920s, had been destined to clash sooner or later. These forces were Chinese nationalism, Soviet communism, and Japanese militarism. The fourth element in the interaction of these forces was the response of the United States, which, defensive in nature, played a minor role in shaping the pattern of international politics in East Asia in the late '20s. But first, an examination of the history of their interplay preceding the incident is in order.

Less than a year after the May Fourth affair (see Chapter 3), which had given birth to a new phase of Chinese nationalism, the Soviet policy declaration on China reached Peking in March 1920. It proclaimed, in part:

> The Soviet Government has renounced the conquests made by the Tsarist Government which deprived China of Manchuria and other areas . . . returns to the Chinese people, without any compensation, the Chinese Eastern Railway, the all the mining, timber, gold, and other concessions . . . renounces the receipt from China of the 1900 Boxer rebellion indemnity . . . abolishes all special privileges and gives up all factories owned by Russian merchants on Chinese soil . . . is ready to discuss all other questions with the Chinese people . . . to wipe out once and for all the acts of coercion and injustice committed in regard to China by [the] former Russian Government jointly with Japan and the Allies.[21]

This policy had been formulated in Moscow by Lenin's Bolshevik regime at a moment when it was seeking friends and fighting foes. Lenin's revolutionary government stood alone, its success or failure very much in the balance. Kolchak's anti-Bolshevik government, which had been accorded formal recognition by the Allied powers, was in control of the Omsk region and the Allied intervention in Siberia posed a grave threat to the very existence of the young regime.

The Soviet overture was favorably received by the Chinese people, who were led to believe that the Soviets had condemned the czarist policy of imperialism and aggression and had decided to pursue a radical, new, enlightened "good neighbor" policy based on the principles of equality, justice, and friendship with China. They appreciated, at least for the time being, Soviet Russia's voluntary, unilateral, and unsolicited renunciation of its special privileges and rights in China.

The Soviet government, having thus laid the groundwork for a new Sino-Soviet relationship, sent Adolf Joffe, a Comintern agent, to China for the purpose of negotiating a treaty including the implementation of Soviet declared policy. Arriving in Peking on August 12, 1922, Joffe enjoyed a most friendly welcome extended to him by the left-wing organizations. Subsequently, he conferred and negotiated in Shanghai with Sun Yat-sen, the head of the Kuomintang (the Chinese Nationalist party) who was favorably inclined to work with Communists. Although Joffe was unable to achieve all the objectives of his mission, he was successful in arriving at an arrangement whereby members of the Chinese Communist party (CCP) were allowed to enter the Kuomintang (KMT) as individuals rather than as a bloc or group. While retaining their CCP membership, the Communists who joined the KMT did not constitute a "party" but were subject to KMT control and discipline. They had to acknowledge the KMT leadership for the national revolution. Yet, since the CCP itself was not dissolved, the Communists held double membership.

The Sun-Joffe negotiations led ultimately to a joint statement on January 26, 1923, which read:

> Dr. Sun Yat-sen holds that the Communistic order or even the Soviet system cannot actually be introduced into China, because there do not exist here the conditions for the successful establishment of either Communism or Socialism. This view is entirely shared by Mr. Joffe. . . . Mr. Joffe has . . .

categorically declared to Dr. Sun Yat-sen that the Russian Government is ready and willing to enter into negotiations with China on the basis of the renunciation by Russia of all treaties and exactions which the Tsardom imposed on China, including... the Chinese Eastern Railway... that it is not and has never been the intention or purpose of the present Russian Government to pursue an Imperialistic policy in Outer Mongolia or to cause it to secede from China....[22]

After the Sun-Joffe agreement, the Soviet government pursued two-front policies on China—diplomatic and political. On the diplomatic front, in September 1923, Leo Karakhan, deputy commissar for foreign affairs, was sent to Peking to assume the post of Soviet ambassador and simultaneously to take charge of negotiations for a Sino-Soviet treaty. When the talks got under way, Karakhan denied that there had been any commitment in the previous policy declaration with respect to the return of the Chinese Eastern Railway to China *without compensation*. The negotiations dragged on until May 1924, when the Sino-Soviet agreement was finally signed.

This agreement formally restored diplomatic and consular relations. It stipulated mutual renunciation of all previous treaties between them affecting their sovereign rights and interests. It also provided for Russian recognition of China's sovereignty in Outer Mongolia and the withdrawal of Russian troops therefrom. It further stipulated that the Chinese Eastern Railway would continue to remain under joint Sino-Soviet control, that it might be redeemed by China with Chinese funds, and that its ultimate settlement would be a matter solely between the two countries to the exclusion of third parties.[23]

On the political front, when Karakhan was on the way to Peking, Mikhail Borodin, an able veteran Bolshevik sent by Lenin, was heading for Canton as top advisor to the Kuomintang.[24] With him came General Galen (Blücher), who was to help train a KMT army, and some forty Soviet advisors.

Following the death of Sun Yat-sen on March 12, 1925, leadership of the Kuomintang began to split: Wang Ching-wei on the left, Hu Han-min on the right, and Chiang Kai-shek as the military leader. Chiang had been sent to Moscow in August 1923 to study Soviet military organization, its political indoctrination in the rank and file, and the party-military relationships. After a three-month stay in the Soviet Union, he returned to China to be commissioned by Sun to found the Whampoa Military Academy, near Canton, which was designed to develop an officer corps to staff the new nationalist army.[25] In this tripartite power struggle, Mikhail Borodin, the Soviet advisor, was on good terms with the Wang faction and began to wield greater influence and power. Dissatisfied with the KMT-CCP collaboration and with Borodin's bias and prejudice, some right-wing KMT executive and supervisory committee members left Canton for Western Hill near Peking to hold their own Central Executive Committee meeting. They demanded the dismissal of Borodin and other Soviet advisors from the KMT. Accusing the Western Hill group of illegal separatist action, the left-wing faction of the KMT convened its own Central Executive Committee meeting, in which it adopted a resolution to censure the Western Hill faction.

As time passed, the left-right wing factional strife deepened. The right-wing nationalists now found their leader in Chiang Kai-shek who, elected chairman of the standing committee of the KMT Central Executive Committee, successfully imposed considerable restrictions on the Communists. He then set out in July 1926 on his Northern Expedition, the first step toward national unification by military means as Sun Yat-sen had prescribed. From the beginning Chiang's military campaign proved swift and successful, and he was steadily building a power base in central, eastern, and southeastern China. In March 1927, Chiang's troops occupied Shanghai and Nanking, and the following month began the wholesale "extermination campaign" of the Communists. Nationalist troops, police, and secret agents sought out and executed the Communists, destroyed the workers' organizations, and eliminated the labor unions.

In the meantime the Canton government had moved in December 1926 from Canton to Wuhan. It was now composed mainly of the KMT left-wing and the Communists and was dominated by Wang Ching-wei and Borodin. In response to Chiang's determined anti-Communist policy, the Wuhan government counteracted by dismissing him as commander-in-chief of the National Revolutionary Army. Scoffing at the Wuhan decision, Chiang Kai-shek organized his own national government in Nanking with the help of Hu Han-min. The split between the left-wing and the right-wing within the KMT became nearly complete, and the struggle between the Communists and the Nationalists came to plague China for decades to come.

Viewed from Moscow, the events unfolding in China spelled failure and disappointment. Hence, in June 1927, Stalin sent to Borodin and the CCP a series of secret directives which, if carried out, would have transformed the Wuhan government into a Communist dictatorship, reducing Wang Ching-wei to a puppet. As Wang came to know of the contents of the Stalin directives, a rift between him and the Communists began to emerge. In July, Borodin announced that the Communists would dissociate the Wuhan government, though not leaving the KMT party. Then the CCP moved its headquarters to Kiangsi Province, and accelerated its attack on Wuhan. Accusing the Communists of violating KMT policies and ideology, Wang's Wuhan presidium, in return, ordered the expulsion of Communists from the KMT and government posts. This retaliatory measure compelled Borodin to leave China, returning to Moscow via Mongolia. Subsequent developments led Wang to carry out an all-out liquidation of the Communists and their front organizations. Now that both Nanking and Wuhan had rid themselves of the Communists, a reconciliation between them appeared logical. A special committee was created for that purpose, and in December 1927 all differences between the two erstwhile factions were formally resolved. The Wuhan government was dissolved in early 1928 and Chiang Kai-shek resumed his Northern Expedition.

Chiang's road to Peking, the ultimate destination for national unification, was blocked by many obstacles: local bandits, regional warlords, and above all, Japanese military interposition in the path of Chiang's advance. Let us briefly survey the backgrounds and motives of this Japanese action.

Japan in the 1920s was a country of contradictions and contrasts. Behind the moderate conciliatory internationalism, an aggressive chauvinistic nationalism was taking shape; within a democratic parliamentary system, the Imperial Army and Navy exerted enormous political power; and after the international disarmament conferences, the nation accelerated its pace toward militarism and expansionism.

When Kato Komei (Takaaki), president of the Kenseikai (Constitutional Rule Society) and a firm believer in the party system, formed his coalition government on June 11, 1924, it was thought that his ministry would promote the cause of parliamentary democracy and would thereby check the growth of militarism and ultranationalism. But it proved quite contrary in the light of the actual performances of his administration.

Premier Kato reduced the armed forces by four divisions, but the money thus saved was used for a universal military training program in schools, providing an excellent opportunity to indoctrinate Japanese youths with militarism. He had the Diet enact the universal suffrage law, removing all property qualifications and giving all male subjects over twenty-five years of age the right to vote. On the other hand, he had the Diet pass a more strict internal security act providing for severe penalty for advocating alteration of the imperial political system or the abolition of private property. Thus, what little benefits the democratic features of his administration might have contributed to the development of a representative government were more than offset by the effects of authoritarian features in the rule of a police state.

Kato's foreign policy was, generally speaking, conciliatory in nature toward both the Soviet Union and China. Such policy appeared to military-expansionists to be "soft and weak." Foreign Minister Shidehara then became the target of their attack and criticism. When, in early 1925, Shidehara reached an agreement with the Soviet Union on the resumption of formal diplomatic relations and on Japanese troop withdrawal from northern Sakhalin, he came under the militaristic attack for his "excessive concession" and his "weak policy" toward the Russians. Similarly, in the same year, when he refused to take advantage of the civil war in Manchuria and failed to obtain special privileges there, the military-expansionists, especially the Kwantung Army, accused him of being an obstructionist, and his policies were considered by them as an anathema to their cause.[26]

The death of Prime Minister Kato in January 1926 was followed by the appointment of home minister Wakatsuki as premier. His ministry lasted until April 1927, when he was forced to resign on account of his financial policies. The fall of the Wakatsuki cabinet paved the way for change in favor of the militarists, as shown by the selection of General Tanaka Giichi, president of the Seiyukai, to the premiership. A surprise to no one, Tanaka's domestic policy was stern and repressive: ultraliberal activities were banned, the press censored, "dangerous thought" controlled, and the death penalty imposed for serious violations of the Internal Security Act.

Likewise, Tanaka's foreign policy, especially with respect to China, was typified by the "positive policy," contrasting to and opposite of Shidehara's. This policy was formulated in consultation with his military and civil officials and advisors. In essence, it was designed to protect Japan's special interests in Manchuria and China and to carry forward the expansionist policy at an accelerated pace. Convinced that chaos, disorder, and disunity in China would facilitate Japanese design, and concerned over the rising tide of Chinese nationalism, Tanaka was determined to foil Chiang Kai-shek's efforts to unify his country. There would be no greater threat to Japan's stake in China and Manchuria than a strongly united China capable of military resistance to Japan's expansion. Against this background, in April 1928 Tanaka dispatched Japanese troops to Shantung to halt the advance of Chiang's Northern Expedition forces toward Peking.

This intervention resulted in a clash between the Japanese and the Chinese troops at Tsinan. The Tsinan incident was localized, but it thwarted Chiang's plan to subdue Chang Tso-lin, the warlord of Manchuria, and to bring Manchuria under Nationalist control. Manchuria was the bone of contention coveted by the three contending forces: China's nationalism, Chang's warlordism, and Japanese militarism. When the Kwantung (Japanese) Army came to conclude that Chang Tso-lin could not be trusted, it conspired, acting entirely on its own initiative and without Tokyo's knowledge, to eliminate him. In June 1928, Chang met his violent death as the result of a bomb explosion which blew up his special train on the South Manchurian Railway near Mukden. A month later his son, Chang Hsüeh-liang, also known as the Young Marshal, pledged his allegiance to the Nationalist government and later, toward the end of the year, he renounced his control of Manchuria in support of the Nanking regime. Thus, as the momentous year of 1928 came to a close, China was more or less unified under the leadership of Chiang Kai-shek.

Stimson in the Sino-Soviet Conflict

The United States policy toward China during the period 1925–28, corresponding to the Coolidge administration, was one of "watchful waiting." It was *watchful* because the general anarchic conditions accompanied by mob riots and antiforeign uprisings in major cities in central China threatened America's vested interests, which the United States was determined to protect; *waiting* because the United States was ready and willing to negotiate with any government which, emerging from civil turbulence, could effectively exercise state power to restore social order.

U.S. policy faced a test in March 1927 when Chiang Kai-shek's Nationalist troops entered the city of Nanking and carried out an organized, systematic attack on the foreign community in what became known as the "Nanking Incident." The consulates of major foreign powers, including those of the United States and Japan, were raided; their property was plundered and destroyed; and a number of their nationals were killed or wounded. Alarmed by the seriousness of the events, American and British gunboats anchored in the Yangtze River laid a protective barrage around the Standard Oil Company compound where surviving foreign nationals had taken refuge. Thus further onslaughts on the foreigners by the KMT troops were prevented. Then in April, the United States in concert with other injured nations presented to the KMT army such demands as an official apology, reparations for damages, punishment of those responsible for the incident, and guarantees against future recurrence of similar outrages. China's reply was evasive, ambiguous, and anything but satisfactory. Yet the powers did not pursue the matter with any degree of firm determination, for such an action would have weakened the Nationalists and, conversely, would have strengthened the left-wing faction of the KMT under Soviet domination, i.e., the Wuhan government. Led by the United States, the powers were united in hoping for the success of a new, right-wing, non-Soviet, national government in Nanking. It soon came to pass that, as discussed earlier, Chiang Kai-shek carried out the "extermination campaign" of the Communists so as to rid the KMT of their influence. This done, Chiang's Nanking government began to show signs of pro-Western orientation.

In February 1928, when Chiang consolidated his power with the dissolution of the Wuhan government, the United States opened negotiations with the Nanking regime for a settlement of the Nanking Incident. The two nations exchanged notes whereby China tendered an official apology and promised full reparations for material damages, and the United States in return deplored the necessity of having to resort to gunboats to protect her nationals in China.

The United States also took the lead in restoring Chinese tariff autonomy. Responding partly to the call of the Nationalist government for the revision of unequal treaties on the basis of the sovereign equality of all states and taking independent steps which shattered the old practice of international joint action toward China, the United States in July 1928 signed a bilateral treaty recognizing China's tariff autonomy.

The Sino-American tariff agreement was followed by similar treaties with other powers. These developments added considerable prestige to the international status of the Chiang regime, which continued to strive for the restoration of China's complete sovereignty and equality. In the summer of 1928 China became a signatory of the Pact of Paris, which renounced war as an instrument of national policy and bound the signatories to settle all international disputes or conflicts by peaceful means. A year later China approached major Western powers, including the United States, requesting them to abolish at the earliest possible moment their extraterritoriality in China. The United States, as well as Great Britain and France, rejected China's request, claiming that China was not ready or entitled to full jurisdictional sovereignty.

China's battle for the elimination of unequal extraterritorial rights of the powers was fought in parallel with her battle for the recovery of territorial rights in northern Manchuria, especially the Chinese Eastern Railway. In the summer of 1929 the accumulated ill feelings and antagonism between the Chinese Nationalist government and the Soviet Union culminated in the outbreak of hostilities along the Siberian-Manchurian border. In accepting the rein of the Young Marshal's control over Manchuria, Chiang Kai-shek had also inherited Chang Hsüeh-liang's and his father's enmity toward the Soviets. During the last years of Chang Tso-lin's control of Peking, Moscow-Peking relations were severely strained. Suspecting Soviet conspiracies in China, Chang Tso-lin had ordered his police to raid the legation quarter in Peking and to conduct a search of various Soviet premises. A similar raid had also been made in Tientsin. These raids produced, apart from a cache of arms, many Soviet documents of an extremely subversive character. The Peking police reported that "the raid established the fact that the compound of the former Imperial Russian legation guard contained the headquarters of the Communists in which most elaborate and detailed plans and preparations had been made for the overthrow of the government in Peking and for the establishment of a Communist regime."

When the Soviet protests to these raids were ignored, the Soviet government withdrew its chargé d'affaires and his entire legation staff from Peking. Then, in May 1929, Chang Hsüeh-liang's police staged a repeat performance. They raided the Soviet consulates in four cities along the Chinese Eastern Railway in northern Manchuria, arresting Soviet consular officials together with Communist agents and seizing their documents. Several weeks later Chinese officials at the city of Harbin took over the entire communications system of the Chinese Eastern Railway and its Russian employees were removed and expelled.

The Soviet Union promptly lodged a poignant protest with both Chang's local government and Chiang's national government, demanding an immediate conference to settle all disputes between the two nations, particularly those involving the Chinese Eastern Railway. Ignored and irate, the Soviet government severed diplomatic relations with China, only to be met with the same action by the Chinese government. They were quick to resort to force, mass-ing troops along the Manchurian-Siberian border, and hostilities broke out. The fact that they were both signatories of the Pact of Paris was of little consequence. To them the pact was as meaningless as an agreement not to take medicine except in case of illness.

One of the two principal architects of the Pact of Paris—the Kellogg-Briand Pact—was American Secretary of State Frank Kellogg.[27] Secretary Henry L. Stimson, Kellogg's successor, felt it was his moral and obligatory responsibility to invoke the Kellogg-Briand Pact—the treaty to outlaw war—to put an end to the Sino-Soviet military conflict. Earlier in July he had reminded both China and the Soviet Union of their obligation under the pact to settle their differences by peaceful means. A few weeks later Stimson had advanced specific proposals for a settlement. All had proved futile. Now in November, as Soviet troops invaded Manchuria, Secretary Stimson for the third time decided to invoke the pact by organizing its major members with a view to taking some form of collective action. He initiated consultations with Great Britain, France, Italy, Germany, and Japan. The last two declined to collaborate. The remaining three powers in early December followed the United States lead in sending an identic appeal to both Nanking and Moscow. The Stimson note repeated what he had stated in his earlier reminder and expressed the hope that the two belligerents would honor their commitments to the letter and spirit of the Kellogg-Briand Pact.

Responding to the appeal, China denied the implication that she had violated the pact and expressed her willingness to negotiate for a peaceful settlement. In fact, Chang Hsüeh-liang's forces had been defeated by and had capitulated to the Soviets. The negotiations which had ensued between the Soviets and Chang's authorities had resulted on December 3 in restoring the status quo antebellum.

The Soviet government, on the other hand, responded with a terse rebuff. Maxim Litvinov, commissar for foreign affairs, rebuked the United States for meddling in the dispute after peaceful negotiations for a settlement had already begun. He believed that no nation or nations, singularly or collectively, would have the right to play the role of protector of the pact. His note to all the powers stated that "the Soviet-Manchurian conflict can be settled only by direct negotiations between the Soviet Union and China on the basis of conditions known to China and already accepted to the Mukden government, and that it cannot admit interference of any other party in these negotiations or the conflict." Pointing to the fact that the United States had not extended a *de jure* recognition to the Soviet Union, the note concluded that "the Soviet Government cannot forbear expressing amazement that the Government of the United States, which by its own will has no official relations with the Soviet, deems it possible to apply to it with advice and counsel."[28]

Secretary Stimson's rebuttal to the effect that his action was motivated solely for the cause of world peace had little effect on changing the Soviet conviction that the United States was prejudiced against the Soviet Union. Only recently the United States and other Western powers had resorted to gunboats in the protection of their rights in China. They still maintained their armed forces there, indicating clearly that they would not hesitate to repeat the same acts should their rights be put in jeopardy. Why then must they show their hypocrisy, the Soviets asked, in invoking the Pact of Paris to thwart Soviet efforts to protect their rights in Manchuria? The Soviet Union had resorted to force in order to protect its vested interests just as other Western powers had done or would have done under similar circumstances.

Stimson's noble experiment in mobilizing world public opinion against war as an instrument of national policy and the collective moral persuasion directed to the alleged violators of the international treaty turned out to be "passing wind to a horse's ears," as a Chinese saying went. The invocation, so soon, of the untested Kellogg-Briand Pact to quench the flaring flame of a Sino-Soviet armed clash in Manchuria proved a painful failure. This failure in turn reinforced the fear that the pact thereafter would be hopelessly inadequate as a basis for some form of collective sanction or action against any nation which would resort to war to execute its national policy. The net effect of the Stimson venture, therefore, was to demonstrate the inherent weakness of the pact in the world of *realpolitik*. Japan, ambitious and aggressive, was quick to pick up the cue and prepared to implement resolutely her expansionist policy in Manchuria. Secretary Stimson was compelled to meet this new challenge—the Manchurian crisis—differently.

The 9-18 Incident

The Japanese drive toward national greatness was manifested in part by her territorial aggrandizement since 1895. Within a few decades Japan obtained the Ryukyus and Formosa, acquired southern Sakhalin and the Kuriles, annexed Korea, secured economic interests in Liaotung and Shantung, and received a League mandate in the Pacific for former German possessions. Japan's next target toward Continental expansion was the whole of Manchuria —vast in area, rich in resources, sparse in population, and weak in defense. The Japanese began to identify this land as the "life line" (seimeisen) of their sprawling empire. When, in April 1923, Secretary Hughes terminated the Lansing-Ishii agreement, the Japanese coauthor, Ishii, could say that "the Agreement may have been cancelled, but Japan's special interests in China continue to live in all their vigor." "Even supposing that Japan's special interests in China had not been admitted by international agreements," he emphatically pointed out, "they were not something which can be abolished."[29] The Japanese considered Manchuria distinct from China proper in terms of historical developments, geographical propinquity, and ethnic composition. They felt psychological affinity with Manchuria. For this reason, "whatever differences may have been observable between the specific policies advocated by the various cabinets in Japan—as, for example, between the so-called friendship policy of Baron Shidehara and the so-called positive policy of the late General Baron Tanaka—they have always had this feature in common."[30]

The overall objectives of Japanese policies in Manchuria were to maintain, develop, and expand her interests and privileges, i.e., to create a de facto colony out of Manchuria. Spearheading this policy were the militarists, who had instilled in the people the euphoria of power, prestige, and prosperity for the empire. In December 1930, Prime Minister Hamaguchi, who had attempted to revert to the "good neighbor policy" toward China and had joined the London Naval Treaty,[31] was fatally shot at the Tokyo railway station by a military fanatic. His death carried with it the remnant of hope in party government and democratic parliamentarianism, and at the same time it signaled the beginning of a reign of violence in Japanese politics. The tide of ultranationalistic militarism began to surge. Manchuria was to be thrown into this whirlpool.

In the summer of 1931, a clash erupted between Chinese and Korean farmers over the ownership of land. A number of farmers on both sides were killed. This incident triggered anti-Chinese riots in Korea and anti-Japanese riots in China, the Koreans being Japanese subjects. Added to the tense situation was the news that a Japanese army captain, Nakamura, during his intelligence mission in Inner Mongolia, had been executed by Chinese troops. The ultranationalists seized upon these incidents and inflamed Japanese public sentiment by agitating for a decisive settlement of the whole Manchurian issue by force. The determination of the Japanese to defend the "life line" was met by the equally vehement determination of the Chinese to resist and foil Japanese designs in Manchuria. Throughout the summer the friction continued and the antagonism intensified. "As September wore on, this tension reached such a point that it was apparent to all careful observers that a breaking point must soon be reached."[32]

Then came an explosion heard all around the world. On September 18, 1931, a portion of the tracks of the South Manchurian Railway near Mukden was blown up. This "9-18 incident," the Kwantung Army claimed, was an act of sabotage by Chinese troops. But in fact, it was engineered and executed by the Kwantung Army to create a pretext to carry out the premeditated plan for an overt and drastic action to occupy by force the whole territory of Manchuria. Exercising the right of "self-defense," the Kwantung Army commenced systematic military action, occupying such major cities as Mukden, Changchun, and Kirin with swiftness and precision. American Minister Johnson in Peking sent the following telegram to the secretary of state:

It seems to me absurd to believe that mere destruction of railway tracks would warrant occupation of Manchuria, and to imply that the chain of events above mentioned was accidental or occurred on the spur of the moment leaves out of consideration the fact that whole series of incidents involving military occupation of places as far apart as Changchun, Newchwang, Antung, Kowpangtze, and Huluato implies a degree of staff work which could not [have been] improvised. Furthermore, it is our understanding here that Japanese military headquarters were transferred almost immediately from Port Arthur to Mukden.[33]

One of the immediate consequences of the open hostilities in Manchuria was that a number of international arrangements were placed on trial for their efficacy in maintaining world order and security. Specifically, the League of Nations with its doctrine of collective security, the Nine-Power Treaty with its incorporation of the Open Door policy, and the Pact of Paris with its declaration of outlawry of war—all these legal devices designed to curb, minimize, or eliminate war had to face a severe test as to whether or not they were functionally effective enough to preserve peace. The Pact of Paris had been found impotent in coping with the Sino-Soviet conflict two years earlier. How would the other two—the League covenant and the Nine-Power Treaty—fare the storm in Manchuria? How did the United States respond to this new challenge?

Three days after the 9-18 incident China made two urgent appeals: one to the United States and the other to the League of Nations. The United States, as sponsor of the Kellogg-Briand Pact, was called on to take steps to restore and preserve peace in East Asia. The League was likewise requested to recognize the serious breach of peace and to exercise its authority under the Covenant to repair it.

Secretary of State Stimson lost no time in expressing his deep concern over the crisis in Manchuria, believing once again that not only was the Kellogg-Briand Pact violated but the Nine-Power Treaty as well. In his communications with the secretary-general of the League, Sir Eric Drummond, Stimson assured the former of his full cooperation and assistance. Henceforth, Stimson was to coordinate his policy closely with the League actions to be taken subsequently.

While on September 22 the League was urging both Japan and

China to disengage from the hostilities and to seek a peaceful settlement, Secretary Stimson sent off a memorandum to his counterpart in Tokyo, Foreign Minister Shidehara. In it Stimson stated that the Sino-Japanese armed clash in Manchuria "brings into question at once the meaning of certain provisions of agreements such as the Nine-Power Treaty of February 6, 1922, and the Kellogg-Briand Pact." With diplomatic subtlety, Stimson gently laid the blame for a "very unfortunate situation" in Manchuria on Japan: "It would seem that the responsibility for determining the course of events with regard to the liquidation of this situation rests largely upon Japan, for the simple reason that Japanese armed forces have seized and are exercising de facto control in southern Manchuria."[34]

As days passed, it became clear that there were no visible results of the endeavors of the League or of the United States in the search for a pacific settlement. Instead, the situation grew worse as Japanese warplanes, on October 8, bombed Chinchow, the Young Marshal's provisional capital. The bombing further hardened Stimson's conviction that Japan was the culprit in the matter, and it also led Stimson to lament that "modern treaties initiated by Western nations, and especially designed to fit the exigencies of the industrialized world of Europe and America, might not be taken very seriously in the Orient."[35] Secretary Stimson began to think in terms of chastising Japan. The actual use of armed forces—coercion—was, however, out of the question, for the United States at that time had neither the capability nor willingness to resort to such measures. The "weapons" at his disposal were the "decent opinion of mankind," diplomatic pressure, and possible "collective economic sanction" against Japan. He instructed Prentiss Gilbert, American consul at Geneva, to participate in League sessions dealing especially with the Kellogg-Briand Pact as applied to the issue at hand. Similar instructions were given later to Charles G. Dawes, American ambassador to England, to consult with the British government and to proceed to Paris where the League council was scheduled to meet on November 16.

Japanese militarists, on the other hand, could not have cared less about all the diplomatic maneuvers in Geneva, Paris, Washington, or even in Tokyo, where their own civil government was trying to find a compromise settlement. The Kwantung Army, now assisted by the troops from Korea under the command of General Hayashi, methodically extended its military operations into northern Manchuria. The general mood among the populace in Japan, incensed by the victory news from Manchuria and inflamed by the "patriotic" hostility to China, was overwhelmingly in support of the military. The fall of the moderate Wakatsuki-Shidehara cabinet appeared imminent.

On December 10, 1931, with Japan's assent, the League Council adopted a resolution calling for the appointment of "a Commission of five members to study on the spot and to report to the Council on any circumstances which, affecting international relations, threaten to disturb the peace between China and Japan, or the good understanding between them, upon which peace depends."[36] The following day Premier Wakatsuki resigned and was succeeded by Inukai Tsuyoshi, a protégé of General Tanaka. Inukai pledged to pursue a firm policy toward China and filled the cabinet post of the minister of war with General Araki Sadao, a recognized expansionist enjoying a tremendous popularity among the aggressive young officers in the Imperial Army.

CHAPTER FIVE

From Manchuria to the Marco Polo Bridge

USA: Alert and Alarmed

The Stimson Doctrine

As the Japanese militarists marched on to the conquest and consolidation of Manchuria in disregard of the Nine-Power Treaty and the Kellogg-Briand Pact and in defiance of the League, the Stimson policy to solve the Manchurian crisis by negotiations and conciliations proved futile. Yet Secretary Stimson refused to relax his efforts to restrain Japan for three reasons—the very three considerations which President McKinley had postulated in seizing the entire Philippines three decades earlier.

In his persistent endeavor to counteract Japanese expansion in Manchuria, Stimson revitalized and advanced the three pillars of America's Asian policy. Namely, his policy was designed to protect the United States from:

First, the direct material damage to our *trade* which would inevitably be caused; . . . Second, the immense blow to the cause of peace and war prevention throughout the world which would inevitably be caused if without *protest* or *condemnation* Japan were permitted to violate and disregard the group of post-war treaties which she had ratified and upon which so many hopes of *our race* and of our part of the world had been predicated. Third, the incalculable harm which would be done immediately to American prestige in China and ultimately to the material interests of America and her people in that region, . . . after having for many years assisted by public and private effort in the education and development of China towards the ideals of modern *Christian* civilization, . . .[1]

Frustrated by the failure of the League to take more positive, effective, and forceful action against Japan and convinced of his own failure in arousing world moral indignation against Japan's breach of peace in Manchuria, Secretary Stimson shifted his strategy of containment of Japan from a multinational, conciliatory approach to unilateral, compulsory action. He realized full well that his many predecessors, in the defense or in the expansion of United States interests, had formulated and executed such indelible policies as the Open Door, the Dollar Diplomacy, the Gunboat Diplomacy, and the Lansing-Bryan Nonrecognition of the Twenty-One Demands. Stimson was to add to this list another cornerstone of America's Asian policy which came to bear his name—the Stimson Doctrine. On January 7, 1932, in response to Japan's de facto conquest of Manchuria, Secretary Stimson felt it to be the duty of his government to notify both China and Japan that:

It cannot admit the legality of any situation de facto nor does it intend to recognize any treaty or agreement entered into between those governments, or agents thereof, which may impair the treaty rights of the United States or its citizens in China, including those which relate to the sovereignty, the independence, or the territorial and administrative integrity of the Republic of China, commonly known as the open door policy; and that it does not intend to recognize any situation, treaty, or agreement which may be brought about by means contrary to the covenants and obligations of the Pact of Paris of August 27, 1928, to which treaty both China and Japan, as well as the United States, are parties.[2]

The roots of the Stimson Doctrine were to be found unmistakably in the Bryan note of May 11, 1915, and ultimately in Hay's Open Door note of 1899. It should be recalled that, with respect to the 1915 Japanese Twenty-One Demands to China, the then Secretary of State Bryan had informed Japan and China that his government "*cannot recognize any agreement* or undertaking which has been entered into or which may be entered into between the Governments of Japan and China, *impairing the treaty rights of the United States and its citizens in China,* the political or *territorial integrity of the Republic of China,* or the international policy relative to China *commonly known as the Open Door policy.*"[3] The Stimson Doctrine was without a doubt nothing more than a redeclaration of the traditional United States China policy—the Open Door—which, initiated by John Hay, had been redefined, reiterated, reaffirmed, and reasserted through the years by Roosevelt, Knox, Taft, Wilson, Bryan, Lansing, and Hughes.

The Stimson Doctrine at its birth appeared anachronistic, unrealistic, and untenable because the East Asia of 1931 had been vastly transformed from that of 1898. The weak, helpless, prostrate Imperial China had been replaced by a new "unified" Republican China imbued with modern nationalism; the ancient, isolated, small kingdom of Korea had been annexed to Japan; and the island empire of Japan had become one of the leading military powers with a firm grip on Manchuria. The Stimson Doctrine was a vain effort to preserve the status quo of bygone decades. Its weakness became all the more painfully evident as the major powers, whose support Stimson had hoped to enlist, remained uninterested or noncommittal. Secretary Stimson was especially critical of the British government for its failure to render wholehearted support for his policy and for its acquiescence to Japanese defiance and aggression. Stimson remained the "lone ranger," so to speak, in the lawless Asian frontiers, attempting to enforce the law and to discharge moral and legal responsibilities.

Rebuffing the Stimson Doctrine, Japan in mid-January expanded the hostilities from Manchuria to Shanghai, where foreign interests became invariably threatened. Stimson decided on the use of *coercion* to protect American nationals and their property and urged Great Britain to join in his plan to send gunboats to Shanghai. Britain, whose interests were not affected by the Japanese bombing of the city, found common grounds for a common action to protect common interests with the United States. London ordered two cruisers and marine reinforcements to Shanghai, while Washington assembled the entire American Asiatic fleet in Shanghai harbor and dispatched troops from Manila to the troubled city. The show of Anglo-American military might appeared to have caused some concern in Tokyo, for Japan expressed her desire to settle the "Shanghai incident" through the good offices of a neutral power. Encouraged by this development, in early February 1932 the United States drew up a five-point peace plan and, with the concurrence of Great Britain, France, and Italy, presented it to Japan and China.[4] China was ready to accept the peace terms, but Japan was not. Stimson once again felt the necessity of *coercion* in the form either of sanctions on Japan by the League or of an embargo of Japanese goods. He proposed an Anglo-American sponsored international conference in conformity with Article 7 of the Nine-Power Treaty. Again Britain showed an indifferent attitude.

A few weeks later, while the Japanese military carried on bombing raids on Shanghai, it carved Manchuria off China and proclaimed the establishment of the sovereign state of Manchukuo, independent of and separate from the Republic of China. Japan's announcement of the creation of Manchukuo was challenged by Stimson's own announcement of another policy determination in the form of an open letter dated February 23, 1932, to Senator William E. Borah, chairman of the Senate Foreign Relations Committee. Summarizing the history of America's Asian policy since the declaration of the Open Door, the letter reaffirmed the nonrecognition policy, emphasized the interrelated and the interdependent character of all treaties made at the Washington Conference a decade earlier, and implied that further violations of treaty provisions by Japan would free the United States and other signatory powers from the limitations and restrictions of those treaties.

The Stimson letter, with its "veiled threat" and *implied coercion,* was designed, as he clarified later, "to encourage China, enlighten the American public, exhort the League, stir up the British, and warn Japan." The full impact of the letter remains unclear, but in

March of 1932 the League Assembly adopted a resolution containing the nonrecognition doctrine, and in May a truce came to Shanghai. These events were considered by many Japanese as a diplomatic and military setback. On May 15, a small group of discontented "patriotic" naval officers and cadets of the military academy assassinated Prime Minister Inukai, attacked other officials, and bombed the Bank of Japan and other governmental buildings. This incident rendered the *coup de grace* to party cabinets and set the stage for the absolute dominance of the military in Japanese politics.

The Saito cabinet, which succeeded Inukai's, followed the normal international procedures in formally recognizing Manchukuo by means of a treaty signed September 15, 1932. On October 2, the Lytton Commission submitted its report. The commission found that the incident of September 18, 1931, "was not in itself sufficient to justify military action" and that "the military operations of the Japanese troops . . . cannot be regarded as measures of legitimate self-defense." As regarded the establishment of Manchukuo, the commission pointed out:

> The evidence received from all sources has satisfied the Commission that, while there were a number of factors which contributed to the creation of "Manchukuo," the two which, in combination, were most effective, and without which, in our judgement, the new State could not have been formed, were the presence of Japanese troops and the activities of Japanese officials, both civil and military. For this reason, the present regime cannot be considered to have been called into existence by a genuine and spontaneous independent movement.

The report concluded with the commission's recommendations for settlement. It proposed: (1) Manchuria, under Chinese sovereignty, should be placed under a special administration with the power of considerable local autonomy, (2) both Japan and China should withdraw their troops from Manchuria, and the maintenance of law and order should be entrusted to a special gendarmerie, (3) a Sino-Japanese treaty designed to protect Japanese interests should be negotiated, and (4) the two countries should try to reconcile their differences and establish stable and firm relations by concluding treaties of commerce, arbitration and conciliation, nonaggression, and mutual assistance. The report had little consequence or influence upon the *fait accompli.* Japan expressed deep dissatisfaction with the report. The American ambassador in Tokyo reported to the secretary of state as follows:

> The Foreign Office spokesman declares that the report favors China and it is unfair to Japan. . . . The findings and recommendations in regard to Manchuria are held impossible for Japan to accept. . . . The War Office professes indignation at the unfairness of the report; particularly at the denial of the Japanese plea of self-defense and at the statement that the existence of the new state is due to the connivance of the Japanese Army. . . . Press urges the Government to carry out its own solution of the Manchurian question. It declares the report will simply aggravate, instead of solving, the situation, and that the labors of the Commission have been useless.[5]

Japanese national indignation was directed not only at the League of Nations, but also at the United States. Hugh Wilson, American minister in Switzerland, reported to Secretary Stimson on his conversations with Matsuoka Yosuke, head of Japan's delegation to the League, who had made statements to the following effect:

> The hostility of Japanese public opinion toward America is dangerous. Public opinion is convinced that several attempts have been made by the United States to check Japanese development in Manchuria and to get control of the railway situation in the area. Rapidly diminishing is the large body of influential Japanese opinion which heretofore was friendly. In spite of the fact that thinking Japanese realize American public opinion has no thought of war, the Japanese Government may be forced to take sides with the already inflamed public opinion in the event of some incident.[6]

The commission report was in fact a post-mortem of the whole Manchurian affair, perhaps prejudicial to Japan, who insisted that her military action had been justifiable self-defense. Japan could cite various provocations on the part of China and Western powers to substantiate her claim. Japan's view could be summarized as follows: (1) China had unilaterally abrogated her treaties with Japan; the Chinese had been arrogant in their conduct, reckless in resort to violence, and scornful of the Japanese. (2) The Western powers sought to promote their selfish interests at the expense of Far Eastern stability which Japan had hoped for and tried to bring about. (3) The policy of the United States was to condone China's behavior and to encourage her intransigence and recalcitrance.[7] (4) The collective security measures contemplated by the treaty powers were usually *against* Japan, not *with* Japan. Therefore, she was compelled to act decisively in defense of the essential prerequisites of her national survival.[8]

In any case, the League convened in late November to study the report and to consider ways of effecting its recommendations. After a long and serious debate, the League on February 24, 1933, adopted the Lytton report. Thereupon, the Japanese delegation dramatically walked out of the assembly. A month later the Japanese government tendered formal notice of her intention to withdraw from the League. Thus Western imperialism in East Asia, which had set an illustrious example for Japan to emulate, failed to tame Japanese imperialism. The latter proved to be more adept and adventurous than the former. Matsuoka made a triumphant return home from Geneva; when queried by reporters on whether he had anything to say, he replied: "I wanted to tell the delegates of the Western Powers to think twice before they dared to cast the first stone at me."

The New Administration with Old Policy

When President Franklin D. Roosevelt took office in March 1933, he and his secretary of state, Cordell Hull, inherited from the Hoover-Stimson administration the unresolved foreign policy problems in East Asia. The new Democratic administration was not about to depart drastically from the old path which Stimson had tread, but would carry on the torch of *continuity* which had been a remarkable characteristic of America's Asian policy since the turn of the century. In fact, Stimson had been assured by his successor that his doctrine, his nonrecognition principle, and his policy of cooperation with the League were to be honored and followed. True to his word, Secretary Hull refused to recognize Manchukuo and accepted the League invitation for a United States membership in an Advisory Committee.⁹ Minister Hugh Wilson in Switzerland was instructed by Hull to participate in the League deliberations as a nonvoting member. Wilson helped the committee in drafting recommendations for a general application of the nonrecognition policy regarding Manchukuo.

The continuity of policy was also evidenced by the Roosevelt administration's adherence to the principle of collective security as a means to bridle aggression and to limit armaments. As the World Disarmament Conference at Geneva was making little progress, in May 1933 President Roosevelt appealed directly to the heads of powers to refrain from the armaments race. Seeing a cause and effect relationship between armaments and aggression, President Roosevelt felt the need for a multilateral nonaggression pact which, together with strict observance of the disarmament pledge, would bind every signatory not to send armed forces beyond their borders. Such a pact, had it been concluded, would have had little impact on Japanese entrenchment in Manchuria. Stimson's invocation of the provisions of the Nine-Power Treaty and of the Pact of Paris in his efforts to deter Japanese imperialism in Manchuria had proved that these treaties were but "scraps of paper" in the face of the determined aggressor. Another nonaggression pact would have made no difference. The new element in Roosevelt's scheme, however, was to tie disarmament to nonaggression. On May 22, Norman H. Davis, the chief American delegate to the Geneva Disarmament Conference, stated that if substantial arms reductions were effected by international agreements, the United States, in consultation with other powers, would be willing to work for peace. He went on to elaborate that, should a nation be found guilty by the powers of breaking peace in violation of its international obligations and should a collective sanction be directed against that violator, the United States would refrain from any action which might jeopardize such a collective effort. The

United States, however, would reserve the right to agree or disagree with "the Judgement rendered as to the responsible and guilty party."

With no progress whatsoever in the World Disarmament Conference in the ensuing months and with no change in the American position, Davis repeated a year later in 1934 that the United States was "willing to negotiate a universal pact of nonaggression," without "any commitment whatever to use its armed forces for the settlement of any dispute anywhere." This position as applied in East Asia meant that the United States would neither condone Japanese actions in Manchuria nor condemn them with continued acridity and severity. As compared with Stimson's stand on Manchuria, the Roosevelt-Hull policy had become low-keyed and flexible without affecting fundamental principles, and the policy sought to avoid a direct confrontation with Japan.[10]

For this reason Secretary Hull appeared undisturbed and made no public protest as Japan proceeded to expand her hegemony over Inner Mongolia and North China. After the creation and consolidation of Manchukuo, Japanese forces directed their military activities toward Jehol Province in Inner Mongolia, which fell under their control in March 1933. Then they proceeded to extend hostilities to North China where they encountered stiff resistance by the Chinese troops. This development resulted in the Tangku Truce of May 1933, which created a demilitarized zone between Peking and the Manchurian border. The Japanese forces were to evacuate from the zone to the Great Wall, while the Chinese troops were to withdraw from the designated area. Further, Chinese police, friendly and acceptable to the Japanese army, were to maintain peace and order.

The truce was, at its best, no more than a temporary respite. Frictions between the two contending forces continued. Anti-Japanese propaganda and activities by the Chinese people drew Japanese suppression and intimidation. Mutual accusations and recriminations never ceased. The Japanese, thereupon, demanded control over the demilitarized zone at a conference held at Dairen in July. This demand being granted, the Japanese had secured their northern access to China proper.

As the United States was unable to check diplomatically the

Japanese penetration into North China, so was the Soviet Union incapable of challenging militarily the Japanese expansion toward north Manchuria. The United States' formal recognition of the Soviet Union in November 1933 was destined, if not designed, to realign the balance of power in East Asia. During the Manchurian crisis Soviet foreign policy toward Japan was defensive and conciliatory. Under the banner of "socialism in a single country," Stalin had first to strengthen Soviet power internally and to harmonize the Soviet position internationally. In late 1931, the Soviet Union offered Japan a nonaggression pact, but no agreement was reached. The Soviet policy of accommodation failed either to minimize Japanese provocations or to curb her expansion into north Manchuria where the Chinese Eastern Railway was still under Soviet control. Alarmed and antagonized as they were, the Soviets were pressed for time in the implementation of the Five-Year Plan, directed primarily at armament. They seemed to have achieved this objective by early 1933, as Stalin would declare:

> In view of the refusal of neighboring countries to sign Pacts of Non-Aggression with us, and in view of the complications that arose in the Far East, we were obliged, in order to improve the defense of the country, to hastily transfer a number of factories to the production of modern weapons of defense. ... The Soviet Union has been transformed into a country mighty in defense, a country prepared for every contingency, a country capable of producing all modern weapons of defense on a mass scale and of equipping its own army with them in the event of an attack from without.[11]

Negotiating on the "position of strength," Soviet diplomatic maneuvers continued at a brisk pace. In December 1932, the Soviet Union had fully restored with China the normal diplomatic and consular relations which had been severed after the Sino-Soviet hostilities in 1929. In May 1933, the Soviets offered to sell the Chinese Eastern Railway to Japanese-controlled Manchukuo in order to remove one of the major sources of Soviet-Japanese friction and, as they had hoped earlier, to "increase the antagonism between America and Japan."[12] While negotiations for the sale of the railway were in progress, in July the Soviet Union signed a series of nonaggression treaties with various nations in eastern Europe, the Near East, and Central Asia. The most significant diplomatic success of the year was the *de jure* recognition extended to her by the United States. This Soviet-American accord might have been intended to dampen Japanese expansion in East Asia, but it had little effect in mitigating Japan's antagonism toward the Soviet Union.

The United States recognition of the Stalin regime, on the other hand, appeared to have created no immediate, special, adverse effect upon American-Japanese relations. If it did, it was not discernible at once. In February 1934, the Japanese foreign minister, Hirota Koki, made an overture in his message to Secretary Hull for the strengthening and expansion of diplomatic and commercial relations with the United States. Hull responded that no question should exist between the two nations that was fundamentally incapable of amicable solution. He emphasized the need for a mutual understanding of the respective positions of each country "in a spirit of amity and of desire for peaceful and just settlement." The Hirota-Hull exchange of notes could have become a basis for further exploratory negotiations aimed at settling the outstanding differences between the two countries. But their respective policy lines and specific means to achieve a "peaceful and just settlement" were fundamentally antithetical. Japan devotedly advocated the international recognition of Manchukuo, while the United States doggedly adhered to the nonrecognition policy. The same day that Hirota sent his message to Hull, Japan established the monopolistic Manchurian Petroleum Company, thus gradually squeezing other powers out of the Manchurian market. As the governments of the United States, Great Britain, and the Netherlands respectively lodged their protests against this discriminatory practice, Japan responded with a notion that formal recognition of Manchukuo would be the *quid pro quo* for equal commercial opportunity in that disputed part of the world.

Meanwhile, behind the low-keyed and flexible Asian policy of the Roosevelt-Hull administration, an unmistakable measure of military preparedness had been taken. When Roosevelt took office, the United States fleet strength was approximately two-thirds of the treaty limitations, as compared to Japan's 95 percent. A strong advocate of sea power, President Roosevelt was determined to pursue naval construction in which he desired to accomplish two important objectives simultaneously: to shore up the navy in order to strengthen national defense on the one hand, and to create employment in order to combat the depression on the other. He had, therefore, written into the National Industrial Recovery Act of June 1933 a stipulation that an appropriation be made for naval construction within the limit of treaty obligations. The president immediately apportioned $238 million for the navy and orders were placed for two aircraft carriers, five cruisers, and a number of lesser vessels. In March 1934, four additional cruisers were authorized, and the Vinson-Trammell Act empowered the president to bring the naval forces to full treaty strength by 1942.

President Roosevelt also kept the battleship fleet in the Pacific, where it had been since 1932. American naval maneuvers had been planned in the summer of 1931, before the Manchurian incident of September 18, and in the winter of 1932 the entire United States fleet had been engaged in maneuvers in the Pacific between California and the Hawaiian Islands. Secretary Stimson had written:

> Thereafter, just when the Japanese were making their attack on Shanghai, the American fleet in the course of these maneuvers came to Hawaii on February 13th. After further careful consideration it was allowed to remain in that neighborhood and was not dispersed or sent back to the Atlantic on the conclusion of the maneuvers.

This decision had been made on the basis of the fear that Japan might launch a surprise attack in "a state of fanatical excitement." Stimson went on to state:

> In such a situation that presence of the entire American fleet assembled at a port which placed it on the flank of any such outbreak southward towards Hong Kong, French Indochina, or the Philippines, undoubtedly exercised a steadying effect. It was a potent reminder of the ultimate military strength of

peaceful America which could not be overlooked by anyone, however excited he might be.[13]

As President Roosevelt and Secretary Hull decided to keep the United States fleet in the Pacific as a deterrent against a possible Japanese rash action, their policy did not materially differ from the Hoover-Stimson policy.

Dual Dramas: In Tokyo and in Sian

Japan was, of course, fully aware of these policies and positions of the United States. At this time Japan was particularly concerned with and irritated by American aid to the Nanking government then under Chiang Kai-shek. The United States had sold fighter planes to China, sent a retired officer to train Chinese combat pilots, and allowed Curtiss-Wright to build an airplane factory in China. Such assistance to China prompted the Japanese government to issue, in April 1934, what was known as the Amau Statement, which stated in part:

> We oppose therefore any attempt on the part of China to avail herself of the influence of any other country in order to resist Japan. We also oppose any action taken by China, calculated to play one power against another. . . . Supplying China with war planes, building aerodromes in China and detailing military instructors or military advisors to China or contracting a loan to provide funds for political uses, would obviously tend to alienate the friendly relations between Japan and China and other countries and to disturb peace and order in East Asia. Japan will oppose such projects.[14]

Thus, in what became inescapably labeled a "Japanese Monroe Doctrine," the Japanese government proclaimed its determination to assume unilaterally the position and the role of political guardian and economic protector of China, rejecting any form of aid or interference by the Western powers in East Asia in general and China in particular. China lost no time in countering the Amau Statement:

China believes that the maintenance of international peace is dependent upon the cooperation of all the nations in the world. Those interested in maintaining long-lasting peace in the world must promote a sincere spirit of mutual understanding and eliminate the basic causes of serious problems. No nation in the world can assert that it alone has the responsibility to maintain international peace.[15]

The United States likewise challenged, in a considerably milder tone, the Amau Statement:

The relations of the United States with China are governed, as are our relations with Japan and our relations with other countries, by the generally accepted principles of international law and the provisions of treaties to which the United States has with regard to China certain rights and certain obligations. . . . In the opinion of the American people and the American Government, no nation can, without the assent of the other nations concerned, rightfully endeavor to make conclusive its will in situations where there are involved the rights, the obligations, and the legitimate interests of other sovereign states.[16]

Secretary Hull's protest was followed by the United States' cancellation of plans for aid to China.[17] This was a great disappointment to China, for the United States appeared to avoid scrupulously the initiative in opposing Japanese expansion.

In fact, Japanese expansion toward China continued with a steady pace. By 1935 the Kwantung Army had successfully pressured the Peiping Military Council to withdraw its troops and officials from Hopei, to end all anti-Japanese activities, and to eliminate the Kuomintang organization in the area. Japan's next move was to detach North China from the rest of the country and to form another "autonomous" region similar to that of Manchukuo. As in the case of the creation of Manchukuo, Japan played on the same theme that a spontaneous and popular demand of the Chinese inhabitants in North China necessitated such a move. In reality, however, there was neither the popular interest of the Chinese people nor the public willingness of the Chinese officials, who saw no special benefit in severing their ties with the Nanking regime. Nevertheless, at the end of the year Japan was able to establish the East Hopei Autonomous Council which came under the complete control of Japanese military authorities. But the council was unable to function properly to fulfill the objectives sought in the face of the newly surging anti-Japanese sentiment.

Japan, for the moment, did not press the issue any further. At this time, in early 1936, Japan was confronted with a domestic political crisis resulting from a power struggle between the two rival factions in the Imperial Army. It appeared to the extremist elements in the army that they were losing ground as evidenced by the rising hostility of the Diet, administration, and large segments of the people. They felt it their "patriotic" duty to rid the government of "corrupt" and "weak-minded" leaders. Before dawn, February 26, 1936, more than a score of radical army officers and fourteen hundred men set out to assassinate the prime minister and his cabinet members.[18] They seized the principal government buildings, such as the war ministry, the police headquarters, the Diet building, and the premier's official residence, and remained in a state of insurrection for three days. In the end, following a personal appeal by the emperor, they laid down their arms and returned to their unit. After the unprecedented coup, which had the effect of strengthening the position of the army and the advocates of a strong foreign policy, Hirota Koki was nominated to form a new cabinet. Under heavy pressure from the military, Hirota instituted a cabinet reform whereby the ministers of the army and the navy should thereafter be high-ranking military officers on *active* duty.[19]

In the summer of 1936, the Hirota cabinet set forth its fundamental national policy. It consisted of (1) economic cooperation and strengthening of ties among Japan, Manchukuo, and China, (2) peaceful penetration of Southeast Asia, (3) the elimination of the Soviet (Communist) threat, and (4) the construction of a powerful Imperial Navy to match the United States Navy in the western Pacific.

Hirota's China policy was focused on securing China's acceptance of the general principles which Japan had advanced in the previous years, which called for China to cease anti-Japanese agitation, to recognize Japan's special position in North China, to promote Sino-Japanese economic cooperation, and to collaborate in the suppression of communism. The Chinese government, on the other hand, insisted on an annulment of the Tangku Truce and abolition of the demilitarized zones both in Hopei and around Shanghai, withdrawal of Japanese troops from Hopei and Chahar Provinces, and elimination of the East Hopei Autonomous Regime. Despite strenuous negotiations between the two countries through the remainder of the year 1936, no agreement was reached to resolve the basic differences.

The insoluble difficulty with Japan was one of the two critical problems with which the Chiang Kai-shek government was faced, the other being an internal Communist threat. Chiang had been waging the "extermination campaign" for years. In October 1934, Chiang had driven the Communists out of their Kiangsi base and forced upon them the year-long retreat of what has become the epochal six-thousand-mile Long March into Yenan in the corner of Shansi Province.[20] Chiang was determined to pursue and liquidate the Communists at their new northwestern lair. He therefore ordered Chang Hsüeh-liang (the Young Marshal) and Yang Hu-cheng to lead their armies in a renewed assault on the Communists. But low morale and serious doubt spread among the rank and file as to why they were fighting fellow Chinese when they should be fighting against the invading Japanese. This sentiment and mood culminated in the "kidnapping" of Chiang Kai-shek on December 12, 1936, at Sian, the headquarters of the Young Marshal and General Yang. Chiang had flown there for the purpose of personal observation and assessment of the military situation.

The captors set forth a number of demands to Chiang; among them were the termination of all internal strife, release of all political prisoners, and reorganization of the Nanking government to include all parties and groups working for national salvation. Chiang adamantly refused to accept any of these demands, and at times his life was feared threatened. This episode at Sian, which stunned the country and the world, came to an end with the release of Chiang on Christmas Day, 1936, presumably through

Chou En-lai's mediation and on Comintern advice. The Comintern was then pressing for the effective implementation of the United Front policy against the aggression and expansion of fascism. Hitler's Nazi Germany had invaded the Rhineland, Mussolini's Fascist Italy subjugated Ethiopia, and the militaristic Japanese Empire dominated Manchuria and North China. The Communist leaders at Yenan and in Moscow came to realize that the Chinese Communists, determined as they were, should not bear alone the burden of confronting the impending aggression of Japan in China. All the Chinese—Communists, Nationalists, peasants, students, proletariats, and bourgeois alike—under the banner of the United Front should put up a strong resistance to Japan. Chiang Kai-shek was thought to be able to provide the leadership for this kind of joint effort of national unity.

Upon release, Chiang flew back to Nanking accompanied by the Young Marshal, who "repented" and volunteered to face any punishment for his action.[21] Although Chiang denied that there was any bargain or concession on his part for his freedom, his release was followed by a Nationalist-Communist accord on the United Front. Chiang terminated, at least for the time being, the anti-Communist extermination campaign and reset the national priority from chasing the Communists to facing the Japanese.

In view of this new development, Japan had to make a choice between (1) proceeding immediately with her design of detaching North China before the United Front became all-effective and (2) temporizing the plan for future optimum conditions. Japan chose the latter course, but ended up with the former alternative.

In the meantime Japan had been resolutely moving toward achieving the goal of naval parity with Great Britain and the United States. In December 1934, Japan had delivered the required two-year advance notice of her intent to withdraw her membership from the Washington Naval Treaty. Japan also refused to renew the London treaty as proposed. By the beginning of 1937, therefore, Japan was no longer bound by any treaty obligations to limit her naval construction and expansion. Her naval budget soared to unprecedented proportions.

Japanese naval policy triggered a chain reaction, plunging the major powers into a naval armaments race. The United States accelerated her shipbuilding schedules with the allocation of an enormous amount of funds. Great Britain likewise greatly enlarged her naval expenditures, including the modernization of the Singapore facilities. France was no exception; she increased proportionately her expenditures to strengthen her navy. These three Western powers had signed in March 1936 a second London treaty imposing qualitative restrictions. But the escape clause in the treaty allowed the signatories to disregard these limitations in war or in peace if they deemed it vital to their national security. On the basis of this convenient leeway, the three treaty powers invoked this very stipulation to run an unlimited naval armaments race when Japan rejected the restriction on maximum gun calibre of capital ships and refused to disclose whether she was building 45,000-ton battleships as rumored. As for the United States, in 1938 President Roosevelt asked Congress to expand the naval fleet beyond the old treaty limits and to strengthen the insular possessions in the western Pacific, as Japan intended to fortify the mandate islands. The fateful test of each other's strength was to come in three years.

Imminent Involvement

Epidemic of World Lawlessness

In early 1937, there was a momentary calm in Sino-Japanese relations. Chiang Kai-shek had just returned to Nanking after the ordeal at Sian and had to revamp his policy, including "cooperation" with the Communists in their United Front. In Japan, the Hirota cabinet, which had enjoyed a temporary respite, fell in February 1937 under the pressure of the military, and General Hayashi formed a new government. His foreign minister, Sato, pursued a conciliatory policy toward China and declared his willingness to settle the differences through negotiations on a basis of equality and friendship. But his policy had little consequence in mitigating the growing anti-Japanese sentiment among the Chinese people.

Unable to satisfy the military-expansionist circles, the Hayashi cabinet was destined to be short-lived. At the end of May it fell.

Prince Konoye Fumimaro was selected to form a new cabinet. With his prestige, popularity, and youth, he was able to establish a government of "national unity" and to pursue a consensus policy as envisioned by the militarists. The calm soon proved to be the lull before the storm.

Fighting broke out between the Chinese and Japanese troops during the night of July 7, 1937, as the latter were conducting maneuvers in the vicinity of the Marco Polo Bridge (Lukouchiao) southwest of Peking.[22] There was no convincing evidence to show that this "incident" had been premeditated by the Japanese as had been the case with the Manchurian incident. In fact, the Konoye government attempted to localize the incident and to settle the controversy through negotiations between the local commanders. But the jingoistic spirit and atmosphere in Japan and the anti-Japanese sentiment in China were too incompatible to bring about a negotiated settlement. Japanese military-expansionists found in the incident an opportunity to secure by force of arms their prime objective in China—the control of North China. After the brief attempt to quench the spark of the Lukouchiao incident, the Sino-Japanese conflagration roared out of control. By the end of July, the invading Japanese forces occupied Peking, and soon thereafter, the provincial capitals of Chahar and Suiyan fell into Japanese hands. The Japanese army quickly succeeded in driving the Chinese out of the entire Peking-Tientsin area. "Three days after the early morning hostilities at Wanping, the [Japanese] cabinet had taken all the necessary steps to secure mobilization of the army, evacuation of Japanese nationals from China, and regimentation of public opinion at home. The scope of these measures, no less than the rapidity with which they were put into effect, suggests the operation of a well-oiled machine which needed only to be thrown into gear at a given signal."[23]

The Japanese militarists had come to the conclusion that the China issue required a military solution rather than political or diplomatic negotiations; Sato's conciliatory policy under Premier Hayashi had amply demonstrated the futility of the course of peaceful settlement. They were convinced that Chinese armed resistance could be easily crushed by the overwhelming Japanese military might, and therefore, Japan would be able to detach the five northern provinces from China and to incorporate them eventually into Manchukuo.[24]

They were further convinced that no third power or powers could successfully intervene on behalf of China. The Soviet Union, which had long been regarded as a nemesis to Japanese interests in Manchuria, was engrossed in treason trials and the execution of high-ranking officers in the Red Army. It should be added that Japan had signed on November 25, 1936, the anti-Comintern pact with Germany. The expressed purpose of the pact was to exchange information on the threat of Communist subversion. A secret protocol, however, provided that in the event of an unprovoked Soviet attack upon either one of the signatories, the two would immediately hold consultation for cooperation against the Soviets. As for the Western powers, they were in disarray. The Japanese leaders had seen that Mussolini had invaded Ethiopia and Hitler had occupied the Rhineland with impunity. The civil war in Spain was drawing the fascist "Rome-Berlin Axis" on the side of France and the Soviet Communists on the side of the Loyalists, while the Western democracies were remaining scrupulously behind the policy of "nonintervention." To the Japanese military-expansionists, therefore, nothing seemed to stand in the way of their conquest of China. They believed that it was now or never for their designs in China.

By mid-August 1937, the hostilities spread to the Shanghai area and the capital city of Nanking was bombed by the Japanese air force. But China could not be bludgeoned into submission. She was no longer the same as the China of 1894, of 1915, or of 1931; she was determined to resist Japanese aggression and to preserve her national integrity. Chiang Kai-shek had declared to his people: "We will trade space for time—once the fighting begins, we will never surrender."

China began to witness an apparent sign of the emergence of national unity. Some powerful local military leaders journeyed to Nanking to offer their services, pledging their loyalty to the Nationalist government. The Communist-Nationalist negotiations resulted in a speedy agreement, whereby the Communist-controlled regions were incorporated into the Nationalist domain and the Red

Armies were renamed as the Eighth Route Armies in the national armed forces. Although this show of unity subsequently turned out to be superficial, it nevertheless demonstrated at that moment of national crisis the determination of the Chinese to take a joint stand.

Japan's assumption as to the attitudes of the Western democracies proved to be accurate. They were divided on their policies with respect to the aggression of the totalitarian fascist states in Europe and East Asia. The United States at first followed the course of impartiality, as recommended by Ambassador Joseph C. Grew in Tokyo, who had advocated noninvolvement in the conflict, maintenance of friendship with both China and Japan, and protection of lives, property, and rights of American citizens in China.

The initial noninvolvement-nonintervention policy of the United States in the "China Affair" was presumably based on the following reasons: (1) The resurgent isolationism at home was clearly against any type of agreement or action which might constitute or suggest alliance; (2) There was no indication that invocation of provisions of the covenant of the League of Nations, the Kellogg-Briand Pact, or of the Nine-Power Treaty against Japan would stop her aggression now any more than it did in 1931; (3) A United States involvement in the form of mediation or of aid to China might prove counterproductive, for such an action might antagonize Japan and further aggravate the situation (hence, on July 12, 1937, Secretary Hull refused China's plea to mediate); (4) A military involvement was unthinkable and undesirable because the United States Asiatic fleet remained a token unit, which could not match the Japanese Imperial Navy in Asian waters; and (5) Finally, believing that the principles of international law and morality were as vital in international relations as the Christian ethics in personal relations, the United States sought to uphold the sanctity of international treaties which had bound the nations to solve their disputes by peaceful means.

Doggedly adhering to the noninvolvement policy, on July 21 Secretary of State Hull refused an Anglo-French invitation for a joint *demarche* toward the Sino-Japanese conflict, but a month later he sent about twelve hundred marines to Shanghai for the protection of American interests in the international settlement. In strengthening the noninvolvement policy, the Roosevelt administration could have invoked the Neutrality Act of May 1, 1937. But the invocation was thought to hurt, rather than help, China, with whom the administration's sympathy lay. China needed arms and supplies to fight the Japanese. The Neutrality Act, if applied to China, would cut off the sources to supply her war needs. In September, President Roosevelt announced that no government-owned vessels could carry war goods to either belligerent, but private shippers were allowed to engage in such trade at their own risk. Thus, the scale of America's impartiality began to tip toward China. This trend became conspicuous as evidenced by the speech of the president and by the positive cooperation with international organizations which condemned Japanese actions in China.

On October 5, 1937, in Chicago, President Roosevelt made the famous "quarantine speech," in which he asserted:

> It seems to be unfortunately true that the epidemic of world lawlessness is spreading. When an epidemic of physical disease starts to spread, the community approves and joins in a quarantine of the patients in order to protect the health of the community against the spread of the disease.

The president was implicitly reminding his audience that "the epidemic" of unprovoked aggressions had victimized the Ethiopians, the Rhinelanders, the Manchurians, and now the Chinese. He appealed to the peace-loving nations to unite in a concerted effort to make world peace (the health of the community) prevail. He warned his countrymen that "mere isolation or neutrality," which the United States was pursuing, was no guarantee against ambitious aggressors, the carriers of the epidemic. The contention that the president was calling for a collective security measure to sanction the aggressor or that the speech marked a drastic change in American foreign policy was debatable. But when he delivered the speech, and as he was thinking of the Sino-Japanese hostilities, there was no doubt in his mind as to who represented the disease and who the patient.

The day after the "quarantine speech," October 6, the League

Assembly at Geneva endorsed its advisory committee's finding that Japan had violated the provisions of both the Nine-Power Treaty and the Pact of Paris. China, therefore, deserved all moral support and sympathy, concluded the assembly, adding that a conference should be convened under the Nine-Power Treaty. Secretary Hull immediately expressed his concurrence with the League position.

The Anglo-American accord quickly cleared the way for a conference. Belgium, acting as host, extended invitations to all the original and new signatories of the Nine-Power Treaty as well as to Germany and the Soviet Union.[25] The conference opened at Brussels on November 3, 1937, without Japan and Germany. Japan declined to participate in the parley on the grounds that the League had already found Japan *guilty* without a fair and impartial hearing from both sides, that the Sino-Japanese conflict was a matter which solely concerned the two countries and which would brook no interference by any nation or nations, and that the Nine-Power Treaty was inapplicable to the fundamentally altered circumstances in East Asia—a claim in complete accordance with the doctrine of *rebus sic stantibus* in international law.

During the three-week conference, each of the major powers acted as though it wished that someone else would pull the chestnut out of the fire. Great Britain thought it unwise to talk about economic sanctions. France was cautious not to antagonize Japan because her colony of Indochina was extremely vulnerable to a Japanese attack. The Soviet Union, which had recently signed a nonaggression treaty with China, offered big rhetoric but little substance. The United States was displeased because other powers attempted to place the blame for the debacle on her. Italy, as expected, acted on behalf of her two absentee partners and announced her intention to join the anti-Comintern pact. The only agreement reached at the conference, with Italy dissenting, was a reaffirmation of the validity of the Nine-Power Treaty and a nudging rebuke to Japan that her actions were contrary both to the letter and spirit of that treaty and to the views held by all other signatories.[26] On November 24, 1937, the conference was adjourned.

The outcome of the Brussels conference might be regarded as China's moral, diplomatic victory. Though the powers assembled shed "Maria-Theresa's tears" for China, she stood alone militarily. The Chinese armies put up a gallant resistance but their cities and towns fell one by one into the hands of the invaders.

By this time, however, Chinese nationalism had become a formidable force which began to play a crucial role in the defense and salvation of the country. The concept of modern state sovereignty and equality, and its concomitant nationalism, both of which were claimed to be Western in origin, were introduced into China through educators, students, missionaries, traders, and diplomats. Merging with this principle of the inviolability and sanctity of a nation-state was the sense of pride and prestige in a brilliant culture which the Chinese had held for centuries. These had come to constitute the foundation of Chinese nationalism. The Boxer Rebellion against foreigners at the turn of the century was the first embryonic manifestation of Chinese nationalism, and in the 1920s Chinese nationalism worked into the thinking of the country as having an intellectual validity in its own right. The famous May Fourth movement of 1919 had already suggested the crystallization of Chinese nationalism because it had, in reality, been a combined intellectual and sociopolitical movement to emancipate the individual, to establish a just society through modernization, and to achieve genuine national independence.

One of the San Min Chu I (Three Principles of the People), which Dr. Sun Yat-sen expounded as the revolutionary philosophy, was nationalism. Dr. Sun had compared China to a sheet of sand and nationalism to cement. Just as cement must be used to bind the particles of sand strongly together, so must nationalism bind the Chinese people together. Chinese nationalism, therefore, aimed at the creation of national unity and the development of national patriotism, raising the level of individual Chinese loyalty and sense of belongingness from family or clan to the nation of China. Imperial China was a universal empire, of which the decline was precipitated by the coming of Western nations to China beginning in the middle of the nineteenth century. As the universal empire gave way to the republican nationalist China, so did universalism give way to nationalism.

The formation of the Kuomintang (nationalist party), the

Northern Expedition aimed at *national* unification, the establishment of a *national* government in Nanking, and the positive policy
to recover lost *national* interests were illustrative manifestations
of Chinese nationalism. In modern times nationalism is usually
spurred most conspicuously by hostile external forces which
threaten national security and integrity. For this reason, the Japanese invasion of Manchuria and North China had the effect of
solidifying Chinese nationalism into a powerful force—the will and
determination "to pay any price, to bear any burden" to resist the
Japanese aggression.

The Open Door vs. the New Order

The expansion and intensification of the hostilities in scope and
scale made it increasingly difficult for the Japanese forces to confine their military operations strictly to the destruction of the
Chinese armies. Intentionally or unintentionally, they inflicted
damage upon foreign interests and property in China. Such was the
case with the U.S.S. *Panay* and H.M.S. *Ladybird.* On December
12, 1937, Japanese war planes bombed, strafed, and sank the
American gunboat *Panay,* which was escorting Standard Oil
tankers, in the Yangtze River near Nanking. Two sailors were
killed and some of the crew wounded. The Japanese government
was deeply disturbed because it feared that such an incident as
this, which it claimed to be an unfortunate accident due to the
mistaken identity of the ships, could trigger an unwanted confrontation with the United States. Japanese officials took prompt and
proper action to meet the contingency. The foreign minister personally visited the United States embassy in Tokyo to offer apolo-
gies and payment of reparations. With no cry for reprisals in the
United States, the crisis was settled in two weeks.

The *Panay* incident took place as the Japanese launched an all-
out attack on Nanking, which fell the same day. The victorious
Japanese troops, as they occupied the Chinese capital, plundered,
pillaged, looted, and destroyed the city in what became known as
"The Rape of Nanking." The barbarity of the Japanese Imperial
Army shocked the civilized world. An American consular officer
reported: "It would seem that the soldiers were let loose like a

barbarian horde to desecrate the city." The sacking of Nanking further forged China's will to resist and to repel the "Eastern invaders."

In January 1938, Japanese foreign minister Hirota Koki (former premier, 1936–1937), in a speech before the Imperial Diet, set forth the course of foreign policy. His four-point conditions for a peaceful settlement of the "China Affair" were:

1. China to abandon her pro-Communist and anti-Japanese and anti-Manchukuo policies to collaborate with Japan and Manchukuo in their anti-Comintern policy.
2. The establishment of demilitarized zones in the necessary localities, and of a special regime for the said localities.
3. Conclusion of an economic agreement between Japan, China, and Manchukuo.
4. China to pay Japan the necessary indemnities.[27]

Fundamentally, these four points were the refined and expanded version of his old China policy during his own premiership.

Hirota added that Japan would not "close the Chinese door," but would "leave the door wide open to all Powers." This was obvious lip-service to the Open Door, for he asserted at the same time that the powers would have to recognize "a New Order in the Far East," and one of the essential principles of the New Order was, as he put it, to "expel the interests of the Powers from China."

Hirota seemed to have perceived no contradictions between the Open Door and the New Order. In his scheme of the New Order, China's door would be open to any nation which would acknowledge Japan's paramount position in the Far East, recognize the legitimacy of Manchukuo, endorse the Amau Statement, and accept the supremacy of Japanese interests in China. The Open Door under the New Order, therefore, would allow the powers to "enjoy" commercial opportunities, not necessarily *equal*, and to promote their interests within the limits of not running counter to those of Japan.

In the summer of 1938, two unrelated events caused Japan to pause for a moment for careful evaluation of her foreign policy:

one was the Soviet-Japanese armed clash, and the other, America's economic pressure. Japan's anti-Soviet and anti-Communist posture to a great degree resulted from her traditional fear and suspicion toward her historical rival since the days of the Russo-Japanese War. A Soviet "surprise attack" constantly haunted Japan, the major Japanese cities and industrial centers being within easy striking distance of Soviet air power. The common borders between the two countries, stretching from Sakhalin to Inner Mongolia for all practical purposes, were guarded by armed forces poised to strike on a moment's notice. In July 1938, fighting broke out between the Japanese and Soviet troops at Chokoho (Chang Kufeng), a strategic height on the Tuman River, Korea. From the beginning it was the kind of war which neither side really wanted. Having committed a large portion of the Imperial armies in China, Japan did not want a two-front war. The Soviet Union, by the same token, had to take into consideration a possible German attack.[28] After two weeks of bitter fighting, they agreed to negotiate their differences, including the fishery controversy.

At the time that Japan and the Soviet Union were testing each other's military capability at Chokoho, the United States started down the road of economic retaliation against Japan. Japanese aerial bombing of major cities in China, such as Nanking, Canton, Shanghai, and others, caused a great number of civilian casualties. Abhorred by the acts which had inflicted suffering upon innocent victims, Secretary of State Hull advised the American aviation industry that his government was strongly opposed to the sale of airplanes to nations guilty of indiscriminatory bombing. The United States Treasury Department, on the other hand, purchased silver to help ease China's dwindling foreign reserve.

Neither Soviet needling at Chokoho nor American economic pressure left any impact on Japanese military operations in China. The Japanese successfully won battle after battle, while the Chinese had to resort to their invincible weapon—the vast territory. After the fall of Nanking, the Chiang Kai-shek government retreated to Hankow; when Hankow fell in October 1938, the Chiang regime moved further into the interior to Chungking, which remained Chiang's wartime capital until the end of World War II.

On November 3, 1938, Prime Minister Konoye officially proclaimed the establishment of the "New Order" in East Asia as his national objective. Konoye's "New Order," an elaborated and systematized version of the original Hirota policy announcement made ten months earlier, was designed to "insure the permanent stability of East Asia" on the basis of a "tripartite relationship of mutual aid and coordination between Japan, Manchukuo, and China in political, economic, cultural, and other fields."[29] The fundamental feature of the New Order was deceivingly simple. It did not rest on a Japanese-Manchukuo-Chinese tripod with the principle of equality as it appeared to be, but rather it purported to create a pyramidal community in East Asia with Japan at the apex exercising unrivaled dominance.

The United States was opposed to the New Order and called Japan's attention to the certainty of infringing on the treaty rights of other powers. Japan retorted with the assertion that no useful purpose would be served by "an attempt to apply to present and future conditions without any changes, concepts, and principles which were applicable to conditions prevailing before the present incident."[30] The United States then counteracted with the same argument expounded in the Stimson Doctrine. American ambassador in Tokyo Joseph Grew, speaking for his government, stated that the United States was not aware of the changed conditions, to which Washington was willing to have existing treaties adapted. Such adaptation, however, would have to be achieved through democratic processes of negotiation and accommodation. There would be no assent to the abrogation of any of his country's rights or obligations "by the arbitrary action of agents or authorities of [any] other country." For these reasons the United States would not recognize the New Order, for it was formulated by Japan alone "in areas not under its sovereignty and to constitute itself the repository of authority and the agent of destiny in regard thereto."[31] Thus, by the end of 1938, Japan and the United States had taken uncompromising and irreconcilable positions toward each other.

In strengthening the New Order, the Konoye government desired to transform the anti-Comintern pact into a military alliance directed solely against the Soviet Union, but not against Great Britain, France, or the United States. The influential industrialists, the diplomats, and the navy shared and supported this view, but the army did not. The internal dissension, coupled with the stalemate in China, caused Konoye to resign in January 1939. Succeeding Konoye, Premier Hiranuma Kiichiro pledged to continue the policy of his predecessor, including that of the New Order.

The first concrete implementation of the New Order was carried out in February 1939, when the Japanese seized the island of Hainan in the South China Sea. A month later Japan also staked out a territorial claim over the Spratly Islands nearby. Because of the strategic value of these islands, the Japanese occupation of them posed a threat to the French and British possessions in the Far East. The earlier nonalienation rights secured by these two Western powers from China now became less than meaningful. Furthermore, the American Philippines, French Indochina, British Malaya, the Dutch East Indies, and even Singapore—Britain's Asian Gibraltar—all began to feel the menace of the approaching tentacle of Japanese power. In addition, the Japanese began to apply pressure to the government and administration of the International Settlements in Shanghai and waged "economic warfare" in the form of a blockade against British and French concessions in Tientsin with the intent of controlling silver bullion held by the British as backing for Chinese currency.

Neither Britain nor France could retaliate in kind. Only the United States decided to act. On July 26, 1939, Washington gave Tokyo the required six months' notice of its intention to terminate the 1911 treaty of commerce with Japan. The United States then established a credit for China of $25 million, followed by Great Britain who also granted China credit of £450,000 for arms and supplies. All too obvious was, in the words of American Ambassador Grew, "an unmistakable hardening of the administration's attitude toward Japan and a marked disinclination to allow American interests to be crowded out of China." In a speech delivered later (October 19, 1939) before an audience of the America-Japan Society in Tokyo, Grew stated that his countrymen "had good reason to believe that an effort is being made to establish control, in Japan's own interest, of large areas of a system of closed economy. It is this thought, added to the effect of the bombings, the indignities, the manifold interference with American rights, that accounts for the attitude of the American people to Japan today."[32]

"Intrusion by the United States"

One of many startling events in international power politics in the second half of 1939 was the signing of the German-Soviet Nonaggression Pact on August 23. It came as a surprise to Japan, for Hitler had ignored the letter and spirit of the Tripartite Anti-Comintern Pact of 1937. Prime Minister Hiranuma felt that his country was in danger of being isolated by her Axis partners. The German-Soviet collusion could not have come at a worse time, because the Hiranuma government was suffering from the stings of the Nomonhan incident. On May 5, 1939, Soviet-Japanese hostilities, like those at Chokoho ten months earlier but on a larger scale, had broken out near Nomonhan on the Outer Mongolian-Manchukuo border. The fighting had all the essentials of a full-fledged war. By the end of August, the Kwantung Army, which had been thrown into combat, was severely beaten, with more than eighteen thousand casualties, by the superior Soviet armed forces.[33] With that enemy, ideologically irreconcilable and politically incompatible, Hitler had signed an agreement. Calling Hitler's diplomatic acrobatics a "complex absurdity," Hiranuma resigned a week after the announcement of the Nazi-Soviet accord and was succeeded by General Abe Nobuyuki.

On September 1, 1939, with the German invasion of Poland, which plunged Europe into the Second World War, the Abe cabinet immediately declared its policy of noninvolvement in the European conflagration and of concentration on a solution of the "China Affair." It, therefore, suspended negotiations for the conversion of the Tripartite Anti-Comintern Pact into a military alliance and obtained a truce settlement with the Soviet Union on the Nomonhan conflict.

The Abe administration, however, was confronted with mounting domestic difficulties. Consumer goods became scarce; rice and fuel shortages became critical; insufficient supply of chemical fertilizer hurt the farmers; and an antiwar sentiment began to emerge. Unable to solve these problems, the Abe government toppled within five months. Admiral Yonai Mitsumasa then became the new premier in January 1940.

The fourth cabinet change in fourteen months was symptomatic of Japan's political instability and lack of sound leadership. Japan was groping for a policy which would unify the people and strengthen the foundations of national power. The seemingly insoluble China affair had been draining national energies. Even the military came to realize that its expansionist policy had cost Japan dearly. The high command of the army decided in a conference held on March 30, 1940, that should the China affair fail to be resolved during the year, a gradual troop withdrawal from China would be carried out beginning in 1941; thus by 1943, the battlefronts would be shortened and consolidated by means of creating military enclaves at the Shanghai delta and at the North China-Mongolian border region.[34]

This decision, however, was reversed within two months, as Hitler's conquest of the Low Countries and France in May and June 1940 left Japan with an added sense of security and confidence that her ultimate objectives might be achieved. Japanese militarists were convinced of Hitler's total victory in Europe and the eventual collapse of Britain, France, and the Netherlands with their vast colonial possessions in Asia. The cry for *Hokushu-Nanshin*—defend the north, advance to the south—became the strategic shibboleth among the military-expansionists. Fearful of a Japanese aggressive move, Secretary of State Hull in April had declared that the status quo should be maintained in the Pacific. To back up the words by deeds, the United States had made Pearl Harbor a base for naval operations, and in May President Roosevelt had ordered the U.S. Pacific fleet, then in Hawaii for maneuvers, to remain there until further notice. This move, defensive and psychological in nature and more political than military, was a show of naval force to Japan in case she might choose to disturb the status quo in Southeast Asia by taking advantage of the events in Europe.

Notwithstanding the American warning, imbued with ever-growing imperial ambition and emboldened by the freedom of action in the Far East, Japan decided to exploit the plight of the stricken nations. She commanded Great Britain to withdraw her troops from Shanghai, to halt traffic from Hong Kong to mainland China, and to close the Burma Road through which a limited quantity of war supplies had been introduced to Chungking. She demanded French concession allowing Japan to station a military mission in northern Indochina to block any aid which might reach Chiang Kai-shek through that route. She told the Netherlands to guarantee the continued flow of raw materials to Japan from the Dutch East Indies. By mid-July most of these demands were met. But these gains were not enough to satisfy the army, which brought down the Yonai cabinet.

On July 22, 1940, Prince Konoye became premier for the second time and formed his cabinet with Matsuoka Yosuke as foreign minister and General Tojo Hideki as minister of the army. With Konoye back at the helm of state affairs, assisted by many staunch advocates of expansionism, Japan appeared to have recovered national unity, goals, and leadership in the new government.

The immediate objective of President Roosevelt's Far Eastern policy at this juncture was to prevent further deterioration of the Anglo-French-Dutch position in Asia in light of the heightened posture of Japan. Thus United States-Japanese relations came to assume a series of moves and countermoves. Only three days after the formation of the Konoye cabinet, the United States government prohibited the export to Japan of petroleum, petroleum products, tetraethyl lead, and scrap metal. A week later aviation gasoline was added to the list. Thereupon Japan protested against the American policy in the following words:

> As a country whose import of American aviation gasoline is of immense value, Japan would bear the brunt of the virtual embargo. The resultant impression would be that Japan had been singled out for and subjected to discriminatory treatment.[35]

At the same time, Japan pressed the French authorities in Indochina to allow Japanese troops, in their military operations against China, to pass through the French colony and to use military bases and other facilities. The United States expressed its deep concern and warned of "the unfortunate effect on American public opinion"—that such demands would interfere with domestic affairs of Indochina and would disturb the status quo in Southeast Asia. The Japanese reaction to America's expressed concern, to put it succinctly, was: *Mind your own business.*

> Under the ever-changing conditions of today, past rules and norms rapidly become inapplicable to actual conditions. It is clear that merely to adhere blindly to such rules and norms is not the way to stabilize world peace. Despite the fact that in the Western hemisphere epoch-making changes are actually being made in the status quo, Japan has as yet expressed no opinion for or against those changes. It has to be pointed out that intrusion by the United States in an area which is so remote from that country as in this case brings about the same effect upon Japan's public opinion as the meddlesome attitude of a third country toward the policy of the United States concerning third-power territories in the Western hemisphere would bring about upon public opinion in the United States.[36]

In this statement the Japanese government clearly indicated its displeasure toward the "intrusion by the United States" in what Japan considered to be her sole sphere of influence—East Asia. Japan claimed to have as much of a free hand in Asia as did the United States in the western hemisphere under the Monroe Doctrine. Based on this consideration, on September 19, 1940, the Konoye cabinet converted the New Order into the so-called Great East Asia Co-Prosperity Sphere—a grandiose territorial limit inclusive of "the former German islands under mandate, French Indochina and Pacific Islands, Thailand, British Malaya, British Borneo, Dutch East Indies, etc. with Japan, Manchuria, and China as the backbone."

It reflected Japan's ambitious drive toward a realization of monopolistic economic autarky by means of securing rich supplies of raw materials from those regions, especially those of oil, rubber, nickel, bauxite, and ore from Southeast Asia.

Japan's first step toward the long-range expansionist policy in Southeast Asia was its immediate strategic plan in Indochina. On

September 22, 1940, the Japanese army signed the Hanoi Convention with the Vichy representatives, whereby France agreed to place her military facilities at the disposal of the Japanese army in return for Japan's promise to respect France's rights and interests in the Far East. Japanese troops immediately landed at Haiphong, moved into northern Indochina, took over military installations, and occupied various strategic points. They were now able to control arms supplies to Chiang Kai-shek via Hanoi and to conduct air assaults on the Burma Road.

Secretary of State Hull lost no time in issuing a statement in response to the Japanese move:

Events are transpiring so rapidly in the Indochina situation that it is impossible to get a clear picture of the minute-to-minute developments. It seems obvious, however, that the *status quo* is being upset and that this is being achieved under duress. The position of the United States in disapproval and in deprecation of such procedures has repeatedly been stated.[37]

This statement was followed by America's tit-for-tat countermeasures. On September 25, 1940, to assist China in meeting her foreign exchange needs, the United States agreed to lend China an additional $25 million which would be liquidated through the sale of tungsten.[38] The following day, President Roosevelt further tightened controls on the exportation of iron and steel scrap with a view to, as well as under the pretext of, "conserving the available supply to meet the rapidly expanding requirements of the defense program" in the United States. The new regulations established the licensing system which permitted shipments of those items to the countries of the western hemisphere and Great Britain only; Japan was to suffer most.

CHAPTER SIX

War Path
to Pearl Harbor

Alignment for Conflict

The Axis Alliance and the "Arsenal of Democracy"

The United States economic warfare of assisting China and of abusing Japan risked an outbreak of American-Japanese hostilities. Japan undertook to deter this threat by transforming the Tripartite Anti-Comintern Pact into a military alliance directed against the United States. This measure of deterrence was accomplished on September 27, 1940, as the Axis powers signed their mutual assistance pact, which provided in part:

> Germany, Italy, and Japan . . . undertake to assist one another [by] all political, economic, and military means, if one of the three Contracting Parties is attacked by a Power at present not involved in the European War or in the Chinese-Japanese conflict. . . .[1]

The pact further stipulated that the "aforesaid terms do not in any way affect the political status which exists at present as between each of the three contracting parties and Soviet Russia." The specification of this clause was intended to give the Soviet

Union an assurance that the Nazi-Soviet nonaggression pact concluded over a year earlier would continue to be honored. With the Soviet Union thus excluded from the framework of applicability of the pact, it was most obvious that the purpose of the Axis Alliance was to deter the United States from entering the war against either Japan or Germany; if she did, she would have to fight all three Axis powers.

The pact also included the principle of mutual recognition of their respective spheres of operation and responsibility. Germany and Italy were to be guardians of the European new order, while Japan was to exercise the complete hegemony in "Great East Asia." The additional understandings as embodied in the exchange of notes were: (1) full applicability of the pact to be decided by consultation, (2) full German aid to Japan in the event of the latter's war with Great Britain, and (3) assurance to Japan of the mandated islands of former German possession. The pact was to come into force immediately upon signing, without ratification, and to remain in force for ten years.

The Nazi regime favored the pact with the conviction that it stood as a deterrent to the United States in Western Europe and as a threat to Great Britain in East Asia. Japanese gains were not so evident. Should the Soviet Union attack Japan, Germany would remain neutral under the Nazi-Soviet nonaggression pact; and if the United States entered the war against Japan, Germany was not and would not be in any position to provide effective military support to Japan. Yet, the Japanese government went to great lengths to trumpet the pact's significance. An Imperial rescript was issued to express "deep gratification" for the conclusion of the pact. Prime Minister Konoye stated that it was "an urgent necessity" to conclude the three-power pact "with a view to joining hands with these powers to establish a new order in the respective regions, and furthermore to cooperate with them toward the restoration of world peace."[2]

Foreign Minister Matsuoka was a little more explicit in defining the purpose of the pact. In a radio address on the day of the signing of the accord, he pointed out:

We should first unite with Germany and Italy which have the same aspirations and policy as ours and later with those powers who can cooperate with us. We should thus go fearlessly forward to carry out our conviction, calling at the same time upon those powers that obstruct us to reconsider their attitude.[3]

Prominent among "those powers that obstruct" Japanese policy were, as Matsuoka remarked in a later statement, the United States and Great Britain, who

... are not only checking Japan's actions through legalistic arguments and treaty pronouncements which have become inapplicable because of changing conditions, but are also oppressing Japan through such means as restriction on the exportation of important commodities to Japan and at the same time are giving positive aid to Japan's enemy, the Chiang Kai-shek regime. These actions spring from hidden motives to keep the Orient under conditions of disorder as long as possible and to consume Japan's national strength.[4]

The Tripartite Alliance Pact, intended to provide a deterrent to the United States, worked to promote the determination of that country to assist her allies. President Roosevelt, after having won an unprecedented third term, told his countrymen in a radio address on December 29, 1940:

Never before since Jamestown and Plymouth Rock has our American civilization been in such danger as now. For, on September 27, 1940, by an agreement signed in Berlin, three powerful nations, two in Europe and one in Asia, joined themselves together in the threat that if the United States interfered with or blocked the expansion program of these three nations—a program aimed at world control—they would unite in ultimate action against the United States.[5]

The president went on to call his nation's attention to the fact that the forces of "the aggressor nations" were being held away from American shores by the British "on the other side of the Atlantic" and by the Chinese "in another great defense" in Asia. He emphatically urged his audience:

We must be the great arsenal of democracy. For us this is an emergency as serious as war itself. We must apply ourselves to our task with the same resolution, the same sense of urgency, the same spirit of patriotism and sacrifice, as we would show were we at war.[6]

As the eventful year 1941 dawned, friction and tensions between the United States and Japan were growing steadily. On January 15, 1941, in testimony before the House Foreign Affairs Committee, Secretary of State Hull asserted that Japan's "new order" in the Pacific area meant her political domination of the entire region by "force of arms," her economic control "of the resources of the area . . . to the ultimate impoverishment of other parts of the area and exclusion of the interests of other countries," and her social hegemony which would bring about "the destruction of personal liberties and the reduction of the conquered peoples to the role of inferiors."[7]

In response to Hull's statement, Foreign Minister Matsuoka declared that the United States, having "no correct understanding of Japan's thoughts and actions," seemed to consider all of Asia and the South Seas as her "first line of defense." Such being the case, he stated, "there is not the slightest hope for improvement of Japanese-American relations."

Clearly then, the geographic point of conflict between the two countries was Southeast Asia. In the formulation of a global strategy, the United States concluded that Britain's survival and an eventual victory would require not only an adequate supply of arms and munitions by the United States, but also an uninterrupted flow to England of foodstuffs and raw materials from her dominions and colonies and the maintenance of her commerce with the outside world. The United States, therefore, could not tolerate the cutting of communications between Britain and her Asian possessions such as Hong Kong, Malaya, Singapore, Australia, and New Zealand. Moreover, these regions together with the Dutch East Indies were the principal sources of rubber, petroleum, and tin for the United States.

Japan's *Hokushu-Nanshin*

Japan, on the other hand, in the pursuit of her *Hokushu-Nanshin* policy, had stationed troops in Indochina and was moving down slowly toward Malaya, Singapore, and the Dutch East Indies. If Japan could occupy these strategically important areas, she could easily break into the Indian Ocean and the South Pacific and pose a grave threat to essential British (and Dutch) lines of communication. Japan's search for an alternative source of supply for essential materials denied by the United States made it imperative for Japan to accelerate her march toward Southeast Asia.

But if Japan's *Nanshin* (advance to the south) were to be overstretched to cover the vast regions of Southeast Asia, *Hokushu* (defense of the north) would be proportionately weakened, thereby strengthening the Soviet temptation to launch an attack on Japan. The Soviet menace in East Asia might have dissipated on account of her primary involvement in Europe with the occupation of Poland and the struggle in Finland. Nevertheless, the potential danger of Soviet-Japanese hostilities remained persistent. A means to temporize this threat had to be found.

Such a policy was provided by Foreign Minister Matsuoka Yosuke, who left for Europe to visit Rome and Berlin the day after the United States Congress had passed the Lend-Lease Act.[8] It was not clear whether Matsuoka, while in Berlin, became aware of Hitler's "Operations Barbarossa."[9] Though he might have known of the plan, he seemed to have failed to grasp the significance of such an event; more likely, he was ignorant of German preparations for an invasion into the Soviet Union. He apparently believed that Hitler and Stalin would continue to honor their nonaggression pact of 1939, and a similar agreement between Japan and the Soviet Union would place the three powers on the best of friendly terms, thus protecting his country's northern flank.

On his way home, Matsuoka proceeded to Moscow and concluded the Soviet-Japanese neutrality pact on April 13, 1941. It provided that "should one of the Contracting Parties become the object of hostilities on the part of one or several third Powers, the other Contracting Party will observe neutrality throughout the duration of the conflict." For Japan this meant that should the vigorous *Nanshin* policy result in an outbreak of war with the United States or Great Britain or both, the Soviet Union would remain neutral. Matsuoka believed that this Soviet-Japanese accord was his diplomatic master stroke. The two countries also signed a supplementary protocol of mutual respect for the territorial integrity and inviolability of the Mongolian People's Republic and Manchukuo.

Upon his return to Tokyo, Foreign Minister Matsuoka turned his attention toward a *détente* in Japanese-United States relations. In fact, before his departure to Europe, Matsuoka had sent a new Japanese ambassador, Admiral Nomura Kichisaburo, to Washington with the assurance that the latter would receive full support in negotiations for a *rapprochement* with the United States. At this juncture, Japan's United States policy was based upon the following assumptions and objectives: (1) despite the Lend-Lease Act, arms production in the United States could not be substantially increased before June 1941, and that the United States would not be in a position to render Great Britain any effective assistance before the end of that year, by which time Britain would have been defeated by Germany; (2) after Britain's collapse the United States would not continue the struggle but would withdraw behind its isolationism, giving its attention to its own domestic affairs and interests; (3) since Chiang Kai-shek was relying heavily upon American aid, President Roosevelt was in the position to use his influence in pressuring Chiang to bring the Sino-Japanese War to a satisfactory conclusion; (4) Japan did not expect that Germany would declare war on the United States, but if that action should come to pass, Japan would decide independently her course of action; and (5) Japan would try to persuade the United States to lift its partial embargo, and in return Japan would promise to use only peaceful means to implement her *Nanshin* policy.

The initial conversations between Ambassador Nomura and Secretary of State Hull began on March 8, 1941. The secretary deplored military conquests in various parts of the world, which had impeded his government's efforts to liberalize international commercial relations. The ambassador expressed the desire of his government to reach a "just and honorable" settlement with China and to reestablish friendly relations with the United States. But Ambassador Nomura could offer no concrete suggestions for dealing with the China issue, nor could he clarify his government's attitude toward the Axis alliance, to which Hull had called attention. A month later, on April 9, Secretary Hull received from unofficial sources a document containing a draft of a proposal for a general settlement in the Far East.[10] On April 14, Secretary Hull requested the Japanese ambassador to clarify his position on the April 9 document and other reports that certain Japanese had been formulating proposals for improving U.S.-Japanese relations and that the ambassador had been participating in such activities. The ambassador promptly acknowledged his awareness of the document and his role in the formulation of proposals. He then expressed his readiness to present it as a basis for negotiations.

Secretary Hull, for his part, set forth on April 16 four fundamental principles which Japan was asked to accept before any final settlement could be reached. These principles were: (1) respect for the territorial integrity and the sovereignty of each and all nations; (2) support of the principle of noninterference in the internal affairs of other countries; (3) support of the principle of equality, including equality of commercial opportunity; and (4) nondisturbance of the status quo in the Pacific except as the status quo may be altered by peaceful means.[11]

It should be noted that these principles were in essence the restatement and reiteration of the same principles that had been incorporated and repeated in the Hay Open Door note, in the Bryan note, in the Nine-Power Treaty, and in the Stimson Doctrine. In remarkable continuity, Secretary Hull was carrying, consciously or unconsciously, the relaying baton of United States Asian policy principles of his eminent predecessors. The continuity meant the status quo and *vice versa*. The status quo policy of the United States was looked upon by Japan as unrealistic, archaic, outmoded, and outrageous because the realities and situations of the Far East had changed drastically from the days of Stimson, Hughes, Bryan, and Hay.

In response to Hull's four principles, on May 12, 1941, Japan presented its own basic position paper. It reaffirmed Japan's determination to adhere to the Axis Alliance, for the Tripartite

Pact was defensive in nature with a view to deterring a third power or powers from entering the European or Asian hostilities then in progress. The Japanese proposal also included: (1) the use of the United States influence upon the Chiang Kai-shek regime to negotiate with Japan a settlement of "the China Affair" on the basis of the "Konoye principles";[12] (2) resumption of normal trade relations between Japan and the United States and mutual supply of commodities in their respective needs; (3) United States cooperation in Japan's production and procurement of such natural resources as oil, rubber, tin, and nickel; and (4) United States acknowledgment and declaration that Japan's *Nanshin* policy was to be of a peaceful nature.

Through the subsequent negotiations between the United States and Japan, a number of points of conflict became crystallized. First, Japan indicated that her troop withdrawal from China would not include her troops which, unspecified in number and undetermined in location, would be retained in China for "cooperative defense against Communism," whereas the United States maintained that the continued presence of Japanese troops in China would jeopardize Sino-Japanese friendship. Second, in view of Japanese relations to the Axis powers, her professed "peaceful intention toward the United States" was no assurance as to Japan's position vis-a-vis the United States should the latter become involved in war with Germany. Third, Japan expressed her desire to enter into a settlement for peace and nondiscriminatory commercial relations in the Pacific area, but, in the light of the statements made by high officials in Tokyo, the United States had to conclude that Japan was seeking a way to extricate herself from the "China Affair" while otherwise employing methods and practices contrary to the said principles.

The German invasion of the Soviet Union on June 22, 1941, made the American-Japanese negotiations further complicated, largely because it had unmistakably changed the balance of power in Europe in favor of the anti-Nazi forces and partly because it had immediately created a crisis within the Konoye cabinet. Japan had neither been consulted in advance nor given prior notice by her Nazi colleague. Foreign Minister Matsuoka, the prime architect of the Japanese-Soviet Neutrality Pact and the chief advocate of the Axis Alliance simultaneously, found himself on the horns of a dilemma. He urged, however, that Japan should enter the war on the Nazi side, disregarding the ten-week-old nonaggression pact with the Soviets. Many of his cabinet colleagues and top military circles did not support his position. There were divergent views and considerable confusion among governmental leaders. With a view to deciding on the basic policy, on July 2 they held a top-level conference in the presence of the emperor himself. They reaffirmed the *Hokushu-Nanshin* policy even at the risk of war with the United States and Great Britain. They were determined to break through by force what they later called the ABCD Line— American-British-Chinese-Dutch encirclement of Japan. They further decided that, on the point of the Nazi's final victory, Japan would intervene in the European war in order to enhance her position in East Asia at the expense of Soviet Russia. In the meantime, they agreed that the Japanese-Soviet Neutrality Pact would be observed. Thus, on that same day, Matsuoka made an oral statement to the Soviet ambassador in Tokyo; the foreign minister said that "Japan finds herself in the most awkward position" in view of the German-Soviet hostilities, that Japan wished the conflict "be confined to regions not immediately adjacent to the Far East where she possesses vital interests," and that Japan did not feel compelled to modify her policy toward the Soviet Union.[13]

Tokyo-Washington Divergencies

On July 18, in an effort to implement successfully the new policy, Prime Minister Konoye carried out a cabinet reshuffle in which a number of dissident members, including Foreign Minister Matsuoka, were replaced. The ministers of the army (General Tojo) and the navy were not affected. Admiral Toyoda was appointed as the new foreign minister. The Konoye government was now ready to take action. After having exerted strong pressure on France and the Vichy government, Japan was prepared to send her troops into French Indochina to occupy airfields in the south and to use Saigon harbor and Cam Ranh Bay for their fleet. The United States was fully aware of this move in advance.[14] In fact, on July 20, 1941, the day before Japanese troops commenced landing, Ambassador Nomura informed Rear Admiral Turner, director of the War Plans Division of the Navy Department, that "within the next few days Japan expects to occupy French Indochina."[15] From the Japanese military occupation of Indochina, the United States drew two conclusions: (1) the Japanese government intended to pursue a policy of force and of conquest; and (2) Japan was now poised to fan out and seize entire regions of Southeast Asia, including Thailand.

Before taking calculated countermeasures against Japan, in a personal conversation with Ambassador Nomura on July 24 President Roosevelt suggested that Indochina should be made a neutralized country in the same way as Switzerland so that none of the powers concerned could undertake any military act of aggression against it. No further exploration followed along the line of this suggestion. What followed was President Roosevelt's executive order freezing Japanese assets in the United States. It was designed to place under governmental control all financial and commercial transactions in which Japanese interests were involved, and its effect was to bring about the virtual cessation of trade between the United States and Japan. Within a few days Great Britain and the Netherlands took similar action. Thus, Japan felt the increasing pain of economic strangulation applied by the Western powers.

Moreover, a number of additional countermeasures were taken by the United States. Military commanders on Pacific outposts, including those at Hawaii, were ordered to take "appropriate precautionary measures"; General Douglas MacArthur was recalled to active duty to command a new Far Eastern force; a military mission under General Magruder was sent to assist the Chiang Kai-shek army; and all Japanese ships were barred from using the Panama Canal. Furthermore, during August 9–12, 1941, President Roosevelt and Prime Minister Winston Churchill of Great Britain held a two-man summit conference on board the *Prince of Wales* in the Atlantic off Argentia, Newfoundland. They drew up the Atlantic Charter and warned Japan that any new moves of aggression would face joint Anglo-American resistance. In the light of these deteriorating developments, Prime Minister Konoye had entertained the idea that "the responsible heads of the two Governments" should meet with a view to breaking the diplomatic impasse. This suggestion had been submitted to the secretary of state. On August 17, Ambassador Nomura again personally conveyed this idea to President Roosevelt: "Prince Konoye . . . would be disposed to meet the President midway, geographically speaking, between our two countries and sit down together and talk the matter out in a peaceful spirit."[16] The president's reply was that "it would be helpful if the Japanese Government would furnish a clearer statement than had as yet been given of its present attitude and plans." If Japan continued her aggression and conquest by force of arms, "we could not," the president told the ambassador, "think of reopening the conversations."[17] In a separate oral statement to the ambassador on the same day, the president declared:

> This Government now finds it necessary to say to the Government of Japan that if the Japanese Government takes any further steps in pursuance of a policy or program of military domination by force or threat of force of neighboring countries, the Government of the United States will be compelled to take immediately any and all steps which it may deem necessary toward safeguarding the legitimate rights and interests of the United States and American nationals and toward insuring the safety and security of the United States.[18]

Premier Konoye continued to press for a summit conference. In response to Roosevelt's demand that Japan should "furnish a clearer statement" on her "attitude and plans," Konoye specified that: (1) His government was prepared to withdraw its troops from Indochina "as soon as the China Incident is settled or a just peace is established in East Asia"; (2) Japan would not take any military action against the Soviet Union so long as the latter remained faithful to the Japanese-Soviet Neutrality Pact; and (3) Japan had no intention of launching an unprovoked attack on any neighboring nation. Furthermore, the prime minister told the American ambassador in Tokyo that Japan would fully and definitely subscribe to the four principles which Secretary Hull had previously set forth as a basis for American-Japanese *rapprochement*.

These qualifications notwithstanding, the leaders of the United

States could not overlook Konoye's close association with the aggressive policies of the military in the past, nor were they convinced of Konoye's ability to influence the military in the direction of policies of peace. Konoye had headed the Japanese government in 1937 when Japan launched the full-scale, undeclared war on China; he had been the author of "the Konoye basic principles" to which his government would adhere in any peace settlement with China; a year earlier under his premiership the Axis Tripartite Alliance Pact had been concluded; and in November 1940, his government had instituted the puppet Wang Ching-wei regime in the Japanese-occupied areas of China and concluded a treaty with it, acquiring the right to station armed forces for a required duration in specified areas of Chinese territory. In light of this record, President Roosevelt and Secretary Hull were unable to disperse the doubt in their minds as to Konoye's sincerity and earnestness in agreeing to a genuine peace settlement, which would have negated his previous achievements.

Meanwhile, in Tokyo, another Imperial conference was held on September 6. At this conference, an Imperial National Policy Outline was drafted: (1) war preparations "for national self-defense against the United States," should be completed by the end of October; (2) simultaneously, every possible diplomatic means should be employed toward the United States and Great Britain so as to make them comply with Japanese demands; and (3) should diplomatic negotiations produce no agreement by early October, Japan would go to war.[19] But the subsequent exchange of diplomatic notes throughout September between the United States and Japan failed to bring about any semblance of accord. By early October the United States became more aggravated by Japanese deeds than mitigated by her words. As the United States assessed the manifestations of Japanese policy and action, they ran exactly contrary to her professed peaceful intentions, as, for example, "the movement of Japanese armed forces into Southern Indochina, the augmentation and speeding up of Japanese military preparations at home, the continuing bombing by Japanese armed forces of Chinese civilian populations, the constant agitation in the inspired Japanese press in support of extremist policies, the unconciliatory and bellicose public utterances of Japanese leaders, and the tactics of covert or overt threat which had become a constant feature of Japanese diplomatic procedure."[20]

The stiffened position of the United States spurred the belligerency of the army faction headed by General Tojo, minister of the army, in the Konoye cabinet. Since the navy was reluctant to go to war with the United States, Premier Konoye was unable to maintain unity within his cabinet, and he resigned on October 18. Expectedly, General Tojo Hideki became prime minister. He nearly consolidated his power by heading simultaneously such important cabinet ministries as interior, army, education, and munitions. Tojo was determined to settle the differences with the United States, either by diplomacy or by force, by the end of the year. On November 5, at another Imperial conference, the Tojo cabinet reaffirmed the previous decision to go to war with the United States and Great Britain if the negotiations in Washington should produce no result by November 25. The Imperial conference further decided that Japan would invite the European Axis partners to join in a war against the United States but would decline if invited to join in the war against the Soviet Union.

On November 7, Secretary of State Hull fully informed the cabinet of recent developments and emphasized that a crisis was imminent in the Pacific area. Thanks to operation "Magic," wherein the United States had broken the Japanese cryptograph, Secretary Hull was in the position to know in advance Japanese true intent and what the envoys from Tokyo would say in their conversations with United States officials. Beginning November 17, Ambassador Nomura was assisted in his negotiations with the United States by a Japanese special envoy, Ambassador Kurusu Saburo, who had arrived in Washington two days earlier.

The Lost Peace

Japan's Search for "Peace with Honor"

By this time the American-Japanese peace negotiations centered primarily on three points: (1) withdrawal of Japanese troops from China, (2) the adoption of a liberal commercial policy, and (3) the question of the Axis Alliance Pact. As to the first point, the

United States demanded total and complete withdrawal of Japanese troops from China, maintaining that "the present situation was one of Japan's own making and it was up to the Japanese government to find some way of getting itself out of the difficulty in which it had placed itself." Japan, on its part, insisted upon stationing residual forces in China; Ambassador Kurusu even called attention to the fact that Japan had the right to station troops in Peking and Tientsin under the Boxer protocol. As to the second point, the United States advocated the principle of unconditional most-favored-nation treatment in general and urged the restoration to China of complete economic, financial, and monetary control in particular. Japan, on the other hand, refused to relinquish preferential or monopolistic commercial or other economic rights in China or in the "Great East Asia Co-Prosperity Sphere."

The Japanese envoy stated that the United States should relax the freezing regulations and lift the embargoes which "had caused impatience in Japan and a feeling that Japan had to fight while it still could." As to the third point, the United States would not be convinced of Japan's clear intention to follow a peaceful course in the event that the United States became involved militarily against Germany. A Japanese assurance of her intent to break off ties with the pact would be an essential prerequisite for a United States-Japanese agreement. Evading a definitive declaration of position on this question, Japan simply repeated that she had the freedom of decision and would make her own interpretation of her obligations should the United States go to war with Germany.

Having exhausted all efforts to arrive at an agreement with the United States, on November 20 the Japanese envoys presented to Secretary Hull a *modus vivendi* referred to in "Magic" as Plan (or Proposal) B—the last possible concessions Japan could offer to the United States. This Plan B contained the following five points:

1. Both the Governments of Japan and the United States undertake not to make any armed advancement into any of the regions in the Southeastern Asia and the Southern Pacific areas except the part of French Indochina where the Japanese troops were stationed at present.

2. The Japanese Government will undertake to withdraw its troops now stationed in French Indochina upon either the restoration of peace between Japan and China or the establishment of an equitable peace in the Pacific area.

In the meantime, the Government of Japan declares that it is prepared to remove its troops now stationed in the southern part of French Indochina to the northern part of the said territory upon the conclusion of the present arrangement which shall later be embodied in the final agreement.

3. The Governments of Japan and the United States shall cooperate with a view to securing the acquisition of those goods and commodities which the two countries need in the Netherlands East Indies.

4. The Governments of Japan and the United States mutually undertake to restore their commercial relations to those prevailing prior to the freezing of assets.

The Government of the United States shall supply Japan a required quantity of oil.

5. The Government of the United States will undertake to refrain from such measures and actions as will be prejudicial to the endeavors for the restoration of general peace between Japan and China.[21]

Secretary Hull thought that this proposal was "of so preposterous a character that no responsible American official could ever have dreamed of accepting."[22] He then drew up a six-point *modus vivendi* of his own, the gist of which was: (1) Both the United States and Japan would pledge to pursue their national policies through peaceful means and not to take any military advancement across any international border in the Pacific area; (2) Japan would undertake to withdraw its troops from southern Indochina and to limit its troop level in northern Indochina to twenty-five thousand; (3) The United States would undertake to remove the freezing restrictions, placing exports from each country under the respective export control measures; (4) The United States would consult with the governments of Great Britain and the Netherlands with a view to having them take similar measures; (5) The United States "would not look with disfavor" upon any Sino-Japanese negotiations for peaceful settlement of their disputes; and (6) This *modus vivendi* would be in effect for a three-month period.[23]

Secretary Hull first showed this draft to General Gerow of the War Plans Division (WPD) of the army and Admiral Stark, the chief of naval operations. They found it satisfactory from a military standpoint, for it would permit them to complete defense preparations in the Philippines. Hull next consulted with the representatives of China, Great Britain, and the Netherlands on the Japanese Plan B and his own *modus vivendi,* requesting each to submit an official response of his respective government. In a few days these governments made their positions known. China was violently opposed to the *modus vivendi*; Great Britain was cautiously reluctant to endorse it; only the Netherlands was reasonably disposed to support it. In the end, in the light of the combination of factors against Hull's *modus vivendi*—the Chinese opposition, the British reluctance, accusations of appeasement at home, Japanese troop movements suggesting that Japan was not negotiating in good faith—on November 26 Secretary Hull decided, with the approval of President Roosevelt, to abandon the *modus vivendi* and to present in its place the Ten-Point Note to the Japanese ambassadors.

The United States' Ten-Point Note, which has since been frequently characterized as America's ultimatum to Japan, contained the following propositions: (1) the conclusion of a multilateral nonaggression pact among the United States, Japan, Britain, China, the Netherlands, the Soviet Union, and Thailand; (2) pledge by each of the six powers mentioned above (except the Soviet Union) to respect the territorial integrity of French Indochina and not to seek or accept preferential treatment in its trade or economic relations therewith; (3) total and complete withdrawal of Japanese armed and police forces from both China and Indochina; (4) recognition of the Chiang Kai-shek regime as the sole, legal government of China; (5) renunciation of all extraterritorial rights in China; (6) negotiations for a new United States-Japanese trade agreement based on reciprocal most-favored-nation treatment; (7) mutual removal of the freezing restrictions; (8) a plan for the stabilization of the dollar-yen rate; (9) mutual understanding that no treaty concluded with any third power or powers would be so interpreted as to conflict with the fundamental purpose of this agreement; and (10) mutual endeavor to use their influence to cause other governments to subscribe to this agreement.

Couched in this proposal were the fundamental United States demands that Japan must withdraw all her armed forces—army, navy, and air forces—from both China and Indochina, dismantle "Manchukuo" and restore Manchuria to China, disband the Wang Ching-wei government in Nanking, discard the notion of the "Great East Asia Co-Prosperity Sphere," disengage from the Tripartite Pact, and declare her genuinely peaceful intentions in the Pacific area, substantiating them by deeds. The United States attempted in effect to restore the *status quo* ante 1931, and, in doing so, had closed the last avenue for the negotiations. Japan, it was argued, was compelled to take decisively to the war path.[24] Through "Magic" the United States had known that Japan had set a deadline, first November 25, later November 29, by which time some kind of agreement had to be reached; otherwise "things are automatically going to happen," so read the intercepted message.

Things indeed moved along, as though predestined, toward the fateful moment of collision. On November 25, at a meeting of the War Council which included General Marshall and Admiral Stark, Secretary of State Hull pointed out the critical nature of United States-Japan relations. He asserted "that there was practically no possibility of an agreement being achieved with Japan; that in his opinion the Japanese were likely to break out at any time with new acts of conquest by force; and that the question of safeguarding our national security was in the hands of the Army and Navy."[25] He emphatically added that any plan for our military defense should include an assumption that the Japanese might make the element of surprise a central point in their strategy and also might attack at various points simultaneously with a view to demoralizing efforts of defense and of coordination for purposes thereof. Secretary of War Stimson described the same meeting in his diary: The president "brought up entirely the relations with the Japanese" and that "we were likely to be attacked perhaps (as soon as) next Monday, for the Japanese are notorious for making an attack without warning." The Stimson diary continued: "The question was how we should maneuver them into the position of firing the first shot without allowing too much danger to ourselves. It was a difficult proposition."[26] On November 28, the War Council agreed that the president had to inform Congress that if the Japanese invaded Singapore or the Dutch East Indies, the security of the United States would be in jeopardy and, therefore, the United States would resist with force Japan's further advance into Southeast Asia.

Meanwhile, a Japanese Imperial Navy task force of six aircraft carriers had been ordered to sail from the Kuriles to attack Pearl Harbor unless recalled. Japanese submarines were on the way to rendezvous at Pearl Harbor. At the same time, a large Japanese convoy was sighted on the South China Sea heading toward Indochina, indicating Japan's military thrust into Southeast Asia—the Dutch East Indies, British Malaya, Thailand, the Philippines, any or all of these. On December 1, an Imperial conference ratified the decision for war.

A Day of Infamy

At this late stage there was not the slightest chance to avert the impending catastrophe. President Roosevelt, however, made one final gesture—if not for permanent peace, at least for a temporary pause. On December 6, he sent a personal message to the emperor of Japan in which he pointed out that the deterioration of American-Japanese relations contained "tragic possibilities." He urged that the two countries "should agree to eliminate any form of military threat," because he and the emperor had "a sacred duty to restore traditional amity and prevent further death and destruction in the world."[27] This presidential telegram reached Ambassador Grew in Tokyo too late, almost at the moment of the commencement of the attack on Pearl Harbor. In fact, this message and the Japanese ultimatum crossed each other.

The Japanese ambassadors Nomura and Kurusu were scheduled to meet Secretary Hull at 1:00 P.M., December 7. Owing to the delay in decoding the message from their home government, they were unable to keep the appointment. Having asked for, and been granted, a postponement, they arrived at the State Department at 2:05 P.M. and were received by the secretary at 2:20. They delivered to the secretary the memorandum of their government, the contents of which Secretary Hull had already known through "Magic." The Japanese envoys did not know that the Pearl Harbor attack had started exactly one hour earlier.[28] The secretary glanced at the document, turned to the ambassador, and said:

> I must say that in all my conversations with you during the last nine months I have never uttered one word of untruth. This is borne out absolutely by the record. In all my fifty years of public service I have never seen a document that was more crowded with infamous falsehoods and distortions— infamous falsehoods and distortions on a scale so huge that I never imagined until today that any Government on this planet was capable of uttering them.[29]

The Japanese ambassador left Secretary Hull's office in silence.

What statements were in the Japanese memorandum which had infuriated the secretary so much? The first half of the document was devoted to a brief review of the Japanese-American negotiations during the preceding nine months. Then it emphasized the five special "points" to which Japan "desires to call the attention of the American Government":

1. The American Government advocates in the name of world peace those principles favorable to it and urge upon the Japanese Government the acceptance thereof.... Of the various principles put forward by the American Government as a basis of the Japanese-American Agreement, there are some which the Japanese Government is ready to accept in principle, but in view of the world's actual conditions, it seems only a utopian ideal on the part of the American Government to attempt to force their immediate adoption. ...

2. The American Government, obsessed with its own views and opinions, may be said to be scheming for the extension of the war. While it seeks, on the one hand, to secure its rear by stabilizing the Pacific area, it is engaged, on the other

hand, in aiding Great Britain and preparing to attack, in the name of self-defense, Germany and Italy, two Powers that are striving to establish a new order in Europe. . . .

3. Whereas the American Government, under the principles it rigidly upholds, objects to settle international issues through military pressure, it is exercising in conjunction with Great Britain and other nations pressure by economic power. Recourse to such pressure as a means of dealing with international relations should be condemned as it is at times more inhumane than military pressure.

4. It is impossible not to reach the conclusion that the American Government desires to maintain and strengthen . . . its dominant position it has hitherto occupied not only in China but in other areas of East Asia. It is a fact of history that the countries of East Asia for the past hundred years or more have been compelled to observe the *status quo* under the Anglo-American policy of imperialistic exploitation and to sacrifice themselves to the prosperity of the two nations. The Japanese Government cannot tolerate the perpetuation of such a situation since it directly runs counter to Japan's fundamental policy to enable all nations to enjoy each its proper place in the world. . . .

5. All the items demanded of Japan by the American Government regarding China such as wholesale evacuation of troops or unconditional application of the principle of non-discrimination in international commerce ignored the actual conditions of China, and are calculated to destroy Japan's position as the stabilizing factor of East Asia. The attitude of the American Government in demanding Japan not to support militarily, politically or economically any regime other than the regime at Chung King, disregarding thereby the existence of the Nanking Government [the Wang Ching-wei regime], shatters the very basis of the present negotiation. . . .[30]

The Pearl Harbor attack was followed by the Japanese declaration of war in the form of the Imperial rescript which stated in part: "Eager for the realization of their inordinate ambition to dominate the Orient, both America and Britain, giving support to the Chung King regime, have aggravated the disturbance in East Asia. . . . For existence and self-defense Our Empire has no other recourse but to appeal to arms." In Washington, on the other hand, Secretary Hull issued a press release announcing: "Japan has made a treacherous and utterly unprovoked attack upon the United States," despite his government's efforts to stand for "all the principles that underlie fair-dealing, peace, law and order, and justice between nations." The following day, Congress declared war on Japan upon the request of President Roosevelt whose message to Congress had described the day of attack, December 7, 1941, as "a day which will live in infamy." Great Britain, the Netherlands, and China likewise formally declared war on Japan. Three days later the other two Tripartite Pact partners—Germany and Italy—declared war on the United States.

Pearl Harbor Controversies

The Pearl Harbor attack was a stunning blow. The attackers either sank or crippled seven battleships, wiped out virtually every plane on the island of Oahu, and inflicted some three thousand casualties. In view of the enormity of the tragedy, historians, political scientists, and politicians alike have attempted to probe facts and truths and locate the responsibilities for the "infamy." Such attempts have, in turn, generated endless controversies in their conclusions or findings, ranging from the theory of *total innocence* on the part of the American government to the *conspiracy theory* on the part of the Roosevelt administration.

According to the *total innocence* theme, which was expounded primarily in various official announcements by government leaders, it was Japan that had launched a "treacherous," "utterly unprovoked," and "dastardly" attack upon Pearl Harbor. While the United States was conducting peace negotiations in good faith, Japan "deliberately sought to deceive the United States by false statements and expressions of hope for continued peace." Japanese desire for peace was "infamously false and fraudulent." The Japanese had been scheming all along for the "sneak attack" upon the United States, but their memorandum "contained no threat or hint of war or armed attack." The United States, caught by a "total surprise at Pearl Harbor, was the innocent victim of Japanese treachery and betrayal."

At the other extreme lies the *conspiracy theory,* which maintains that President Roosevelt deliberately lured the Japanese into the Pearl Harbor trap so that the United States could enter the European war through the "back door."[31] The exponents of this theory argue that President Roosevelt and his advisors took advantage of "Magic" and skillfully maneuvered to create a diplomatic impasse from which there was no escape for Japan but to resort to force. For instance, the top officials in Washington knew that "things are automatically going to happen" after the negotiation deadline date in late November. Secretary Hull delivered his Ten-Point Note to the Japanese ambassador, anticipating that it would be rejected; then he told Secretary of War Stimson: "I have washed my hands of it, and it [the eventuality] is now in the hands of you and Knox [Secretary of the Navy], the Army and Navy." Secretary Stimson's diary revealed his firm belief in the inevitability of war: "The question was how we should maneuver them [the Japanese] into the position of firing the first shot." In 1946, Commander Lester Schultz, a naval aide at the White House who had delivered those "Magic" intercepts to the president the day before Pearl Harbor, testified before the Joint Congressional Committee as to Roosevelt's reaction. Commander Schultz stated:

The President read the papers . . . Then he handed them to Mr. [Harry] Hopkins . . . Mr. Hopkins then read the papers and handed them back to the President. The President then turned toward Mr. Hopkins and said in substance . . . "This means war." Mr. Hopkins agreed. . . . Mr. Hopkins . . . expressed a view that since war was undoubtedly going to come at the convenience of the Japanese, it was too bad that we could not strike the first blow and prevent any sort of surprise. The President nodded and then said in effect, "No, we can't do that. We are a democracy and a peaceful people." Then he raised his voice, and this much I remember definitely. He said, "But we have a good record."[32]

Neither the *total innocence theory* nor the *conspiracy theory* explains adequately or accurately the complex event of Pearl Harbor, for each of these extreme views, lacking in objectivity, contains considerable bias and prejudice. The truth of the matter can obviously be found somewhere between these two extremities. That truth, however, would have to reflect the following known facts:

1. In November, when negotiations were reaching the critical stage, Ambassador Grew warned Washington that Japanese military actions might come "with dangerous and dramatic suddenness."

2. Secretary Hull suspected that the Japanese "might make the element of surprise a central point in their strategy, . . . [they] might attack at various points simultaneously."

3. The Japanese Imperial Navy task force under the command of Admiral Nagumo had been assembled in absolute secrecy near Etorofu Island in the Kuriles. On November 25, it had set out for Pearl Harbor to launch the attack, unless recalled, at dawn December 7. During its voyage through the North Pacific it had never been detected. "Magic" never deciphered Tokyo's last order to Admiral Nagumo.

4. On November 27, "war warnings" were dispatched to the Army and Navy commanders in Hawaii and in the Philippines but they were not specific or emphatic enough to perceive the imminent surprise attack.

5. Through "Magic," high officials in Washington were aware of impending Japanese hostile acts, but they were uncertain as to exactly when, where, or how the Japanese would commence such acts. They expected that the Japanese punch would fall on the Philippines, the Dutch East Indies, British Malaya, and Thailand, scarcely on Pearl Harbor.

CHAPTER SEVEN

Road to *The Missouri*

The Pacific Front

Japan's Blitzkrieg

When Japan struck Pearl Harbor, she enjoyed all the initial military advantages—careful planning, meticulous execution, high morale, and first strike with the element of surprise. Synchronized with Pearl Harbor, coordinated Japanese attacks were launched from Formosa, Indonesia, the Caroline Islands, and later from Thailand. The immediate targets were Hong Kong, Malaya, Burma, the Philippines, and subsequently the Dutch East Indies (Indonesia). In a massive *blitzkrieg,* Japan tore the ABCD Line asunder.

Britain suffered no less humiliation than the United States. Only two days after Pearl Harbor, the British Far Eastern Fleet was crippled when Japanese planes bombed and sank the "unsinkable" *Prince of Wales* and the *Repulse.* Within three weeks the British crown colony of Hong Kong, which she had acquired from China after the historic Opium War (1839–1842) was captured by the Japanese. Using Indochina and Thailand as staging areas, the Japanese Imperial Armies launched the Malayan campaign, entering the peninsula through the "impenetrable" jungles and moving southward toward Singapore, which fell on February 15, 1942.

Simultaneously with the Malayan operation, the Japanese invaded Burma from Thailand in an effort to cut the Burma Road. Thailand had been forced to sign an alliance treaty with Japan and on January 25, 1942, "dutifully" declared war against the United States and Great Britain. With the fall of all Burma by June 1942, the United States could supply Chiang Kai-shek only by air, over the "Hump" (the Himalayas).

The Japanese assault on the Philippines came only a few hours after Pearl Harbor. They landed on Luzon Island in late December and drove toward Manila, which, declared to be an open city, fell into the hands of the invaders on January 3, 1942. Meanwhile, after days of fierce Japanese bombing of the capital and in the face of the approaching defeat and disaster, Philippine President Quezon and Vice-President Osmena moved their government, together with American and Filipino defense forces under the command of General Douglas MacArthur, to the fortified island of Corregidor. Soon, upon the fall of Bataan and the inevitable Japanese attacks on Corregidor, they moved to Australia.

In the meantime, the United States, galvanized by Pearl Harbor but galled by its own unpreparedness, was helpless to blunt the surge of Japan. One of the important questions confronting the American leaders was to decide which of the two war theatres— the European or the Pacific—should be given a higher priority. Many Americans, including military commanders in the Pacific, considered Japan the main enemy and advocated the concentration of national effort on her defeat. Keenly tuned to the American mood, British Prime Minister Winston Churchill expressed his apprehension: "We are conscious of a serious danger that the United States might pursue the war against Japan in the Pacific and leave us to fight Germany and Italy in Europe, Africa, and the Middle East."[1]

In a series of Roosevelt-Churchill meetings, they decided that the war in Europe should be given priority, while executing a holding operation in the Pacific with the ultimate objective of defeating Japan in cooperation with the Chinese. This decision meant simply to defer aid to the Chinese, but did not intend entirely to neglect them.

In contrast to Japan's dazzling military conquests of various regions in Asia, the United States and Great Britain took the lead in building the diplomatic foundations for the unity of those nations resisting the Axis powers. On New Year's Day, 1942, at the White House, the representatives of the United States, Great Britain, the Soviet Union, China, and twenty-two other nations united in war against the Axis brought their common objectives into formal existence by signing the Declaration of the United Nations. Subscribing to the Atlantic Charter, the declaration bound each signatory "to employ its full resources, military or economic, against those members of the Tripartite Pact and its adherents" and "to cooperate with the governments signatory hereto and not to make a separate armistice or peace with the enemies." Other nations adhering to these principles could subsequently become signatories. The Declaration of the United Nations was a grand performance to form "the Grand Alliance." Furthermore, it laid the cornerstone for a new international organization for peace and security—the United Nations.

The military setback in Europe and in the Pacific compelled President Roosevelt and Prime Minister Churchill to define war objectives for their own peoples and for the world. They declared that both Hitler's Nazism in Germany and Tojo's militarism in Japan were "seeking to subjugate the world" by use of "savage and brutal forces." Against these policies of armed conquest, free men the world over should be committed "to defend life, liberty, independence, and religious freedom, and to preserve human rights and justice in their own lands as well as in other lands."

While the Allied powers were getting ready to translate their unity in principles and purposes into fighting strength, the Japanese continued to achieve military successes. After the conquest of the Dutch East Indies in March 1942, they pushed toward Australia. They reached as far south and southwest in the Pacific as parts of New Guinea and the Bismarck and Solomon Islands. This thrust was clearly designed to cut Australian supply lines from the United States. At this point two encouraging events developed, signaling the beginning of American prowess. First, the United States Navy executed a tactical offensive on the Japanese outposts in the Marshall and Gilbert Islands and was able for the first time to halt the Japanese advance. Second, on April 18, 1942, a small group of American bombers commanded by Colonel James Doolittle raided Tokyo. This raid, more a moral than a military victory, more psychological than strategic in nature, demolished the myth of Japanese invincibility.

The first major naval battle between Japan and the United States took place in the Coral Sea on May 7–8, 1942. Both sides suffered considerable losses in men and ships, but it "marked the high tide of Japanese conquest in the Southwest Pacific."[2] The more definite turning point of the war came within a month with the naval engagement near Midway, June 3–6, when the United States forces inflicted heavy losses on the Japanese navy and thwarted the Japanese plan to occupy Midway and possibly the Hawaiian Islands. Midway climaxed America's "first half year of war and marked the opening of a new phase of operations in the Pacific." These two battles "restored the balance of sea power in the Pacific to the United States and lessened a grave threat" to her Pacific possessions.[3]

The Battle of Midway had commenced with a Japanese diversionary attack on the Aleutian Islands which was designed to lure the United States fleet north. Knowing the Japanese tactical plan via "Magic," the American naval forces did not respond to this move. The Japanese, however, went on to occupy the islands of Attu and Kiska in an attempt to extend their defense perimeter into the northern Pacific. But their occupation of these islands did not pose any serious threat to the American defense. Only Japanese probing operations from the bases on the Solomons and New Guinea constantly harassed the supply lines between the United States and Australia. To secure these lines, the American forces began to assume the initiative in offensive operations in the central and southwest Pacific. After a series of fierce, costly battles, they captured Tulagi on August 7, 1942, and established beachheads on Guadalcanal, where a grisly war of attrition was to last for six months. At the same time, joint American-Australian forces fought bitterly against the Japanese at Port Moresby in New Guinea and succeeded in halting the Japanese advance. During the remainder of the year, land, air, and sea battles continued to rage with heavy losses on both sides. By the end of 1942, however, the

United States could claim to have gained air and naval supremacy in the southwest Pacific.

As the year 1943 rolled in, the Japanese were to face more misfortunes ahead. In February, unable to keep their supply lines open, they were forced to abandon Guadalcanal. On March 3–4, a convoy of sixteen ships was attacked by American planes in the Bismarck Sea and all but four ships were sunk. Then in April, Admiral Yamamoto was killed in what was described by a Japanese naval officer as "an ambush in the sky." The news of his death stunned the Japanese people and came as "an almost unbearable blow to the morale of all the military forces."

American Military and Diplomatic Strategies

In early May, the United States formulated a three-phase offensive strategy to defeat Japan. The first phase was to clear the Aleutian Islands of the Japanese. On May 11, American troops began landing on Attu, which they captured by the end of that month. The island of Kiska, known to be heavily fortified, was taken by the Americans in mid-August without a fight; the Japanese had evacuated before the American landing. The second phase of the offensive was placed under the command of General Douglas MacArthur. In June, his forces launched an offensive against the Japanese bases in eastern New Guinea. From there he was to advance through Luzon and Okinawa, following the "leapfrog" strategy—taking important islands and bypassing unimportant or too heavily fortified ones. The third phase was a naval offensive in and through the Central Pacific, commanded by Admiral Nimitz. In November, his armada launched an attack on the atolls of Makin and Tarawa in the Gilbert Islands. The four-day battle of Tarawa was one of the most ferocious of the war. By the end of 1943, United States forces were well on the offensive route to Tokyo.

America's successes in its comprehensive offensive strategy in 1943 were matched by those in its diplomatic grand strategy. The scope of the globe-girdling diplomacy covered a number of pivotal issues, ranging from Chinese extraterritoriality to Korean independence and from Soviet entry into the war to the unconditional surrender of Japan. Since Pearl Harbor, China had become an indispensable ally of the United States. The Chinese people, for years reeling under the tortuous war with Japan, had expected a speedier rescue by the United States with its unqualified and unlimited aid. But they were less than fully satisfied with the American strategy of giving first priority to the war in Europe, although they realized that the United States would, after the defeat of Germany, fight the Japanese in full cooperation with China. In fact, the United States' China policy at this point had two principal objectives: (1) to assist China as much as possible so as to ensure her cooperation in carrying on an effective war against Japan, and (2) to elevate China to the status of a great power with a strong democratic government so as to replace Japan as the dominant stabilizing force in a postwar East Asia friendly to the United States.

The substantiation of these objectives, especially the second, would require that the United States free China from the stigma of inferiority and inequality which had characterized American-Chinese relations for over a century. Even before Pearl Harbor, Japan had accused Chiang Kai-shek's China of being a lackey of Anglo-American imperialism which, hiding behind the protective screen of those two powers, shamelessly obstructed Japan's effort to establish the New Order in Asia. In October 1942, the United States agreed to negotiate a new treaty with China in order to promote mutual friendship and trust on the basis of sovereign equality, thereby renouncing the last remnants of the unequal treaties. A few months later, on January 11, 1943, the United States formally signed a treaty with China which (1) relinquished America's rights of extraterritoriality and other unilateral privileges held in China since the 1844 Cushing Treaty, (2) terminated rights accorded to the United States under the 1901 Boxer protocol, including the administration and control of the diplomatic quarter at Peking, and (3) restored to China the international settlements at Shanghai and Amoy and the jurisdiction thereof. Great Britain signed a similar treaty with China on the same day. Other Western treaty powers soon followed the Anglo-American lead. Furthermore, in October, President Roosevelt urged Congress to pass a law ending Chinese exclusion so as to "correct an historic mistake." Congress responded in December by enacting a law which made Chinese aliens in the United States eligible for citizenship and permitted 105 Chinese immigrants to enter yearly on a quota basis. However, the discriminatory provisions of the 1924 immigration act against other Orientals, including Japanese, still remained in force. It should be added that, after Pearl Harbor, about 110,000 Japanese-Americans living on the Pacific Coast were herded into "detention camps," though about two-thirds of them were American-born citizens.

China now assumed "among the powers of the earth the separate and *equal* station" in principle, if not in substance. Earlier in August, China had been invited as a great power to participate in the Quebec Conference to map the Allied global strategy. Roosevelt and Churchill dealt primarily with European strategy, but at this conference it was decided to defeat Japan by providing greater aid to China and to create a Southeast Asian Command under Lord Mountbatten separate from the Chinese theatre under Chiang Kai-shek. The president and the prime minister also took up the question of Soviet entry into the Pacific war. Stalin had hinted at this issue a year earlier, and Roosevelt and Churchill had discussed the very subject in January 1943 at their meeting in Casablanca.

As a sequel to the Quebec Conference, the foreign ministers of the United States, Great Britain, and the Soviet Union met in Moscow in October 1943, and issued, with China joining, a declaration on general security. The Moscow Declaration contained, among its many general and vague principles, three important specific pledges: (1) to prosecute the war until the "unconditional surrender" of their respective enemies, (2) to establish a general international organization for the maintenance of peace and security, and (3) to bring about a general agreement on arms regulation in the postwar period.[4] Since the Soviet Union was not then at war with Japan and the Soviet-Japanese Neutrality Pact was in force, the Moscow Conference did not take up specific military plans regarding Japan. Stalin, however, told Secretary Hull in secrecy that the Soviet Union would join the war against Japan after the defeat of Germany.

Military and political strategy respecting Japan was left to the subsequent meeting of the heads of government—Roosevelt, Churchill, and Chiang Kai-shek—at Cairo the following month (November 22–26, 1943). In a joint communiqué, the three leaders announced their agreement to the following four key points: (1) Japan would be stripped of all her mandate islands in the Pacific, (2) Manchuria, Formosa, and the Pescadores were to be restored to China, (3) Korea would become free and independent "in due course," and (4) they were resolved to continue their war efforts "to procure the unconditional surrender of Japan."[5]

Scarcely had the Cairo Conference been closed when Roosevelt and Churchill flew to Teheran, the capital of Iran, to confer with Stalin. At this conference (November 28–December 1, 1943), the Big Three made two important military decisions. First, in Europe, the Anglo-American cross-channel invasion into "Hitler's Fortress"[6] should be undertaken in May or June 1944, with a simultaneous Soviet offensive on the Eastern European front. Second, in Asia, Stalin repeated his intent to enter the war against Japan upon the final collapse of Germany. As to the specific conditions for Soviet entry into the war, Stalin did not elaborate at this time. He did so later at Yalta.

Tojo's Woes

In a striking contrast to the series of summit meetings and international conferences among the Allied leaders, the Axis Powers conducted the war independently—Germany in Europe and Japan in Asia. From the very beginning, neither took prior consultation with the other before acting. As Germany had not given Japan any formal or informal indication of her attack on either Poland or on the Soviet Union, so Japan gave no hint of the Pearl Harbor plan to either of her European partners. Throughout the war, there was never any meeting of the heads of state: Tojo, Hitler, and Mussolini never held a conference to coordinate their tactics and strategy or to cooperate in their policies and objectives. Tojo considered war the highest form of diplomacy. He believed that the quickest way to solve complex political problems lay in the battlefield, not at the conference table. He saw little value in formal diplomacy and consequently reduced the Ministry of Foreign Affairs to a mere adjunct of the Imperial Army. When his foreign minister, Tani, resigned in frustration, Tojo assumed the post himself. He soon discovered inadequacies and inefficiencies for the conduct of foreign affairs in his manner and attitude. He then appointed Shigemitsu Mamoru foreign minister. An experienced career diplomat who had served as ambassador to Nanking, Moscow, and London, Shigemitsu tried to convince the Asian people that the New Order sought to establish a permanent peace and security in Asia on the basis of equality for all nations. Believing that the "China Affair" could be brought to an honorable and fair end, he strove for its settlement, but to no avail.

The major theme of the Tojo-Shigemitsu diplomacy was *Asian Unity*—Asia for Asians. As a means to achieve this goal and as an answer to the Declaration of the United Nations, in November 1943 they convened a Great East Asian Conference in Tokyo. Intended to be an august summit meeting of the heads of "new governments," the conference was attended by Wang Ching-wei of China, Jose Laurel of the Philippines, Ba Maw of Burma, Chandra Bose of India, and the representatives from Thailand and Manchukuo. All of them had accepted, by choice or by force, Japanese leadership in the "brave new world" of the Great East Asia Co-Prosperity Sphere. The conference produced the "Declaration of the Principles" which included: mutual respect of one another's sovereignty and independence, mutual cooperation and assistance toward friendship and common prosperity, cultural exchange and the promotion of reciprocal economic benefits, and the elimination of discriminatory practices on the basis of race and nationality.

As the war moved into the third year, the Japanese military situation became ever grimmer. On February 1, 1944, United States marines landed on Kwajalein in the Marshall Islands, capturing it after three days of fighting. Eniwetok also fell. The heavily fortified island of Truk in the Carolines, though not taken by Americans, was rendered virtually useless by massive air and naval attacks which blasted Japanese military equipment and facilities out of existence. In March, MacArthur occupied the Admiralty Islands and, in April, he attacked Hollandia in Dutch New Guinea. In May, American troops landed on the tiny but strategically important island of Biak near western New Guinea.

Early in June, the United States Fifth Fleet was steaming toward the Mariana Islands—Saipan, Tinian, and Guam. From June 15, the day the first American marines went ashore on Saipan, to August 10, the day the last marines captured Guam, bitter and heartbreaking battles in air, on land, and sea were fought with ruthless ferocity and intensity. The Japanese suffered the terrible human toll of fifty thousand men killed,[7] against America's four thousand. The fall of Saipan in early July 1944 into the hands of Americans brought about two immediate consequences.

First, it touched off a political crisis in Tokyo. Anti-Tojo feelings ran high among naval officers who were angered by what they considered the mismanagement of war production, misallocation of arms supplies, and misplacement of strategic priority. Some of the powerful political leaders such as Konoye, Okada, and Hiranuma were also dismayed by Tojo's policies and by the interservice rivalry between the army and the navy. At this point Tojo asked Kishi Nobusuke,[8] minister of commerce and industry, to resign so as to make room for Admiral Yonai and General Abe, both of whom Tojo desired to add to his cabinet. Kishi challenged Tojo by refusing to resign and advocated, instead, the resignation of the entire cabinet. On July 18, 1944, faced with dissension within his own cabinet, Tojo was forced to resign, succeeded by General Koiso Kuniaki. The Koiso administration was to last for nine months, during which time Japan suffered military defeats in the Philippines, Iwo-Jima, and Okinawa.

Second, the American capture of Saipan brought the Japanese mainland within striking distance of United States strategic bombers (B-29s). On November 24, 1944, the first group of these flying superfortresses left Saipan for Tokyo on a bombing mission. Thence, American air raids systematically demolished military installations, industries, communication centers, harbors, and marshalling yards. In addition, American submarine operations were so complete and effective that Japan was virtually unable to transport needed arms supplies to its troops overseas or to bring in required raw material from abroad.

In the China-Burma-India (CBI) theatre far to the west, the Allies won a battle of logistics. At the early stage of the war, the Japanese had gained complete control of this area. But the long distance supply lines from the homeland, unbearable tropical heat and disease, rugged terrain, lack of medical supplies, shortage of rations, and devastating monsoons all worked against them. In the winter of 1943–1944, the Anglo-American airborne invasions had been launched on northern Burma. Later, during the spring of 1944, while the British were waging fierce battles on the Manipur-Imphal front, American-Chinese forces under General Joseph Stilwell attacked Japanese troop positions in northern Burma and captured Myitkyina. At the same time Chinese troops advanced from Yunan and occupied Bhamo. Thus the Allies secured the overland supply routes into China, linking the Ledo Road (India-China supply line) with the Burma Road.

By the late summer of 1944, Japan's outer defense perimeter began to crumble as the Allied offensive accelerated with an added fury. In the Southwest Pacific, General MacArthur's forces were about to be joined by Nimitz's Central Pacific force. Their next objective was the invasion and liberation of the Philippines. The massive invasion of Leyte began at dawn, October 20. "At 10 A.M. the first ground forces were ferried to the shore and by sundown more than sixty thousand Allied soldiers were on the beaches with one hundred thousand tons of supplies."[9] It was just the beginning; bitter and costly battles were ahead. It was not until Christmas that the Americans took Leyte, paving the way for the realization of MacArthur's pledge—"I shall return." In January 1945, the United States Sixth Army landed at Lingayen Gulf and fought its way to Manila. On March 4, the Americans recaptured Manila and enabled MacArthur to proclaim: "I have returned."

The Historic Year, 1945

Implications of the Yalta Agreements

Meanwhile, the Allied leaders met once again, in February 1945, at Yalta to refresh their decisions at Teheran, to reaffirm their determination for the final victory and, above all, to reshape the destiny of the postwar world. The Yalta Conference, February 4–11, attended by Roosevelt, Churchill, and Stalin, produced the most important, and most controversial, wartime agreements. In addition to military matters, they dealt with four main topics: the Polish and Eastern European issues, the future of Germany, the

United Nations organization, and the Far East. Since the first three subjects are beyond the scope of this study, the last—the Far East—is discussed here.

The Far East agreement at Yalta, kept in top secrecy for a full year, proved so critical to the future of East Asia that it deserves to be quoted in its entirety.

The leaders of the three Great Powers—the Soviet Union, the United States of America, and Great Britain—have agreed that in two or three months after Germany has surrendered and the war in Europe has terminated, the Soviet Union shall enter into the war against Japan on the side of the Allies on condition that:

1. The status quo in Outer Mongolia (The Mongolian People's Republic) shall be preserved;
2. The former rights of Russia violated by the treacherous attack of Japan in 1904 shall be restored, viz.:
   (a) the southern part of Sakhalin, as well as all the islands adjacent to it, shall be returned to the Soviet Union,
   (b) the commercial port of Dairen shall be international, the preeminent interests of the Soviet Union in this port being safeguarded and the lease of Port Arthur as a naval base of the U.S.S.R. restored,
   (c) the Chinese Eastern Railroad and the South Manchurian Railroad which provides an outlet to Dairen shall be jointly operated by the establishment of a joint Soviet-Chinese Company, it being understood that the preeminent interests of the Soviet Union shall be safeguarded and that China shall retain full sovereignty in Manchuria:
3. The Kurile Islands shall be handed over to the Soviet Union.

It is understood that the agreement concerning Outer Mongolia and the ports and railroads referred to above will require concurrence of Generalissimo Chiang Kai-shek. The President will take measures in order to obtain this concurrence on advice from Marshal Stalin.

The Heads of the three Great Powers have agreed that

these claims of the Soviet Union shall be unquestionably fulfilled after Japan has been defeated.

For its part the Soviet Union expresses its readiness to
conclude with the Nationalist Government of China a pact
of friendship and alliance between the U.S.S.R. and China
in order to render assistance to China with its armed forces
for the purpose of liberating China from the Japanese yoke.[10]

A number of questions could be raised to clarify some of the
provisions in this agreement:

First, why was President Roosevelt so anxious to bring the
Soviet Union into the Pacific war? He was told by his military
advisors that it would take as long as eighteen months after Germany's surrender to defeat Japan, with perhaps a million casualties. Alarmed by the possible necessity of having to commit a large
number of American ground troops to an Asian land war, the
president and his military advisors desired the Soviet entry into the
war "at as early a date as possible."

Second, what was the status quo in Outer Mongolia at this
time? The Sino-Soviet Treaty of 1924 had recognized officially
China's sovereignty in Outer Mongolia, but the Soviet Union continued to deal separately with the government at Ulan Bator.
During the years of Japanese expansion and pressure in this region, especially in the 1930s, the Soviet Union and Outer Mongolia moved even closer together, culminating in the conclusion of
the mutual assistance arrangements of 1934 and 1936. After the
Marco Polo Bridge and the Nomonhan incidents, Soviet troop
introduction into Outer Mongolia was accelerated, and so was
Soviet influence there. In 1940, under Soviet auspices, the new
constitution of the "Mongolian People's Republic" was promulgated. Throughout the war the Soviets tightened their grip on
Outer Mongolia.[11]

Third, why had Chiang Kai-shek not been invited? Stalin me-
ticulously maintained the appearance, if not the intention, of strict
neutrality as bound by the Soviet-Japanese neutrality pact of 1941.
The presence of Chiang at Yalta might have had two adverse
effects. In the first place, it would have aroused Japanese suspicion
that Stalin was planning an attack on Japan in cooperation with

China. As, indeed, the Big Three actually planned such a move, Chiang's participation, they feared, would become the source of a leak to the Japanese of their plan. President Roosevelt said to Stalin and Churchill that anything told to the Chinese "was known to the whole world in twenty-four hours." In the second place, some of the political and territorial arrangements which the Big Three were bound to make might run into Chiang's strong opposition, even risking the danger of wrecking the conference. They thought that no consultation with Chiang Kai-shek on matters concerning China might be morally wrong but politically wise. Apart from these considerations, in view of the Big Three, China was not a full-fledged Great Power, although technically she had been elevated to one. Again President Roosevelt was reported to have said: "Three generations of education and training would be required before China would become a serious factor."[12]

Fourth, in the absence of Chiang Kai-shek, had those concessions in Manchuria made to Stalin not infringed upon China's territorial and administrative integrity and sovereignty? It could be argued that Chiang had done little to expel the Japanese from his country. He had lost control of Manchuria since 1931. Hence, the restoration of Russian rights in the territory which he did not possess could not constitute a concession. The entire territory of Manchuria could have been taken away from Chiang; but this the Big Three did not undertake. Since they agreed that "China shall retain full sovereignty in Manchuria," the concessions made to the Soviets were in reality in the form of a *servitude* which, within the framework of international law, was not a total impairment of national prestige. Such being the case, the "preeminent interests of the Soviet Union" at the port of Dairen should not, as Mr. Harriman[13] believed, "go beyond Soviet interests in the free *transit* of exports and imports to and from the Soviet Union." As to Port Arthur, President Roosevelt regarded its lease for a naval base, according to Ambassador Harriman, "as an arrangement similar to privileges which the United States has negotiated with other countries for the mutual security of two friendly nations." With respect to the Chinese Eastern Railway, the American leaders at Yalta seemed to have had in their minds only transit traffic without any general Soviet interest in Manchuria.

On the other hand, critics of the Yalta agreements charge that, by complying with Stalin's demands, President Roosevelt had violated his own pledge to Chiang at Cairo. Moreover, the president's action was tantamount to an undoing of the Portsmouth treaty of 1905, in the making of which another American president of the same name, Theodore Roosevelt, had played an important role. Ever since the turn of this century, the United States' China policy has evolved around the central theme of the "maintenance of territorial and administrative integrity" of that country, as exemplified by the Open Door, the Bryan note, the Nine-Power Treaty, and the Stimson Doctrine. In fact, the United States had to go to war with Japan largely on that principle. At Yalta, President Roosevelt substituted the Soviet Union for Japan in Manchuria, just as at Versailles President Wilson had substituted Japan for Germany in Shantung. In each case the United States decided to placate the strong-willed potential adversary at the expense of the weaker ally.

Fifth, and finally, why did the Big Three take up the question of Korea? The Cairo declaration had promised a Korean independence *in due course.* Implicit in this phrase was the understanding that Korea would not be given an immediate, outright independence after the surrender of Japan, but that Korea would have to go through a period of a certain form of political tutelage. With this in mind, the Big Three, independent of the written agreement, subscribed to a four-power (American-British-Soviet-Chinese) international trusteeship for Korea.

If the future shape of East Asia had been molded at the Yalta Conference table, the ultimate realization of that plan was predicated upon military success in the Pacific battlefield. The relentless destruction of Japanese defenses by the Allied forces was certain to guarantee the fulfillment of those objectives. Shortly after the Yalta Conference and concurrently with the liberation campaign in the Philippines, the United States forces began to battle on Iwo-Jima and Okinawa. The former was taken on March 16, and the latter on April 8, 1945. Both islands provided the Americans with advance bases for air operations against the Japanese on their mainland, in Korea, China, and even Manchuria.

When the Americans were landing on Okinawa, the Koiso cabinet fell. General Koiso, having succeeded Tojo nine months earlier, had been a compromise choice. He had been prosecuting the war with renewed determination, but at the same time exploring the possibility of a negotiated peace. These fundamentally incompatible courses of action made it impossible for him to achieve either of these objectives. He had to resign, succeeded by Suzuki Kantaro, another compromise choice.

In Europe, on April 30, 1945, Adolf Hitler committed suicide in the basement of his Chancellery in Berlin, marking the end of his Third Reich. A week later in Rheims, France, Hitler's successor government signed an unconditional surrender for all fronts. President Truman declared May 8, 1945, V-E Day.[14] Great Britain now was able to add her full military strength to the offensive operations in the Pacific. In June, mop-up operations in Okinawa officially came to an end when the Japanese commanding general committed hara-kiri. The complete liberation of the Philippines came in July when American and Filipino forces broke the backbone of Japanese resistance. In the same month, the Australians and the Dutch made their triumphant return to Borneo.

The Surrender of Japan

Thus, by the summer of 1945, America's massive air assaults and naval bombardments upon Japanese industrial and population centers from Hokkaido to Kyushu, from Tokyo to Taiwan, made Japan's military position utterly hopeless.

At this time, the Japanese leaders were divided into two groups: those who insisted on the continuation of the war to the bitter end, such as Tojo and other militarist diehards, and those who favored a search for negotiated peace, such as Kido Koichi and several other senior statesmen. Premier Suzuki, himself, was leaning toward the "peace group." Japan literally stood alone: her European Axis partners had been vanquished, the Soviet Union had informed her that the Soviet-Japanese neutrality pact would not be renewed, and those "puppet" regimes she had created in Asia had either disappeared or deserted her. Premier Suzuki, like his predecessor, had been pursuing a dual policy of diametrically opposed goals: an effective prosecution of the war, and a desperate search for "a peace with honor." At a Supreme Council meeting in May 1945, Foreign Minister Togo had proposed that, in view of Japan's forlorn position, the government should endeavor to improve Japanese-Soviet relations and at the same time to approach the Soviet Union with a request for her mediation in the war on behalf of Japan. The Council had endorsed the first point, but divided on the second, and had appointed Hirota Koki to negotiate with Jacob A. Malik, the Soviet ambassador in Tokyo.

The Hirota-Malik conversations proved inconsequential, lacking Soviet enthusiasm or encouragement. In fact, the Soviets were transporting their troops from the European theatre to the Siberian-Manchurian-Korean borders in preparation for the attack on Japan. Worsening conditions of war, meanwhile, forced the Japanese leaders to employ desperate, fanatic, last-ditch tactics—the Kamikaze suicide attacks.[15] The man-made Kamikaze, it was hoped, would inflict such staggering casualties on the Allies as to force them to retreat or reconsider their stiff demands for unconditional surrender. Contrary to their expectations, the Kamikaze raids proved insufficient to halt the Allies' advance or to hurt their morale. On June 22, at another Supreme Council meeting, it was decided to initiate peace negotiations through Soviet mediation. Again Hirota was chosen to negotiate with Malik, who subsequently conveyed the Japanese peace overture to Moscow. Malik then suggested to Hirota that their meetings be postponed until instructions had arrived from Moscow.

Days and weeks passed without any response from the Soviets. On July 8, 1945, the Supreme Council chose ex-Premier Konoye as a special envoy—a personal representative of the emperor—to be sent to Moscow to perform what the Hirota-Malik conversations had failed to accomplish. The Japanese ambassador in Moscow, Sato Naotake, was instructed to inform the Soviet leaders of Japan's desire for Konoye's Moscow visit. While Ambassador Sato was negotiating with the Soviets so that they would act before the forthcoming Potsdam Conference, Stalin and Molotov left for Potsdam, Germany.

The Potsdam Conference, the last in the series of wartime summit conferences, was held from July 17 to August 2, 1945, and attended by the new Big Three—President Truman of the United States, Prime Minister Attlee of Great Britain[16] (assisted by Winston Churchill), and Premier Stalin of the Soviet Union. At Potsdam, Stalin informed Truman that he had been approached by Japan requesting him to offer his good offices for peace negotiations, but he did not respond because he thought Japan was making a diplomatic maneuver to prolong the war. What Stalin did not know was the fact that the United States had known all about Tokyo's efforts to secure Soviet mediation to end the war.[17]

On July 26, 1945, the United States and Great Britain, with China joining, issued the Potsdam Declaration, calling upon Japan either to surrender unconditionally or to face "prompt and utter destruction."[18] They laid down the specific terms from which they would not deviate: (1) the elimination of the authority and influence of irresponsible militarism which misled the Japanese people to the path of world conquest, (2) the Allied occupation of Japan to ensure conditions for achieving their basic objectives—the establishment of a new order, peace, security, and justice, (3) the implementation of the terms of the Cairo Declaration and the limitation of Japan's sovereignty to the four major islands and such minor ones as determined by the Three Powers, (4) the total disarmament of the Japanese armed forces and the repatriation of Japanese military personnel, (5) the punishment of war criminals, the revival and strengthening of democratic tendencies in Japan, and the establishment of such fundamental human rights as freedom of speech, of religion, and of thought, (6) the restriction of Japanese industries to a peacetime economy, a payment of reparations in kind, and eventual Japanese participation in world trade, and (7) eventual withdrawal of the occupation forces upon the accomplishment of these objectives and upon the establishment of a peaceful and responsible government instituted by the freely expressed will of the Japanese people.

The following day, in Tokyo, the Supreme Council and the cabinet held a meeting to discuss the Potsdam Declaration. The military advocated an outright, unequivocal rejection of the declaration. Foreign Minister Togo was opposed to such a move but favored a delaying action, maintaining that the government should wait for a Soviet reply to Japan's request for mediation. The indecisive attitude of the government and the absence of an official announcement caused the Japanese news media to report that the government considered the declaration to be of little significance and that it would pay no attention to it. Prime Minister Suzuki appeared to have confirmed the news report at a press conference held on July 28, as he stated: "I consider the joint proclamation of the three powers to be a rehash of the Cairo Declaration. The Government does not regard it as a thing of any great value; the Government will ignore it. We will press forward resolutely to carry the war to a successful conclusion."[19]

In Washington, in the absence of any official Japanese response through diplomatic channels, President Truman and his top advisors concluded that the Suzuki statement was tantamount to a contemptuous rejection of the Potsdam Declaration. Then they decided to use the atomic bomb on Japan. On the morning of August 6, 1945, a lone B-29 (*Enola Gay*) dropped on Hiroshima the first atomic bomb in warfare; a new era dawned—the atomic age. In a statement President Truman said, "That bomb had more power than 20,000 tons of T.N.T. It had more than two thousand times the blast power of the British 'Grand Slam,' which is the largest bomb yet used in the history of warfare. . . . With this bomb we have now added a new and revolutionary increase in destruction to supplement the growing power of our armed forces. . . . It is an atomic bomb. It is a harnessing of the basic power of the universe. The force from which the sun draws its power has been loosed against those who brought war to the Far East."[20] That single bomb over Hiroshima killed more than eighty thousand persons instantly and wounded hundreds of thousands of Japanese.[21] Two days later the Soviet Union declared war against Japan, stating in part: "The demand of the three powers, the United States, Great Britain, and China, of July 26 for the unconditional surrender of Japanese armed forces was rejected by Japan. Thus the proposal made by the Japanese Government to the Soviet Union for mediation in the Far East has lost all foundation."

The issue at hand for Japan at this critical moment was no longer whether she should continue the war to the "last drop of blood," but whether she should accept the surrender conditionally or unconditionally. On August 9, the Supreme Council meeting was deadlocked on this issue. The military members in the Council had suggested that Japan should accept the Potsdam Declaration on four conditions: The emperor to retain his throne and sovereignty, no Allied occupation of Japan, their disarmament and demobilization by themselves, and the trial of war criminals by the Japanese themselves. The peace faction, including Premier Suzuki, favored the acceptance of the Potsdam terms with only one exception—the preservation of the Imperial system. In the midst of agony and anxiety, the conference was informed of the second atomic bomb raid over Nagasaki. In addition, Soviet troops poured into Manchuria and Korea, where the Japanese defense collapsed ignominiously. Yet, these events appeared to have little effect upon the adamant attitude of the military, and the council remained deadlocked. Premier Suzuki, thereupon, appealed to the emperor to make the final decision. In the dark hours of 3:00 A.M., August 10, until which time the Council meeting had lasted, the emperor sided with the peace faction and decided to accept the Allied terms and to end the war.

The Japanese government transmitted to the Allied powers, via the Swiss and Swedish governments, its official decision to surrender and to accept the Potsdam Declaration. In doing so, it was made clear that the decision was made "with the understanding that the said declaration does not compromise any demand which prejudices the prerogatives of His Majesty as a sovereign ruler." When this formal message was received, the United States government, on behalf of itself and other parties to the Potsdam Declaration, took an unequivocal position on the Japanese "reservation" concerning the status of the emperor. On this point the Allied statement, drafted by Secretary of State Byrnes, asserted: "From the moment of surrender the authority of the Emperor and the Japanese Government to rule the state shall be subject to the Supreme Commander of the Allied Powers who will take such steps as he deems proper to effectuate the surrender terms."[22]

Upon receipt of this reply, the Supreme Council again met, discussed, and divided. Did the Allied statement mean to allow the emperor to retain the throne and remain as sovereign of the state? Or, did it mean the Imperial system, as the national policy, would be abolished at the will of the Supreme Commander of the Allied Powers when he deemed necessary? The military held the answer to the first question to be negative, and the second, affirmative. The peace group was inclined to believe that the reply was not repugnant to the Imperial system. For three days they pondered and argued without arriving at any consensus view. On August 14, the emperor concluded that the war should be terminated and ordered the immediate and unconditional acceptance of the Allied demands.

At about the same time (August 15, Tokyo; August 14, Washington), when President Truman received the final acceptance note from the Japanese government, the emperor of Japan was addressing his people on a nationwide radio broadcast: Japan had been defeated and forced to accept the terms of the Potsdam Declaration. He said: "The enemy has begun to employ a new and most cruel bomb, the power of which to do damage is incalculable. Should we continue to fight, it would not only result in an ultimate collapse and obliteration of the Japanese nation, but it also would lead to the total extinction of human civilization." He went on to invoke the will and determination of his people to survive with patience and perseverance: "It is according to the dictate of time and fate that we have resolved to pave the way for a grand peace for all generations to come by enduring the unendurable and suffering what is insufferable."

Thus came the end of World War II. The grand finale of the "Great Tragedy" was performed on September 2, 1945, when the Instrument of Surrender was signed on board the U.S.S. *Missouri,* which was anchored in Tokyo Bay—the same place where nearly a century earlier Commodore Matthew Perry's "Black Ships" had steamed in to open Japan to the West.

Lessons of World War II

Are there any lessons to be learned from the experience of World War II, especially with respect to the war-making process? War as an instrument of national policy is not limited to totalitarian states. Any nation, of democracy or of dictatorship, tends to take up arms either to promote or to defend what is broadly termed "national interests." National security and well-being constitute without a doubt essential elements of national interests and, therefore, national self-defense of those elements is recognized in international law as the inherent right of a nation-state. The crucial question lies in the indistinguishable difference between *de-*

fensive and *offensive* policies taken in the name of self-defense. For this reason aggression is extremely difficult to define qualitatively.

Which country, Japan or the United States, was responsible for the Pacific war? Perhaps neither or perhaps both. In any event, in waging the war as they did with the United States, the Japanese militarists had made a number of fundamental miscalculations and misjudgments.

First, they overestimated their own military power in terms of men and material. Their blind confidence in the morale, patriotism, and military skill of the Imperial armed forces obscured the reality that they had been fatigued by the war of attrition with China since the Marco Polo Bridge incident of July 1937. Having committed hundreds of thousands of troops in the vastness of China—the "quicksand of Asia"—Japan was unable to withdraw from her ambition to conquer China or to withstand the endless drain of her national energy for that adventure. The Japanese leaders believed that once they had secured the seemingly inexhaustible natural resources (oil, rubber, tin, etc.) of Southeast Asia, they could infinitely strengthen their national economy and arms production, enabling them to carry on any protracted war. As it turned out, however, within a year Japan lost most of her navy and, consequently, the control of the sea lanes to transport these raw materials to Japan. At the onset of the war Japan had a considerable amount of arms stockpiled, sufficient for limited military operations, but once they were drained, resupplies could not meet the needs. This problem had been anticipated by only a handful of military leaders, including Admiral Yamamoto who had said to Premier Konoye:

> If you tell me that it is necessary that we fight, then in the first six months to a year of war against the U.S. and England I will run wild, and I will show you an uninterrupted succession of victories; I must also tell you that, should the war be prolonged for two or three years, I have no confidence in our ultimate victory.[23]

By comparison, in 1941 the United States had nearly eighty times the strategic materials that Japan had and during the wartime years the former produced a total of 260,000 aircraft as against the latter's 58,000.

Second, Japan overestimated the power of her alliance partners in Europe—Germany and Italy. Hitler's conquest of Poland, his march through the Low Countries into France, his occupation of Norway, his invasion of the Soviet Union, his domination of the Balkans, and even Mussolini's adventure in Albania—all these events glamorized and mesmerized the Japanese militarists into believing that the European New Order was a *fait accompli* which would last for some time. With the Soviet Union vanquished, with Great Britain defeated, and with France subjugated by the Nazis, the United States would be isolated geographically, politically, and diplomatically. They believed time was on their side; the age of democracy had given way to the era of totalitarianism symbolized by the principles of Teutonic supremacy in Europe and *Yamato Tamashi* (Spirit of Japan) in Asia.

Third, they grossly underestimated the potent power of American nationalism. They were convinced that the heterogeneity of American society would scarcely bring about national unity in the face of a grave national crisis. Reared and disciplined in a society of Spartan mold, the Japanese militarists failed to comprehend the resiliency of a free people in a free society. They convinced themselves that the Americans were so accustomed to an "easy life" with material luxuries and comforts that they could not long endure the hardships and shortages of consumer goods which a war would entail. The devastating attack on Pearl Harbor pulverized the American fleet, but it galvanized the American people into acting as one nation to defeat what they were led to believe to be "treacherous, sneaky, and cruel" enemies.

Fourth, and finally, during the war itself, the Japanese failed to appreciate the incipient Asian nationalism in various regions of their occupied territories. Ironically, the Japanese themselves had helped foster the rise of Asian nationalism by way of smashing the myth of the "white man's invincibility" in the early stages of the war, but they were unable to perceive or to direct its potent force in their favor. The basic Japanese war objective was a realization of *Hakko-Ichiu,* which in essence amounted to world conquest. The specific terms of this goal included: the establishment of the new order in East Asia to the exclusion of the interests and influence of the Western colonial powers, the formation of a strong East Asian defense system on the perimeter of the Great East Asian Co-Prosperity Sphere, the creation of a self-sufficient economic community within the sphere, and the eventual granting of "independent governments" friendly to Japan in the former Western colonies.

Where in this scheme was found the principle of the sovereign equality of all nations or of all peoples? The Japanese were to maintain their undisputed supremacy. With the coming of the Japanese, the peoples of the former Western colonies discovered that they had simply traded one master for another; they were liberated from the Western colonial yoke only to be shackled by a new Asian chain. Led by small groups of nationalists, they took up arms to resist the Japanese brand of the new order.

In Indochina, some Vietnamese were influenced by the Japanese propaganda of the "independence of Vietnam" from the French colonial rule and of an "Asia for Asians," but the anti-Japanese activities of nationalistic, underground resistance groups like the Vietminh never ceased. In the last stages of the war, when the inevitable defeat had become evident, the Japanese allowed Vietnam, Laos, and Cambodia each to declare her independence. In Malaya and Singapore, the indigenous people were urged to collaborate, but only minor offices were open to them. In 1943, the Malay People's Anti-Japanese army was organized under the guerrilla leader Chin Peng, who successfully harassed the Japanese occupation forces until the end. No movement toward national independence emerged during Japanese control. In Burma, a puppet regime headed by Ba Maw and Thakin Nu was formed with nominal "independence." They soon discovered their disenchantment. Thakin Nu, who had served as minister of foreign affairs, wrote: "We hoped that we would get independence, but all we got was slapped faces, ruined homes, looted property, and forced labor."[24] The Japanese renamed the Burma Independence army, under the leadership of Aung San, the Burma Defense army. Aung San also discovered that the Japanese were worse than the British, and in the summer of 1944, he transformed his army into the Anti-Fascist People's Freedom League to fight the Japanese on the side of the Allies. In the Dutch East Indies, the Indonesians first welcomed the Japanese as liberators who had emancipated

them from three centuries of Dutch colonial rule. But they likewise found that Japan wanted their country for exploitation; the
Japanese began to seize petroleum, nickel, bauxite, rubber, and
food supplies. They were banned from political discussions, sup-
pressed in their expression of nationalism, and conscripted into
labor forces. Again, only when the defeat became imminent did the
Japanese allow the Indonesians to form, in March 1945, a committee in preparation for independence. Two days after the surrender of Japan, the Indonesian nationalists—Sukarno, Hatta,
Sjahrir—proclaimed their independence. In the case of the Philippines, the Japanese were equally unsuccessful in inducing the
Filipinos to render wholehearted collaboration. Their treatment
of the occupied people with the "stick and carrot" method produced
more guerrilla fighters than genuine collaborators.[25] In October
1943, the Philippines were granted "independence" and the puppet
regime duly declared war on the United States, who never recognized the validity of this act. President Manuel Quezon of the commonwealth government died in exile and was succeeded by Sergio
Osmena. President Osmena landed on Leyte with General Douglas
MacArthur and later achieved a triumphant return of his government to Manila in February 1945. But the capital lay in a heap of
rubble and the country in the depth of ruin.

All these miscalculations and misjudgments contributed in part
to the ultimate collapse of the Japanese empire.

CHAPTER EIGHT

Bearing the Victor's Burden

A Chinese Gordian Knot

The Chiang-Stilwell Controversy

The history of China from the surrender of Japan in August 1945 to the establishment of the People's Republic of China by the Communists in October 1949 was a panoramic unfolding of the struggle for power between the Nationalists and the Communists. These contending rivals cast off all pretense of the wartime "United Front" and resumed the deadly contest for survival and supremacy.

Traditionalists might assert that, in the pattern of China's dynastic cycles, it was a transitory period in which the decadent and corrupt Nationalists had lost the "Mandate of Heaven" to the more dynamic and courageous Communists. The Communists, on the other hand, might claim that their victory was predicated upon the correct historical inevitability of the triumph of Marxism-Leninism-Maoism, which is founded upon the "scientific" law of dialectic materialism.

Irrespective of various interpretations and assessments of the causes and outcomes of the historic event, one indelible fact remained undisputed. That was, the United States had been deeply involved in the Chinese struggle and unable to shape the course of

189

events toward a "strong, united, and democratic" China within the framework of United States global policy.

When, in early 1942, the Japanese launched an attack on Burma with the intent to cut the Burma Road, through which arms supplies reached Chungking, the Allies hastily established the China-Burma-India (CBI) theatre under the command of Generalissimo Chiang Kai-shek with the American general, Joseph Stilwell. General Stilwell's assignment was made in accordance with an earlier agreement between the two governments of "sending to the Generalissimo a high ranking United States Army officer to act as his Chief of Staff and as Commanding Officer of the United States Army office." The functions of such a U.S. Army representative were:

To supervise and control all United States defense-aid affairs for China.

Under the Generalissimo, to command all United States forces in China and such Chinese forces as may be assigned to him.

To represent the United States Government on any International War Council in China and act as the Chief of Staff for the Generalissimo.

To improve, maintain and control the Burma Road in China.[1]

The Allies' military operation commanded by General Stilwell to thwart the Japanese offensive at this time ended in failure. The British were quickly driven out of lower Burma and the Chinese out of upper Burma. By the middle of May 1942, the victorious Japanese army occupied Burma entirely, forcing the Anglo-American troops' retreat into India and the Chinese back to their own borders. To Stilwell the Burma campaign was a military disaster and a terrible personal nightmare. As he said later, the Japanese had given him "a hell of a beating." He was particularly disappointed with the Chinese whose "morale was low, discipline poor, leadership inferior, and supplies squandered." He noted that "they were too busy hauling goods to China to haul soldiers. Trains were blocked or stalled, commanders were out of touch, military discipline was dissolving."[2] He was convinced that this deplorable state of affairs was attributable primarily to Generalissimo Chiang Kai-shek, who was in his view an "amateur tactician" and who "has made it impossible" for him to do anything.[3] Thus the genesis of the Chiang-Stilwell conflict could be found in the campaign in Burma.

After the Burma fiasco, the Allies undertook the program of training some sixty thousand Chinese troops in India with advanced weapons and techniques so as to raise the combat standard to a level befitting modern warfare. Simultaneously, under American advisors, thirty divisions of Chiang's armed forces received training in southwest China and were equipped adequately with arms and matériel which had been flown in over the Hump. The construction of air bases in this area and of the Ledo Road from Assam through northern Burma to link with the upper Burma Road were also undertaken. These operations were carried out under the direct supervision of General Stilwell.

Yet the CBI theatre remained at the bottom of the Allied priority list. The grand strategy of the Allied Powers had determined that "the war against Germany came first. Second came the great 'triphibians' movement across the Pacific toward the Japanese Empire. The China-Burma-India theatre was a poor third." Accordingly, in Europe, Anglo-American forces executed such remarkable campaigns as the occupation of Morocco and Algeria (operation Torch) and the invasion of Sicily (July 10, 1943); on the Russian front, the Soviets won the costly but decisive battle of Stalingrad with arms and supplies furnished by the United States; and in the Pacific, the United States forces were relentlessly prosecuting counteroffensives against the Japanese in the Aleutians, in the Central Pacific, in the Coral Sea, and in New Guinea.

In the aftermath of the Burma campaign, Chiang Kai-shek felt that "the United States would sacrifice China's interests to Britain's whenever necessary," and "he [Chiang] let it be known that such diversions from the China theatre coupled with further Allied war reverses could make China go 'completely antiforeign overnight' and quit the war."[4] Chiang demanded increased aid and accelerated action. Toward the end of 1943, General Stilwell launched his "back to Burma" offensive against the Japanese.

After nearly eight months of dogged fighting, the Allies captured portions of upper Burma and were poised to retake the Burma Road.

At this time, the Japanese launched an all-out offensive throughout the entire China theatre. Their immediate objectives were to cut off any possible source of aid to Chiang's armies and to capture, if they could, such Nationalist strongholds as Sian in the northwest, Kunming in the southwest, and even Chungking itself. In the face of these general offensives, the Chinese suffered a calamitous military defeat, coupled with civic and economic paralysis. In 1944 Chiang's China was progressively deteriorating; official life was infected by corruption; the military, ineffective and demoralized, was writhing under the heavy losses in untold casualties, and its bases were either taken or destroyed by the enemy; disunity among the leaders and discontent among the people rose to an alarming peak.

It was only in the CBI theatre, where the Chinese troops were under the direct command of General Stilwell, that they were making substantial military gains. Washington, therefore, conceived a plan to put Stilwell in command of the Chinese armed forces with authority to direct and revitalize their military effort. In a message to Generalissimo Chiang, in July 1944, President Roosevelt stated:

> The critical situation which now exists in my opinion calls for the delegation to one individual of the powers to coordinate all the Allied military resources in China, including the Communist forces. . . . I recommend for your most urgent consideration that you recall him [General Stilwell] from Burma and place him directly under you in the command of all Chinese and American forces, and that you charge him with the full responsibility and authority for the coordination and direction of the operations required to stem the tide of the enemy's forces. I feel that the case of China is so desperate that if radical and promptly applied remedies are not immediately effected, our common cause will suffer a disastrous setback.[5]

The president's message, straightforward in tone and stringent in substance, contained three significant features: (1) it expressly proposed to bring within the scope of American aid Chiang's most feared domestic enemies—Chinese Communists—who had been regarded by Stilwell as better and more effective fighters than the Nationalists; (2) it clearly questioned Chiang's ability to govern as head of a great power, accepting Stilwell's view of Chiang as incapable of running his country in the war; and (3) it sought to place a foreigner in a high position in the Chinese government, thus violating by implication the principle of the national sovereignty of China.

Chiang Kai-shek, agreeing to this proposal *in principle,* "proposed modification, shifted ground, insisted on control of Lend-Lease, twisted and temporized." General Stilwell, reporting in September to the chief of staff in Washington, stated that "he [Chiang] believes the war in the Pacific is nearly over, and that by delaying tactics, he can throw the entire burden on us. He has no intention of instituting any real democratic regime or of forming a united front with the Communists."

Added to the major Chiang-Stilwell feud was the minor Stilwell-Chennault friction. General Claire Chennault, commander of the Fourteenth Air Force operating in China against Japanese troop movements, installations, and shipping, contended that he deserved a lion's share of military goods and hammered at Stilwell for more planes, bombs, fuel, arms, and supplies. Chennault claimed that his air war against the Japanese was a decisive factor, whereas Stilwell believed that it could hamper but not halt the enemy offensive. Moreover, because of Chinese weakness on the ground, Stilwell contended, air resistance to Japanese advance proved limited and ineffective. He accused Chennault of "trying to prepare an out for himself by claiming that with a little more, which we won't give him, he can still do it." Chiang Kai-shek preferred Chennault's strategic view to Stilwell's, for the former would involve less extensive use of his ground forces.

By the end of September, the incompatibility between Chiang and Stilwell had reached a point beyond conciliation. Chiang demanded Stilwell's recall on the grounds that he refused to cooperate with, but attempted to command, Chiang, that he was unfit for the vast and complex duties which the new command would entail, and that his appointment would do "irreparable injury" to Sino-American cooperation. Endorsing Chiang's demand, Patrick J.

Hurley, who had arrived in Chungking a month earlier as President Roosevelt's personal representative to China, advised the president: "If you sustain Stilwell in this controversy you will lose Chiang Kai-shek and possibly you will lose China with him." The president was not prepared to insist on imposing an unwanted American commander against the expressed wish of a recalcitrant chief of state. Stilwell had to be recalled and replaced by General Albert C. Wedemeyer.

The Chiang-Stilwell controversy did not necessarily damage Chinese-American cooperation in the attainment of common goals, but it conspicuously represented a policy difference with respect to the Chinese Communists. The Communists were steadily expanding their area of occupation and building up the foundation of their power, military as well as political, especially among the rural population. Wherever they went, they carried out land reform, eliminated rent to landlords, rectified the local administration, and offered protection and security to the peasants, who felt for the first time freed from extortion and exploitation. As the Communists won allegiance from the peasantry and their territory expanded, their position relative to the Chiang regime was strengthened and their confidence grew apace.[6] They entertained no illusion either in the failure of the Nationalist-Communist united front or in the inevitability of the final contest for survival.

The prospect of an all-out civil war in China after Japan's surrender had worried the United States. President Roosevelt, with a view to bringing about a compromise settlement of the Nationalist-Communist antagonism, in June of 1944 sent Vice-President Wallace to Chungking. Wallace was to persuade Chiang to negotiate with the Communists. But his personal diplomacy, added to the prestige of his office, could not change Chiang's conviction and attitude toward the Communists. Chiang, rejecting the prevalent notion that the Communists were "agrarian democrats," steadfastly maintained an unswerving conviction that they were determined to seize power in China and were as dangerous, perhaps even more so, to the independence and peace of China as were the Japanese because they were primarily serving the Soviet cause. The primary purpose of Wallace's mission was unattained, but he recommended to the president the compliance with Chiang's request for "a personal representative to serve as liaison" between the two leaders.

The Hurley Mission

In August 1944, President Roosevelt sent General Patrick Hurley to China as his personal representative. As Hurley understood, his mission involving the implementation of American policy in China was: "(1) to prevent the collapse of the Nationalist Government, (2) to sustain Chiang Kai-shek as president of the republic and generalissimo of the armies, (3) to harmonize relations between the generalissimo and the American commander, (4) to promote production of war supplies in China and prevent economic collapse, and (5) to unify all the military forces in China for the purpose of defeating Japan."[7]

En route to Chungking General Hurley stopped in Moscow to confer with the Kremlin leaders. Soviet Foreign Minister V. M. Molotov assured Hurley that the Soviet government would be pleased to see the United States assist the Chinese in unifying their country, in improving their military and economic conditions, and in choosing for these tasks their best people. Molotov further made it clear that until Chiang's government made sincere efforts to improve Sino-Soviet relations by changing its policies, the Soviet Union would take no interest in Chinese governmental affairs.

Upon his arrival at Chungking in September, Hurley conveyed this assurance to Chiang Kai-shek in the hope that Chiang would mitigate his antagonism toward the Communists. In this Hurley appeared to be successful because Chiang came to believe, sincerely or seemingly, that the Soviet government did not recognize the Chinese Communist party as Communist at all, contrary to his earlier conviction that the Chinese Communists were serving the Soviet cause. Molotov had expressed to Hurley a similar view that many impoverished Chinese people called themselves Communist, but were related to communism in no way at all; it was merely a way of expressing dissatisfaction with their economic condition, and the Soviet government should not be concerned with these "Communist elements." Chiang further expressed his view that the

Soviet Union was neither supporting the Chinese Communist party nor desiring dissensions or civil war in China, but wanted more harmonious relations with China.

The apparent change in Chiang's attitude gave rise to the possibility and hope that a compromise settlement might be reached with the Communist party on the basis that it was to be recognized as one of the internal political parties without external entanglements. The Communists, however, made their position quite clear: they would not relinquish their military power unless their political position was unequivocally secured.

Hurley's mediation was directed primarily toward strengthening the national government by means of democratic reform which would broaden the basis of participation in the government of various political parties and groups, including the Communists. Chiang Kai-shek was urged to allow Communist participation in his government on conditions acceptable to both sides; the Communists were likewise urged to allow the integration of their troops into the Nationalist armies so as to form more effective fighting forces against the Japanese.

Hurley played a significant role as mediator. After consultation with Chiang and Chinese Communist representatives in Chungking, on November 7 he flew to Yenan, the Communist stronghold in Shansi, for a two-day conference with Mao Tse-tung, chairman of the Chinese Communist party. Their discussions resulted in a tentative plan envisaging the establishment of a coalition government on the basis of Nationalist-Communist cooperation. The plan consisted of a five-point proposal: (1) The government, the Kuomintang, and the Communist party would cooperate in achieving the unification of military forces for the prompt defeat of Japan and the reconstruction of China; (2) Chiang's government was to be reorganized into a coalition National government made up of representatives of all parties, and a United National Military Council was to be formed with representatives of all anti-Japanese armies; (3) The coalition National government would promote progress and democracy and guarantee all the democratic principles such as the Bill of Rights; (4) The foreign-secured supplies would be equitably distributed among all fighting forces under the direction and control of the coalition National government; and

(5) The coalition government would recognize the legality of the Kuomintang, the Chinese Communist party, and all other anti-Japanese parties. It was signed by Mao Tse-tung as chairman of the Chinese Communist party and Hurley as personal representative of the president of the United States. In his appreciation for American initiative, Chairman Mao wrote to President Roosevelt on November 10: "It has always been our desire to reach an agreement with President Chiang Kai-shek which will promote the welfare of the Chinese people. Through the good offices of General Hurley we have suddenly seen hope of realization."[8]

When this plan was presented to Chiang Kai-shek, he found it unacceptable and made a three-point counterproposal: (1) The Nationalist government would agree to incorporate, after reorganization, the Chinese Communist forces in the National Army and to give legal recognition to the Chinese Communist party; (2) The Communist party would fully support the Nationalist government in the present war effort and in the postwar reconstruction and give over control of all their troops to the Nationalist government; and (3) The Nationalist government, to which the Communist party would subscribe, would carry out Dr. Sun's Three Principles of the People so as to establish a democratic government designed to guarantee all civil liberties.

The fundamental differences of position between the two parties, as demonstrated in the proposals, could be reduced as follows: the Nationalists insisted upon the incorporation of the Communist forces into the Nationalist army first, followed by recognition of the political and legal status of the Communist party, whereas the Communists insisted upon the guarantee of political and legal status of their party first, followed by the integration of their military forces into the Nationalist army.

On November 22, Chiang's counterproposal was presented to Chou En-lai, the Communist representative in Chungking. Early in December, Chou left Chungking for Yenan, where he wrote to Hurley:

The refusal of the Generalissimo and the National Government of our minimum five point proposal . . . and the submission of the three point counter-proposal, preclude the

possibility of my returning to Chungking for further negotiations. We find it impossible to see any fundamental common
basis in these new proposals.[9]

General Hurley, who was now appointed American ambassador
on November 17, 1944, following the resignation of Clarence E.
Gauss, continued to mediate. After a series of exchange letters,
Ambassador Hurley succeeded in persuading Mao Tse-tung to
send Chou En-lai back to Chungking to negotiate with the government. Chou arrived at Chiang's capital on January 24, 1945, and
Nationalist-Communist negotiations resumed with Hurley attend-
ing on the invitation of both parties. Their negotiations were, however, unable to break the impasse. The deep-rooted suspicion and
distrust of each side toward the other were too great to iron out
their differences. Neither side was ready or willing to make any
substantive concession to or reasonable compromise with the
other. Months of negotiations, failing in narrowing their differences, only broadened the scope of their discussions which further
complicated the original issues.

In the meantime, in February at Yalta, the Big Three had made
many historic decisions, the exact terms of which were kept from
Chiang and Hurley. In April President Roosevelt died and Harry
S. Truman became the president of the United States. In May,
while the United Nations Conference was in progress in San Francisco, the war in Europe came to an end with the total collapse of
Hitler's Nazi regime. In July, Churchill's party lost the general
elections, and while the new Big Three (Truman, Stalin, and
Attlee) were meeting at Potsdam, the first atomic bomb exploded
over the New Mexico testing grounds, heralding a new era in
man's history. The whole world was changing all around China,
but the Nationalist-Communist impasse remained unchanged. It
was during this impasse in August that Japan surrendered.

The sudden surrender of Japan compounded another complex
problem with already existing difficulties. The issue was which of
the feuding parties was to accept the surrender of more than two
million Japanese troops in the occupied territories. Chiang was
given authority to accept for the Allies the surrender of the Japanese in China, Formosa, and northern Indochina above the sixteenth parallel, but not in Manchuria where the Soviet Red Army

had vanquished the Japanese. The Soviet Union had entered the war against Japan a week earlier in accordance, it should be recalled, with the provisions of the Yalta Agreement.

No mention of Chinese Communists was made in General MacArthur's order of August 17, 1945, specifying the forces to which the Japanese had to surrender. Protesting the omission in the order and disobeying a directive to remain in Shantung and Chahar, the Communists lost no time in exercising their "belligerent right" to accept the surrender of troops and territory from the Japanese. Chiang Kai-shek sharply denounced this unilateral "unauthorized" action of the Communists and began to deploy his own Nationalist troops to various locations to ward off the Communist move. In this Chiang was backed by General Wedemeyer, who had been instructed to use all means at his disposal to airlift the Nationalists. Moreover, fifty thousand U.S. marines had to be landed to help Chiang recapture Peking, Tientsin, and Tsingtao.

The principal bone of contention in this race was North China and Manchuria, highly industrialized regions of the country, owing to Japanese investments of capital and technology over the years. Here also were substantial stocks of Japanese arms and supplies. The Communists' objectives were to occupy Manchuria and to secure those arms, most of which were in the hands of the Soviets who had overrun Manchuria following their declaration of war on Japan.

The Communists began their carefully planned infiltration into Manchuria and organized themselves into armies equipped with Japanese arms which had been surrendered to the Soviets. The Nationalist troops, on the other hand, were unable to enter Manchuria on account of the very presence and noncooperative, obstructionist tactics of the Soviet troops. Chiang's armies were subsequently transported into Manchuria by the United States military planes and ships in conformity both with the principle of the United States official policy to assist the *legitimate* government of China and with the spirit of the Sino-Soviet treaty of August 1945, whereby the Soviet Union had agreed to render moral support and military aid entirely to the "National Government as the central government of China" and had recognized Chinese sovereignty in Manchuria.

By the time the Nationalist troops were admitted, the Communist forces were well prepared and ready to challenge them in battle. Meanwhile, the Soviets had stripped Manchuria of industries and equipment on the grounds that such property was "war booty" because it had been used to operate the Japanese military in the war.

On the political and diplomatic front, Ambassador Hurley had persuaded Chiang Kai-shek to invite Chairman Mao to Chungking for a conference which might lead to a negotiated settlement. The Mao-Chiang meetings, which took place during Mao's six-week stay in Chungking in the fall of 1945, produced little agreement on substantive issues. Even their calculated cordiality and friendliness to each other were more apparent than real. What came out of it, however, was a vague and broad agreement on general principles such as the preservation of peace, national unity, integration of armies, creation of an all-party Political Consultative Conference (PCC), and preparation for establishing a general democratic government. But there were insurmountable differences and discrepancies in the specific measures to implement these principles.

The inevitable armed clash between the Nationalists and the Communists took place, and on November 11 the military attaché in Chungking reported, "The fighting is becoming more bitter and larger numbers of men are becoming involved." Ambassador Hurley was further instructed to mediate. But his effort was now regarded by the Communists as *intervention* rather than mediation because the United States appeared committed to one side—the Nationalist side. To the Communists the American lifting of Chiang's troops to the north by United States military air transport and warships, the landing of American marines to hold cities in advance of the Nationalists' arrival, and the continued American arms supply solely to the Kuomintang armies were all clear evidence that the United States had ceased to be an impartial, objective, unbiased mediator.

On his part Ambassador Hurley came to feel increasingly that his government's support of the Chiang regime was less than positive and that some officials in the Department of State and in the Foreign Service were actually undermining his efforts. The Foreign Service experts, convinced of prevalent corruption and inefficiency in the Chiang government, had for some time wanted the United

States to stop *carte blanche* support of Chiang Kai-shek. Hurley, frustrated and infuriated, announced his resignation on November 26, 1945.

In his letter of resignation to President Truman, Ambassador Hurley stated: "Of all the assignments China was the most intricate and the most difficult." He continued:

> The professional foreign service men sided with the Chinese Communist armed party and the imperialist bloc of nations whose policy it was to seek China divided against herself. Our professional diplomats continuously advised the Communists that my efforts in preventing the collapse of the Nationalist Government did not represent the policy of the United States. These same professionals openly advised the Communist armed party to decline unification of the Chinese Communist Army with the National Army unless the Chinese Communists were given control.[10]

Hurley returned home. "His accusation captured the spirit of the time. Since the dissolution of wartime alliance with the Soviet Union, innate fear and hate of Communism reasserted itself in America. . . . Hurley opened the journey toward the tawdry reign of terror soon to be imposed with such astonishing ease by Senator Joe McCarthy. The time of hysterics had arrived."[11] China, meanwhile, was worsening day by day: society demoralized, economy ruined, and finance bankrupted. Worst of all, China stood on the brink of a full-scale civil war. Then, the Nationalists launched an attack on the Communists in their interior strongholds; fighting began to spread over various regions in China.

End of a Mission: Birth of a Nation

The Marshall Mission

At this critical juncture, the United States had four possible options in its China policy:

First, the United States could deactivate Wedemeyer's command, cease Lend-Lease, and withdraw its marines and other military support units. In the face of the rising power and confidence of the Communists, however, such a total hands-off policy would be certain to allow the entire American hope and effort for a unified, friendly, and democratic China to collapse in disaster. Such a course of action was thought to be unrealistic and unacceptable by both the United States and the Nationalist Chinese.

Second, the United States could make an all-out commitment, politically and militarily, with a view to helping achieve a unified China under the Nationalists. Such a total involvement policy would undoubtedly require the enlargement of the American troop commitment, run the risk of military confrontation with the Soviet Union, and face the likelihood of direct entanglement in the Chinese civil war. Having endured so much sacrifice in WW II, which had just ended, the war-weary American public would not tolerate their leaders dragging their country into yet another massive land war in Asia. It would be unwise, undesirable, and tragic.

Third, the United States could write off the Nationalists and instead render moral and material support to the Communists in the revolutionary efforts to reform and reconstruct a new China. But in view of the new world alignment, in which Communists had loomed as the deadly new enemy, such a turnabout was believed to be self-defeating and self-destructive; to abandon the legitimate government for the Communists would mean political betrayal and immorality, which would have amounted to a treasonable act at home.

Fourth, and finally, the United States could continue to support the Nationalist government within the framework that the latter would strive to carry out a reform within itself and to reach a settlement with the Communists, and it would not employ American arms and aid to conduct a civil war.

The United States chose the fourth course of action, on the basis of which the Marshall mission was undertaken. At the request of President Truman, in December 1945 General George C. Marshall, who had just retired as Chief of Staff, flew to China as the president's personal envoy to carry out a specific mission: to bring about an immediate cessation of hostilities and a unification of the country on democratic principles. Continued American aid was conditioned on the cooperation of the Nationalists in achieving these ends.

At the same time, President Truman declared his governmental policy on China, which also constituted a part of the guidelines for General Marshall. The president prefaced that world peace and prosperity depended on the stability of all nations to work for collective security within the framework of the United Nations, and reiterated that a "strong, unified and democratic China is of the utmost importance to the success of this United Nations organization and for world peace." He went on to state:

A China disorganized and divided either by foreign aggression, such as that undertaken by the Japanese, or by violent internal strife, is an undermining influence to world stability and peace, now and in the future. The United States Government has long subscribed to the principle that the management of internal affairs is the responsibility of the peoples of the sovereign nations. Events of this century, however, would indicate that a breach of peace anywhere in the world threatens the peace of the entire world. It is thus in the most vital interest of the United States and all the United Nations that the People of China overlook no opportunity to adjust their internal differences promptly by means of peaceful negotiations.[12]

The presidential statement set forth two essential objectives to be effected immediately: (1) a cessation of hostilities between the Nationalists and the Communists so as to complete the return of all China to effective Chinese control, and (2) a creation of a national conference of representatives of major political elements so as to end the internal strife and to bring about the unification of China.

Marshall's active mediation resulted in an apparent, quick success. On January 10, 1946, he was able to arrange for the ceasefire between the two warring parties. It provided for the cessation of hostilities and all troop movements, for the prohibition of destruction of all lines of communication, and for the establishment of an executive headquarters at Peking to carry out the truce terms. The truce, however, provided for the movement of Nationalist troops into and within Manchuria in order to restore Chinese sovereignty there. Marshall welcomed this stipulation because he wanted to see Manchuria firmly restored to the sovereign jurisdiction of a unified, democratic China friendly to the United States. Manchuria was, in American diplomatic history, the land which had given birth to the Knox neutralization proposal, the Bryan notes, internationalization of the Open Door, and the Stimson Doctrine. Manchuria had been the land pregnant with international rivalries. It was no exception in early 1946. Soviet Defense Minister Rodion Malinovsky declared: "It is hoped that the question of economic cooperation in Manchuria can be quickly settled. Soviet Russia does not wish to have any third party come in. She is particularly opposed to Manchuria being turned into an anti-Soviet base." The Soviet Union sought economic cooperation with the Chiang government through the establishment of joint Sino-Soviet commercial enterprises in Manchuria. The United States protested such undertakings in a note to Moscow and Chungking on February 9, 1946, invoking the old Open Door policy and warning against any exclusive Sino-Soviet monopolistic enterprises which might preclude American commercial interests. But only a year earlier at Yalta had the United States committed to endorse such Sino-Soviet joint undertakings in Manchuria. The note of February 9, therefore, incompatible as it was with the Yalta terms, sufficiently demonstrated that the United States desired to keep Manchuria from falling into the hands of the Soviets. General Marshall was inescapably bound to conduct mediation and negotiations within the framework of these considerations and contradictions.[13]

Marshall's added success came on February 25, 1946, when an agreement on military reorganization and the integration of the Communist forces into the National army was reached. The terms of the agreement envisaged the reduction, in an eighteen-month period, of the Nationalist armies to fifty divisions and the Communist forces to ten divisions, the total of sixty divisions of not more than fourteen thousand men each to be formed into twenty armies. For the purpose of integration and deployment, China was divided into five general military areas and a specific number of both armies was provided for each area. During the negotiations leading to this agreement, Marshall had emphasized the necessity of creating in China a national, nonpolitical armed forces as a democratic army and not as authoritarian weapons. The same day in Washington, President Truman announced the establishment of a United States military mission in China consisting of a thousand officers and men under General Wedemeyer. It was understood that the Communist forces would receive American training and American supplies before their integration into the Nationalist armies.

Although the cease-fire agreement had the obvious effect of preventing, for a time, a full-scale civil war, there ensued a number of infractions of the terms committed by both sides. The Nationalist commander at Canton, for instance, refused to recognize the authority of the executive headquarters in his area of command, and the Nationalist supreme headquarters in Nanking failed to report all Nationalist troop movements to the executive headquarters in Peking. The Communists, on their part, continued to strengthen their forces in Manchuria through troop reinforcement and the acquisition of weapons and supplies surrendered by the Japanese and made available to them by the Soviet army. They also carried out a most effective political infiltration. Through it all the Nationalist government hardened its position and seemed determined to pursue its freedom of action and to execute a policy of complete military occupation of Manchuria by exterminating the Chinese Communist forces even though its military capability of achieving these goals was doubtful.

On March 11, 1946, General Marshall left China for Washington for consultation. It was during his absence from China that the nexus of the precarious truce began to give way. The Communists, as determined as the Nationalists, steadily extended the area of their control. They were moving both into areas from which Soviet troops were withdrawing and into the zones where there had been no occupation forces. Soviet troop withdrawal from Manchuria had been scheduled to be completed by December 3, 1945, but it was postponed because the presence of "non-governmental troops made it difficult to introduce Chinese [government] troops and administration into Manchuria." After months of delay, the Soviets began their troop evacuation in April 1946.

The Chinese Communist forces commenced the attack on the city of Changchun in the heart of Manchuria on April 15, 1946, the day after the withdrawal of Soviet troops, and seized it on April 18. On that day, General Marshall returned to China and resumed his mediation. Chiang now insisted repeatedly that any settlement must be conditioned on the Communist evacuation of Changchun and Nationalist occupation thereof, and on the complete restoration of Nationalist sovereignty in Manchuria. In an effort to persuade Chiang to seek a compromise, Marshall pointed out the fact that:

> The Government's military position was weak in Manchuria and the Communists had the strategic advantage there. The psychological effect of a compromise on the part of the Government to achieve peace would not injure its prestige but would indicate that the Generalissimo was making every effort to promote peace. The proposal to utilize the Executive Headquarters in Changchun would bolster the conviction that the Generalissimo was striving for peace. Finally some compromise must be reached as quickly as possible or China would be faced with a chaotic situation, militarily, financially, and economically.[14]

The same line of reasoning was presented to Chou En-lai. In response, Chou expressed his doubt as to Chiang's sincerity and demanded the right to station five Chinese Communist army divisions in Manchuria instead of one as authorized in the military reorganization agreement reached earlier.

In May, General Marshall presented to Chou En-lai a proposal calling for the evacuation of Communist troops from Changchun, admission of the advance section of the executive headquarters into the city, and the cessation of further advances of government forces. The Communists accepted the proposal and withdrew from Changchun, and the Nationalist army entered the city without difficulty. Then the Nationalist forces continued to advance toward Harbin to the northeast and toward Kirin to the east. Consequently, Communist suspicion and distrust of Nationalist promises became intensified and Marshall's position as an impartial mediator became suspect insofar as the Communists were concerned. Thereupon, Marshall sent to Chiang a message urging him to desist military offensive and to send an advance section of the executive headquarters to Changchun; otherwise the integrity of his position would be untenable as a fair, impartial, and objective mediator. Chiang indicated that he would comply with the proposal.

On June 6, 1946, Marshall's tireless mediation brought about another cease-fire agreement for a fifteen-day period, in which time the two parties conducted more negotiations that were marked by tardiness and bitterness. As the Nationalists made sweeping demands which were totally unacceptable to the Communists, another impasse developed, and at the suggestion of General Marshall, the time period was extended to June 30. The extension, however, had little consequence in reaching any important agreement, although in July both parties issued orders to their respective forces to refrain from taking aggressive action. For a moment a de facto truce appeared to take effect but, on the contrary, intensified hostilities began to flare up across the country. A week later the Chinese Communists issued a manifesto bitterly attacking the American China policy and protesting against what they termed American military and financial aid to Chiang Kai-shek, encouraging him to pursue the civil war policy.

In mid-July, the first significant incident took place between the United States marines and the Chinese Communists. The latter kidnapped seven American marines and held them for several days before their release. This incident was followed at the end of the month by a more serious clash in which the Communists ambushed a U.S. marine-escorted motor convoy bound from Tientsin to Peking, causing American casualties of three killed and twelve wounded.

Meanwhile, President Truman appointed Dr. J. Leighton Stuart as American ambassador to China at the recommendation of General Marshall, who had become convinced "of the desirability of obtaining the assistance in the mediation effort of an American of unquestioned character and integrity and with long experience in

China." Ambassador Stuart, former president of Yencheng University in Peking, was then given the principal responsibility in mediating political issues involving specifically the implementation of the Political Consultative Conference (PCC) resolutions. The PCC, composed of representatives of the Kuomintang, the Communist party, the Democratic League, and nonparty delegates, had earlier passed many resolutions concerning such questions as those of governmental organization, national construction, military issues, the National Assembly, and the draft constitution.

Through the latter half of July, Marshall and Stuart held frequent conferences with the leaders of both parties in an effort to help create the state council and to put an end to their hostilities, to little avail. At this juncture, President Truman, on August 10, 1946, sent to Chiang Kai-shek a personal message stating in part:

> The rapidly deteriorating political situation in China, during recent months, has been a cause of grave concern to the American people. While it is a continued hope of the United States that an influential and democratic China can still be achieved under your leadership, I would be less than honest if I did not point out that the latest developments have forced me to the conclusion that the selfish interests of extremist elements, both in the Kuomintang and the Communist Party, are obstructing the aspirations of the people of China. . . . It will be necessary for me to redefine and explain the position of the United States to the people of America.[15]

In response, Chiang placed the blame for the worsening situation on the Communists, who, he claimed, were determined to seize political power through the use of armed forces, to overthrow the government, and to install a totalitarian regime. He minimized the blame on his part by stating that mistakes had also been made by some subordinates on the government side, of course, but compared to the flagrant violations on the part of the Communists, they were minor in scale.

The general tone of Chiang's reply was taken favorably by Washington and on August 30, 1946, it signed an agreement with the Chiang government for the sale to China of American surplus property in the Pacific regions. This agreement together with United States military aid programs placed Marshall and Stuart in the untenable position of impartially mediating, on the one hand, between the two Chinese antagonists while, on the other, the United States was continuing to supply arms and ammunition to one of the two parties, namely, the Nationalists. Certain portions of these programs, therefore, had to be suspended temporarily. The suspension, however, had little effect on curbing the Nationalist military campaign which had reached in November what turned out to be its highest point, occupying most of the areas covered by its demands to the Communists in June and during later negotiations.

As expected, the Communists charged United States aid to the Chiang government as contributory to civil war, and demanded that the United States freeze all supplies and shipping to China pending the establishment of a Nationalist-Communist coalition government and the restoration of peace in China. At the same time, during negotiations, the Communists insisted upon two points: the assurance of fourteen seats in the state council and the early issuance of a cease-fire order by the Nationalists. Chiang Kai-shek was equally adamant in insisting that the Communists should have thirteen seats[16] in the state council and that he had no reason to issue a cease-fire order because the Communists had provoked the fighting. Since it became abundantly clear that the positions of the two parties were hopelessly irreconcilable, General Marshall, on October 1, sent to Chiang Kai-shek a memorandum stating in part:

> I wish merely to state that unless a basis for agreement is found to terminate the fighting without further delays of proposals and counterproposals, I will recommend to the President that I be recalled and that the United States Government terminate its efforts of mediation.[17]

General Marshall was convinced that Chiang was following a definite policy of force under the cover of the protracted negotiations. Although Chiang expressed his apparent concern by stating that Marshall's departure from China was "unthinkable," he failed to promise to halt the Nationalist offensive toward Kalgan. Chiang had previously agreed in June that the Communists would be permitted to retain possession of this city of Kalgan, which they had occupied shortly after V-J Day.

On October 10, the Nationalist forces captured Kalgan and Chihfeng. On the same day, the Chiang government announced the resumption of nationwide conscription and the following day Chiang proclaimed the convening of the National Assembly on November 12, 1946. The latter announcement was regarded by the Communists and other minority parties as evidence of unilateral and dictatorial action on the part of the Nationalist group, violating an earlier agreement reached in August that the date for convening the Assembly would be decided by discussion among all parties.

The National Assembly was formally convened on November 15, with an unquestionably limited representation from non-KMT groups; the Communist party and the Democratic League were not represented. The next day Chou En-lai issued a statement accusing the Nationalists of violating PCC resolutions, and added:

This unilateral National Assembly is now afoot to adopt a so-called 'constitution,' in order to 'legalize' dictatorship. . . . We, Chinese Communists, therefore, adamantly refuse to recognize this National Assembly. The door of negotiation has now been slammed by the single hand of the Kuomintang authorities. All the shows that are going to be staged during the National Assembly, even the reorganization of the Government, are not worthy of our slightest attention.[18]

Chou En-lai left Nanking for Yenan on November 19 in a United States Army plane provided by General Marshall. Chou's departure brought to an end the long period of mediations, negotiations, and discussions begun in January 1946. Marshall's attention was now centered chiefly on the National Assembly and the type of constitution it might produce. The assembly adjourned on December 25 after having adopted a constitution of a democratic nature, on its face reasonably in line with the PCC resolutions; but

Marshall's apprehension remained as to the degree and manner in which it was to be implemented.

By this time Marshall's usefulness as a mediator had virtually ceased. On January 6, 1947, President Truman directed him to return to Washington to report in person on the situation in China. In a public pronouncement on his mission, General Marshall stated that the greatest obstacle to peace in China was the complete, almost overwhelming distrust and suspicion with which the Nationalists and the Communists regarded each other. The primary causes for the breakdown of negotiations were, he believed, the opposition of the dominant group of Kuomintang reactionaries to a coalition government on the one hand, and the efforts of the extreme Communists to wreck the national economy in order to hasten the overthrow or collapse of the Chiang government on the other. "The salvation of the situation," Marshall suggested, "would be the assumption of leadership by the liberals in the Government and in the minority parties and successful action on their part under the leadership of the Generalissimo would lead to unity through good government."

General Marshall became the secretary of state, and a decision was reached not to make any further attempt, by sending a special envoy, to seek a solution of this Chinese Gordian Knot.

The People's Republic of China

Shortly after Secretary of State Marshall assumed the office, the decision was made to withdraw American personnel from the executive headquarters at Peking. This move allowed the withdrawal of all United States marines from North China, except for a guard contingent at Tsingtao, where American naval officers were engaged in training Chinese naval personnel. The state of affairs in North China had thus returned to that prior to the surrender of the Japanese—the Communists had been fighting the Japanese then; they were fighting the Nationalist troops now.

The Communists took the initiative in both North China and Manchuria in the manner which Mao Tse-tung had prescribed: "Enemy advances, we retreat; enemy halts, we harass; enemy tires, we attack; enemy retreats, we pursue." These kind of guerrilla tactics sufficiently fatigued the Nationalist armies who were ill-prepared to counter them with large-scale organized attacks. The Nationalist troops, equipped with relatively heavy arms for conventional warfare, placed high priority on major cities and communication centers which were of vital importance to them, whereas the Communist guerrillas, equipped with light arms for rapid mobility and concealment, operated with ease in small villages and rural towns which were of great value to them.

In the early stage of the civil war, however, the Nationalists, enjoying more than a three-to-one military superiority, won many battles. By the time of Marshall's recall, they had wrested many towns and much territory from Communist control. The zenith of the Nationalists' military glory came in March 1947, when government troops attacked and captured the Communist capital of Yenan. The seizure of Yenan, which had been already largely evacuated, had psychological and propaganda value, but from a long-range military standpoint it was costly, insignificant, serving only to overextend government supply lines. The Communists had followed their long-developed tactics—*enemy advances, we retreat*—drawing their enemies into a pocket, and thereafter they began to destroy the Nationalists with guerrilla strategies. Yet, the Nationalists, at the apparent peak of their triumph, could claim that the Communists would be defeated in six months. Chiang Kai-shek confidently told Ambassador Stuart that by the end of August or September the Communist forces would either be exterminated or driven into the remote hinterland.

Within months, however, in May and June, symptoms of the growing popular discontent erupted, spearheaded by student demonstrations and violence, demanding an end to the civil war. A government edict banning student demonstrations was immediately disobeyed in major cities at the loss of government prestige. In contrast, as general discontent and disillusionment spread, Communist prestige became enhanced largely through their reputed rectitude and increased military success in North China and Manchuria.

The anti-civil war sentiment was not limited to students, business groups, or peasants, but it equally affected Chiang's troops. They did not understand what the civil war was all about; they could see some point in endless fighting when the enemy was the Japanese, but they saw little sense in fighting when the enemy was their fellow Chinese. By the summer of 1947 government troops were demoralized; there was dissension among officers in the high command, disunity and unrest among men, and friction between troops and local populace. Apathy, defeatism, and resentment were spreading like the plague among the Nationalist troops, who chose either to surrender or to desert.

On July 9, 1947, President Truman, on Secretary Marshall's recommendation, instructed General Albert C. Wedemeyer to "proceed to China without delay for the purpose of making an appraisal of the political, economic, psychological and military situations—current and projected." After a two-month fact-finding mission, General Wedemeyer submitted a lengthy report, a part of which read:

> The Communists have the tactical initiative in the overall military situation. The Nationalist position in Manchuria is precarious, and in Shantung and Hopei Provinces strongly disputed. Continued deterioration of the situation may result in the early establishment of a Soviet satellite government in Manchuria and ultimately in the evolution of Communist-dominated China.
>
> China is suffering increasingly from disintegration. Her requirements for rehabilitation are large. Her most urgent needs include governmental reorganization and reform, reduction of military budget and external assistance.

He then recommended that

> The United States Government provide as early as practicable moral, advisory, and material support to China in order to ... protect United States strategic interests against military forces which now threaten them.... It is recognized that any foreign assistance extended must avoid jeopardizing the American economy.[19]

By mid-summer the Communists had commenced a southward

movement across the Lunghai and toward the Yangtze. Taking advantage of the fact that the Nationalist forces were committed to positional warfare, were overextended, and for reasons of prestige would not withdraw or consolidate, the Communists had concentrated by late 1947 a formidable force in central China for an eventual showdown. They also controlled the rail lines from north China to Manchuria, occupied portions of the Tsinan-Tsingtao Railroad in Shantung, and, as the year closed, the South Manchuria Railroad near Mukden. The Communist control of these lines of communication and transportation meant that it was nearly impossible for the Nationalist forces, which had not succeeded in developing local resources, to procure reinforcements and to maintain logistics by rail, and as a result, all the major Nationalist garrisons in Manchuria became isolated and compartmented.

As the year 1948 rolled in, the Communists kept their offensive going, and in mid-April they reoccupied Yenan by destroying or capturing the Nationalist units which had originally taken Yenan. In fact, the Communists met little resistance in this operation, during which many Nationalist troops defected to the Communists. The problem of defection was only a part of the Nationalist woes which were compounded by inferior leadership, poor strategy, and low morale. The following observations would sufficiently illustrate the case in point:

> The Nationalists' commander, in order to preserve his forces intact, withdrew them from the main areas of conflict into the east city. In a subsequent attempt to evacuate the forces, he was caught and his troops were destroyed.
>
> The Nationalists, however, clung to their defensive strategy, making possible a major Communist victory in Shantung at Tsinan, where 85,000 to 100,000 Government troops took refuge behind the strong natural and constructed fortifications of the city.... After a brief period of fighting, marked by the defection of units of the Nationalist 84th Division, the Communists took the city.... With this victory they acquired an estimated 50,000 rifles and considerable stocks of ammunition.

Nationalist soldiers and [the] population [of] Shantung in general no longer consider the Nationalist Government merits continued support in civil war, loss of lives and economic chaos. These factors expressed themselves in outright defection to the Communists, immediate surrender, and failure to stand and fight.[20]

Meanwhile, the United States government followed a policy of *limited assistance* to the Chiang regime. In October 1947, a sum of $27.7 million was earmarked for a China program. In December, an additional sum of $18 million was expended for food and medical supplies in China's coastal cities. The United States government was drifitng away from its earlier position to encourage and accept Communist participation in a coalition government of China. In March 1948, in a press conference, President Truman stated that "we did not want any Communists in the Government of China or anywhere else if we could help it." The following month, the China Aid Act of 1948 was passed by Congress, providing for a $400 million aid program for the Nationalist government. This program was designed to give the Chiang regime "a breathing spell to initiate those vital steps necessary to provide the framework" for economic recovery and for its survival. But the aid was too little and too late. The Nationalists were in shambles, and United States disappointment in them had proportionally hardened its attitude toward the Communists. In August, Secretary of State Marshall sent policy directives to Ambassador Stuart, emphasizing the following two points:

1. The United States Government must not directly or indirectly give any implication of support, encouragement or acceptability of a coalition government in China with Communist participation.
2. The United States Government has no intention of again offering its good offices as mediator in China.[21]

At this time the most frequently raised question was whether or not the Truman Doctrine should be applied to China in the way Greece and Turkey were receiving United States military aid and advisory assistance. In view, however, of the enormity of China's needs and the incalculable risk involved, supporters for America's direct military involvement in China lost out. It was argued that direct armed intervention in the internal affairs of China would run counter to traditional American policy toward China and would be contrary to the clearly expressed intent of Congress not to have United States combat troops fighting in China's civil war.

In late October Manchuria was lost to the Nationalists. At the beginning of 1949 there was practically nothing to sustain the crumbling Nationalist forces. The hopeless situation prompted Chiang Kai-shek, in his New Year's message to the nation, to propose what appeared to be peace overtures. "If the Communists are," said Chiang, "sincerely desirous of peace, and clearly give such indication, the Government will be only too glad to discuss with them the means to end the war." A week later the Chinese foreign minister requested the United States, Great Britain, France, and the Soviet Union to mediate on China's behalf Nationalist-Communist negotiations toward peace. The United States replied to the Chiang request in an *aide-mémoire*: "It is not believed that any useful purpose would be served by the United States Government's attempting . . . to act as an intermediary in the present situation." And when the Communists responded with what amounted to a demand of unconditional surrender, including the trial of Chiang as a war criminal, Chiang retired on January 21 to his birthplace, Fenghua, and turned over the government to his vice-president, Li Tsung-jen.

Meanwhile, Tientsin fell on January 18, 1949, and Peking on February 3. On April 20, the Communists crossed the Yangtze, seized Nanking four days later, captured Hankow on May 16, occupied Shanghai on May 25, took Tsintao on June 2, and reached Chungking on November 30.

Flushed with successive military victories, Mao Tse-tung and his comrades began the task of building a new China on the foundation of the "New Democracy." Mao Tse-tung had written in 1940:

Under all circumstances, the proletariat, the peasantry, the intelligentsia and other sections of the petty bourgeoisie in

China are the basic forces determining her fate. These classes, some already awakened and others on the point of awakening, will necessarily become the basic component parts of the state structure and of the structure of political power of the democratic republic of China with the proletariat as the leading force. The democratic republic of China which we now want to establish can only be a democratic republic under the joint dictatorship of all anti-imperialist and anti-feudal people led by the proletariat, that is, a new democratic republic.[22]

In June 1949, Mao declared that only through a people's representative government could China "free herself from a semicolonial and semifeudal fate and take the road of independence, freedom, peace, unity, strength, and prosperity," and in July he stated: "We must have the people's democratic dictatorship led by the working class [through the Communist party] and based upon the alliance of workers and peasants." The Communist party then formed its own Chinese People's Political Consultative Conference (CPPCC), replacing the previous PCC at Nanking. The CPPCC convened in September 1949 and approved the draft Organic Law of the CPPCC and of the Central People's Government.

On the basis of these laws, on October 1, 1949 the establishment of the People's Republic of China together with its executive agency—the Central People's Government—was formally proclaimed in Peking. Mao Tse-tung became the head of the new regime and Chou En-lai its prime minister. Mao's People's Liberation Army carried out the mop-up operation to eliminate pocket resistances of the Nationalists, and on December 8, Chiang Kai-shek, returning from his temporary retirement, retreated to Formosa (Taiwan) with what was left of his government and his armies that had survived the Communist onslaught.

The Soviet Union immediately extended *de jure* recognition to the People's Republic of China and most of the Communist states followed Soviet suit. The Soviet formal recognition of the Central People's Government in Peking meant *ipso facto* the termination of all relations with the Chinese Nationalists, and consequently the

Sino-Soviet treaty of August 1945,[23] which had been concluded in conformity with the Roosevelt-Stalin understanding at Yalta, was abrogated.

Burma became the first non-Communist country officially recognizing the new regime at Peking. By the end of January 1950, other non-Communist countries which had established formal diplomatic relations with the People's Republic of China were: India, Pakistan, Great Britain (January 6), Ceylon, Norway, Denmark, Israel, Finland, Afghanistan, Sweden, and Switzerland.

The United States' official position regarding the question of recognition of the Peking government had been made clear on October 12, 1949, by Secretary of State Dean Acheson, who had listed three conditions: (1) the new regime in Peking must exercise effective control in the country, (2) it must recognize its international obligations, and (3) it must govern with the consent of the people. The secretary expressed his grave doubt as to the second condition, and when in January the Chinese Communist authorities seized American, French, and Dutch compounds in Peking on the grounds that they were military barracks, his doubt appeared to be confirmed; United States recognition moved a step further away.

The People's Republic of China, on its part, was determined to resume its station among the great powers. On January 8, 1950, Premier Chou En-lai sent a telegram to the United Nations Security Council demanding removal of the Nationalist delegation. A few days later, when a Soviet resolution to this effect was introduced to the Council, it was rejected. The Nationalist Chinese delegate, on the other hand, told a Security Council committee that he would veto any resolution designed to recognize the right of the Communist regime to represent China in the world organization. Whereupon, the committee decided that the General Assembly would have to solve the problem of Chinese representation. In March the People's Republic of China heard a friendly and influential voice in the United Nations. UN Secretary General Trygve Lie implied in a memorandum to all the delegations that the People's Republic of China should be permitted to take China's seat at the United Nations, whose policy, he said, should be to exercise "effective authority" in a country which was "habitually obeyed by the bulk of its population."

In the meantime, Mao's personal diplomacy and his nine-week negotiations in Moscow with the Soviet leaders resulted in a series of agreements. On February 14, they signed a treaty of friendship, alliance, and mutual assistance; an agreement on the Changchun Railway, Port Arthur, and Dairen; and an agreement by which the Soviet Union was to extend long-term credits to China. The Sino-Soviet thirty-year military alliance treaty stipulated:

> In the event of one of the High Contracting Parties being attacked by Japan or states allied with it, and thus being involved in a state of war, the other High Contracting Party will immediately render military and other assistance with all the means at its disposal.

This provision subsequently attracted the considerable attention of the American policymakers as they had to decide on the question of military countermeasures against Chinese Communist intervention in the Korean War.

CHAPTER NINE

Loser's Bliss or Burden

U.S. Occupation of Japan

Democratization Policy

The defeat and surrender in World War II left Japan prostrated and exhausted. National morale sank to the lowest level, economic life was crippled, urban centers were reduced to rubble by Allied bombing, industrial production reached a standstill, and the once sprawling empire was stripped to four home islands. Territorially, Japan became the same island country which Commodore Perry had found nearly a century earlier. In spite of, perhaps because of, all these eventualities the Japanese were ready to accept the victor's military occupation with an amazing tractability and stoic flexibility.

The guidance for the occupation was set forth in the United States Initial Post-Surrender Policy for Japan. This policy document, formulated by joint effort and cooperation among the State, War, and Navy Departments, determined its ultimate objectives to be: (1) to ensure that Japan would never again become a menace to the United States or to the peace and security of the world, and (2) to help establish a peaceful, responsible, and democratic self-government based on the freely expressed will of

221

the people. The principal means to achieve these objectives were: the limitation of Japan's sovereignty to the four home islands, complete disarmament and demilitarization, inculcation of individual liberties and respect for fundamental human rights, and the development of a peacetime economy.

Technically, the military occupation of Japan was an Allied affair. In December 1945, in Moscow, the foreign ministers of the United States, Great Britain, and the Soviet Union, with the concurrence of China, agreed to establish the Far Eastern Commission and the Allied Council as control machinery for Japan. The primary responsibility of the thirteen-nation Far Eastern Commission with its seat in Washington, was the formulation of policies for occupied Japan. The commission, supreme policymaking body in theory, could review directives of General Douglas MacArthur, the Supreme Commander for the Allied Powers (SCAP), and his action on policy matters. Yet it could not direct any military matters or discuss any peace treaty problem such as territorial settlements. The commission recognized the exclusive right of the United States government to communicate officially with SCAP.

The Allied council for Japan, located in Tokyo, consisting of the representatives of the United States, the British Commonwealth, the Soviet Union, and China, was not a control body and had no authority over the execution of policy by SCAP. The council was an advisory organ with which SCAP could consult when he so desired. As he seldom did so, it simply turned into a forum with little influence over him. SCAP, therefore, was the sole authority in Japan for executing the policies as well as general and specific operations of the occupation, which more and more came to be a reflection of United States policy.

As the occupation began, SCAP's immediate task was to disarm and demobilize the Japanese forces at home and to repatriate Japanese troops and residents abroad. Simultaneously the occupation authorities undertook to implement the basic policy of democratization of Japan by way of eliminating all institutions which were the sources as well as the consequences of militarism and aggression. On October 14, 1945, SCAP issued a directive ordering the release of political prisoners and the removal of restrictions on political, civil, and religious liberties. This directive also brought about a drastic shake-up in Japan's police organization which had exercised authoritarian and arbitrary power for a long time.

Believing, moreover, that one of the essentials to better safeguard individual rights and liberties was democratic constitution, SCAP authorities decided to have the old Meiji constitution revised or, if necessary, to institute a new one. At first SCAP instructed the Japanese government to revise the existing constitution under the general supervision and guidance of the occupation authorities. On February 1, 1946, the Shidehara cabinet submitted the official draft to SCAP, who found it inadequate to meet the fundamental requirements for a democratic state. Thereupon, the government section of SCAP undertook to draft a new constitution incorporating such principles as popular sovereignty, responsible government, consent of the governed, separation of powers, guarantee of civil liberties, and outlawry of war. On March 6, 1946, the new constitution was published. On this occasion General MacArthur declared in a statement:

> It is with a sense of deep satisfaction that I am able today to announce a decision of the Emperor and the Government of Japan to submit to the Japanese people a new and enlightened Constitution which has my full approval. This instrument has been drafted after painstaking investigation and frequent conference between members of the Japanese Government and this headquarters following my direction.[1]

The new constitution, formally promulgated on November 3, 1946, became effective May 3, 1947. One of the most significant changes in the new constitution was the determination of the new identity and role of the emperor, as stipulated in Article 1: "The Emperor shall be the symbol of the State and of the unity of the people, deriving his position from the will of the people with whom resides sovereign power." This was a radical change in contrast with the old Meiji constitution which had declared: "The Empire of Japan shall be reigned over and governed by a line of Emperors unbroken for ages eternal." Thus, the people of Japan, not the emperor, came to exercise the sovereign power of the state. Furthermore, in theory at least if not in reality, if the people should desire to abolish the Imperial system, they would have the power to do so. Again, this was a drastic departure from the old constitutional provision: "The Emperor shall be sacred and inviolable." It came as little surprise because the myth of divinity in the person of the emperor had been renounced, on SCAP's urging, by Emperor Hirohito in his 1946 New Year's rescript as he had referred to "the false conception that the Emperor is divine."

The unique and prominent feature of the new constitution could be found in Article 9 on the renunciation of war:

> Aspiring sincerely to an international peace based on justice and order, the Japanese people forever renounce war as a sovereign right of the nation and the threat or use of force as means of settling international disputes.
>
> In order to accomplish the aim of the preceding paragraph, land, sea, and air forces, as well as other war potential, will never be maintained. The right of belligerency of the state will not be recognized.

It was the first such attempt for any sovereign state not to maintain armed forces and to proclaim in its domestic constitution the renunciation of war as national policy.[2] In view, however, of subsequent developments in internal and international scenes, Article 9 came to be interpreted as having not repudiated Japan's sovereign right of unilateral or collective self-defense.

In other articles of the new constitution, the peerage was abolished, and the Diet was made "the highest organ of state power," to which the cabinet became collectively responsible. The members of the bicameral Diet (House of Councillors and House of Representatives) were to be elected directly by the people. The franchise was extended to all men and women of twenty years of age and over. The judiciary was made independent and the Supreme Court, with a provision for popular review of its membership, was made "the court of last resort with power to determine the constitutionality of any law, order, regulation or official act." Also included in the new constitution were the basic rights and liberties of the people, such as those found in the American Bill of Rights, plus academic freedom, equal rights of husband and wife, right to maintain minimum standards of wholesome and cultural living, right to an education, right to work, right of collective bargaining, and right to own property. In addition, it provided for the guarantee of due process and equal protection of the law.

Changes were invariably introduced on a local level in an effort to enhance the autonomy of local government on democratic principles. The prefectural governors, unlike the old practice of being appointed by the central government, were to be elected by the prefectural voters and made responsible to the prefectural assemblies. Mayors were, likewise, to be elected directly by the constituents. Moreover, the principles and procedures of recall, initiative, and referendum were instituted at the prefectural and municipal levels.

Demilitarization Policy

The democratization policy carried with it the elimination of a key undemocratic feature—Japanese militarism. The demilitarization of Japan, therefore, was believed to be essential to the prevention of a resurgence of militarism in Japan and to the future peace and security of Asia and the Pacific.

The implementation of the demilitarization programs covered many fields and took various forms: total disarmament of the Japanese armed forces, destruction of military installations and equipment, the abolition of the War and Navy departments, the elimination of the Imperial supreme headquarters including the general staff organization, the dissolution and prohibition of paramilitary organizations, and the inauguration of trials for war criminals.

As a partial fulfillment of the Potsdam Declaration, the war crimes trials were designed to discourage a revival of Japanese militarism and aggression and to punish those leaders who were responsible for "crimes against peace and humanity." For this purpose, in January 1946 SCAP issued a special proclamation for the creation of the International Military Tribunal for the Far East. The tribunal, made up of eleven judges, began its deliberations in May. Twenty-eight major war criminals were arrested, indicted, and tried for "the planning, preparation, or waging" of aggressive war. Among them were former prime ministers, militarists, and ultranationalists. The emperor himself was not included in the list of war criminals in spite of Soviet insistence. General MacArthur later wrote: "I believe that if the Emperor were indicted and perhaps hanged as a war criminal, military government would have to be instituted throughout all Japan, and guerrilla warfare would probably break out."[3] The prosecution's presentation of the case took nine months and the sentences were finally handed down in November 1946. All defendants were found guilty as charged. The punishment pronounced to each individual criminal ranged from the death penalty by hanging to imprisonment for several years.[4]

What impact did the war crimes trials have on the people of Japan? The efficacy of having achieved the professed objectives of discouraging a revival of Japanese militarism by such trials remained questionable. After the defeat and surrender, the Japanese as the vanquished were prepared to accept any dictates of the victors, including the punishment of their wartime leaders. The crimes of their leaders, they believed, consisted not so much in losing the war or in violating the rules of war as in having waged an unwinable war in the first place and in misleading the people through the years. To the Japanese the guilty verdict for the accused was a foregone conclusion because they assumed that justice was at the victor's disposal. The long, tedious trial procedures, sifting through complex legal technicalities of "due process" and "the right of the accused" were little understood or appreciated by the Japanese. In brief, they regarded the trials as the process of legalizing Allied vengeance rather than meting out justice in the truest sense. Had they won the war, they would have had war crimes trials for Allied leaders.

Economic Reform

A successful implementation of democratization and demilitarization of Japan was deemed unobtainable without a comparable reform in the economic foundations of the country. For this reason the initial policy statement declared that "the existing economic basis of Japanese military strength must be destroyed and not be permitted to revive."

Specifically, SCAP intended to eliminate munitions plants and the aircraft industry and to reduce or reshape such key industries as steel production and shipbuilding. Japan was permitted to restore her economic level which would be "reasonable and peaceful" enough "to meet the needs of the occupying forces to the extent that this can be effected without causing starvation, widespread disease and acute physical distress." But the wrecked state of the post-surrender Japanese economy did not necessitate the immediate execution of such policies. Physically and economically, Japan was in ruins. There were not many munitions plants left to be dismantled, or aircraft factories to be destroyed, or steel mills to be shut down, or shipyards to be closed. Over 40 percent of the nation's urban areas had been destroyed. Industrial production sank to a level of less than one-third of that of 1930 and one-seventh of the total in 1937. The acute food shortage was about to cause mass starvation.

Under these circumstances SCAP's initial economic reform was inescapably centered on conceptual, structural, and organizational aspects of the Japanese economic system. For example, the reform policy to promote "democratic forces" stated:

> Encouragement shall be given and favor shown to the development of organizations in labor, industry, and agriculture, organized on a democratic basis. Policies shall be favored which permit a wide distribution of income and of the means of production and trade.[5]

One of the means to achieve this end was "to favor a program for the dissolution of the large industrial and banking combinations which have exercised control of a great part of Japan's trade and industry."

There were a number of reasons for favoring the dissolution of those gigantic family combines, known as the *zaibatsu*.[6] Through the history of Japan's modernization, industrialization, and expansion in the period from the Meiji Restoration to the end of World War II, the *zaibatsu* represented economic imperialism, while the militarists stood for territorial conquests. The *zaibatsu* and the military were occasional rivals in their respective strategies and tactics but they were united in their ultimate national objectives—

Japan's hegemony in Asia. In light of this fact, the *zaibatsu* could not escape from war responsibility and aggression. Furthermore, the continued concentration of economic, industrial, and financial power in the hands of minority oligarchs was essentially a totalitarian feature contrary to the economic goals of democratization. In fact, an official United States report had described the *zaibatsu* as the greatest war potential of Japan; i.e., the *zaibatsu* had made all of Japan's conquest and aggression possible.

As the SCAP authorities began to undertake the task of dissolving the *zaibatsu*, they were immediately confronted with a number of practical, circumstantial, and inherent difficulties. One of them was to find qualified buyers of the *zaibatsu* securities. Owing to postwar inflation, high prices, unemployment, and other factors of economic instability, the "little men" simply could not afford to absorb these securities. Another difficulty lay in the fact that most executives of *zaibatsu* companies remained under the personal influence and dominance of the *zaibatsu* families, in spite of the "economic purge," which was directed at ultranationalists in business and industry. The strong personal ties among the *zaibatsu* families continued to maintain unofficial chains of control after the official linkage had been severed.

Nevertheless, the *zaibatsu* liquidation had been ordered for the five major firms and later extended to additional combines and their subsidiaries. A special holding company was organized to hold and dispose of the securities of these concerns. The Japanese criticized the United States authorities for regarding the *zaibatsu* as the same business institutions as American trusts or corporations, ignoring the traditional feudal character of the Japanese family combines.

The *"zaibatsu busting"* did not go very far before it began to reverse its course. The change in policy was brought about partly by a clearer understanding of the inherent difficulties in carrying out the original program and partly by the sharp criticism from American financial and business circles that SCAP had been pushing the dissolution measure with undue and unrealistic severity. But the change in direction largely reflected the crystallization of United States global policy in the light of what it considered as the rising menace of communism in the world, and in China in particular. Having failed in the effort to help foster a "strong, united, democratic" and friendly China, the United States decided to restore Japan's industrial capacity to its prewar level and to make a *strong, united, democratic* Japan as a future "bastion against Communism" in Asia.[7]

Another area of economic reform was to promote an independent trade union movement in Japan. SCAP urged the Japanese government to enact a number of labor laws, among which was the trade-union law of December 1945, which guaranteed the workers' right to organize, to engage in collective bargaining, and to strike. The following year the Diet passed legislation establishing grievance procedures for the settling of labor disputes. In 1947, another law was enacted to set minimum standards for working hours, safety regulations, sick leaves, sanitation requirements, accident compensation, vacations and work rules for women and children. It should be pointed out that workers' protection and their rights guaranteed by these laws had been denied under the prewar regime.

Still another area of economic measure dealt with the land reform. Although there were no exceptionally huge landowners in Japan at the time when the occupation began, it was estimated that about 70 percent of the farmers were tenants and that nearly half of the cultivated land was tenanted. The land reform was designed, therefore, to allow tillers to own the land they tilled so as to bring about a more equitable distribution of national wealth. Under the direction of SCAP, a detailed reform program was drawn up and studied by the Allied council for Japan. In October 1946, the Diet passed two land reform laws which compelled absentee landowners to sell their land to the government. The land thus purchased by the government was sold to former tenants in thirty annual installments at low interest rates. A landlord who lived on his land could retain 2.5 acres. Active cultivators were allowed to own farmland up to 7.5 acres. Finally, all landowners were required to give written leases to the tenants, whose rentals could not exceed 25 percent of the crop. There were undoubtedly certain obstacles and difficulties in the implementation of the land reform program, but as it turned out, it was the most effective and enduring postwar economic reform executed by SCAP.

The question of reparations constituted a part of the basic economic policy of the United States and its allies. They were to exact reparations from Japan, for its acts of aggression, through the transfer of Japanese capital equipment and industrial facilities. This policy had a twofold purpose: (1) to effect the economic, industrial, and military disarmament of Japan, and (2) to compensate the Allied powers for the expenses, damages, and destruction caused by Japanese aggression.

As the first step, the United States drew up the interim reparations removals policy, but no agreement was reached either on the percentage of reparations to be allocated to each Far Eastern Commission country or on the total amount of industrial reparations to be removed from Japan. In an effort to find an early solution to the problem, the United States proposed to establish an inter-Allied reparations commission and hold a reparations conference. Nothing resulted from these moves because of the Soviet refusal to permit the conference to discuss Japanese external assets, especially the industrial facilities which the Soviet army had dismantled in Manchuria and transported to the Soviet Union as "war booty."

By 1947, in view of the heightening pace of the Cold War, the United States government regarded the unsettled reparations issue as one of the key factors which had impeded Japan's economic rehabilitation, and felt it necessary to execute an interim directive on "Advance Transfers of Japanese Reparations." SCAP was authorized to transfer 30 percent of Japan's surplus industrial facilities for advance reparations to China, the Philippines, the Dutch Indies, Burma, and Malaya. Both the United States and the Soviet Union were excluded from the list. This program was carried out for two years, then the United States announced that it had reached the conclusion that no further reparations should be required from Japan.

Occupation Reassessed

By early 1948, the United States leaders concluded that the greatest threat and danger to their national interests in East Asia would not come from Japan but from the Soviet Union and from the ascendant communism in the area. This conclusion and the concomitant policy of the "containment of communism" compelled the United States to reassess the occupation policy, for Japan could not be considered independently of this global strategy to combat communism. The United States had hoped that the Soviet Union would cooperate with the Western democracies in the postwar reconstruction of international peace and security in the spirit of their wartime comradeship. But it became painfully evident that the end of World War II only heralded the beginning of the Cold War, replete with mutual suspicion and distrust. Soviet words and deeds were assessed by the United States by a single criterion that the Soviet Union was bent on world revolution along the Marxist-Leninist-Stalinist line.

Viewed in this light, Soviet policies and actions were explained away in the clearest terms. The Soviets sought to achieve their objectives by setting up Communist governments in those countries which they had occupied and by aiding Communists and their sympathizers in other countries to gain power by armed revolt, insurrection, and subversion. Hungary fell into the hands of the Communist party which had polled less than 20 percent of the popular vote in a postwar free election. In Poland a number of non-Communist leaders had to seek political exile in order to escape from inevitable persecution or imprisonment. In Greece and Turkey the Communist insurgents waged guerrilla warfare against their governments in an effort to seize power. The prospect that these two countries might fall into the Soviet orbit alarmed the United States. On March 12, 1947, President Truman went before a joint session of Congress and delivered a speech which later became known as the Truman Doctrine:

> One of the primary objectives of the foreign policy of the United States is the creation of conditions in which we and other nations of the world will be able to work out a way of life free from coercion. . . . We shall not realize our objectives, however, unless we are willing to help free peoples to maintain their institutions and their national integrity against aggressive movements that seek to impose upon them totalitarian regimes. This is no more than a frank recognition that totalitarian regimes imposed on free peoples, by direct or in-

direct aggression, undermine the foundations of international peace and hence the security of the United States.[8]

The Comintern (Third International), which had been formally dissolved during the Grand Alliance, was revived in 1947 as the Cominform (Communist Information Bureau or the Fourth International). This organization, designed to be a powerful weapon for the world Communist movement, acted as a propaganda agent directed at the capitalistic Western democracies. In February 1948, the Communist-armed minority in Czechoslovakia seized state power with the blessing of the Soviet army. Then in June, the Soviet Union blockaded the passage of Allied personnel and matériel through the Soviet zone of occupied East Germany into the Allied zones of Berlin.

In the context of Soviet global strategy those developments in Europe were equally matched by an immense increase in Soviet strategic strength and political influence in East Asia. Not only were the Soviet frontiers pushed eastward to embrace Sakhalin and the Kuriles, but Soviet presence in Mongolia and Manchuria had understandably created mounting influence and an enduring impact. In Korea the Soviet and American forces confronted each other across the thirty-eighth parallel.

Under these circumstances the United States never had more urgent and greater need of an ally in East Asia friendly and strong enough to stand as a bastion against the threat of Communist expansion. When Japan was defeated and occupied, it was hoped that the Chinese Nationalist regime under Chiang Kai-shek or even a Nationalist-Communist coalition government of China would form this point of stability, but China itself was in the throes of a civil war in which Chiang's Nationalist government eventually collapsed.

In addition to these international factors which had effected the change of policy for Japan, there were a number of internal issues which equally impelled SCAP to revise his policy. When Katayama became premier in May 1947, he was confronted with such deplorable economic conditions as rampant inflation, black markets, high prices, labor disputes, and so on. He, therefore, immediately strengthened the Economic Stabilization Board of the cabinet, which had responsibility for economic controls and re- habilitation. While the board was enforcing drastic measures in an attempt to avert an impending economic crisis, voices of discontent and alarm were heard from industrial sectors. Labor unions made vociferous demands for real wage increases; business circles ex- pressed their desire for lessened reparations payments; and indus- trialists began lobbying for the release of those who had been re- stricted in their activities by the "economic purge." They argued that a strong and healthy economic rehabilitation of Japan was essential for the salvation of Japan from *hunger communism*. Ja- pan's industrial potential and its economic recovery were now viewed in the light of the ideological war of the "free" world against communism in the Cold War.

The United States government, the occupation authorities, and the Japanese leaders came to the conclusion that a reexamination of the occupation policy requiring decisive measures had to be taken in order to solve Japan's basic economic problems and to restore that country to the position of the "workshop of Asia." With this in view, SCAP began to revamp its economic policy. It came to realize that the enforcement of the Antitrust Law and the Elimina- tion of Excessive Concentration of Economic Power Law, which had been enacted in April and December 1947, respectively, for the purpose of preventing the concentration and recurrence of the monopolistic system, and the *zaibatsu* dissolution had weakened and impeded Japanese economic power and progress more than necessary.

Restoration of Sovereignty

Peace Treaties with Japan

In the wake of the outbreak of the Korean War on June 25, 1950, and the ensuing arms production and procurement, the Japanese economy made a remarkable recovery. The rate of recovery far outran the original rehabilitation program established before the hostilities in Korea.

At this juncture, Prime Minister Yoshida Shigeru of Japan be- lieved that the opportune moment had arrived for a peace settlement with the United States. Although some of his political opponents feared that such a separate peace treaty with the United States and its "free" Allies might unnecessarily antagonize the Soviet Union and other Communist nations, Yoshida felt that such a course of action "is not necessarily a question of either dogma or philosophy, nor need it lead to a subservient relationship; it is merely the quickest and most effective—indeed the only way—to promote the prosperity of the Japanese people."[9] In this respect, his view coincided with that of General MacArthur who believed that "the consummation of a just peace for Japan is one way— possibly the most dramatic and dynamic way open at this time— of asserting our leadership and regaining our lost initiative in the course of Asian affairs." The Canadian foreign minister echoed that view in a statement expressing the "need for seizing every opportunity that might lead to a satisfactory early settlement with Japan." It became more and more apparent that a revival of Japanese militarism was so remote, while a rebirth of a prosperous, democratic, independent and sovereign Japan so urgent. Thus the desire for a peace treaty with Japan became increasingly conspicuous among the leaders of the United States and several other nations directly involved.

Earlier in 1948, there had been an attempt to conclude such a treaty, but it failed because of Soviet insistence on four-power (USA, UK, USSR, and China) control of negotiations and on the rule of unanimity among them in reaching agreement. With this experience in mind, the United States, in September 1950, began informal discussions with its Allies on the subject. President Truman, in a spirit of bipartisan foreign policy, assigned John Foster Dulles, a Republican, to carry on the necessary negotiations. Dulles's fundamental attitude on the issue was to make a peace treaty conciliatory, not punitive, and to enable Japan to become a member of the free world on its own free will, not by coercion.

In October 1950, Dulles further specified his approach in seven principles: (1) all the belligerents at war with Japan to sign the treaty, (2) Japan to be admitted to the United Nations, (3) Japan's recognition of the independence of Korea and Japan's renunciation of special interests in China, (4) United States-Japanese cooperative defense for security, (5) Japan to be granted most-favored-nations treatment, (6) reparations from the Japanese mainlands to be waived, and (7) all international disputes to be settled by peaceful means.

In the course of the series of bilateral as well as multilateral negotiations that followed, the United States encountered a number of thorny issues. The United States proposals for a trusteeship of the Ryukyus and for a formation of a multilateral security pact among the Pacific Powers including Japan were both rejected. The question of representation to the peace negotiations of China, whether the Peking government (the People's Republic of China) or the Taipei regime (Nationalist China), was never resolved. A number of Allies led by the Philippines and Australia expressed their strong opposition to the draft treaty which lacked a provision on the limitation of Japanese rearmament.

The United States continued to work throughout the first half of 1951 in an effort to resolve the conflicting views and the policy differences among the Allies. The major obstacles were Soviet refusal to discuss the draft text of the peace treaty and British insistence on the Peking representation.

Finally, in June 1951, Anglo-American joint invitations were extended to fifty-five nations, excluding China, requesting them to participate in the peace conference to be convened in San Francisco on September 4, 1951. All but three (India, Burma, and Yugoslavia) accepted the invitation. India's refusal was based on two reasons: the People's Republic of China was not represented and the proposed draft treaty was believed to leave Japan overly dependent upon the United States. Burma felt that the treaty was too lenient and too liberal to Japan and that the reparations clause was inadequate.

During the conference the most vehement attack on the proceedings and on the draft treaty came from the Soviet Union. Andrei Gromyko, the Soviet delegate, demanded that the People's Republic of China be invited, deplored the inadequate safeguards against a revival of Japanese militarism, and accused the United States of perpetuating its dominance in Japan. He charged that the treaty would violate the territorial rights of both the Soviet Union and the People's Republic of China.

The peace treaty was formally signed on September 8, 1951, by

Japan and forty-eight other former belligerents. As expected, the Soviet Union—along with Czechoslovakia and Poland—refused to sign the treaty. On the same day the United States and Japan signed a security agreement providing for joint defense against external aggression and internal insurgency supported by external forces. For this purpose United States troops continue to be stationed in Japan. These treaties were ratified by the Japanese Diet in October and became effective on April 28, 1952, ending the historic period of the American occupation.

Economic Recovery

With the termination of the American occupation in 1952, Japan was faced with many complex problems and important tasks, especially that of making the transition from an occupied country to a sovereign state with all its rights and responsibilities. One of the most crucial tasks was to maintain and continue to promote a stable and prosperous economy for a nation which has a teeming population and is poor in natural resources.

In postwar Japan, democracy and economic progress were considered almost synonymous, and a review of the economy of Japan revealed phenomenal growth in those years, once the initial difficulties had been overcome. As in the Meiji era, economic growth was fostered by a combination of government and private enterprise. Governmental success depended on a strong popular conviction that economic progress constituted a supreme objective; so long as the economy was healthy and strong, there was a sense of security. Harding's dictum, "the business of a government is business" was applicable to Japan. This was the reason Prime Minister Yoshida was willing to accept the continuation of United States military bases in Japan, placing his country under the American nuclear umbrella, but he balked at American suggestion that Japan should rearm. Yoshida strongly felt that conventional rearmament would only jeopardize Japan's economic prosperity, not to mention its futility in a nuclear war.

Economic recovery and growth was fastest in basic industries and engineering, which also had suffered the worst destruction during the Pacific war. They regained their prewar importance in the economy by 1953, when output per capita was close to the level of the mid-1930s. In terms of per capita real income of the average Japanese wage earner, the figure of 1946 was half of that of 1934 and the 1953 figure equals the 1934 figure. The overall rate of economic growth averaged 10 percent annually from 1950 up to 1965, with a high rate of 12.1 percent in 1963 and a low of 7.5 percent in 1965.[10] The post-surrender high rate of growth which enabled Japanese output roughly to double by 1953 could be attributed to a number of factors: (1) economic assistance from the United States, both governmental and private, (2) the Korean War boom, (3) high levels of Japanese technology, and (4) Japanese trade policy.

First, technical know-how acquired from the United States, embodied in hundreds of contracts with firms, contributed extensively to the fast-growing economy. Coupled with it was an immense inflow of American credit to Japan, largely in the form of bank loans, but more and more as investments in Japanese securities. Second, by the time of the outbreak of the Korean War, the Japanese economy was stabilized and functioning in a relatively healthy manner; and her industry was in a position to profit from the large flow of United States procurement orders for the military in Korea. American expenditures, both direct aid and special procurement, reached approximately $800 million a year in 1952–1953 and continued at an annual rate of more than $500 million through 1957. These expenditures provided a powerful stimulus to Japan's economic development and enabled her to build a surplus in foreign exchange. Third, high levels of technology in Japan were measured by the quality, competence, and experience of Japanese engineers, technicians, and industrial managerial personnel. They were well trained and well disciplined in the hard-work ethics of the Japanese tradition. Their skill and production efforts accelerated Japanese economic growth. Furthermore, bomb-wrecked or dilapidated industrial machinery was systematically replaced with the most advanced equipment, which gave the Japanese an advantage over their international competitors. Finally, the expansion of Japan's foreign trade was a planned operation. Japanese officials analyzed the conditions of particular industries, conducted market research, planned desirable export goods and their destinations, and encouraged quality control. They indeed decided what to produce, how to produce, and for whom to produce. The Japanese banks had made commercial loans easy to acquire, and the government offered tax incentives and high depreciation allowances.

The first industrial and trade successes were in textiles and other light industries which Japan had mastered in the 1920s and 1930s. Then they moved into more advanced and complex new fields, such as optical industries, automotives, motorcycles, shipbuilding, electronics, and steel production. They achieved high productivity in these areas by means of a combination of their labor forces with advanced industrial skills and relatively low wages. This also meant that they had an advantage over their competitors who had less skill or who paid high wages in international markets.

While manufacturing quality products, Japan not only recaptured the old Asian markets but also developed new ones in the United States and throughout the world. She began to be described as a performer of an "economic miracle," as a "workshop in Asia," and as an "economic giant." This will be discussed further in later chapters.

Search for Identity

After the conclusion of the peace treaty, Japan, as a sovereign and independent state, was confronted with a host of urgent issues which, domestic and foreign, she had to solve for herself. One of such issues which drew immediate national attention was concerned with a constitutional amendment designed to restore the position of the emperor and to revise the renunciation of the war clause.

The conservatives who had firm control of the Japanese Diet and government were anxious to amend the constitution so as to restore the prewar principle of the sanctity and sovereignty of the emperor. They argued that the emperor should be the *de jure* ruler, not just a symbol of the nation. At the same time they also wanted to revise Article IX of the constitution. To them the renunciation of the right to maintain armed forces for national defense and as an instrument of national policy seemed folly in a world of power politics. National independence or national sovereignty meant little to them as Japan was overly dependent on the "American umbrella" without military autonomy.

The conservative proponents of a constitutional amendment were met by vehement opposition from the Left—primarily Socialists and Communists. Fearing that any attempt to change the constitution might trigger a legislative landslide to undo the occupation reforms and to sweep the country back to prewar military totalitarianism, the Left opponents argued that the constitution was a sound document which should not be tampered with. They bitterly opposed the conservatives in the Diet and staged street demonstrations eliciting popular support for their position. By the late 1950s, however, the issue slowly faded away.

The advocates of rearmament on the other hand nearly achieved their desired goal through de facto armament without having to amend Article IX. The first step to rearm Japan had been taken immediately after the outbreak of the Korean War. It had taken the form of the creation of the 75,000-man National Police Reserve to replace American occupation troops sent to the Korean front. Then, in August 1952, shortly after the peace treaty became effective, Premier Yoshida added to it a National Safety Force which included a small naval unit. In February 1954, he further expanded these units, renaming them the Ground Self-Defense Force and Maritime Self-Defense Force, and added a small Air Self-Defense Force. All three were placed under a Self-Defense Agency. The rationale behind all such moves was that the constitution, in renouncing war, had not renounced the inherent right of self-defense.

As to the foreign relations of post-treaty Japan, there were three alternative courses open to her: (1) to commit herself to the "free" world camp, (2) to align with the Communist bloc, or (3) to remain uncommitted or nonaligned. Let us examine each of these courses in reverse order.

First, the advocates of neutralism came primarily from the center of Japan's political spectrum. They argued that Japan's interests would be better served by establishing equally friendly relations both with the free world and with the Communist powers. To them greater safety for Japan lay in complete, unarmed neutrality, rather than in a military alliance either with the arch-Capitalist United States or with the arch-Communist Soviet Union. They felt extremely uncomfortable with so many American military bases in Japan, which would naturally become Soviet military targets in the event of a United States-Soviet war. But this neutral course was clearly untenable. The Japanese leaders, barely emerging from the American political shadow, were in no position to cast off completely American pressure and influence. United States foreign policy at this time was committed to waging an anti-Communist "crusade," wherein the policy of neutralism was considered "immoral" and unfriendly to the United States in the struggle against "godless" international communism.

Neutralism notwithstanding, Japan began normalizing her relations with her Asian neighbors. In April 1952, Japan and Nationalist China on Taiwan signed a peace treaty, establishing full diplomatic relations. This was a clear indication that Japan was following the United States policy of nonrecognition of the Peking regime of the People's Republic of China. In 1954 the Philippines ratified the San Francisco peace treaty after having reached an agreement with Japan on reparations. Toward the end of that year Japan likewise signed a peace treaty with Burma. At the same time Japan joined the Colombo Plan with a view to contributing to international programs of economic assistance to developing nations in Asia. The following year Japan also became a member of the GATT (General Agreement on Tariffs and Trade).

As to the possibility of taking the second alternative course of action, Japan had to deal primarily with the two Communist giants—the Soviet Union and the People's Republic of China. Japan's relations with the Soviet Union were characteristically restrained. The pro-Communist oriented Left in Japan denounced the peace settlement which, in their view, had made Japan too subservient to the United States, and therefore they demanded a policy of friendship, or alignment if necessary, with the Communist bloc led by the Soviet Union. They took to the streets for protest demonstrations by the thousands against the peace treaty, against the security treaty, against the presence of American military bases in Japan, and against American dominance. In the years to come, this "politics of protest demonstrations" became a familiar feature in Japanese political life.

Behind the scenes of such anti-American sentiment was the towering image of the Soviet Union. In an attempt to entice Japan away from the United States, the Soviet Union and the People's Republic of China in late 1954 announced their readiness for a normalization of their relations with Japan:

> The Governments of the Soviet Union and the Chinese People's Republic in their policy with regard to Japan, are moved by the principle of the peaceful coexistence of states, irrespective of their social systems, being confident that this is in accord with the vital interests of all peoples. They stand for the development of extensive trade relations with Japan on mutually profitable terms and the establishment of close cultural relations with her. They also express their readiness to take steps to normalize their relations with Japan and declare that Japan will meet full support in her striving to establish political and economic relations with the U.S.S.R. and the Chinese People's Republic and that all her steps to provide conditions for her peaceful and independent development will meet full support.[11]

In response, Japan cautiously approached the Soviet Union for negotiations, in the course of which the Soviets refused to make any concessions on Japan's requests such as the fishing rights in the waters closed by the Soviets, the return of certain small islands at the southernmost of the Kurile chain, Soviet support for Japan's UN membership, and the repatriation of Japanese prisoners of war still held in the Soviet Union.

The Soviet Union remained adamant on these issues until October 1956, when the Japanese-Soviet "peace treaty" was finally signed. The treaty provided for the reestablishment of diplomatic and consular relations between the two nations, and the Soviet Union agreed to the aforementioned Japanese requests except the return of those small islands. In this respect this treaty was not exactly a formal peace treaty in the conventional sense, but was a rapprochement between the two countries. A genuine peace treaty was yet to be signed.

Japan's relations with the People's Republic of China were dictated more by the necessity for commerce and trade than the complexity of politics. Japanese leaders, in government and in business, concerned with Japan's economic future, favored expanded trade with China. They hoped that their diplomatic recognition of the Nationalist government on Taiwan would not impede or jeopardize their trade relations with the Peking regime. They would like to consider that "politics is politics and trade is trade." But the Peking leaders were not very cooperative. There was a clear tendency on the part of the People's Republic of China to put pressure on Japanese politics by manipulating the Japanese desire for trade into political profit for Peking. Many discontented Japanese believed that this uncooperative attitude of Peking resulted from the intransigent China policy of the United States with which Japan had identified herself.

Finally, the only remaining alternative for Japan to pursue was, therefore, to ally with the free world led by the United States. In fact, one of the underlying prerequisites for the peace treaty was to have Japan solidly wedded to the United States. The advantages Japan would derive from the alignment with its former occupation mentor were far greater than those which might have been drawn from the other two alternatives. Japan was freed from the economic burden of rearmament and was able to create a favorable political atmosphere for economic recovery and growth. The United States continued to aid Japan for the development of industries, for the construction of power plants, for the improvement of agriculture, and for the building of a marine fleet.

The official position of friendship and alliance notwithstanding, the American-Japanese relations were often strained. The most conspicuous source of irritation was the continued presence of American troops in Japan. There were constant flare-ups of anti-American sentiment triggered by American soldiers' mischief, ranging from traffic accidents to crimes committed by them against the Japanese. One of the much-publicized incidents was the case in 1956 involving an American soldier on duty who shot and killed a Japanese woman gathering scrap metal on a rifle range. The subsequent jurisdictional question as to which authorities—the Japanese or the American military—should handle the case became a highly emotional issue in Japan as well as in the United States.[12]

The Japanese were also extremely sensitive and concerned with the nuclear tests conducted by the United States in the Pacific. An incident which fanned anti-American sentiment in this regard occurred in 1954 when radioactive fallout from an American nuclear test at Bikini resulted in the death of a crew member of a Japanese fishing vessel some distance away. The Japanese public reacted with indignation, linking it with the atomic bombings of Hiroshima and Nagasaki.

Another source of friction resulted from disputes over land. For overpopulated Japan, the problem of effective land use is a deep national concern. Therefore, whenever the American military conducted maneuvers or bombing practice or constructed runway extensions of air bases at the expense of farmland, the embittered farmers and their supporters "battled" the Americans. In a larger vein, the American base in the Ryukyus constituted the same source of friction. By virtue of the 1951 peace treaty, the United States retained the powers of legislation, administration, and adjudication in the Ryukyus. As years passed, agitation for more indigenous autonomy and demonstrations for more land (no more runway constructions) were frequently staged against the United States military authorities in Okinawa, the largest island in the chain. The United States was determined to retain Okinawa as a frontier outpost in East Asia so long as international tension continued to exist in the region, while Japan was allowed to retain "residual sovereignty" over this island.

It should be emphasized that these sources of conflicts and irritation, poignant as they were in many instances, never jeopardized the basically friendly American-Japanese relationships.

CHAPTER TEN

Two Wars
in Two Decades

The Korean War

Genesis of the Conflict:
Two Regimes in a Single Nation

Perhaps the earliest official expression of United States interest in Korea came in 1834, when Edmund Roberts, a special agent of the government exploring East Asia, reported to the secretary of state upon his return that trade with Korea would be possible after the opening of trade with Japan. No official action or contact was made for decades until 1866 when the *General Sherman,* an American schooner seeking to open up trade with Korea, went aground off Pyongyang and was burned by the Koreans.[1]

Several years later, in 1871, a United States expedition arrived off the Korean coast with a fleet of five steamships. They were fired upon from the Korean forts and in the ensuing engagement both sides suffered casualties without any decisive results. Over a decade later, in 1882, the first United States-Korean treaty of "peace, amity, commerce and navigation" was signed. This treaty provided for the appointment of diplomatic and consular representatives; it stipulated further that American vessels in stress or in need of provisions could seek aid at any Korean port and that United States citizens in Korea would enjoy the protection of local authorities.

The United States-Korea treaty set the tone for such agreements with other Western powers: Britain, Germany, France, Italy, and Russia. They appeared successively on the Korean scene. Korea became the center of international power rivalry, of which the Sino-Japanese contest over Korea loomed most ominous. A United States appeal, supported by Britain, France, and Russia, to both China and Japan to withdraw simultaneously their troops from Korea went unheeded. Inevitably, in August 1894, the Sino-Japanese War broke out. Thereupon, Britain made an inquiry as to whether the United States would join other Western powers in intervening in the war; the United States rejected the move.

The war ended in a Japanese victory, and, in the subsequent Treaty of Shimonoseki signed on April 17, 1895, China recognized Korean independence, disclaiming the age-old notion of her suzerainty over Korea. But Korea as an arena of major power rivalry remained unchanged. Having removed China, Japan was now confronted with a new foe—Russia. The Russo-Japanese rivalry was so intense that Korean independence and sovereignty was at the mercy of those two imperialist powers. At this juncture, in 1899, the king of Korea requested the United States to take the initiative in obtaining from the powers an agreement guaranteeing the integrity of Korea. President McKinley, however, made a negative response.

There were diplomatic efforts between Japan and Russia to resolve their differences by negotiations. On one occasion, it should be recalled, Russia proposed to establish a neutral zone in the north of the *thirty-ninth* parallel.[2] The Japanese counterproposal was to create a neutral zone along the Korean-Manchuria frontier and to declare Manchuria and Korea as outside their special interests.

The diplomatic impasse resulted in the outbreak, on February 8, 1904, of the Russo-Japanese War. Within two weeks, Japan and Korea signed a treaty, making the latter a virtual protectorate of the former in return for guarantees of Korea's integrity. After the war, in late 1905, when the Japanese government informed the United States that Japan was in full charge of the foreign affairs of Korea, the United States government withdrew its legation in Korea and ordered the Korean legation in Washington closed.

The Japanese annexation of Korea in 1910 came as no surprise. Japan was determined to make Korea an integral part of its empire. Thus, from 1910 until August 1945, Korea did not exist as a sovereign nation-state. The United States, as other powers, accepted the new situation. Later, in 1916, in response to a United States senatorial request for correspondence between the officials of the Korean and American governments, Secretary of State Robert Lansing made a "judicious selection" of the documents and submitted it to President Wilson, who in turn transmitted it to the Senate.

Japanese rule over Korea, after the annexation, was primarily militaristic in character and oppressive in nature. Korea as a new colony was placed under the full control of a governor general, a high-ranking career military officer, who was personally appointed by the emperor of Japan. His colonial policies were exploitative and suppressive, and they accelerated the process of disintegration of the old social order of Korea. The accumulating discontent and the pent-up resentment against Japanese rule, coupled with the mounting nationalism among Koreans, exploded on March 1, 1919, in what became known as the Samil (3–1) Movement.

The Samil Movement was a spontaneous outburst of the desire of Korean people to regain their national independence. It was not planned in advance, nor was it designed to be an armed struggle. Appealing to "the opinions of Mankind," the leaders of the movement believed that through the goodwill of the peacemakers at Versailles, who had hoisted the banner of "national self-determination," the Koreans would be allowed to achieve their goal. The Koreans appealed to the United States for help as the Japanese military and police began to suppress them by force. The United States, however, refused to respond; instead, the Department of State instructed the American ambassador in Tokyo on April 14, 1919, that the consulate in Seoul "should be extremely careful not to encourage any belief that the United States will assist the Korean nationalists in carrying out their plans." The movement was crushed by the Japanese, but Korean nationalism went on to survive.

During the next two decades, the United States' relations with Korea were limited to missionary activities and to trade through

Japanese channels. With the Japanese attack on Pearl Harbor, the United States began to reassess Korea as deserving the principle of "self-determination" incorporated in the Atlantic Charter. In March 1942, a State Department official announced that the Korean question was receiving due consideration. Then, late in 1943, in the Cairo Declaration, the Big Three (Roosevelt, Churchill, and Chiang) unequivocally declared that, "mindful of the enslavement of the people of Korea, [they] are determined that in due course Korea shall become free and independent." Later, with Stalin's endorsement of the Cairo Declaration, all four powers became publicly committed to the ultimate independence of Korea.

Japanese rule in Korea came to an end on August 15, 1945, as Japan surrendered to the Allied powers. At this time Soviet troops had moved into Korea and they were in the position to overrun the entire peninsula, where there were no American forces. To prevent a unilateral Soviet occupation of all of Korea, the Joint Chiefs of Staff instructed General MacArthur, SCAP, to issue an order directing the Japanese to surrender their troops north of the thirty-eighth parallel to the Soviets and those troops south of this line to the Americans. This division of Korea by the thirty-eighth parallel was intended presumably to be a temporary military measure in order to expedite the disarming and repatriating of the Japanese troops.

Korea became America's new frontier in the context of the Cold War. Here two opposing political, social, and economic ideologies —democracy and communism—converged face to face to test the superiority of one over the other. The "temporary" nature of the demarcation line became "permanent" in the pattern of bipolarization of world politics. The United States established an American military government in the south and the Soviet Union its counterpart in the north. As the thirty-eighth parallel came to assume more and more the character of a permanent "international" boundary rather than a local geographical line, the issue of territorial unification became the ardent national aspiration of all the Korean people. This issue was taken up in December 1945, at the Moscow Conference of Foreign Ministers. There they reached an agreement, to which China later adhered, to establish a four-power trusteeship of Korea for a period of up to five years. In addition, in order to discuss the establishment of a provisional Korean government, they agreed to set up a United States-Soviet Joint Commission, which, subsequently formed, met for the first time on March 20, 1946.

It became immediately clear that the respective positions of the United States and the Soviet Union were diametrically opposite with respect to the question of the Korean political parties and social organizations which were to participate in the conference and to the question of the process of unification. The Soviet representatives on the Commission insisted that any political party or social organization that was opposed to the trusteeship plan should be excluded from consultations. This meant that the Communist minority in Korea, which had supported the trusteeship, would have a predominant voice in the consultation, whereas the moderate to rightist majority, which had previously opposed the trusteeship, would have been totally excluded. The United States rejected the Soviet view, arguing that the democratic principle of freedom of speech and of assembly necessitated the participation of all parties and groups and that, therefore, either pro- or anti-trusteeship position should not be a criterion for consultation.

As to the question of unification, the Soviets proposed to create a provisional government first, followed by unification at a later date. The United States, quite contrarily, wanted first to remove all the barriers—social, economic, administrative, communication, and physical—between North and South Korea, followed by the establishment of a provisional government based on the freely expressed will of the people.

These two problems clearly indicated that the Soviet Union wanted a unified Korea under a pro-Soviet communistic regime, whereas the United States hoped for a unified Korea under a pro-American democratic government. Deadlocked as they were on those issues, the first joint conference broke up in May 1946. One year later, in May 1947, the second joint conference was held only to be terminated in failure. In August the United States proposed to have a four-power conference to find means of implementing the Moscow Agreement, but the Soviet Union in September rejected this proposal on the grounds that it would not be within the scope of the Moscow Agreement.

Frustrated in bilateral negotiations with the Soviet Union, the United States brought the Korean question to the General Assembly of the United Nations, which in November 1947 adopted United States proposals despite Soviet objection. The proposals called for, among others, the formation of the United Nations Temporary Commission on Korea (UNTCK) to supervise general elections to be held throughout Korea. The commission, duly formed, began its work in January 1948. For months the commission undertook preparations for a general election, but its activities were partially hampered by the Soviets who denied it access to Soviet-occupied North Korea. Thereupon, the United Nations decided to proceed with elections in the South where the commission's supervision was possible. Accordingly, a general election was held on May 10, 1948. In the following month a National Assembly was formed and in July a constitution was promulgated. Thus, the Republic of Korea (ROK) came into being to assume, "among the powers of the earth," the separate, equal, and sovereign station. American-educated Syngman Rhee was elected president and his government was formally recognized first by the United States and later by many of its allies.

The creation of the Republic of Korea did not end the difficulties of the Korean issue, but perhaps it heralded the beginning of their intensification. In theory, and by claim, the sovereignty of the Republic of Korea would prevail over the entire peninsula, from the Yalu to the Korean Straits, but in reality it only covered the territory south of the thirty-eighth parallel.

In the North, meanwhile, a completely different type of regime had grown up. At the time when the United States-Soviet joint conferences were held, a North Korean People's Committee led by Marshal Kim Il-sung was formed. Later, in July 1945, the North Korean Democratic People's Front and the North Korean Labor Party (Communist party) were organized. Under their control and supervision, land reform was carried out, the nationalization of major industries was implemented, and labor laws were put into effect, giving equal rights to men and women. In October 1947, the People's Committee drew up a constitution, the draft of which was made public in February 1948. In August, a general election was held to form the Supreme People's Assembly, which convened in September and accepted the constitution. Following the adoption of the constitution, the Democratic People's Republic of Korea (DPRK) was officially established, with Soviet-trained Marshal Kim Il-sung chosen as premier. Kim's government was formally recognized in October 1948, first by the Soviet Union and later by other nations of the Soviet bloc. The DPRK likewise claimed that its sovereignty would prevail over the entire peninsula, though in fact it controlled only the territory north of the thirty-eighth parallel.

In this way, the one nation of Korea came to have two governments—one in the south and the other in the north. The territorial dividing line between the two hostile regimes was the thirty-eighth parallel, which in reality became the line separating the two super powers—the United States and the Soviet Union.

Across the Thirty-eighth Parallel

After the formation of Kim's Communist regime in North Korea, the Soviet Union on September 18, 1948, informed the United States of its intention to withdraw all Soviet forces from Korea by the end of that year. At this time the North Korean government had at its disposal formidable armed forces on which the Soviets could count. They had equipped the North Korean Army with tanks, planes, artillery pieces, and automatic weapons of their own as well as those of the Japanese.

The United States, on the other hand, during its occupation of South Korea, had concentrated its efforts not so much on arms build-up as on economic rehabilitation of the country. At the time when the Soviet announcement was made, the military balance between North and South Korea was overwhelmingly in favor of the former. For this reason, as the United States began preparations for troop withdrawal, the National Assembly of the Republic of Korea in November 1948 adopted a resolution requesting the United States to postpone the plan until the country could develop a sufficient defense capability. Street demonstrations against troop withdrawal were seen and unified cries of "Yankee *don't* go home" were heard in the South.[3]

Despite the Korean opposition to the troop withdrawal, the first contingent of United States forces departed from Korea in

May 1949, and the last contingent on June 29, 1949. Left behind was the Korean Military Advisory Group (KMAG), a handful of American military advisors, to be in charge of the military defense training of the infant Korean constabulary. Still, the military question was not the American priority in Korea, but the economic issue was. The United States continued to provide financial, material, and technical assistance toward economic recovery and by mid-1950 Korea became substantially self-sufficient in food production and remarkable gains were made in such sectors as fisheries, coal mining, electric power, textile manufactures, railroad construction, and other industries. This optimistic outlook was shattered by the North Korean attack.

On the dawn of Sunday, June 25, 1950, the North Korean armed forces launched a sudden full-scale attack against South Korea, prepared with secrecy in consultation with the Soviets. Kim Il-sung had been in Moscow at the end of 1949. He had expressed to Stalin his intention "to prod South Korea with the point of a bayonet." Nikita Khrushchev, former Soviet premier, wrote:

The North Koreans wanted to give a helping hand to their brethren who were under the heel of Syngman Rhee. Stalin persuaded Kim Il-sung that he should think it over, make some calculations, and then come back with a concrete plan. Kim went home and then returned to Moscow when he had worked everything out. He told Stalin he was absolutely certain of success. I remember Stalin had his doubts. He was worried that the Americans would jump in, but we were inclined to think that if the war were fought swiftly—and Kim Il-sung was sure that it would be won swiftly—then intervention by the USA could be avoided.[4]

Khrushchev remembered further:

Stalin decided to ask Mao Tse-tung's opinion about Kim Il-sung's suggestion. . . . He [Mao] approved of Kim Il-sung's suggestion and put forward the opinion that the USA would not intervene since the war would be an internal matter which the Korean people would decide for themselves.

The Communist attack, then, was made on the basis of two crucial assumptions. First, the Communist leaders believed that once an attack was launched against the South with the overwhelmingly superior North Korean military might, it would "touch off an internal explosion in South Korea" against the Syngman Rhee regime, and the South Koreans would flock to the northern "liberators." What, in fact, happened was that the northern invaders behaved as conquerors, cruel and brutal, rather than as brethren, compassionate and benevolent. Their conduct and behavior alienated the masses and galvanized the South Koreans against their policy and their ideology—communism. Again in the words of Khrushchev:

> The attack was launched successfully. The Koreans swept south swiftly. But what Kim Il-sung had predicted—an internal uprising after the first shots were fired and Syngman Rhee was overthrown—unfortunately failed to materialize.[5]

Second, they assumed that the United States would not intervene with armed forces. The United States had excluded Korea as well as Taiwan from its defense perimeter, as evidenced by the public statement of Secretary Dean Acheson. On January 12, 1950, in a speech before the National Press Club in Washington, he defined the American defense line in East Asia as running from the Aleutians through Japan and the Ryukyus to the Philippines. In the event of an attack outside this line, he suggested that "the initial reliance must be on the people attacked to resist it and then upon the commitments of the entire civilized world under the Charter of the United Nations."[6] Many critics of Secretary Acheson charged that his speech had been an open "invitation" for North Korea to attack the South. It might have convinced the Communist leaders of American nonintervention. Even if the United States should intervene, the North Korean *blitzkrieg,* they were convinced, would make their occupation of the entire South a *fait accompli* before any meaningful intervention by the United States.

But, contrary to their assumptions, both the United States and the United Nations acted as swiftly as they could to repulse the aggression. Within five days after the attack, the United States armed forces—army, navy, and air force—were all committed to combat actions against the invaders. These actions were taken in accordance with the United Nations Security Council resolution of June 27, which had requested that "the Members of the United Nations furnish such assistance to the Republic of Korea as may be necessary to repel the armed attack and to restore international peace and security in the area." The Security Council further adopted on July 7 another resolution requesting members to contribute military forces and other assistance to be placed under a unified United Nations Command, which was subsequently headed by General Douglas MacArthur. Sixteen UN members, including the United States, provided armed forces to the UN Command.

The United States' determined response to the North Korean attack was a *volte-face* from the Acheson speech several months earlier. President Truman later clarified the reasons for the policy change:

> If the Communists were permitted to force their way into the Republic of Korea without opposition from the free world, no small nation would have the courage to resist threats and aggression by stronger Communist neighbors. If this was allowed to go unchallenged, it would mean a third world war, just as similar incidents had brought on the second world war.[7]

Despite the unforeseen turn of events, North Korea continued its military operations and by the middle of September 1950 the United Nations forces were compressed into a small beachhead perimeter around the city of Pusan, a southern port of Korea. A Korean "Dunkirk" appeared to be in the making; but, on September 15, 1950, the UN forces executed an amphibious landing at Inchon, splitting the enemy forces in the middle. From then on, in the face of the all-out offensive by the UN forces, the North Korean army began to collapse.

When the United Nations forces reached the eventful thirty-eighth parallel in pursuit of the retreating North Korean troops, the United States and the United Nations had to decide whether to halt at this line, with their proclaimed objectives accomplished, or to attempt to unify Korea by military means just as North Korea had attempted to do. There had been warnings from Peking that the People's Republic of China would intervene if the United States forces drove on into the north across this line. Nevertheless, the UN forces were given the order to carry the war into the North, as implied in the General Assembly resolution of October 7, 1950, recommending that *"all* appropriate steps be taken to ensure conditions of stability *throughout* Korea" (author's italics).

The victorious UN forces captured Pyongyang, the North Korean capital, on October 19, 1950, and continued to advance toward the Yalu with a confident anticipation of unifying Korea by the end of the year. Suddenly, however, they came to face fresh and new fighting forces—the Communist Chinese "volunteers" armies. The Chinese intervention created a new situation calling for a new strategy, new policy, and new objectives. General MacArthur advocated a naval blockade of the entire China coast, strategic bombing of Manchuria, and a Chinese Nationalist invasion of the mainland. The Truman administration, on the other hand, believed that such policies would certainly lead to a third world war contrary to the "limited" objectives of the Korean War. A full-scale, all-out war with China would involve the United States, in the words of General Omar Bradley, chairman of the Joint Chiefs of Staff, "in the wrong war, at the wrong time, in the wrong place, and with the wrong enemy."[8]

The UN forces, therefore, retreated southward, back to and beyond the thirty-eighth parallel. General MacArthur, with his strategic recommendations rejected, was unwilling to accept the limitation of the war to the Korean peninsula. He challenged the administration in a letter to a congressional leader.[9] Thereupon, President Truman, convinced that his constitutional authority as the Commander-in-Chief could no longer tolerate the general's insubordination, in April 1951 relieved General MacArthur of his Far Eastern Commands and appointed General Matthew B. Ridgway as his successor. The war itself now turned into a series of seesaw battles along the thirty-eighth parallel, and a stalemate developed.

Armistice and After

The United States policy to limit the war and the Communist inability to achieve a total victory created a military impasse fraught with frustration, anxiety, and even the danger of escalation to a larger war. It was in this situation, on June 23, 1953, that Jacob A. Malik, the Soviet ambassador to the United Nations, suggested that "discussions should be started between the belligerents for a cease-fire and an armistice providing for the mutual withdrawal of forces" from the thirty-eighth parallel. The United Nations Command decided to explore the Malik proposal and made direct arrangements for the initiation of armistice negotiations.

The first formal meeting was convened on July 9, 1951, at Kaesong; later meetings were held at Panmunjom, a farm village in "no man's land." From the beginning, the basic United Nations position was that military realities would determine the line of demarcation, appropriate assurances should be taken to prevent either party from increasing military potential, and the exchange of prisoners of war (POW) should be undertaken on the principles of humanitarianism, international law, and the provisions of the Geneva Conventions. The question of prisoners of war exchange turned out to be a major barrier to be overcome. The United Nations Command had taken a stand against forcible repatriation. The Communist side, on the other hand, insisted that *all* Chinese and North Korean POWs under United Nations custody must be returned. To their embarrassment, a preliminary screening revealed that more than a third of those held by the UN Command refused repatriation.

While the negotiations were deadlocked on this issue, fighting raged on with relentless intensity. It appeared that both sides were attempting to achieve on the battlefield what they failed to settle at the conference table. In the process the casualties in both camps were rising steadily.

Such conditions inevitably generated uneasy domestic repercussions. Charges were made against the Truman administration for the so-called no-win policy in Korea and for allegedly being "soft on communism" in general. The Republican party nominated General Dwight D. Eisenhower, one of the better-known World War II heroes, as its presidential candidate for the 1952 elections. During his election campaign, Eisenhower made a public pledge that he would go to Korea in search of an "honorable" settlement.

Upon his successful election, the president-elect visited Korea. After his inauguration in January 1953, President Eisenhower began to apply pressure on the Communists by way of strengthening the Republic of Korea army and of lifting the interposition of the United States Seventh Fleet on the Taiwan Straits.

The change of hands on the reins of power in Washington was soon followed by a similar event in Moscow on account of the death of Stalin on March 5, 1953. The new leaders in the Kremlin under collective leadership began to show signs of a policy change in what was described as a "New Look" in world politics. Within two weeks the Communists agreed to the exchange of sick and wounded prisoners, and they further expressed their desire to resume the armistice talks which had been deadlocked over the POW issue.

Once the negotiations were resumed, the Eisenhower administration applied an added pressure on the Communists. In May, the new secretary of state, John Foster Dulles, warned Moscow and Peking, through Nehru of India, that unless a Korean armistice was agreed upon soon, the United States might bomb Manchuria and might have to employ tactical atomic weapons in Korea against the Communist troops. There was no way of knowing just how much such a "nuclear intimidation" had influenced the Communist leaders in their subsequent actions. In any case, the truce negotiations began to show signs of progress and success.

At this juncture, a strong opposition to the prospect of a successful armistice came from an unexpected source—the Syngman Rhee government. President Rhee came to believe that a Korean armistice would be nothing but a facade to cover up the defeat of the United States and the United Nations on the military and diplomatic fronts. In his view the United States and the United Nations lacked the will and courage to carry out the intent of the General Assembly Resolution of October 7, 1950, which had declared unification of Korea by all means as the ultimate objective. To him, a nonmilitary peaceful unification of his country was as remote and unattainable as a nonviolent peaceful fusion between capitalism and communism. Military means were the only possible way to achieve unification and an armistice would negate that possibility.

President Rhee, therefore, threatened to withdraw all of the South Korean forces from the United Nations Command if those terms unacceptable to his government were to be incorporated in the armistice agreement. The United States confronted a formidable task of placating a recalcitrant Rhee. After a series of frank and earnest negotiations, the United States acquired Rhee's nonobstruction pledge to an armistice in exchange for a United States-Korea defense treaty. The last obstacle thus removed, on July 27, 1953, the Korean Armistice Agreement was finally signed at Panmunjom. The Republic of Korea, however, was not a signatory.

The Armistice Agreement provided for a cease-fire, a ban on reinforcements, a demilitarized zone (DMZ) of four kilometers in depth, and a military demarcation line which, along the actual battle line, followed natural geographic configurations rather than the straight thirty-eighth parallel. It also created a Military Armistice Commission, made up of military officers from both sides, to supervise the armistice and to handle any alleged violations. The agreement dealt strictly with military issues alone and contained no provisions for the settlement of political questions, except a brief statement to the effect that within the near future a political conference of a high level should be held to settle through negotiations the political question of Korea and the question of foreign troop withdrawal.

Simultaneous with the signing of the armistice agreement, the sixteen nations whose combat troops were in Korea under the UN Command met in Washington and announced their joint declaration:

We affirm, in the interest of world peace, that if there is a renewal of the armed attack, challenging again the principles of the United Nations, we should again be united and prompt to resist. The consequences of such a breach of the armistice would be so grave that, in all probability, it would not be possible to confine hostilities within the frontiers of Korea.[10]

In addition, as had been agreed on, the bilateral United States-Korea Mutual Assistance Agreement was signed in Washington on October 1, 1953, to safeguard Korea's future security.[11]

The Korean War was one of the most hotly contested military struggles in modern history. During the thirty-seven months of fighting the United States suffered total casualties of over 150,000, while those of the other fifteen members of the United Nations Command were about 17,000. It cost the United States over $20 billion. But the Koreans, both South and North, suffered the most. Total casualties of the South Korean Army exceeded 400,000. The heavy toll in death and injuries to the civilian population and in destruction of their property was inestimable. Their country lay ruined and scarred, and remained still divided. The total casualties suffered by the Communist forces were estimated at nearly two million.

In spite of the enormous losses and sacrifices in men and material, virtually nothing was accomplished by the Korean War, although each side claimed a victory. The Communists extolled their "victory" on the ground that they had successfully blunted American imperialism in Asia and destroyed the myth of American invincibility throughout the world. The United States, meanwhile, claimed success because the collective security measures taken by a group of United Nations members had saved not only the Republic of Korea from the Communist aggression but the United Nations itself from meeting the fate of the League of Nations. At the same time, a third world war was avoided.

The Korean War, in any case, had left a confused and beguiled national psyche to the American people. Their proud nation, which had crushed Hitler's *wehrmacht* and defeated the seemingly invincible Japanese Imperial Army only a few years earlier, had to acquiesce in a dubious "victory"—a "draw" at best—in a war against what they considered to be third- or fourth-rate military powers. After a postmortem examination of the Korean War, some Americans came to believe that the sad episode was a political defeat resulting from pusillanimous leadership plagued with Communist conspiracy in all levels of their government. They helped foster a domestic scene that was filled with recrimination, self-doubt, and suspicion. They accentuated the emotional and irrational atmosphere, which the extremists and demagogues successfully exploited to create what became known as the era of McCarthyism. A residual element of McCarthyism was to restore

American omnipotence by defeating Communists—whoever and wherever they might be—so as to settle the score of the Korean War. Conveniently, Vietnam was waiting in the wings.

The War in Indochina

French Colonial War

In the year of 1787, when the Founding Fathers of the United States assembled in the city of Philadelphia to draft the Constitution for their infant Republic, in a remote corner of Asia the king of Hue, Gia Long, enlisted the aid of French volunteers against his rival for the imperial throne of Annam.[12] His successor, Emperor Minh Mang, a dedicated Confucian traditionalist, was opposed to the spread of Christianity, which he considered to be anathema to Confucianism. In 1833, Minh issued an imperial edict declaring the profession of Christianity a crime punishable by death. Thereafter the French missionaries were hounded out of his empire, imprisoned, or executed. The persecution of Christians became the established imperial policy which succeeding emperors adhered to with added vigor.

In the 1840s the French government dispatched naval vessels to Vietnam to secure by force the release of imprisoned missionaries. But France soon became engulfed in domestic and international turmoils in Europe such as the 1848 revolutions, the creation of the Second Empire in 1852, and later involvement in the Crimean War. It was not until early 1859 that France was able to redirect her attention to Vietnam. A joint Franco-Spanish task force was sent to Vietnam to occupy Tourane [Da Nang] and Saigon. The French proceeded to capture the three provinces around Saigon and this territorial conquest was formally confirmed in 1862 by a treaty signed with the Vietnamese ruler.

Five years later the French occupied Cochin China, then they began to move to the north. A small French contingent captured Hanoi in 1873, but the French government soon disavowed it. Ten years later, in 1883, a French naval squadron took Haiphong and Hanoi and by the terms of the treaty signed on August 25, 1883, the Vietnamese ruler formally recognized the French protectorate over his kingdom. Entire Vietnam became a French colony and Vietnamese independence came to an end. In 1887 Vietnam and two other protectorates—Laos and Cambodia—were organized into the Indochinese Union which was placed under the absolute French colonial administration.

The Vietnamese lost their sovereign national identity, but, precisely because of it, their nationalism became even more fervent in the form of an anti-French, anticolonial independence movement. In 1939 Vietnamese nationalists organized the Vietminh, the League for the Independence of Vietnam, a coalition of various groups, democrats, socialists, Communists, and so on. Their common objectives were national independence and social reform based on democratic principles.

After the outbreak of World War II, Hitler defeated France in June 1940, and he created a puppet government at Vichy to be in charge of the unoccupied part of France. All the French colonies overseas were placed under the jurisdiction of this Vichy regime headed by Marshal Pétain. In September 1940, under pressure from Berlin, the Vichy authorities in Indochina signed the Hanoi Convention with the Japanese Army, allowing the Japanese to use their facilities in return for Japan's promise to respect French interests in Asia. Japanese troops immediately moved in and began their occupation of Indochina. The Vietnamese were now subjected to "double oppression" and the Vietminh under the leadership of Ho Chi Minh carried on strong underground resistance with the slogan: "Neither the French nor the Japanese as masters."

In March 1945, as the Japanese came to realize their imminent defeat in the war, they ousted the French officials and allowed Vietnam, Laos, and Cambodia each to declare its independence. French Indochina was thus broken into three states which went their separate ways. Vietnam was headed by Emperor Bao Dai of Annam, the nominal ruler under the French and now the same under the Japanese; whereas the Vietminh, with its headquarters in South China and aided by the OSS,[13] organized its own provisional government for Vietnam. When Japan surrendered to the Allied powers, Bao Dai too surrendered his throne to Ho Chi Minh's provisional government, which assumed state power, moved into Hanoi, and, on September 2, 1945, declared national independence. The declaration of independence by the provisional government read in part as follows:

> 'All men are created equal. They are endowed by their Creator with certain inalienable rights, among these are Life, Liberty, and the Pursuit of Happiness.' This immortal statement was made in the Declaration of Independence of the United States of America in 1776.
>
> ... Nevertheless for more than eighty years, the French imperialists ... have acted contrarily to the ideals of humanity and justice ... they have deprived our people of every liberty.... They have enforced inhuman laws ... they have founded more prisons than schools.... We are convinced that the Allied nations which have acknowledged at Teheran and San Francisco the principles of self-determination and equality of nations will not refuse to acknowledge the independence of Vietnam.... For these reasons, we, members of the provisional government of Vietnam, declare to the world that Vietnam has the right to be a free and independent country. We also declare that the Vietnamese people are determined to make the heaviest sacrifices to maintain its independence and its liberty.[14]

The Vietnamese determination "to make the heaviest sacrifices" for their national independence was ominously prophetic. As it turned out, they had to wage a modern-day Thirty Years' War for independence.

As in Korea, for occupation purposes, French Indochina was divided at the sixteenth parallel. North of that line was occupied by the Chinese Nationalist forces, south of it by the British. Their task was to assemble, disarm, and repatriate the defeated Japanese armies and to restore "law and order." The British further assumed that their occupation entailed the overthrow of Ho's provisional government and the restoration of the French to power. They rearmed about five thousand French troops who had been released from Japanese captivity. In September 1945, in an attempt to seize power, these troops attacked the Saigon headquarters of the provisional government and fighting broke out between the two forces. This was the beginning of the French Indochina War and it set the tone for all that followed. By the end of the year, when the British were prepared to withdraw, there were about fifty thousand French troops in the southern zone to carry on by force the reestablishment of French rule.

In the north the Chinese occupation authorities recognized the de facto jurisdiction of the rovisional government at Hanoi and they kept several thousand French troops found in Hanoi under their strict control. In February 1946, after three-way negotiations among the Ho government, the French, and the Chinese, the Kuomintang troops left Vietnam. At this time Ho Chi Minh also appealed to the United States and other major powers to "intervene and stop the war in Indochina in order to mediate fair settlement."[15]

On March 6, Ho Chi Minh and the French government arrived at an agreement whereby France would recognize Vietnam as a free, but not independent, state within the French Union and the Indochinese Federation. In reality, however, this agreement was nothing more than a truce because French determination to restore her absolute control over all of Indochina and to wrest power from Ho had never been changed. Consequently, French-Vietnam relations worsened during the remainder of the year to the extent that the French bombarded Hanoi on November 23, killing thousands of Vietnamese. A full-scale war spread steadily throughout Tonkin and northern Annam and flared up again in Cochin China.

Despite occasional French victories, it became abundantly evident that the French could not hope to win by military means alone. Only by a political offensive could they hope to defeat Ho's followers. Out of this consideration, in 1949 France managed to install Bao Dai, who had been self-exiled in France after his abdication, as Chief of State of Vietnam with Saigon as his capital. Bao Dai, neither powerful nor popular, was a poor substitute for Ho Chi Minh who symbolized Vietnamese nationalism. The great majority of Vietnamese regarded Ho Chi Minh as their only possible leader in the struggle against the French, whereas Bao Dai was clearly a creature of French colonialism and imperialism.

The composition of combatants on each side could tell the nature of the conflict. The French fighting forces, about 150,000 by the end of 1949, consisted not only of French regulars but also of German mercenaries, French Foreign Legionnaires, Moroccans and Bengalese from overseas France, and Bao Dai's troops. They barely managed to hold only the centers of major cities. The Ho Chi Minh forces, in contrast, were mostly young, dedicated Vietminh fighters with high morale who held the countryside and enjoyed the loyalty of a large segment of the rural population. Unlike the North Koreans who behaved as ruthless conquerors in South Korea, Ho's men showed kindness, generosity, compassion, and fairness so as to marshal widespread public support for their cause. Their use of violence and terrorism against those who collaborated with the French or Bao Dai was not wanton but selective.

The Vietnam War, from its inception, was an historic struggle between the reactionary old order of colonialism and the progressive new order of nationalism. But the French insisted that they were not fighting a colonial war but an anti-Communist war. They projected themselves to be the defenders of Western civilization and Christianity in Asia against Eastern paganism and atheistic communism. These arguments were geared to the United States, which began to believe what it wished to believe: "Bao Dai seemed to represent the wishes of the majority of the Vietnamese and was daily gaining new support."[16]

On February 7, 1950, the United States extended *de jure* recognition to the Bao Dai regime and in May it announced that:

The United States Government, convinced that neither national independence nor democratic evolution exist in any area dominated by Soviet imperialism, considers the situation to be such as to warrant its according economic aid and military equipment to the Associated States of Indochina and to France in order to assist them in restoring stability and permitting these states to pursue their peaceful and democratic development.[17]

President Truman, only two days after the outbreak of the Korean War, reiterated his policy of "acceleration in the furnishing of military assistance to the forces of France and the associated states in Indochina and the dispatch of a military mission to provide

close working relations with these forces."¹⁸ But the war in Indochina was to be sidetracked by the Korean War which occupied
the top priority of the United States.

By the time the United States emerged from the frustrating, "no
win" war in Korea, the French Union forces in Indochina were on
the verge of total collapse. In April 1954, they were under siege
in the fortress of Dienbienphu. At this juncture, Secretary of State
John Foster Dulles attempted to initiate a United States military
intervention, but he was unable to enlist congressional support or
British cooperation for a "united action." Dienbienphu fell on
May 7, 1954. It marked the end of the French colonial war in Indochina. Ho Chi Minh felt that his nation's independence was at
last in his grasp. But it was only the first installment of his "heaviest sacrifices."

The 1954 Geneva Agreements

At the time when Dienbienphu was under the Vietminh siege,
on April 3, 1954, Secretary of State John Foster Dulles held a
high-level National Security Council (NSC) meeting attended also
by military and congressional leaders. He stated that President
Eisenhower needed a joint congressional resolution permitting him
to use air and naval power to rescue French efforts in Indochina.
The congressional leaders were puzzled and skeptical of such a
course of action and urged Dulles to explore the possibility of enlisting active support and cooperation from other Allies, especially
the British, for "united actions." A week later Secretary Dulles flew
to London to confer with Anthony Eden, the British foreign minister. Unable to gain British support, he flew back to Washington
via Paris where he talked briefly with Georges Bidault, the French
foreign minister.

British refusal to go along with the Dulles plan had the effect
of preventing an immediate American intervention in the war in
Indochina. But it also heightened the anxiety and bellicosity of
some members of the Eisenhower administration as expressed by
Vice-President Richard M. Nixon when he said: "The United
States as a leader of the free world cannot afford further retreat
in Asia. It is hoped the United States will not have to send troops
there, but if this government cannot avoid it, the Administration

must face up to the situation and dispatch forces."[19] Public reaction to the Nixon speech was so hostile that the attitude of the "hawks" in the administration was somewhat dampened. Secretary Dulles flew back to Paris—his shuttle diplomacy—to confer further with Georges Bidault. Anthony Eden joined them. During their meeting, Bidault requested a massive American air attack on the enemies to save Dienbienphu.[20] Secretary Dulles was assisted by Admiral Arthur Radford, chairman of the Joint Chiefs of Staff, who favored the air strike, believing that the loss of Indochina "would be the prelude to the loss of all Southeast Asia and a threat to a far wider area." By this time the American military aid program had reached over $1.1 billion, paying for 78 percent of the French war burden.[21]

British foreign minister Eden was deeply concerned and visibly uneasy with the apparent American determination to intervene unilaterally in Indochina in the name of "united action" of the Western Allies. He felt that the United States, on the eve of a conference at Geneva for a negotiated settlement of the Indochina war, was recklessly proposing military action which might uncontrollably lead to a general war in Asia, if not a World War III. It was incredible that the bitter lesson of Korea had been forgotten so soon. Eden flew to London for a consultation with his government and returned on April 25 with a firm, negative answer. The following day the Geneva Conference opened in a gloomy mood of American "sour grapes."[22]

The Geneva Conference had two distinctive phases: one on the Korean question, and the other on Indochina. It should be recalled that the Korean Armistice Agreement did not provide for any specific means to solve the political question of Korea, but it stated simply to hold a political conference for that purpose. In February 1954, at the four-power (USA, UK, USSR, and France) Foreign Ministers Conference in Berlin, designed to deal with German and Austrian problems, they had agreed to convene a conference at Geneva beginning on April 26, 1954, for the purpose of bringing about a peaceful unification of Korea and restoring peace in Indochina. The Korean question became deadlocked soon enough and it was shelved for good. The second phase of the conference began on May 8, the day after the fall of Dienbienphu.

The moment the conference took up the Indochina problem, and whatever settlement it might ultimately bring thereon, it was destined to be doomed from the standpoint of the United States. Secretary Dulles felt that the French were negotiating a settlement in the hope of escaping an unpopular war. In the same week the conference opened, the National Security Council urged President Eisenhower to inform the French government that its appeasement of the Communists would jeopardize not only its Big Power status but also continued United States aid. The council's policy paper had stated that the United States should consider continuing the war itself, with the associated states, if France negotiated an unsatisfactory settlement. The United States' objective was set at nothing short of a "military victory," which had eluded the American grasp so humiliatingly in Korea. Secretary Dulles refused to become personally involved in the work of the conference and returned to Washington, leaving the under-secretary of state, Walter Bedell Smith, in charge of the American delegation.

In the course of negotiations, replete with the usual proposals and counterproposals, deadlocks and *demarche,* on June 12 the Laniel government of France fell and Pierre Mendes-France was nominated to form a new government. Five days later his government was formally invested and the new premier declared that he would resign if he failed to conclude a peaceful settlement in Indochina by July 20. He met his deadline.

On July 20, 1954, the cease-fire agreement was signed between the French forces and the Vietminh forces (Democratic Republic of Vietnam). The highlights of this armistice agreement were:

1. Provisional military demarcation line to be established at the seventeenth parallel for the purpose of regroupment of troops as well as civilians in the period of 300 days.
2. Civilian administration in the regroupment zone to the north of the demarcation line to be in the hands of the Vietminh and that to the south in the hands of the French.
3. Banning of the introduction into the whole of Vietnam, North or South, of troop reinforcements or of all forms of arms; and the prohibition of any establishment of new military bases.

4. Neither party to be permitted to adhere to any military alliance or to allow any foreign power to use military bases in its own zone.

5. International Control Commission (ICC), composed of representatives of Canada, India, and Poland, to be formed to supervise the proper execution of the provisions of the Agreement.[23]

The following day, the final declaration was announced, endorsing the preceding armistice agreement for Vietnam as well as those for Laos and Cambodia. Two of the most important statements in the final declaration were (paragraphs 6 and 7):

6. The Conference recognizes that the essential purpose of the agreement relating to Vietnam is to settle military questions with a view to ending hostilities and that the military demarcation line is provisional and should not in any way be interpreted as constituting a political or territorial boundary. The Conference expresses its conviction that the execution of the provisions set out in the present declaration and in the agreement on cessation of hostilities creates the necessary basis for the achievement in the near future of a political settlement in Vietnam.

7. The Conference declares that, so far as Vietnam is concerned, the settlement of political problems, effected on the basis of respect for the principles of independence, unity and territorial integrity, shall permit the Vietnamese people to enjoy the fundamental freedoms, guaranteed by democratic institutions established as a result of free general elections by secret ballot. In order to secure that sufficient progress in the restoration of peace has been made, and that all the necessary conditions obtain for free expression of the national will, general elections shall be held in July 1956, under the supervision of an international commission composed of representatives of the Member States of the International Supervisory Commission, referred to in the agreement on the cessation of hostilities. Consultations will be held on this subject between the component representative authorities of the two zones from July 20, 1955, onwards.

With the military defeat of the French forces, Ho Chi Minh was confident that he could easily unify his country by continued military operations. But the Soviets and the Chinese, fearing a massive American military intervention in the event of a collapse of the Geneva Conference, persuaded Ho Chi Minh to accept the above-mentioned declaration providing for the 1956 general elections. It should also be pointed out that Ho's interests were further safeguarded by Article 27 of the armistice agreement: "The signatories of the present Agreement and their successors in their functions shall be responsible for ensuring the observance and enforcement of the terms and provisions thereof." As it turned out, however, the founders of the Republic of Vietnam (South Vietnam), replacing the Bao Dai regime and the French, refused to observe this rule, and partly because of it the whole Geneva system began to crumble.

When the final declaration was made public, the United States, as expected, refused to endorse any of the Geneva work, but it made a unilateral announcement specifically relevant to the subject of elections. Walter Bedell Smith stated:

In connection with the statement in the Declaration concerning free elections in Vietnam, my government wishes to make clear its position which it has expressed in a Declaration made in Washington on June 29, 1954, as follows: 'In the case of nations now divided against their will, we shall continue to seek to achieve unity through free elections, supervised by the United Nations to ensure that they are conducted fairly.'

The United States also declared, in a form of self-pledge, that it would "refrain from the threat or the use of force to disturb" the agreements and that "it would view any renewal of the aggression in violation of the aforesaid agreements with grave concern and as seriously threatening international peace and security."

Thus was ended the epoch-making Geneva Conference. It remained to be seen how effectively those agreements would fulfill the stated objectives. In the words of Anthony Eden, the chairman of the conference, the agreements were the best that their hands could devise: All will now depend upon the spirit in which those agreements are observed and carried out." From the standpoint of the United States, the Geneva settlement was, according to Walter Bedell Smith, the best which the United States could have possibly obtained under the circumstances. Publicly, the United States held the view that Geneva was not a "Munich"; however, it could be another Panmunjom. Privately, however, the United States regarded it as a "disaster" that "completed a major forward stride of Communism which may lead to the loss of Southeast Asia."[24] Geneva was worse than Panmunjom, so it went, because in the latter case negotiations had bridled a war in which the mighty United States military power had been engaged to repulse Communist aggression, whereas in the former case negotiations had brought an end to a war in which no United States armed forces were involved to contain Communist expansion. Such being the case, a "disaster" was an anticipated outcome of the Geneva Conference, for "diplomacy has rarely been able to gain at the conference table what cannot be gained or held on the battlefield."[25] The underlying thought in this was that military means or war is the determinant of diplomacy, i.e., war is an instrument of national policy.

The United States, by refusing to endorse the Geneva Agreements which it labeled as disaster, set the stage to go it alone, like a lone ranger in Indochina, to assume the burden of defending South Vietnam. In the process, knowingly or unknowingly, the Eisenhower administration began to undo the Geneva settlement and sowed the seeds of another war in Asia.

United States Involvements

The Korean War was America's fourth frontier military involvement in Asia in this century.[26] The Demilitarized Zone (DMZ) separating North and South Korea became the farthest frontier outpost of the United States in the continent of Asia. The United States defense perimeter then ran from Alaska to the Philippines through the Aleutians, Japan, Korea, and Taiwan. In view of the United States global strategy of containing the spread of communism, the Eisenhower administration came to the conclusion that the weakest link in this structure was Southeast Asia.

As early as February 1950, when the National Security Council

decided to extend military aid to the French in Indochina, it enunciated what later became known as "the domino theory"—the
basic rationale for American involvement in this region. The council stated that it was important to United States security interests
that all practicable measures be taken to prevent further Communist expansion in Southeast Asia. The council had described
how the domino effect would endanger even European security:

The loss of any of the countries of Southeast Asia to Communist aggression would have critical psychological, political
and economic consequences. In the absence of effective and
timely counter-action, the loss of any single country would
probably lead to relatively swift submission to alignment
with Communism by the remaining countries of this group.
Furthermore, an alignment with Communism of the rest of
Southeast Asia and India, and in the longer term, of the
Middle East (with the probable exceptions of at least Pakistan and Turkey) would in all probability progressively follow.
Such widespread alignment would endanger the stability and
security of Europe.[27]

President Eisenhower spoke of the "row of dominoes" at a press
conference on April 7, 1954; and on July 7, two weeks before the
final signing of the Geneva agreements, Secretary Dulles seemed
to have foreseen the toppling of the first domino in the 1956
general elections that were to be proclaimed in the final declaration. It would be undoubtedly true, Dulles said, "that elections
might eventually mean unification [of] Vietnam under Ho Chi
Minh."[28]

The urgency of the post-Geneva United States policy in Southeast Asia, therefore, was to strengthen the weakest link and to
prevent Red Dominoes from sweeping the area. Out of this consideration came the finalization of the forming of the Southeast
Asia Treaty Organization (SEATO) less than two months after
the Geneva agreements. The SEATO was a hastily contrived
modern-day "covered wagons," assembled in a circle against the
threatening Red hordes in the Southeast Asian frontier of the
United States.

During the crisis over Dienbienphu, Secretary Dulles had tried hard to gain British support for a military intervention under "united action." Failing in this, he came up instead with an idea of creating some form of collective self-defense mechanism which could lead to "united action." Time ran out quickly and the "disastrous" Geneva settlement became a reality.

On September 6, 1954, Secretary Dulles convened the Manila Conference attended by representatives of Britain, France, Australia, New Zealand, the Philippines, Thailand, and Pakistan. To avoid the appearance of a "white man's party,"[29] more Southeast Asian nations, such as Indonesia, India, Burma, and Ceylon, had also been invited, but they declined to attend the conference, preferring to pursue their policy of neutralism. Two days later, the delegates from the eight nations signed the Southeast Asia Collective Defense Treaty and Protocol (the Manila Pact). The treaty stipulated that in cases of external aggression by means of armed attack each treaty power was "to meet the common danger in accordance with its constitutional processes" (Article IV, para. 1). It should be noted that, as far as the United States was concerned, this provision would be applied "only to Communist aggression." In case of subversion, each party was to "consult" with the other signatories "in order to agree on the measures to be taken for common defense" (Article IV, para. 1). The SEATO powers, by an additional protocol, designated the states of Cambodia and Laos and the "free territory under the jurisdiction of the State of Vietnam" to come under the protection of the above-mentioned article.

What were some of the implications of the SEATO arrangements? First, by the protocol designation "the free territory under the jurisdiction of the State of Vietnam," Vietnam was given the status of statehood equal to that of Laos. Since the Geneva agreements had recognized that there was only one political entity of a single Vietnam with two regroupment zones divided by a provisional demarcation line at the 17th parallel, the State of Vietnam would become by inference *the* Vietnam having the "free" territory (South) and the *unfree* territory (North). Here the United States attempted to apply the Korean formula to the Vietnam situation. There were some similarities between the two. To begin with, the original purposes and the nature of thirty-eighth and seventeenth parallels were identical. Both the Koreans and the Vietnamese had suffered from colonial rules from which they were liberated. They had regained their national independence and were fighting for their national unification. Both Korea and Vietnam became international arenas for the Cold War struggle between the free world and the Communist bloc. There were, however, some fundamental dissimilarities which the United States failed to distinguish or ignored deliberately. The Republic of Korea was legally established under the auspices of the United Nations, which recognized its sovereignty throughout the Korean peninsula. The United States could, therefore, justifiably label the North Korean regime as an illegal creation of the Soviet occupation forces.

When North Korea launched an attack on South Korea, the United States and fifteen other UN member states formed the United Nations Military Command in order to repulse the attacker in conformity with the provisions of the UN Charter. The United States was able rightly to claim moral as well as legal obligations in the effort to save the Republic of Korea by way of implementing the principles of collective security of the United Nations. In Vietnam, on the other hand, the Vietminh forces had been fighting an anticolonial, national liberation war against the French and they finally succeeded in defeating their former overlords. Indeed, the Vietminh independence war was comparable to the American War of Independence. The fact that Ho Chi Minh was widely regarded as Vietnam's George Washington indicated more substance than superficial rhetoric. In short, the United States created a self-deceiving illusion that the State of Vietnam was a legitimate, sovereign nation over the entirety of Vietnam.

Second, since the State of Vietnam was unable to exercise its jurisdiction over the *unfree* territory north of the seventeenth parallel, the United States implicitly permitted this line to become a permanent political and territorial demarcation line contrary to the intent and spirit of the Final Declaration.

Third, nowhere in the Manila Pact could there be found any mention of *commitment,* either by the United States or by any other signatories, to any government designated by the protocol. An explicit pronouncement to that effect would have violated the Geneva agreements. Yet, *American commitment* to protect South

Vietnam against whatever sources of threat to its security became the central theme of American leaders who continued to accelerate their involvement in Vietnam.

Fourth, unlike NATO, SEATO had no combined military command, i.e., there were no SEATO forces made up of armed forces contributed to it by its member nations. The "teeth" of the organization were solely the United States military power armed with nuclear weapons.

Fifth, and finally, SEATO was a poor substitute for the Geneva settlement. A critic wrote:

SEATO was the product of Dulles' compulsion to combine the practical tenets of international law, which he had studied and practiced, with the singular fervor of his own anti-Communist crusade—one that, in a political sense, matched de Lattre's military crusade. His mistake lay in trying to shove SEATO down the throats of America's principal allies —particularly Great Britain and France as well as a rather motley and suspicious group of other nations—in such a hurry that they couldn't possibly digest.[30]

Earlier, in August 1954, the United States had adopted a threefold program for South Vietnam: (1) militarily, to train and build up indigenous armed forces, (2) economically, to provide aid directly to the Vietnamese, not as before through the French channel, and (3) politically, to work with Premier Ngo Dinh Diem, who had taken office July 7, just two weeks before the signing of the Geneva agreements which he had refused to endorse. Diem was not, according to President Eisenhower's special ambassador General Lawton Collins, qualified to handle the staggering task of solving such critical problems as a disorganized administration, a bankrupt economy, a corrupt social order, chronic factional strife, a chaotic political system, and swarming refugees. Collins recommended Diem's removal to Secretary Dulles, who replied: "We have no other choice but to continue our aid to Vietnam and support of Diem."

In October 1955, by a national referendum, Bao Dai was deposed and with the American blessing a republic was proclaimed by Diem, who became the first president of South Vietnam. And, in July 1956, as the Geneva-provided date for general elections throughout Vietnam rolled in, Diem refused to hold elections, asserting that the South Vietnam government had not signed the Geneva accords and therefore was not bound by them. Whether or not the United States had actually "conspired" with Diem to sabotage the elections was a moot question. What was evident at this time was that United States aid to South Vietnam was focused almost entirely on arms supplies, and much of what was intended for agriculture, education, or transportation actually went to military-oriented programs. Such being the case, the massive American aid money seldom touched the lives of the predominately rural populace, while providing Diem with a degree of financial independence. Diem was little interested in bringing about changes for the disadvantaged classes and isolated himself from the basic economic and political realities of his people.

After the uneventful passing of the date for elections in 1956, anti-Diem insurgency began. Most of those who took up arms were South Vietnamese and the causes for which they fought were by no means contrived by Hanoi. Those insurgents regarded the United States as having adorned itself with the French colonial mantle and they looked upon the Diem regime as an American puppet just as much as the Bao Dai government had been for the French. In October 1957, Vietcong (Vietnamese Communists) guerrillas bombed the United States Information Agency (USIA) and the Military Assistance Advisory Group (MAAG) institutions; and in July 1958, they attacked the Vietnam military base at Bien Hoa, killing and wounding several United States MAAG personnel.

By the end of 1959, the Vietcong controlled about a third of the countryside. Within a year they were claiming half the country and Diem's forces were everywhere on the defense. As dissatisfaction and discontent with his government mounted, Diem relied more and more on his family, particularly his brother Ngo Dinh Nhu, for advice and guidance in state affairs. He became increasingly authoritarian, moralistic, inflexible, bureaucratic, suspicious, and isolated. The United States officials in Saigon, secretly pessimistic as they were, publicly presented to the American people and Congress the picture of "continuing progress, virtually miraculous improvement, year in and year out."[31]

Inside of the other half of Vietnam, from 1954 to 1958, the Ho Chi Minh government in Hanoi concentrated on its internal development, confidently hoping to achieve reunification either through the general elections provided for in the Final Declaration at Geneva or through the inevitable demise of the feeble Diem regime. As to Ho's southern strategy, he had cautioned and ordered the Communist cadres left behind in the South not to wage subversive activities against Diem. When these Vietcong cadres found themselves caught in the predicament between being wiped out by Diem's program of extermination of Communists and following Ho's orders not to fight back, they chose the road to insurgency. As the insurgence showed growing success, only then did North Vietnam's leaders decide in May 1959 to take control of the insurgents and they allowed southern cadre members who had been taken north to infiltrate back to the south. In October 1960, in the jungles of South Vietnam, the National Front for the Liberation of South Vietnam was organized "to overthrow the U.S.-Diem clique" and "to liberate the South." The tempo of the war was suddenly accelerating.

That was the situation that confronted President Kennedy when he took office in January 1961.

CHAPTER ELEVEN

Storm and Lull in Asia

The Vietnam War

The Kennedy Burden

"Ask not what your country can do for you; ask what you can do for your country." So spoke President Kennedy in his inaugural address on that cold January day of 1961. He went on to call on the American people to "pay any price, bear any burden, meet any hardship, support any friend, oppose any foe to assure the survival and the success of liberty."[1] Kennedy's call for American determination, pledge, and sacrifice in his inaugural address and Ho Chi Minh's call for "heaviest sacrifice" in his Declaration of Independence had been destined by a twist of historic irony to converge on a deadly conflict in Vietnam—the conflict between the forces of indefatigable Vietnamese nationalism and the forces of American frontier adventurism.

By the time President Kennedy came to office, Vietnam was approaching a crisis. In contrast to Diem's rapidly deteriorating position, the numerical strength of the Vietcong guerrillas steadily increased. At the time of the Geneva cease-fire in 1954, about ten thousand Vietcong cadres were left behind among the peasant population in the South.

These men became the nucleus of the new force which the Communists have built. The number expanded by local recruitment as well as by infiltration from the North until it has reached an estimated 22,000 to 24,000 regulars with a supplement of local irregulars of over 100,000. The force is equipped largely with primitive, antiquated, and captured weapons. In recent months, some sophisticated equipment has been employed in battle against the government forces.[2]

President Kennedy felt that the United States had been overcommitted in Southeast Asia in general and in South Vietnam in particular. The previous administration had gradually developed a special commitment; certainly it was not absolutely binding, but the commitment was there nevertheless. Without United States support and aid, the Diem regime could not survive. In March 1961, more than one-half of the entire region around Saigon, the capital of South Vietnam, was under Vietcong control and they began to move closer on the city.

In May, President Kennedy sent Vice-President Lyndon B. Johnson on an Asian tour to reassure the Asian allies of America's continued support. In Saigon, despite his unfavorable private assessment of Diem, Vice-President Johnson hailed him publicly as the "Winston Churchill of Southeast Asia."[3] Upon his return, Johnson recommended a U.S. move forward promptly in support of those nations in Southeast Asia, otherwise the United States had to "pull back our defense to San Francisco and a 'Fortress America' concept."[4] Rhetoric and exaggeration notwithstanding, Johnson visualized the Red Dominoes toppling across the Pacific to the shores of California. Secretary of State Dean Rusk was likewise convinced that the northern dominoes were about to fall on the south by way of "the determined and ruthless campaign of propaganda, infiltration, and subversion by the Communist regime in North Vietnam to destroy the Republic of Vietnam."[5] He then developed the theme of "aggression from the North," an apparent reminder of the North Korean attack on South Korea.

In October, President Kennedy sent General Maxwell D. Taylor, then the president's personal military advisor, and Walt W. Rostow, then the senior White House aide, to Vietnam on a fact-finding mission. The Taylor-Rostow report and its recommendations emphasized the military aspect of the problem, which could be solved by an added American commitment including, if necessary, the introduction of United States armed forces. By accepting most of the recommendations, as they did, the frontiersmen of the Kennedy administration who considered defeat unthinkable produced a broad commitment to Vietnam's defense, rendering priority to the military aspects of the war over political reforms. The basic flaw in this policy, which was doomed from its inception, was that the United States was bent on solving political issues by military means. The United States failed to persuade or prod Diem into undertaking the kind of political, economic, and social reforms which would, in the maxim of a popular government, "win the hearts and minds of the people."

All in all, the Taylor-Rostow report is an extraordinary document and provides a great insight into the era. It shows a complete misunderstanding of the nature of the war (there was no discussion of the serious political problems of the war in Taylor's cables). It was arrogant and contemptuous toward a foe who had a distinguished and impressive record against a previous Western challenger. It was written by a general who had seen the limits of air power in Korea and now said that if things went wrong, air power would handle Hanoi any time we wanted. . . . When Ridgway in 1954 investigated the possibility of U.S. troops in Indochina, he maximized the risks and minimized the benefits; now Taylor was maximizing the benefits and minimizing the risks.[6]

In conjunction with military operations, United States officials in Vietnam and the Diem regime developed the "strategic hamlet" program as an all-embracing, counter-guerrilla strategy. Under this program the Vietnamese peasants were regrouped into fortified hamlets in which the Diem officials were to carry on political, social, and economic measures designed both to weed out Vietcong sympathizers and to gain popular allegiance through better security and better services. It was a kind of collective farm or a commune in the Diem style and he saw it as a means of controlling his people, Communist or non-Communist, while American officials saw it as a means of winning the loyalty of the Vietnamese peasants. Those peasants involved, on the other hand, saw it as a means of forcing them to move against their will from their fields and their ancestral homes. To them it was the same old method of harassment employed by the French. The result of the program was dismal failure, coupled with increased resentment and hostility of the people.

By the end of 1962, the United States' policy proved ineffective militarily as well as politically. American forces in Vietnam had reached eleven thousand men; the number of American combat casualties increased from 14 in 1961 to 109 in 1962 and to 489 in 1963. Yet, through the year of 1962 and after, almost all official American pronouncements were expressed in glaring optimism. Secretary of Defense Robert S. McNamara stated on his first tour to Vietnam in 1962, "Every quantitative measurement we have shows we're winning this war."[7] President Kennedy in his third State of the Union message declared that "the spearpoint of aggression has been blunted in South Vietnam" and that "we have maintained the frontiers of freedom from Vietnam to West Berlin."[8] Secretary Rusk asserted that the strategic-hamlet program was producing "excellent results . . . morale in the countryside has begun to rise."[9]

The veil of official optimism was torn asunder by the Buddhist revolt which erupted in the summer of 1963. The Buddhist crisis highlighted and intensified a widespread, long-standing dissatisfaction with Diem and his style of government. It plunged the nation into the nadir of internal political turmoil. Through political ineptitude, religious intolerance, and cruel repression, the Diem regime failed to mollify inflamed Buddhist feelings. Their protests in the form of mass demonstrations and the immolations of their fellow monks were met by police truncheons and indiscriminate arrests. The shock waves spread abroad, especially in the United States, bringing the Kennedy administration under strong public criticism for its support of the Diem government. By the end of August, the United States was at its wits' end.

On September 2, 1963, in a television interview with CBS correspondent Walter Cronkite, President Kennedy declared that the

United States was prepared to continue its aid to South Vietnam, "but I don't think that the war can be won unless the people support the effort, and, in my opinion, in the last two months, the Diem Government has gotten out of touch with the people."[10] A week later, in another television interview, President Kennedy stated that he would not reduce American aid to South Vietnam because that might bring about its collapse similar to Chiang's downfall in China after WW II.

The dilemma for the United States was this: war was not winnable with Diem at the helm of South Vietnam; aid to Diem was inconsequential; but South Vietnam would collapse without American aid. Robert F. Kennedy, the president's brother and attorney general, raised the question of disengagement, suggesting that if the war was unwinnable it was time for the United States to get out of Vietnam. With a view to finding an answer, the National Security Council decided to send to Vietnam a fact-finding mission led by Major General Victor H. Krulak, the Pentagon's top-ranking expert in counter-guerrilla warfare, and Joseph A. Mendenhall of the Bureau of Far Eastern Affairs of the Department of State. They made an exhausting four-day tour of Vietnam and on September 10 presented to the National Security Council such diametrically opposed assessments that President Kennedy quizzically asked: "You two did visit the same country, didn't you?"[11]

The inconclusive results of the Krulak-Mendenhall mission simply nurtured a renewed urge for another fact-finding mission. In late September, Secretary of Defense McNamara himself visited Vietnam, accompanied by Maxwell Taylor, then the chairman of the Joint Chiefs of Staff. On the basis of their report, the National Security Council announced that the major part of the United States military task could be completed by the end of 1965 and that in view of the rapid progress the United States was making in training Vietnamese, one thousand U.S. military personnel assigned to South Vietnam would be withdrawn by the end of 1963. At this time the U.S. military personnel in Vietnam exceeded sixteen thousand and official optimism or miscalculation began to revive.

Two tragic events in November 1963 catapulted the war in

Vietnam onto an intractable path. On November 1, a U.S.-sup-
ported military coup, organized by key generals in South Vietnam
armies, overthrew the Diem regime. Rebellious troops laid siege
to the presidential palace in Saigon, which was captured by the
following morning. President Diem and his brother-advisor, Ngo
Dinh Nhu, escaped through a secret tunnel and hid in Cholon, the
Chinese quarter of Saigon. Soon they were captured by the rebels
and on the way to coup headquarters were shot and killed in what
was officially described as "accidental suicide" in an armoured
carrier.

The new government—the military junta—headed by General
Duong Van Minh, recognized by the United States on November 7,
would be heavily dependent on American advice and aid not only
for the war effort but also in the practical problems of running the
country. The central implication and the essence of the U.S.-
endorsed military coup were:

> The United States, through its participation in the overthrow
> of the Diem regime and the establishment of a successor
> government, became more directly involved in managing the
> political, economic, and military problems of Vietnam. With
> the increase in U.S. involvement came an increase in the
> commitment of U.S. prestige to victory in South Vietnam.
> This in turn made a U.S. withdrawal from Southeast Asia
> more unlikely.[12]

The death of Diem appeared to have given rise to a hope that
the conflict in Vietnam could be solved by negotiations between
the parties involved. The National Liberation Front (NLF) on
November 8 issued a manifesto calling on the new regime in South
Vietnam to take such a course so as to reach a cease-fire and to
foster conditions conducive to free general elections with a view
to establishing state organs and to forming a national coalition
government. The manifesto also advocated a policy of neutralism,
the creation of a neutral zone in Indochina, and the reunification
of North and South step-by-step.

The junta's response was, in line with United States policy, outright suppression of neutralist movements. The junta generals de-

clared that they, having no political ambitions, would continue to fight Vietcong to a successful conclusion. But this coup was only a curtain-raiser for the political drama yet to be unfolded in South Vietnam.[13] Three weeks later President Kennedy was killed by an assassin's bullets in Dallas, Texas.

The Johnson Escalation

Upon the death of President Kennedy, Vice-President Johnson succeeded to the presidency with a firm public pledge to "let us continue" and that "this nation will keep its commitments from South Vietnam to West Berlin."[14] So did he continue the war in Vietnam. He rejected both Ho Chi Minh's proposal for a negotiated settlement, which was conveyed to him through the secretary-general of the United Nations, U Thant, and Prince Sihanouk's proposal for a neutralization of South Vietnam. President Johnson felt that neutralization of South Vietnam was tantamount to a Communist take-over. He was determined to prosecute the war, rejecting any compromise or any peace proposals. "We shall maintain in Vietnam," the president assured in his message to General Duong Van Minh "American personnel and material as needed to assist you in achieving victory."

Victory was hard to achieve. The military coup which had overthrown Diem was not a revolution; Duong Van Minh was not a revolutionary leader. The junta had no policy or plan to run the country. The junta generals replaced many officials of the old regime, but nothing was really changed. The Buddhists demanded a clean sweep of the old order, while the Catholics denounced discriminations against them. The Vietcong and their sympathizers saw no difference between the old Diem regime and the new military junta—both were American puppets, reactionary oppressors of the people. Most importantly there was no change at the grassroots, in the villages where the local impact of oppression was most severely felt in the form of petty officials and tax collectors who had been engaged in graft, corruption, extortion, and often physical brutality on the peasants. Within a month after the coup, government forces suffered their heaviest casualties of the year, losing key provinces in the Mekong delta. This defeat should be attributed primarily to the old regime which used to exaggerate the progress that was being made in the strategic-hamlet program, concealing the truth of the deteriorating military situation. It was significant that one of the decisions the junta made was to put an end to the building of new strategic-hamlets.

On January 30, 1964, Duong Van Minh was overthrown by a military coup staged by General Ngyuen Khanh who thought that General Minh was inclined to accept neutralism. Vietnam's political instability, coupled with Vietnamese apathy toward their government, accentuated American frustration and anxiety. The more Americans there were in Vietnam, the less they accomplished. Stunned and confused, the United States appeared to have no clear aims or policies in Vietnam.

We dealt repeatedly in tired shibboleths, in continued bland expressions of optimism; and in consequence our policy, if indeed we had one, was obscured in a welter of words that unfortunately soon became involved in a Presidential political campaign. The admission must be made that we had no more of a post-coup plan than the Vietnamese had.[15]

Against these backgrounds, voices advocating a wider war were frequently heard, as in Senator Barry Goldwater's campaign speeches for the presidential nomination. Earlier, such a course of action had been proposed to President Johnson by the Joint Chiefs of Staff:

Currently we and South Vietnamese are fighting the war on the enemy's terms. He has determined the locals, the timing and the tactics of the battle while our actions are essentially reactive. One reason for this is the fact that we have obliged ourselves to labor under self-imposed restrictions with respect to impending external aid to the Vietcong. These restrictions include keeping the war within the boundaries of South Vietnam, avoiding the direct use of U.S. combat forces, and limiting U.S. direction of the campaign to rendering advice to the Government of Vietnam.[16]

In Saigon, Vietnamese generals were boasting of their readiness to attack enemies "outside South Vietnam's frontiers" and to bomb and destroy Hanoi. What the American public did not know at this time was the fact that President Johnson had ordered an elaborate program of covert military operations against North Vietnam, begun on February 1, 1964, under the code name Operation Plan 34A. The clandestine operations ranged from U-2 flights over North Vietnam and parachuting sabotage agents into the North, to abduction of North Vietnamese for intelligence information, and commando raids and bombardments from the sea to destroy North Vietnam coastal installations. In May, the Johnson administration drew up the target list for Air Force bombings of North Vietnam, together with a draft of a congressional resolution.

While Americans were kept in the dark, Hanoi knew, of course, of the 34A activities and was convinced of the United States intent to escalate the war. So did the rest of the world. Fearing an imminent, major escalation of the conflict, Secretary-General U Thant in July 1964 proposed to reconvene another Geneva Conference in search of a peaceful settlement in Vietnam. President de Gaulle of France welcomed the U Thant initiative, urging at the same time that the parties involved should observe and comply with the Geneva agreements reached ten years earlier. France, the Soviet Union, and North Vietnam sent communications to the fourteen participants of the previous Geneva Conference, inviting them to attend another conference to deal with the war in Vietnam. The People's Republic of China, Cambodia, and the National Liberation Front promptly endorsed the move. The United States' rejection of their efforts was swift and scornful. President Johnson stated, "we do not believe in conferences called to ratify terror."[17] One might wonder whose terror he had in mind. He then increased American troops in South Vietnam from sixteen thousand to twenty-one thousand.

The major escalation of the war was occasioned by what became known as "the Tonkin Gulf incident" in early August 1964. At midnight on July 30, a South Vietnam naval commando under General Westmoreland's command staged an amphibious raid on two North Vietnamese islands—Hon Me and Hon Niew—in the Gulf of Tonkin. The Hanoi government immediately lodged a protest with the International Control Commission. On August 2, while three North Vietnam torpedo boats were still searching the seas around the islands for the raiders, the United States destroyer *Maddox* appeared in the vicinity. The torpedo boats began their high-speed run at the *Maddox,* which they apparently had mistaken for a South Vietnamese escort vessel. In the ensuing engagement, one of the PT boats was sunk by a direct hit from *Maddox's* guns and the other two were damaged by planes launched from the aircraft carrier *Ticonderoga.*

The following day, August 3, President Johnson ordered the destroyer *C. Turner Joy* to reinforce the *Maddox.* He also instructed another aircraft carrier, the *Constellation,* to join the *Ticonderoga.* That night two more clandestine 34A attacks were made on a radar installation at Vinhson. On the night of August 4 (Hanoi time), North Vietnam torpedo boats allegedly attacked both the *Maddox* and the *C. Turner Joy* in what subsequently became a confused and controversial incident. Hanoi denied there ever was any second attack. Neither of the two American destroyers suffered any casualty or damage. Senator J. William Fulbright, Chairman of the Senate Foreign Relations Committee, later observed:

> But this Gulf of Tonkin incident, if I may say so, was a very vague one. We were briefed on it, but we have no way of knowing, even to this day, what actually happened. I don't know whether we provoked that attack in connection with supervising or helping a raid by South Vietnamese or not. Our evidence was sketchy as to whether those PT boats, or some kind of boats, that were approaching were coming to investigate or whether they actually attacked. I have been *told* there was no physical damage. They weren't hit by anything. I heard one man say there was one bullet hole in one of those ships. One bullet hole![18]

In any case, President Johnson immediately invited sixteen congressional leaders from both parties to the White House and told them that because of the second unprovoked attack on the American destroyers, he had decided to launch reprisal air strikes against North Vietnam and to ask for a congressional resolution.

There was no indication that the president told the lawmakers about the 34A activities. The resolution the president requested was passed on August 7 by a vote of 88 to 2 in the Senate and 416 to 0 in the House. It authorized the president to "take all necessary measures to repel any armed attack against the forces of the United States and to prevent further aggression" and at the same time allowed him to "take all necessary steps, including the use of armed forces, to assist any member or protocol state of the Southeast Asia Collective Defense Treaty requesting assistance in defense of its freedom." Four days after the passage of the resolution, Johnson officials drew up a policy memorandum which outlined graduated steps toward a full-scale air war against North Vietnam. On September 7, 1964, they reached a "general consensus" at a White House strategy meeting that air attacks would commence early in 1965.

The administration's strategy consensus came in the midst of the presidential election campaign. President Johnson was projecting himself as a man of reason, restraint, peace, and perseverance as opposed to Barry Goldwater who, rash and temperamental, was advocating all-out bombing of North Vietnam. Johnson stated that he would not commit "a good many American boys to fighting a war that I think ought to be fought by the boys of Asia to help protect their own land."[19]

President Johnson won a landslide election victory and convinced himself that he was given the "mandate of the people" to achieve peace through a larger war. He was ready to bomb the North and was waiting only for appropriate *casus belli,* which the Vietcong guerrillas provided on February 7, 1965. They attacked a United States military compound at Pleiku, inflicting considerable casualties. The United States response was swift and severe. American warplanes bombed preselected North Vietnam targets. The war became escalated into a new phase with an added intensity.

The escalated war in Vietnam brought the world a step closer to the danger of a wider international conflagration. Secretary-General U Thant, President de Gaulle, and the Soviet Union each once again attempted to persuade the United States to agree on a negotiated settlement in Vietnam; all in vain.[20] Secretary-General

U Thant lamented: "I am sure the great American people, if only they know the facts and the background to the developments in South Vietnam, will agree with me that further bloodshed is unnecessary. . . . As you know in times of war and of hostilities the first casualty is truth."[21]

President Johnson and his advisors had high hopes for the air war against the North, but after over a month of bombing with no sign of yielding from Hanoi, the president decided on April 1, 1965, to use American ground troops for offensive action in South Vietnam. This "Americanization of the war" was to be carried out with "as little prominence as possible," for it would violate not only Johnson's campaign pledge that American boys should not fight an Asian boys' war, but also an American policy maxim held since the Korean conflict that the United States should not fight a land war in Asia.

On September 7, 1965, in a speech at Johns Hopkins University, President Johnson offered to discuss "without posing any preconditions" and suggested that once the Communists agreed to a settlement in which the independence of South Vietnam was guaranteed, the United States would be prepared to provide a $1 billion economic development program for the Mekong River basin in which North Vietnam might participate. This move was geared more to quiet domestic critics and to obtain public support for the air war than to offer acceptable terms to Hanoi.[22] This offer contained in itself a built-in, objectionable condition to which North Vietnam would never agree—the independence of South Vietnam. The United States, as before, insisted on the permanent division of Vietnam and its self-assumed right to protect this "separate" and "sovereign" state of South Vietnam—the creation of the United States in violation of the Geneva agreements. The Hanoi government rejected the offer, calling it "dollar bait" hooked on "American imperialism."

Throughout 1965 the character of the war changed vastly. As the South Vietnam armies continued to lose ground in the face of Vietcong offenses, the United States troops were ordered to fight Communists in the search-and-destroy strategy, unlike the earlier years when they served only in the role of "advisors" and "supporting units." By the end of the year, United States forces in

South Vietnam reached the total of 185,000. Vietcong strength in South Vietnam at this time was estimated at 230,000. Despite the heavy casualties, they had the capacity of substantially increasing their numbers at any given moment through local recruitment in the South and infiltration from the North.

In 1966, a number of high officials in the Johnson administration, including Secretary of Defense McNamara, began to have serious doubts about the effectiveness of the air and ground war in Vietnam, but they kept recommending escalation as the only available policy. They seemed to have become helpless victims of their baseless optimism, meaningless rhetoric, groundless fear of "dominoes," exaggerated sense of omnipotence, and above all, their insensitivity to Vietnamese nationalism. Consequently, the escalation resulted in a steady increase in casualties on both sides, the U.S. bombing of Hanoi-Haiphong areas, Ho's general mobilization for war efforts, U.S. troop level to 400,000, the emergence of the antiwar movement in the United States, and the death of the Great Society.

The pressures of a protracted, frustrating, and unwinnable war began to force the high-ranking policymakers in the Johnson administration to regroup into three identifiable camps on the basis of their perceptions of the war: (1) the "disillusioned doves"—the McNamara group who tried to set limits on the war and then gradually disengage; (2) the insatiable hawks—the military group led by the Joint Chiefs of Staff and General William C. Westmoreland, the commander in Vietnam, who wanted to step up the air war and to consider invasions into Laos, Cambodia, and even North Vietnam; and (3) the cautious owls—some senior officers at the White House and the State Department who took a middle position. This troika division of views within the administration put an end to the "consensus" politics of President Johnson, who became increasingly irritated by it and tended to regard it as a sign of disrespect to his leadership.

During the course of 1967 the Johnson administration continued to assure the American public that it was winning the war with a victory at "the end of the tunnel." The truth was that the United States was losing the battle on every front. The "search-and-destroy" strategy failed because the South Vietnam army was unable to hold the territory cleared of Vietcong by American forces. The "harassment and interdiction" or the "free-fire zone" tactics, designed to deny the Vietcong access to habitable areas, served only to drive peasants out of their farmlands into ever-swelling refugee camps. The widespread use of chemical defoliants, intended to eliminate Communist food supplies and cover, destroyed farm crops of the peasants, creating starvation. The policy of "rooting out the NLF infrastructure" resulted in the destruction of much of South Vietnam's rural society.

The year of 1968 was one of the most turbulent years in modern American history. In Vietnam, at the end of January, the Communist forces launched full-scale, well-prepared attacks upon American and South Vietnamese positions in what became known as "the Tet offensive." (Tet is the Vietnamese Lunar New Year.) It began with an attack on the United States embassy in Saigon; for a day the Vietcong guerrillas held the embassy compound. The ferocious attacks spread rapidly to almost all the cities and towns of South Vietnam—thirty-four provincial towns, sixty-four district towns, and all of the autonomous cities. Communist forces held major portions of Saigon for more than two weeks; when they were driven out, Saigon lay in ruins. Hue, the ancient capital of the Annamese kingdom, was captured by the Communists and was occupied by them for nearly two months until they were forced to evacuate in the face of a massive American counterattack.

The Tet offensive took the White House and the military "by surprise, and its strength, length and intensity prolonged this shock."[23] But President Johnson told reporters three days after the initial attack that the Communist offensive had been "anticipated, prepared for and met" and that the enemy had suffered "a complete failure." It became increasingly apparent that the Johnson administration, as though suffering from a "split personality" syndrome, was not telling the American public the whole truth about Vietnam; the credibility gap was widening ever greater. In the midst of growing domestic dissent, dissatisfaction, and disillusionment about the purposes and the conduct of the war, coupled with the military failure in Vietnam, President Johnson decided to de-escalate the war. On the evening of March 31, 1968, in a telecast to the nation he declared that he was ordering a halt to the bombing and was inviting North Vietnam for peace talks. He went on to say: "Tonight, in the hope that this action will lead to early talks, I am taking the first step to de-escalate the conflict. We are reducing—substantially reducing—the present level of hostilities. And we are doing so unilaterally, and at once." In closing his speech, he added: "I shall not seek, and I will not accept, the nomination of my party for another term." A few days later North Vietnam agreed to peace negotiations which subsequently began on May 3, 1968, in Paris.

The Paris peace talks were reminiscent of Panmunjom—fighting while talking. The deep-rooted suspicion and distrust of one party against the other was difficult to overcome. There was every indication that the talks would be prolonged affairs. President Johnson was unable to win peace any more than war. Time ran out on him. He left his presidency in January 1969, succeeded by Richard M. Nixon who had claimed to have a "secret formula" to end the war in Vietnam "with honor."

The Nixon Policies

During the 1968 election campaign, the Republican presidential candidate, Richard M. Nixon, espoused three goals in his campaign theme: (1) domestic tranquillity by a strict observance of "law and order," (2) national unity by "bringing the American people together," and (3) international peace by "ending the war in Vietnam." Nixon won the election by a narrow margin over Hubert H. Humphrey, Johnson's vice-president.

In his inaugural address in January 1969, President Nixon reemphasized those themes in the following words:

We are caught in war, wanting peace. We are torn by division, wanting unity. We see around us empty lives, wanting fulfillment. . . . The peace we seek to win is not victory over any other people, but the peace that comes 'with healing in its wings'; with compassion for those who have oppressed us; with the opportunity for all the people of this earth to choose their own destiny.

The irony of it all was that none of these goals were fulfilled during his first term in office; quite contrarily the United States was dragged deeper into the nadir of turmoil and anguish, demonstrating the basic weakness in Nixon's leadership and reviving the old doubts about his tricky and manipulative politics with accelerated rhetoric. Even more ironic and cynical was the fact that in the same speech he had warned:

> In these difficult years, America has suffered from a fever of words: from inflated rhetoric that promises more than it can possibly deliver; from angry rhetoric that fans discontents into hatreds; from bombastic rhetoric that postures instead of persuading.

Also during the campaign, Nixon had told some of the Republican leaders that if he was elected he would end the war within six months. After his election, however, he was unable to come up with a bold, new policy to make a clean break with the past. Instead, he clung to the past United States assumptions and policy premises that South Vietnam was a "sovereign," "independent" state which had been subjected to North Vietnam "aggression." Politically and psychologically President Nixon was incapable of acknowledging the fact that the "State of Vietnam" was a creation of the United States in controvention with the Geneva agreements of 1954. If only he could have seen a comparable situation between Manchukuo and South Vietnam! In 1931, Japanese military-imperialists carved off Manchuria from China and created what they claimed to be a "sovereign" and "independent" state of Manchukuo based, as they insisted, on the "freely expressed will of the people." Henry Stimson, then the secretary of state, refused to recognize Manchukuo and declared in what became known as the Stimson Doctrine that the United States "does not intend to recognize any situation, treaty, or agreement which may be brought about by means contrary to international law and agreements." Had the Nixon administration or its predecessors had historic insight, political perspicacity, and moral rectitude, the Vietnam War would not have come about nor would it have been protracted so long so uselessly.

At his first press conference, about a week after his inauguration, President Nixon stated: "There will be new tactics. We believe that those tactics may be more successful than the tactics of the past." The new tactics he spoke of turned out to be his policy to strengthen Nguyen Van Thieu's Saigon government which had been established in September 1967. This policy, later known as "Vietnamization," in essence signified the continuation of the Johnson policy and no real change forthcoming in American objectives in Vietnam. Senator George McGovern viewed the policy as "the same as proposing that we stay in Vietnam indefinitely." President Nixon failed to honor Santayana's maxim: "Those who do not learn lessons from history will repeat the same mistake again." Specifically, the Japanese and the French had Bao Dai; Presidents Eisenhower and Kennedy had Ngo Dinh Diem; President Johnson had Generals Minh, Khan, and Ky; and now President Nixon, Nguyen Van Thieu!

The Thieu government in Saigon was convinced that the Nixon administration would render it wholehearted support and assistance, while pursuing a hard-line, uncompromising policy in dealing with North Vietnam and the National Liberation Front. This conviction was reflected by Thieu's repressive measures toward domestic opponents, non-Communist and anti-Communist alike, knowing that Washington would approve of his actions. He was boasting of the result of the "Phoenix program,"[24] while asserting disparagingly that the Communists had lost their offensive capability.

Thieu had scarcely finished his remarks when Communist forces launched in February 1969 a new general offensive inflicting heavy casualties on Vietnamese and American forces. President Nixon immediately responded by warning North Vietnam that the United States would not tolerate continued attacks and would take appropriate retaliatory measures. At this time the United States forces in Vietnam had reached the peak level of 541,500 men.

In a May 14, 1969, telecast President Nixon told the American people that the situation he was faced with was far different from what it had been in earlier years and said:

One difference is that we no longer have the choice of not intervening. We have crossed that bridge. . . . We can have honest debate about whether we should have entered the war in Vietnam. We can have honest debate about how the war has been conducted. But the urgent question today is what to do now that we are there. . . . We have ruled out attempting to impose a purely military solution on the battlefield. We have also ruled out either a one-sided withdrawal from Vietnam, or the acceptance in Paris of terms that would amount to a disguised American defeat.[25]

In essence, what the president was saying to the American people was this: Never mind that we made a mistake in entering the war in Vietnam; never mind that we made many mistakes in conducting the war; but now that we are there, let's stay there and continue to make more mistakes and see what would happen.[26] The president did not present any real change in the fundamental positions held so long by the United States. For instance, in declaring that "our essential objective in Vietnam" was to "seek the opportunity for the South Vietnamese to determine their own political future without outside interference," President Nixon clearly insisted that South Vietnam was an independent, sovereign state and North Vietnam—the outsider—interfered with South Vietnam's domestic affairs. His statement that "confrontation with the United States is costly and unrewarding" was an implied threat and a covert intimidation which would serve no purpose or leave no impact on the determined Vietnamese nationalists who had been waging war for their national independence for thirty years with "heaviest sacrifices." Furthermore, his offer for American troop withdrawal was conditioned upon a simultaneous departure of North Vietnam from the South. Viewed from Hanoi, such a condition was tantamount to a burglar's insistence that he would leave the house he broke into only if the owner of the house abandoned his premises. Both the Ho government and the NLF denounced any suggestion of mutual troop withdrawal as an infringement on Vietnam's fundamental national rights and demanded "total and unconditional United States withdrawal."

Through the summer of 1969 and well into early 1970, the Nixon strategy began to take a discernible shape, though fuzzy and confusing as it was. The Nixon administration waged a two-front war—the Vietnam front and the domestic front—and resorted to two related tactics on each front.

Regarding the Vietnam front, he devised two interrelated tactics: the Nixon doctrine and the "Vietnamization" policy. In July, at Guam, President Nixon enunciated the "Nixon Doctrine," the essence of which was that in the future the United States would avoid involvements such as in Vietnam by limiting its support to economic and military aid rather than active combat participation with its armed forces. In cases involving non-nuclear aggression:

We shall furnish military and economic assistance when requested in accordance with our treaty commitments. But we shall look to the nation directly threatened to assume the primary responsibility of providing the manpower for its defense.[27]

The Nixon Doctrine, as a *future* strategy for global application, had no immediate effect on a desired policy change on Vietnam because Nixon insisted that "we will respect the commitments we inherited,"—the commitments predicated upon the erroneous premises and the faulty judgments discussed earlier. "Our interests," said the president, "must shape our commitments, rather than the other way around."[28] Yet, to our nation's chagrin, he was neither wise enough to perceive the past mistakes nor brave enough to declare that our *commitments* in Vietnam were contrary to our *interests*. Unfortunately, he let this rational assertion become another victim of the rhetoric syndrome he had warned against.

The Nixon Doctrine was inapplicable to Vietnam and, therefore, President Nixon had to reshape his doctrine to fit in with the situation at hand; it took the form of "Vietnamization" of the war. Two concurrent methods were employed to achieve this goal: stepped-up training and equipping of Thieu's armies so as to shift the burden of actual combat from Americans to the South Vietnamese and gradual withdrawal of United States ground troops from Vietnam. In early June, President Nixon met Thieu on Midway Island and pledged his continued support for the Thieu regime and at the same time he announced that twenty-five thousand

American troops would be withdrawn from South Vietnam by the end of August.

Neither the Nixon Doctrine nor the Vietnamization policy showed any indication that President Nixon really understood Vietnamese realities or that he truthfully intended to end the war. Johnson's war simply turned into Nixon's war, and its critics in Congress and on campuses grew in numbers, intensity, and determination. Antiwar demonstrations in major American cities increased. The moratorium against the war in November drew huge crowds to Washington to demand an immediate end of fighting and rapid withdrawal of American troops from Vietnam. This domestic turmoil was Nixon's second front.

President Nixon employed two tactics to cope with this domestic turmoil. First, in a televised speech on November 3, 1969, he appealed to Middle America or the Silent Majority:

And so tonight—to you, the great silent majority of my fellow Americans—I ask for your support. I pledged in my campaign for the Presidency to end the war in a way that we could win the peace. I have initiated a plan of action which will enable me to keep that pledge. The more support I can have from the American people, the sooner that pledge can be redeemed; for the more divided we are at home, the less likely the enemy is to negotiate at Paris. Let us be united for peace. Let us also be united against defeat. Because let us understand: North Vietnam cannot defeat or humiliate the United States. Only Americans can do that.[29]

The problem with the Silent Majority was that the majority remained silent for many diverse reasons. True, a majority of Americans were good, decent people and they trusted their governmental leaders who, they believed, would place the nation's interests above individual gains; hence, any opposition to governmental policy, they felt, would be *ipso facto* unpatriotic. Some Americans remained silent because they were uninformed, kept from facts, and confused with realities. In some cases, political apathy also kept them silent. Worst of all, they were driven into silence because they had been misinformed, misled, and lied to by their leaders who took advantage of their simplicity, naivety, and gulli-bility. It was immoral and indecent for the national leaders to manipulate the people. It was presumptuous for them to equate the silence of the people with the consent of the governed. It should be remembered that blind and uncritical obedience of the people to their government is a basic feature of totalitarianism.

Second, President Nixon unleashed his vice-president, Spiro Agnew, to attack peace demonstrators, war critics, news media, and campus antiwar youths. Of peace demonstrators Agnew said, "The Mob, the Mobilization, the Moratorium have become some-what fashionable forms of citizen expression . . . [but they are] negative in content, disruptive in effect." Of war critics and news media, he declared, "A spirit of national masochism prevails, en-couraged by an effete corps of impudent snobs who characterize themselves as intellectuals." And of antiwar students, he stated, "We can, however, afford to separate them from our society—with no more regret than we should feel over discarding rotten apples from a barrel."[30] Thus, Agnew became Nixon's Nixon and the field commanding-general on the domestic front. The strategy was to isolate the antiwar groups from the Silent Majority and to sup-press and attack them, identifying them as the real "enemies" who could only "defeat and humiliate the United States." So, the war returned home to nest, while in Vietnam bombs were dropped at the rate of seventy thousand tons a month.

In Spring 1970, the war took a new upturn when, on April 30, President Nixon ordered United States combat troops into Cam-bodia in an effort to destroy Vietcong sanctuaries and supplies. When this incursion was publicly announced, the reaction of anti-war protesters was instantaneous and furious. They disdained the Nixon logic: To end the war was to expand the war. Only ten days earlier the president had declared in a broadcast, "We finally have in sight the just peace we are seeking." It seemed in Nixon's terminologies as well as his deeds, war and peace were interchange-able. Student protesters throughout the country caused one third of the nation's colleges to shut down or be disrupted. On May 4, tragic and deplorable incidents shocked the nation. Four students were shot and killed by National Guards at Kent State University in Ohio and two at Jackson State University in Mississippi. The killings were the final acts to set into motion national expressions of bitter rage and disgust.

President Nixon's two-front war became increasingly intertwined by the Cambodian invasion, which had dubious military results in Indochina but had disastrous political consequences at home. The invasion heralded the opening phases of the Cambodian civil war. The South Vietnamese forces sent in to help the Cambodian government under Lon Nol, who had recently ousted Prince Norodom Sihanouk, indulged more in looting and plundering of villages than in fighting the Vietcong. The tiny Khmer Rouge (Cambodian Communist party) was growing in numbers and in power. For the first time since independence in 1953, Cambodians were forced to choose sides and were killing fellow Cambodians. At home, the chain of events leading from the invasion and the Kent State killings to public outrage drove Nixon into isolation in the "Fortress White House" and set him on the road to Watergate.[31]

President Nixon's assertion that the war was winding down was challenged on the grounds that he simply had switched from a land war to an air war in which, by the end of 1971, more bombs were dropped on Indochina after he had taken office than the total dropped (2.9 million tons) during WW II and the Korean War combined.[32] By this time Vietnamese civilian deaths were estimated at 325,000, and six million became refugees as a result of air raids and artillery fire. In addition, the air war brought severe damage to all the natural ecological systems of Indochina, destroying rice fields, forests, and animals, and creating a moonscape with bomb craters. A group of researchers at the Center for International Studies of Cornell University reached the following conclusion:

> Decision-makers in Washington remain isolated from the effects of their decisions; military commanders are similarly separated from the consequences of their actions. The reasons for this collective failure of the American imagination are manifold, but two seem particularly relevant to the use of air power. First the United States has never suffered aerial bombardment. Suppose the North Vietnamese had been in a

position to carry out occasional air raids in retaliation for the bombing of their country, say against Seattle. Who can doubt that the tenor of the bombing discussions would have changed radically? Second, the very availability of an advanced technology tends to inhibit the imagination. If powerful tools are at hand, it is almost a reflex to reach for them first—and how much greater the temptation to do so if the cost is low. A reassessment of our position is long overdue.[33]

End of an Era

The Vietnam Disengagement

The year 1972 marked an historic turning point in American foreign policy in three important respects: (1) rapprochement with the People's Republic of China, (2) détente with the Soviet Union, and (3) the beginning of disengagement in Vietnam. President Nixon's visit to Peking in February 1972 (which shall be discussed later) and his travel to Moscow in May were designed to lay the foundation for Nixon's "lasting peace." In the context of a global strategy, it became obvious to the Nixon administration that a "lasting peace" could not be achieved without the mutual understanding, open communication, cooperation and accommodation among major powers, especially among the three great powers—the United States, the Soviet Union, and the People's Republic of China.[34] President Nixon reassessed the war in Vietnam in the light of this tricentric balance of power.

He came to the conclusion that there were two alternative means to end the war and to bring about peace in Vietnam. First, he could continue to escalate the war to a finish until a total Communist defeat had been achieved and then dictate peace terms much as the United States did to Germany and Japan after WW II. The inadvisability of this policy was self-evident in view of the French experience of nearly a decade of futile fighting from 1946 to 1954 and America's own experience thereafter. Strictly from a military viewpoint, there was no doubt that, in the short run, the United States had the military capability of bombing Vietnam into the Stone Age or leveling the country into uninhabitable wastelands with all its awesome modern weapons, including nuclear bombs. Such a course of action, in the long run, would have generated irrevocable political fallouts which would smother the United States internally as well as internationally. Worse yet, it might set off a global conflagration which none of the major powers would care to risk. Therefore, the first alternative had to be ruled out.

Second, and the only alternative means, was for the president to seek a negotiated settlement. He had stated often enough that he wanted a "peace with honor," or a "peace we can live with," or an "enduring peace." What he meant by these terms and what he wanted was a kind of peace settlement carrying no odium of American defeat and humiliation wrought by North Vietnam, which he considered a third- or fourth-rate military power. And any peace settlement acceptable to him would not be "enduring" unless the People's Republic of China and the Soviet Union—two principal suppliers of arms to North Vietnam and to the NLF—were prepared to cooperate with, to consent to, or at least to acquiesce in such a settlement.

President Nixon, therefore, embarked upon a personal diplomatic mission to open dialogue with the two mentors of North Vietnam. Nixon critics disparaged his visit to Peking as Nixon's "journey to Canossa,"[35] while Nixon supporters lauded his *demarche* as Disraelian wisdom and courage. In any case, it could be seen that the president, having successfully achieved sufficient rapprochement with the Peking regime, was able to resort to aggressive but limited military power in Vietnam without the fear of bringing China into the war.

Since the peace talks in Paris, secret and otherwise, had made little progress, in March 1972 the United States broke off the formal talks on the grounds that the Communists refused to negotiate seriously. In fact, in February, North Vietnam had protested that the United States, in spite of its official announcement that the new series of air attacks had ended, continued to bomb the North. Hanoi had accused President Nixon of "inconsistency" and "treachery" in that he was making peace proposals in private and was ordering in public air strikes which he characterized as "protective reaction."[36] The fact of the matter was, as disclosed later, that General John D. Lavelle,[37] commander of the United States

Air Force in Vietnam, had waged a "private air war" in which he had ordered unauthorized air raids on North Vietnam between November and March. North Vietnam had repeatedly claimed that American war planes had bombed civilian populated areas under the guise of "protective reaction," causing heavy loss of civilian lives.

The U.S. bombing of North Vietnam was largely designed to make its leaders realize that the United States was negotiating from a "position of strength." Only too well did the Communists realize it; after all, they were the disciples of Mao Tse-tung who had epigrammatized that "political power comes out of the barrel of guns." To demonstrate to President Nixon that they too wanted to negotiate from a "position of strength," they launched their heaviest offensive since the Tet of 1968 in South Vietnam, crossing the DMZ in force with armor and artillery. President Nixon's response was to order the U.S. Air Force to execute massive air raids on the Hanoi and Haiphong areas, thus ending a four-year de-escalation of the air war against North Vietnam. Shortly thereafter the United States announced that it would resume Paris talks.

The North Vietnam forces continued their offensive and took Quang Tri in May and were in the position to control the northernmost province of South Vietnam. Thereupon the United States once again called off formal peace talks in Paris indefinitely, and in a nationwide speech on May 8, President Nixon announced that in retaliation he had ordered the mining of Haiphong harbor and six other major ports in North Vietnam as well as a blockade of supplies destined for North Vietnam. It was designed to prevent Soviet ships from reaching North Vietnamese ports and, therefore, was fraught with elements of risk and unpredictability. Nevertheless, it was a carefully calculated measure based on the conviction that the Soviets had a larger stake in reaching arms limitation agreements with the United States than in supplying arms to North Vietnam. Indeed, the Soviet protest to the American action was mild and in no way jeopardized Nixon's scheduled visit to Moscow.

On May 26, 1972, at the Kremlin, President Nixon and Leonid Brezhnev, general secretary of the Soviet Communist party, signed the Strategic Arms Limitation Talks (SALT) Agreements. The two leaders were thus able to alleviate their economic burden of the arms race and to reduce the threat of nuclear war, demonstrating at the same time that the Vietnam War should not be in the way of their cooperative efforts to achieve mutual advantage and to promote their respective interests. The North Vietnam leaders were not unaware of the patterns of big power politics. But the Sino-American rapprochement highlighted by the Nixon visit to Peking had mystified them, and now the Soviet-American détente culminating in the Nixon trip to Moscow and the signing of the SALT I puzzled and displeased them. Why didn't the Kremlin leaders, Hanoi asked itself, cancel their invitation to Nixon to visit Moscow, as Khrushchev had done to President Eisenhower in 1960 after the U-2 incident? Why didn't they resist more stringently the various treaty proposals of the United States, as the North Vietnam negotiators were doing at the Paris peace talks? Why didn't they openly challenge the U.S. mining of harbors and bombing of cities in North Vietnam? Why didn't they refuse to sign a Soviet-American agreement on the prevention of incidents at sea, while President Nixon had just ordered the mining and blockading of North Vietnam ports? The Hanoi leaders knew the answers to these questions, but they were in no position to criticize the Soviets publicly.

When the Paris peace talks resumed in July 1972, the United States insisted on the earlier "package" proposal, including: (1) an immediate cease-fire, (2) exchange of prisoners of war, (3) withdrawal of United States and North Vietnam forces from South Vietnam within six months, and (4) new elections under international supervision. In this, North Vietnam saw no basic change in United States policy. There had also been a series of private, secret talks between Henry Kissinger and Le Duc Tho, North Vietnam foreign minister. These talks likewise proved unsuccessful until October 26 when, just before the 1972 presidential election in the United States, Kissinger announced that "peace is at hand." But peace was as elusive and illusory, at least for a while, as Neville Chamberlain's "peace in our time."

After Nixon's reelection, Kissinger returned to Paris for more talks with Le Duc Tho, but no final agreements were reached. Kissinger charged that Hanoi was procrastinating, making a "just and fair agreement" unattainable. Hanoi, on the other hand, ac-

cused the United States of backing off from the October draft
agreement and of attempting to reopen the issue and to force
Hanoi to recognize the sovereignty of South Vietnam. President
Nixon decided as before to break the diplomatic impasse by military means. On December 18, he ordered a renewal of air raids on
North Vietnam, including massive round-the-clock B-52 "carpet
bombing" of the Hanoi-Haiphong areas. The bombings were the
heaviest, most extensive, and most destructive of the entire war.
Reduced to a heap of rubble were military and industrial installations, communication centers, marshaling yards, power plants,
POL storages as well as homes, schools, and even hospitals. Hanoi
characterized the raids as a "diabolical, last gasp of American imperialism" and declared it would never resume negotiations until
bombing ceased. After twelve days of relentless air assaults, in
which fifteen B-52s were shot down by enemy SAM missiles (until then, in the previous eight years of bombing, only one B-52
bomber had been lost) and ninety-three airmen were killed, captured, or missing, on December 30 President Nixon ordered a
halt in bombing above the twentieth parallel and announced the
resumption of the secret peace talks in Paris. The memorable year
of 1972 came to a close with a higher number of Vietnamese
casualties, both North and South, than in any previous year of the
war.[38]

Finally, on January 27, 1973, representatives of the four parties
—the United States, North Vietnam, South Vietnam, and Vietcong's Provisional Revolutionary Government—signed an "agreement on ending the war and restoring peace in Vietnam." Some
of the significant provisions of the agreement were:

1. The United States and all other countries respect the independence, sovereignty, unity, and territorial integrity of
   Vietnam as recognized by the 1954 Geneva Agreement on
   Vietnam (Article 1).
2. Within 60 days ... there will be a total withdrawal from
   South Vietnam of troops, military advisors, and military
   personnel ... of the United States (Article 5).
3. Pending the reunification [of Vietnam] ... the military demarcation line between the two zones at the 17th parallel

is only provisional and not a political or territorial boundary, as provided for in paragraph 6 of the Final Declaration
of the 1954 Geneva Conference (Article 15).[39]

In addition, there would be an immediate cease-fire and an exchange of prisoners of war within sixty days.

Thus, the twin causes for the whole tragedy in Indochina—
United States refusal to accept the 1954 Geneva agreements and
its self-induced illusion that South Vietnam was a sovereign, independent state—were finally rectified with a staggering cost in men
and matériel. American casualties exceeded 55,000 killed and
300,000 wounded. Tens of thousands of young Americans, refusing to serve in an unpopular war, deserted their military units,
dodged the draft, and sought refuge abroad. The American people
were torn in division and tormented in despair. The total war
expenditures of the United States surpassed $350 billion.[40] Viet-
namese death tolls, both North and South, reached 1.5 million. The
land itself could not escape injuries: 80 percent of the timber
forests and 10 percent of all the cultivated land in Vietnam were
treated with herbicides. American bombing created in South Vietnam alone 23 million craters measuring twenty-six feet deep and
forty feet in diameter.[41]

The cease-fire was designed to disengage the United States from
the war, but it did not bring peace in Indochina. In Vietnam fighting continued just the same between the Thieu forces and the
Communists. In Cambodia, the United States Air Force continued
to bomb in an effort to save the shaky Lon Nol government from
being overrun by the Khmer Rouge forces. It appeared that President Nixon had switched the American air war from Vietnam to
Cambodia. The U.S. Congress protested Nixon's war policy and
set August 15, 1973, as a deadline for the complete cessation of
all American military activity in Indochina, including the bombing
of Cambodia. Nixon ordered a halt to the bombing only at the last
minute of the deadline.

While the longest frontier war in American history came to a
slow stop, President Nixon's political fortunes at home began a
steady decline. Just as the war had tainted President Johnson's
political career with disfavor so it put President Nixon's political

career in disgrace in connection with the so-called Watergate scandal[42] which had had its roots in the war in Vietnam. In July 1974, the House Judiciary Committee voted to recommend the impeachment of President Nixon, charging him with (1) obstruction of justice by way of covering up the Watergate crimes, (2) misuse of federal agencies in such a manner as to violate the constitutional rights of citizens, and (3) failure to produce "papers and things" which the committee had subpoenaed. As the impeachment recommendation would be accepted by the House and a subsequent trial and conviction appeared inevitable, he resigned in August 1974, succeeded by his vice-president, Gerald Ford.

In the spring of 1975, in the face of North Vietnam's powerful offensive, the Thieu forces retreated in rout, leaving behind huge quantities of arms supplies, including most of their planes and helicopters, tanks and trucks, and artillery pieces. The monetary value of this abandoned military equipment, which had been supplied by the United States and which now fell into the hands of the Communist forces, reportedly exceeded a billion dollars.[43] President Ford appealed to Congress for $722 million in emergency military aid in the vain effort to honor Nixon's secret pledge to Thieu that the United States would come to his aid as needed. Congress, reflecting the feeling of a great majority of Americans, took a firm stand that further military aid to the Thieu government should be reduced to a limited amount. Secretary of State Kissinger insisted that it was America's moral obligation to help Thieu: "The problem we face in Indochina is an elementary question of what kind of a people we are." To do otherwise, he declared publicly, would "deliberately destroy an ally by withholding aid from it in its moment of extremity." He should have realized that American aid to Thieu at this juncture would have made no difference because the Thieu forces were low in morale, had lost the will to fight, and lacked military discipline.[44] The American people and Congress began to realize that the Vietnam adventure was a mistake to begin with and they felt "enough is enough." Thieu's cause was hapless and helpless. Nothing could stop the precipitous collapse of his government; he resigned on April 21, 1975. The fall of the Saigon government irrefutably demonstrated the ultimate failure of the Nixon-Kissinger policy of "Vietnamization" and the inefficacy of the Nixon Doctrine insofar as South Vietnam (and Cambodia) was concerned.

After twenty-five years of adventurous intervention, the United States at last was completely disengaged from Vietnam. North and South Vietnam, after a Thirty Years' War of "great sacrifices," were reunified under the aegis of the Hanoi government. Saigon was renamed Ho Chi Minh City and the Vietnamese took up the task of national reconstruction. But genuine peace was yet to be achieved in Indochina. As though war was a natural way of life, in early 1978 the Vietnamese-Cambodian border skirmishes erupted into a full-fledged war between the two Communist neighbors. The United States had no immediate stake in the outcome of this new Indochina war. But the Pol Pot regime in Cambodia was supported by Peking, while the Hanoi government was backed by Moscow. Hence, it was a "proxy war," as some observers called it, between the People's Republic of China and the Soviet Union. Phnom Penh accused Hanoi of employing Soviet advisors, of attempting to annex Cambodian territory so as to become a dominant, expansionist power in the region. The new war dragged on, and a year later, on February 17, 1979, Peking invaded Vietnam to "punish" it for its invasion of Cambodia. The Vietnamese forces put up stubborn resistance and the fighting raged on for four weeks until the Chinese decided that they had achieved their declared objectives and withdrew their troops. Then the two warring neighbors agreed to negotiate their differences, including immediate exchanges of prisoners of war. There was little indication, however, that Vietnam learned a "lesson"; in May it launched a major offensive in western Cambodia to annihilate the remnants of Pol Pot guerrillas and to secure firm grips on both Cambodia and Laos. Since Vietnam was allied with the Soviet Union, China felt boxed in by the Moscow-Hanoi encirclement. China's annoyance with Vietnam was amply demonstrated when Deng Xiaoping told American officials that "Vietnam is China's Cuba."

Korea: Search for Unification

As discussed earlier, the Korean War settled virtually nothing, and when the Geneva Conference convened in April 1954 there was little hope that it would resolve the fundamental question of a peaceful reunification of Korea. After all, there was a grain of truth in the statement that "diplomacy has rarely been able to gain at the conference table what cannot be gained or held on the battlefield."

As the conference took up the Korean issue, the representatives from the countries which had formed the United Nations Command during the war insisted on two key principles: (1) the establishment of a unified Korean government based on UN-supervised free elections, and (2) the recognition of the authority and competence of the United Nations to deal with the Korean question. The Communists found these principles unacceptable. First, since South Korea had more than two-thirds of the total population in the peninsula and in view of the prevalent anti-Communist feeling in the South, the numerical superiority would work against the Communists. Second, since all the UN collective security measures in Korea had been undertaken on the basis of various UN resolutions adopted in the absence, or over the protest, of the Soviet Union, the recognition of the UN's authority and competence would have negated the previous Soviet position which had regarded the UN action as illegal. Furthermore, since the UN General Assembly had adopted a resolution condemning Communist China as an "aggressor" in Korea, such a recognition would imply China's acquiescence in, if not acceptance of, that verdict.

The Communists, therefore, presented their own proposals calling for, among others, the creation of two main bodies: (1) an all-Korean commission to draft an electoral law for nationwide elections, and (2) a "neutral nations supervisory commission" to oversee the all-Korean elections. The UN side found these proposals unacceptable. First, the proposed all-Korean electoral commission would provide North Korea and South Korea equal weight, despite the population discrepancy, and with a "built-in veto." Second, the proposed neutral nations supervisory commission, consisting of an equal number of Communist and non-Communist governments, was to function only on the basis of unanimity—another source of Communist veto. The Communists deliberately failed to mention any role for the United Nations. Any elections which might be held under these conditions would, in the words of British foreign secretary Anthony Eden, "come first on paper, but last in practice . . . [and] would be free in name but rigged in fact."

After two months of discussion and debate there was no indication of any compromise or agreement between the Communists and the United Nations allies. The impasse was so crystallized that further negotiations would serve no useful purpose. The Allied delegations, therefore, issued the Sixteen Nation Joint Declaration, stating in part:

> It is clear that the Communists will not accept impartial and effective supervision of free elections. Plainly, they have shown their intention to maintain communist control over North Korea. They have persisted in the same attitudes which have frustrated United Nations efforts to unify Korea since 1947. We believe, therefore, that it is better to face the fact of our disagreement than to raise false hope and mislead the peoples of the world into believing that there is agreement where there is none.[45]

The Korean question was then transferred from Geneva back to the United Nations in New York. Both the secretariat and General Assembly were informed of the failure of the Geneva talks on Korea and in December the latter adopted a resolution reaffirming the United Nations objective of achieving a peaceful reunification of Korea. Ever since, this theme has been repeated ritualistically year after year by the General Assembly without any progress in that direction.

The United States, on the other hand, in November 1954, agreed to carry out an extensive economic aid program for the war-torn country and reiterated its intention to use its military power against any renewed aggression. At this time, the United States-Korea Mutual Defense Treaty signed in the previous month entered into force. Two years later the United States and the Republic of Korea signed a treaty of friendship, commerce, and navigation. Each of the two signatories agreed to give the other most-favored-nation treatment, to observe the principles of nondiscrimination in commerce and trade, and to abide by the rules to protect persons, their property, and interests.

During the ensuing few years, occasional exchanges of notes and communications between the UN representatives and the Communists took place, but they failed to produce any agreement on the Korean unification issue. Neither side demonstrated any change in its basic position. The Communists insisted on UN troop withdrawal from Korea. The UN Command refused to accommodate, while urging the Communists to recognize UN authority and competence as embodied in the General Assembly resolution of November 14, 1958. The Communists refused to endorse the resolution, claiming that it had no validity.

The Korean question could not be isolated from the bipolarized Cold War politics any more than the questions of other divided peoples—Germans, Berliners, and Vietnamese. In fact, the Koreans constituted crucial focal points of the Cold War struggle between the United States and the Soviet Union and consequently, they were hardly in the position to pursue independently the course of their own national "self-determination." To the Koreans, both North and South, national reunification came to represent the supreme goal of their nationalism. But, since international political realities of the East-West confrontation in which they were interposed were beyond their control, the unfulfilled national aspiration resulted in fostering national frustration. While the North Korean leaders skillfully steered this frustration toward anti-American "imperialism," the Rhee government in the South not only failed to manage it properly, but made it worse by way of the corruption, inefficiency, and injustice that permeated his regime. As a result, a series of domestic political upheavals began to erupt. In March 1960, President Syngman Rhee was reelected to a fourth term in the rigged elections. Mass demonstrations against the election frauds shook the nation for weeks and Rhee was forced to resign in April, followed by the formation of a new government led by Chang Myun. During this period of political turmoil President Eisenhower visited Korea. Addressing a special session of the Korean National Assembly, he reaffirmed full American support as stipulated in the Mutual Assistance Agreement and reassured the Koreans of his continued effort for the ultimate unification of their country.

A year later, on May 16, 1961, the Chang Myun government was overthrown by a military coup engineered by General Park Chung Hee, who subsequently became the head of the revolutionary government. The Park government pledged to eliminate corruption, to carry out social and economic reforms, and to combat communism. The United States endorsed his pledge and recognized the revolutionary government. North Korea condemned the Park government as a Fascist military dictatorship bent on intensifying the anti-Communist struggle. In July, North Korea concluded a mutual defense treaty with the Soviet Union, providing for reciprocal military and other assistance with all means at their disposal in case either party should become the object of an external armed attack. Within a week a similar military pact was signed between North Korea and the People's Republic of China, thus culminating in the formation of the Moscow-Peking-Pyongyang triple alliance in East Asia.

Park's military rule, fundamentally undemocratic, was not what President Kennedy hoped to see in America's farthest frontier in Asia. There were a number of outstanding differences between Washington and Seoul. In November, Park Chung Hee made a state visit to Washington to confer with President Kennedy to iron out some of those differences. After their talks, they issued a joint communique wherein, among other things, President Kennedy reaffirmed the American commitment to defend South Korea and Park promised to return the government to civilian rule by the summer of 1963. That promise was reluctantly kept, under the pressure and persuasion of the United States, in October 1963, when presidential elections were held in South Korea. Park was elected president. The following month, in separate elections, the legislators of the unicameral National Assembly were elected. A parliamentary democracy, in theory at least, if not in practice, was thus established in the (third) Republic of Korea.

Park's election to the presidency meant no basic changes in either domestic or foreign policy. His domestic priority was focused on economic growth and expansion. His foreign policy objectives were centered on strengthening further the ties with the

United States and on establishing normal relations with Japan. The former was imperative and the latter was necessary. In May 1965, President Park visited Washington to confer with President Johnson, and the two leaders reiterated the solidarity between the two countries. The following month, a Korea-Japan treaty, long overdue as Park felt, was signed, providing for restoration of diplomatic relations, mutual trade, and Japanese investment which would help boost the Korean economy.

President Park's economic policy was well on the way to success and he desired to establish the image of South Korea as a "partner," rather than a "little brother," of the United States. He agreed to dispatch some fifty thousand troops to Vietnam to help fight Communists, as comrades-in-arms of the United States. He also embarked upon a series of foreign visits to Southeast Asian and European nations. These policies and activities were designed to exert the sovereign equality of his country among the powers of the world and, in so doing, to outmatch the North Korean policy of *juche* (self-reliance).

Marshal Kim Il-sung of North Korea had espoused the concept of *juche* which, rejecting subservience and dogmatism, adhered to the principles of self-reliance in ideology, politics, economics, and military affairs. The principle of *juche,* he claimed, would be the true manifestation of the genuine independence and sovereignty of the Korean people. Being caught in the ongoing Sino-Soviet conflict, Marshal Kim Il-sung found the *juche* doctrine useful and convenient, for he was linked ideologically to Peking but was tied to Moscow economically. *Juche* dispelled any notion of a total dependency on either of the two Communist giants. One of the most important, demonstrative acts of *juche* was carried out on January 23, 1968, when North Korea seized a United States intelligence vessel, the *Pueblo*. In terms of the magnitude and the potential danger involved, the *Pueblo* incident was far more serious than either the Tonkin Gulf incident of 1964 or the *Mayaguez* case of 1975. Hence, it should deserve more than a superficial treatment with respect to the circumstances, probable motives for the seizure, and the United States response thereto.

The U.S.S. *Pueblo* was one of America's "elint" (electronic intelligence) ships with a nine-hundred-ton hull equipped with some of the most advanced, sophisticated, and ultrasecret radio, radar, sonar, and other multimillion-dollar instruments. At the time of the seizure the *Pueblo*'s specific missions were to collect electromagnetic intelligence information along the east coast of North Korea, with emphasis on determining the battle order of the North Korean army, the range of the naval force activities, and the locations of radars, naval bases, and commands. At the same time, the *Pueblo* was to detect communication observation posts and to undertake oceanographic research including underwater sound measurements useful for submarine operations. In addition, it was to uncover various military installations along the North Korean shores and to investigate the accommodation capacities of the ports as well as the size of ships visiting these ports.

January 23, 1968, the *Pueblo* appeared off the port of Wonsan and was approached by North Korean patrol boats. The ship and its crew of eighty-two were captured by the North Koreans and taken to Wonsan harbor. The immediate reaction of the American people to the *Pueblo* seizure ranged from a demand for swift retaliation to a caution for rational restraint. Concentrating on "precautionary measures," President Johnson reactivated about fifteen thousand air force and navy reserves and ordered the nuclear-powered aircraft carrier *Enterprise* to the Sea of Japan. This move had two key objectives: (1) to strengthen America's power position in its diplomatic search for a solution by hinting at military action which might be taken against North Korea if it refused to release the ship and its crew, and (2) to provide additional muscle for possible military action in the event of the failure of all diplomatic efforts.

What prompted the North Koreans to take such a potentially dangerous and explosive action? Several possible motives could be advanced and examined. First, it was designed to test the willingness and readiness of the United States, so deeply embroiled in Vietnam, to resist a broadened Communist offensive in Asia. Ever since the Korean Armistice in 1953, the North Korean regime had never abandoned the ambition to unify the divided country under Communist rule by military means if necessary. Premier Kim Il-sung had made a public pledge in 1957 to bring South Korea under his control by the beginning of the 1970s. In October 1966 at a meeting of the Korean Workers' party (Communist party), he had issued an order to intensify the pace of militarization, and a year later, before the Supreme People's Assembly, he called for a national determination "to liberate South Korea at all costs." At that time North Korean war preparedness was reported to be complete. Marshal Kim Il-sung would not necessarily mount another 1950s-type invasion that might be met by a massive U.S. retaliation, including the use of nuclear weapons. He would continue, as he had tried, to stir up a Vietcong-style guerrilla movement in South Korea, although the kind of rural support and cooperation which had rendered the Vietcong their political base in South Vietnam was almost totally missing in South Korea.

Second, confident in their military preparations and convinced that the United States could not afford a two-front war at a time when it was already overextended, the North Korean leaders put out a lure by way of seizing the *Pueblo*. As they had ruled out the advisability of an all-out, unprovoked military assault on South Korea, the Pyungyang leaders created a situation which could have infuriated the United States into taking a rash and reckless retaliatory military measure. Such an action would not have been limited to mere one-act retaliation but could have readily triggered a series of escalatory reactions leading ultimately to the resumption of the war along the Demilitarized Zone in Korea. In these events, North Korea would accelerate its infiltration of trained guerrillas, political cadres, propagandists, and other subversive elements into the South so as to carry out the "national liberation" struggles, thus dragging the United States into the same military and political quagmire as in the Vietnam War.

Third, the capture of the *Pueblo* was regarded as a diversionary tactic aimed at mitigating the Vietnam War efforts of both the United States and South Korea, the latter having some fifty thousand fighting troops in South Vietnam. The Pyongyang leaders hoped that the *Pueblo* crisis would compel the Seoul government to recall some or all of its expeditionary forces from South Vietnam in order to meet the new tension in Korea. At the same time it would divert America's attention from Vietnam where the preparations for the Communist Tet offensive, which came a week later, had been well in the making. There was also a domestic diversionary tactic. In view of the failure in fulfilling the ambitious goals of the Seven-Year Plan (1961–1967), the Pyongyang government capitalized on the *Pueblo* incident to remind its own people of the constant threat of the "American imperialists and their lackey" and to unite them behind its leadership for hard work, higher production, stronger morale, and added vigilance.

Fourth, North Korea's daring and successful seizure of the *Pueblo* was conducted on the basis of propaganda considerations. North Korea was steering a middle course in its relations with the two feuding Communist giants—the Soviet Union and the People's Republic of China. The Pyungyang regime demonstrated and enjoyed a great degree of independent stance—*juche*—which was to prove that it was not a "puppet" or "satellite" either of the Soviet Union or of China. In fact, there seemed to be no prior notice to or consultation with either of the two powers in regard to its intention of seizing the *Pueblo*. The seizure took them by surprise as it did the United States. Indeed, North Korea sought to enhance its stature and prestige at home and abroad by challenging the United States, whose power and influence permeate the world. The North Korean demand for a United States public apology for the "criminal violation" of its territorial waters was designed to humiliate the United States—a feat that even former Soviet Premier Nikita Khrushchev had failed to do.[46]

Finally, the *Pueblo* seizure was an audacious scheme to camouflage North Korea's abortive attempt to assassinate President Park Chung Hee of South Korea and to inject dissension and irritation into United States-Korea relations. On January 21, 1968, just two days before the *Pueblo* incident, a band of North Korean infiltrators armed with modern weapons and grenades attempted to execute a commando raid on the presidential palace in the heart of Seoul. They were detected by the palace guards only a few blocks from the palace, and in the ensuing exchange of gunfire most of them were killed and the rest captured. While South Koreans were in a state of shock and disbelief, the incredible episode of the *Pueblo* compounded their consternation. What caused greater apprehension, even resentment, among the South Koreans, however, was Washington's preoccupation with the fate of the *Pueblo* crew. To the South Koreans, much more critical problems

—the safety of their government and the security of their nation —were at stake, but the United States appeared to have overlooked the real danger stemming from the North Korean bellicosity. For a moment the assassination attempt and the *Pueblo* fiasco created an unpleasant discord between Washington and Seoul. The leading newspapers in Seoul ran editorials which reflected public sentiments. The *Tong-A Ilbo* (the East Asian Daily) warned: "The United States must realize that the connivance with the Communists over the recent intrusion of a North Korea Commando unit into Seoul in exchange for the release of the U.S.S. *Pueblo* and its crew will result in the fall of U.S. prestige as well as the loss of confidence by Koreans in the United States." In the same vein, the *Chosun Ilbo* (the Korean Daily) echoed: "We are learning a good lesson: we, the Korean people, must guard our land for ourselves against Communist aggression and not rely upon any ally." The *Korean Herald* pointed out that the United States would at least have enhanced North Korean prestige internationally at the expense of the Seoul government by "dancing to the Communist propaganda tune."

The sudden appearance of an anti-American mood in South Korea prompted President Park to request President Johnson to send a special envoy for talks. Cyrus Vance, one of the most able and trusted troubleshooters, was dispatched to Seoul. During his four-day stay in South Korea, some of the more fundamental differences were ironed out and a formula was agreed upon for "immediate consultation" in the event of renewed North Korean attack. With the "family quarrel" settled, the United States continued to conduct direct negotiations with North Korea until December 1968, when the *Pueblo* crew was released in exchange for the United States' public apology for, and official admission of, the violation of North Korean territorial waters.[47]

The *Pueblo* incident was a highly successful operation from Pyungyang's point of view. Marshal Kim Il-sung was able to produce "irrefutable proofs" to his thirteen million people that the United States was a "paper tiger" and that the ultimate victory of the North was merely a matter of time. Kim's aggressiveness was further demonstrated on April 15, 1969, by the shooting down of a United States Navy EC-121 reconnaissance aircraft over the Sea of Japan. The added bellicosity prodded President Nixon to send a Navy task force to the Sea of Japan to protect continued reconnaissance flights. The twenty-nine-ship armada was far larger than would be necessary simply to protect the planes, but it was clearly intended to show to North Korea that the "paper tiger" had deadly, awesome claws.

Marshal Kim's daring challenge of American power appeared to be encouraged by the Vietcong's successful conduct of the war in Vietnam. He was confident of unifying the country only if he could emulate a Vietcong-style war in South Korea. He spoke with increasingly belligerent impatience in calling for a new military means to "liberate" the South. He realized, however, that his strategy could not be immediately implemented for three critical reasons: (1) neither the Soviet Union nor the People's Republic of China was willing to endorse his scheme or to render assistance to his effort; the Moscow-Peking-Pyungyang triple alliance was in fact disintegrating, if not dissolved, (2) there was no visible sign that many South Koreans were ready to form their version of Vietcong; all evidence indicated quite the opposite, and (3) some fifty-five thousand United States troops still stationed in South Korea constituted an insurmountable deterrence; there was no way for him to get them out of the country despite the growing antiwar sentiment in the United States.

In the South, meanwhile, President Park Chung Hee had been reelected in a landslide victory on June 8, 1967, for a second four-year term, though not without an allegation that the elections had been rigged. The Korean constitution limited the presidency to two terms and in 1969 President Park was considering a constitutional issue affecting the country's future. The basic issue was whether he should propose to amend the constitution so that he could run for a third term and, when elected, would continue to take a strong anti-Communist stance which, he believed, was essential for the further economic growth of South Korea in the face of North Korea's overt belligerence, or whether he should faithfully observe the constitutional provisions by serving only two terms as stipulated so as to establish the principles of "government by law" and of a "constitutional democracy." He chose the former alternative. He ordered his own ruling Democratic Republican Party (DRP) to try to amend the constitution, enabling him to run for a third term in 1971. In a de Gaullian style, he told the nation that the constitutional amendment would be put to a "national referendum" and that if the people should vote against it, he would interpret it as a vote of nonconfidence and would resign immediately.

After having put the constitutional amendment in motion, on August 21, 1969, President Park visited President Nixon at the western White House in San Clemente. Park intended to convey his three important views to the American president: (1) the Nixon administration's new Asian policy with emphasis on Asians solving their own problems should not in any way lessen United States commitment to South Korea which still needed maximum possible American military and economic assistance, (2) the continued presence of United States military forces in Asia was essential to an Asian stability; the scaling down of the American military presence, as evidenced by the troop reduction in Vietnam and the eventual return of Okinawa to Japan, should not weaken the American power position and defense capability in Asia, especially in South Korea where the threat of a renewed attack by the North was persistent and mounting, and (3) South Korea needed a strong and firm leader, like Park himself, who could provide domestic stability and security for the country where American fighting men were stationed and where vast amounts of American money were invested. His trip was fruitful.

In 1970 the national referendum approved the constitutional amendment and in April 1971 President Park was elected for his third term. His declaration in the last days of his election campaign that he would not seek a fourth term was regarded as a vote-getting campaign ploy. In fact, in 1972 he proclaimed martial law, suspended the constitution, and had a new one drafted, making the term of presidency six years, but through complex legal provisions and procedures his presidency for life was virtually guaranteed.[48] In the North, likewise, a new constitution was promulgated, giving Marshal Kim Il-sung the title of President for the Democratic People's Republic of Korea.[49]

The two leaders—Park in the South and Kim in the North—were in firm control of their respective domains and began to approach the question of national unification from a vastly changed international perspective. President Nixon's visits to Peking in February and to Moscow in May 1972 had created a new international climate of *rapprochement* and *détente* which looked beyond differences in social, political, and economic systems as well as ideologies. Presidents Park and Kim saw no reason why they could not explore the possibility of a domestic *détente* leading to a national reconciliation and reunification. Seoul and Pyongyang carried out secret conversations in May and June, and on July 4, 1972, they announced the dramatic joint communique. It promised to achieve seven goals: (1) peaceful reunification without external interference, overcoming differences in ideologies and political systems, (2) renunciation of military provocations, (3) South-North exchanges in various fields, (4) cooperation for the early success of the South-North Red Cross talks, (5) installation of a "hot line" between Seoul and Pyongyang, (6) establishment of a South-North Coordinating Committee, and (7) adherence to terms of the agreement.[50]

From antagonism to accord was one thing, but from promise to performance was quite another. The implementation of their agreement for success required mutual trust, good faith, statesmanship with moral courage, and political wisdom to overcome the virulence of accusations and propaganda hurled against each other for nearly three decades. They had left so great a degree of psychological scars, emotional bitterness, and irreducible suspicion that they could not be wiped clean in a short period of time. Regretfully to all concerned, the South-North "thaw" proved a short-lived affair. Their dialogue made no substantive progress, and only a year after the communique, Red Cross talks on reuniting divided families became stalled. Hostilities resurfaced. In February 1974, the North Korean Navy sank a South Korean fishing vessel and captured others. The North resumed labelling President Park a "traitor" and the South calling the North "puppet." The return of vituperations, antagonism, and suspicion made South-North relations more rigid, icy, and irreconcilable than ever.

In April 1975, President Kim Il-sung visited Peking. His trip was prompted by the reality of what he called the "great transformation" of the Asian scene, characterized by the ascendancy of Communist revolutionary forces as evidenced by the collapse of Saigon and by the waning of imperialist forces as demonstrated by American troop withdrawals. President Kim saw fresh opportunities for him to unify his country by force of arms and he reportedly solicited Peking's endorsement, support, and assistance. Peking gave Kim less than a wholehearted approval of his enthusiasm but reaffirmed the status of the People's Democratic Republic of Korea "as the sole legitimate sovereign state of the Korean people."

The Peking-Pyongyang reassurance parley with emphasis on a joint communique on the South Korean people's "struggle for the democratization" gave cause for alarm and anxiety to President Park Chung Hee who was under heavy criticism at home and abroad for his violations of the basic human rights of his people. Park's suppression of his political opponents and limitations on people's freedoms were carried out in the name of national security in the face of the ever-present threat of a North Korean attack. In this situation the United States found itself caught on the horns of a dilemma: the continued presence of American troops in South Korea and its concomitant military and economic aid would contribute to the security and perpetuation of the Park regime, while a troop withdrawal from South Korea in repudiation of Park's policy would hasten political instability and even invite a North Korean armed incursion.

The United States approach to this problem was with calculated caution. In 1969, a total of about fifty-five thousand military personnel had been deployed in South Korea. In 1970–1971, the Nixon administration reduced U.S. ground force levels to thirty-four thousand men. During the presidential election campaign in the summer of 1976, candidate Jimmy Carter pledged to pull United States forces out of Korea. After winning the election and following his inauguration, President Carter kept his campaign pledge by announcing his plans for troop withdrawals, which would commence in 1978 and be completed in 1982. In April 1978, President Carter ordered some thirty-four hundred men brought home and another twenty-five hundred in 1979. There was a strong indication that President Carter modified his troop withdrawal schedule in view of substantially larger and more offensively oriented North Korean armed forces than previously assumed. Some sixteen thousand U.S. fighting men were slated to remain in the American frontier of South Korea even after the withdrawal program would be completed in 1982.

President Carter had the first opportunity to visit Korea to have a personal assessment of the situation and to confer with President Park. At the conclusion of the seven-nation summit conference in Tokyo, President Carter flew to Seoul on June 29, 1979, for a three-day visit. While in Korea, he gently rebuked the Park government for its authoritarian character tinged with violations of basic human rights. He said to his host: "There is abundant evidence in Korea of the dramatic economic progress a capable and energetic people can achieve by working together. I believe that this achievement can be matched by similar progress through the realization of basic human rights." President Park, for his part, defended his policy by stating that a democratic system had to be formulated to best suit the actual circumstances and that in his country there were no more urgent human rights than personal securities from war and hunger.

Different views on human rights aside, the two leaders jointly invited North Korea to a tripartite conference for the purpose of reducing tensions between North and South and possibly leading to a peaceful reunification of the country. The Pyongyang government promptly rejected the invitation, stating that the Korean question was a domestic affair which the Koreans should solve by themselves without any external interference.

Korea is the revolving door of Asia. It is a divided nation whose strategic importance is deeply felt by four great powers of the world—the United States, the Soviet Union, the People's Republic of China, and Japan. And the Korean people's search for national unification goes on into the unknown future with marked uncertainty and anxiety.

A case in point was the assassination of President Park on October 26, 1979, by the head of the Korean Central Intelligence Agency (KCIA). South Korea was plunged into a state of uncertainty, fearing that North Korea might exploit the political turmoil by way of another invasion. The United States promptly dispatched its airborne warning and control aircraft to Korea, followed by a U.S. Seventh Fleet task force including the aircraft carrier *Kitty Hawk.* This action had, to a degree, the effect of calming South Korean anxiety. In Seoul the army-backed civilian government and its opposition leaders showed, at least momentarily, signs of national unity in revising Park's undemocratic constitution, with amendments offered to the people in a national referendum. Their hope was to promote democratic political development commensurate with miraculous economic and social growth. This hope was short-lived. The army's tight grip on government machinery, and its ascendancy, coupled with the martial law rule of political power under the leadership of Lieutenant General Chun Doo Hwan, Park's protégé, left little prospect for a constitutional amendment or for political democracy. Student demonstrations against the army rule began to emerge in major cities, and in May 1980 the city of Kwangju was seized by the demonstrators who turned into insurgents. The insurrection was ruthlessly crushed by the army in the midst of national agony and despair. To the Koreans, development of political democracy was as far removed as unification of their country. Chun Doo Hwan, subsequently elected president, visited Washington, D.C. in February 1981 to confer with President Ronald Reagan, who reaffirmed U.S. defense commitments and assured continued stationing of American troops in Korea.

Japan Inc.

The 1850s was an historic decade for Japan: Commodore Perry's "Black Ship" shook Japan from its isolationist slumber and the Tokugawa regime began to crumble, paving the way for the birth of a new Japan. A century later, the 1950s became another historic decade: a conquered nation regained its national sovereignty through a peace treaty, assumed full membership in the United Nations, and found its place in the sun, paving the way for the birth of an industrial giant of the world.

The decade of the 1960s began with the signing of a United States-Japan Treaty of Mutual Cooperation and Security, whereby "the United States of America is granted the use by its land, air and naval forces of facilities and areas in Japan" (Article 6). To many Japanese, this security treaty would have a questionable benefit to Japan because it meant that in time of war involving the

United States, Japan would become a staging area for the United States armed forces and, consequently, would be subject to enemy attack. They were deeply incensed by the "doomsday" prospect that, in the event of a nuclear war between the United States and the Soviet Union or Communist China or both, their country, an unarmed innocent bystander, would be drawn into the holocaust. Their fear coincided with, or perhaps resulted from, the fact that their total confidence in American military and technological superiority had been shaken by the Soviet Sputnik and their trust in American integrity eroded by the U-2 incident. The Japanese feared that they would be used as a mere shield by and for the United States. Furthermore, the immediate consequence of such close ties with the United States would necessarily negate the possibility of normalizing relations with mainland China for expanded trade, commerce, and contacts. There was a surge of antitreaty sentiment among Japanese leftists, socialists, pacifists, antiwar intellectuals, and anti-American agitators who took the lead in opposing ratification of the security treaty.

In May 1960, President Eisenhower was scheduled to visit Japan, and Prime Minister Kishi Nobusuke, who had negotiated the treaty, desired to complete ratification of the new security pact before Eisenhower's arrival. Capitalizing on his Liberal Democratic Party (LDP) majority, Premier Kishi rammed the ratification through the House of Representatives while opponents were not even on the floor. His high-handed, dictatorial tactics and his authoritarian attitude further inflamed the antitreaty sentiment, causing mass demonstrations so violent and vehement as to paralyze Tokyo. The demonstrators were from all walks of life, expressing their displeasure and discontent which stemmed from their attitudes of anti-Kishi, antitreaty, antiarmament, and anti-America. Daily demonstrations in May and June fostered turbulence and chaos and created a political crisis so grave that Eisenhower's planned visit had to be cancelled. But he went on to visit Korea as discussed earlier.

Kishi was compelled to resign in July and was succeeded by Ikeda Hayato, another LDP leader. In November 1960, Ikeda and his LDP won general elections, which indicated that his party was not adversely affected by the tumultuous May–June demonstrations.

In a conscious effort to calm the national mood and to show his sincere concern for the plight of the common man, Premier Ikeda announced his economic policy of "income doubling," whereby Japanese personal incomes would be doubled by the end of the decade. This was a modest, down-to-earth program as compared with President Kennedy's grandiose "New Frontier" project of "landing a man on the moon and returning him safely to the earth" before the end of the decade. Thus, a quiet, unintended, and unnoticed race was on between the United States and Japan: the former to a better understanding of the moon in the solar system and the latter to a betterment of life here on earth.

In June 1961, Prime Minister Ikeda visited Washington to confer with President Kennedy. Their talks covered a wide range of topics and issues: Communist China, Korea, the nuclear test ban treaty, general disarmament, aid to developing nations, and the world economic situation. They stressed the need for "promoting the growth of international trade and financial stability" and agreed that their countries "should pursue liberal trade policies looking to an orderly expansion of trade between the two countries."[51] They also agreed to create a new joint United States-Japan committee on trade and economic affairs, a body composed of cabinet-rank officers to deal with trade issues, which began its work in November 1961.

In foreign affairs Japan was not yet an imposing figure. But its growing self-confidence and national pride enabled Ikeda to strengthen Japan's important position in the world community and to seek an equal "partnership" with the United States. Japanese and European leaders began the exchange of visits. Ikeda visited Europe in 1962 and spoke of the need for "trilateral cooperation" among the United States, Western Europe, and Japan. This theme was officially taken up fifteen years later by the Carter administration. In July 1963, Japan was admitted to the Organization for Economic Cooperation and Development (OECD), an exclusive international organization composed of highly industrialized Western nations. Japan was confident and capable enough to host the 1964 Olympic games, which helped boost Japanese prestige abroad. With respect to American-Japanese relations, President Kennedy's appointment of Edwin O. Reischauer, a Harvard historian and an expert on Asia, especially on Japan, as American ambassador to Japan contributed greatly to the promotion of friendship and goodwill between the two countries. Japan settled to its favor the debt owed to the United States for relief supplies it had received during the occupation. The Japanese in Okinawa were granted by the United States a greater degree of autonomy. President Kennedy's popularity in Japan, enhanced by his brother's (Robert Kennedy) visit to Japan in 1962, also helped improve the American image among the Japanese.

Ikeda's "low posture" of a conciliatory approach to his Socialist opponents avoided confrontation politics and sufficiently achieved domestic tranquillity. Under his leadership Japan left the days of demonstrations behind and enjoyed peace and prosperity, making substantive progress toward a parliamentary, constitutional democracy similar to that of Britain. Politics in Japan came to assume such characteristics as parliamentary supremacy, a responsible cabinet system, and bipartisanship—the two principal political parties being conservative (LDP) and socialist (SP).

On October 25, 1964, Ikeda resigned the premiership on account of his poor health and was succeeded by Sato Eisaku, the younger brother of former prime minister Kishi Nobusuke.[52] As expected, Sato's succession assured the continuity of the Ikeda policy. Sato visited President Johnson in June 1965. The two leaders reaffirmed American-Japanese friendship and cooperation in the maintenance and promotion of their common interests. Premier Sato also continued to expand Japan's role in Asia. Tokyo and Seoul normalized their relations in the midst of public misgivings in both Japan and South Korea. Japan provided economic aid to Southeast Asian nations in the form of reparation payments, capital investments, and technical assistance, while enjoying expanded trade with these countries. Upon the establishment of the Asian Development Bank in 1965, Japan contributed $200 million to its capital, matching the United States. Japan's "partnership" policy vis-a-vis the United States also resulted in tangible gains: in 1968, the United States returned the Ogasawara (Bonin) Islands to Japan and the following year the United States agreed to revert Okinawa to Japanese rule in 1972.[53]

As the decade of the 1960s was coming to a close, the Ikeda

"income doubling" program more than accomplished its goal and the race to a better life was won in what was described as an "economic miracle." The gross national product had doubled before the target date and continued to grow at a phenomenal average rate of about 19 percent faster than any other national economy in the world and about three times as fast as the United States. Per capita income exceeded $1,000[54] and Japan accumulated a trade surplus of over a billion dollars. Japan came to rank as the third largest economy in the world, behind only the two known super powers—the United States and the Soviet Union. Japan led the world in shipbuilding and other manufactured goods—automobiles, motorcycles, television sets, electronic equipment, cameras, and precision machines—all of which were eagerly demanded in the world market because of their reputation as high quality products.

One may wonder what made this remarkable performance possible. What were some of the contributing factors to the success of this "economic miracle"? Three major factors could be cited: (1) so-called work ethics involving Japanese workers' attitudes, (2) managerial skills, and (3) governmental policies and guidance.

First, the Japanese are a homogeneous people, consisting basically of a single ethnic group speaking a single language. For this reason it has been historically true that consensus was rather easily obtained in Japanese society. A Japanese tends to identify himself with the group instead of considering himself an individual above it. Japanese factory workers—skilled, dedicated, and efficient—usually carry this attitude into their firms. They tend to identify strongly with their companies and to think foremost of their firm's overall well-being. Even when labor unions were formed, they were typically enterprise unions consisting of all the employees of a single company, and they seldom went on such crippling strikes as in the United States or in Great Britain. Labor-management relationships in Japan were complementary rather than competitive. The lifetime employment system further enhanced workers' loyalty to their firms, making employer-employee relations a kind of extended family.

Second, Japan witnessed the rise of a new generation of business leaders who mastered the art of business management with both traditional and modern techniques. Many private firms were run by professional managers who stressed the firms' continued growth by plowing profits back into capital and plant expansion. The Japanese are great renovators: they absorbed "things Western," while retaining "things Japanese." Industrial managers and technicians alike refined and improved upon even the most advanced Western techniques just as they had done throughout their national history. Even the wartime destruction of Japanese industrial facilities proved beneficial because new factories were built with the most advanced technology for maximum efficiency.

Third, and finally, from the days of the Meiji rule, close cooperation between government and big business was a tradition. The basic policy of government was to promote exports in order to pay for the importation of raw materials. The powerful Ministry of International Trade and Industry (MITI) exercised careful controls in these areas as well as in overall national productivity because Japan relied so heavily on foreign sources of essential raw materials such as oil and iron that planning for balanced economic expansion was needed. The government also protected domestic industries by means of import controls, limitations on foreign investment inflow, and tariffs. Most private firms with high growth potential received governmental assistance in the form of special tax relief, rapid depreciation allowances, low interest loans, subsidies, and government purchase of stock. It should be added that Japan, placed under a United States "protective umbrella" by the security treaty and, therefore, relieved of the burden of military expenditures, could concentrate its energy, skill, and capital on the growth and expansion of the civilian economy.

Thus, the small island country became "Japan, Inc." and a "workshop of Asia," as it used to be called, now turned into a "workshop of the world." To substantiate this claim, it should be noted that "Japan's steel industry could bring together Australian or Indian iron ore with American coking coal and produce steel that could be sold in the United States in competition with the products of domestic American iron ore and coal."[55]

Behind the scene of Japan's miraculous success in economic growth, in the second half of the 1960s there were paradoxes and dilemmas in Japanese-American relations in two principal areas:

defense arrangements and trade relations. The fears and resentments that had erupted in the form of mass demonstrations against the security treaty of 1960 were never really removed, but they continued to subsist under the surface of the dazzling national prosperity. The economic expansion, in turn, provided the Japanese with a rising sense of national pride, prestige, and self-confidence. The Japanese then began to raise the old nagging question of how genuinely they were sovereign and independent. They realized that no sovereign nation would endure the indignity of the presence of foreign (American) troops and no independent government would be subservient to the policies of a foreign (American) power. The man in the street basically disliked American bases in his country and seriously doubted the benefits of the defense arrangements which appeared to protect primarily American interests.

The fundamental paradox or dilemma was that if Japan wanted to remove American bases and to restore its military sovereignty, it had to carry out a policy of rearmament which had been prohibited by its constitution, notwithstanding the fact that Japan has already come to possess a considerable self-defense force. Would an armed Japan, including nuclear weapons, with two essentially hostile nuclear neighbors—the Soviet Union and Communist China—at its front and side doors be more secure than an unarmed Japan? Japanese leaders thought not. Premier Ikeda had adhered to three so-called nonnuclear principles: nonproduction, nonpossession, and nonintroduction of nuclear weapons. His successor, Prime Minister Sato Eisaku, further refined the Ikeda policy and formulated a four-principle nuclear policy calling for: (1) worldwide nuclear disarmament, (2) maintenance of the three nonnuclear principles, (3) reliance on United States nuclear deterrence, and (4) nuclear energy for peaceful purposes. Thus, the path Japanese leaders had taken to place Japan under the American "nuclear umbrella" ultimately led the country to an "economic miracle," partly because Japan had spent only less than one percent of its GNP annually for its national defense. In brief, American military presence in Japan was regarded by the Japanese as their emotional burden and their economic bliss at the same time.

This dilemma was further enhanced by American military presence in Asia as a whole. During the latter half of the 1960s, the Vietnam War was dangerously escalated. What the Japanese saw in Vietnam was a disturbing, tragic affair in which the United States—Japan's "partner" or her "mentor"—was so deeply involved. The war appeared to give credence to Lenin's dictum that "imperialism is the highest state of capitalism," and it could easily spread to Communist China and possibly even to the Soviet Union, making the worst fear that Japan would be dragged into the doomsday struggle a dreadful reality. Premier Sato during his visit to Washington told President Johnson, "I sympathize with your plight in Vietnam, but . . ." He left his comment unfinished. After his return to Tokyo he said before a Diet assembly, ". . . but I do not agree with his [Johnson's] policy in Vietnam." Japan wanted to see the United States disengage from Vietnam.

Japan's sincere concern and fear, on the other hand, was that the United States might make a rash decision to effect military withdrawal from Asia which would leave Japan extremely vulnerable. America's frustration in Vietnam, rising waves of anti-Americanism in Asia, mounting domestic antiwar sentiments, and soaring war expenditures and inflation could conceivably drive the United States into an isolationist posture which would draw the frontier line of defense perimeter from Alaska, the Aleutians, through the Marianas, to Australia, excluding Japan, Korea, Taiwan, and the Philippines. This was most unlikely, but not impossible. In such an event, the political and military vacuum created by American withdrawal would immediately be filled by Communist powers and consequently Japan's economic lifeline, the sea lanes, would be subject to their mercy.

As the decade wore on, there loomed also a growing friction in American-Japanese trade relations. United States officials and businessmen came to feel that the Japanese economic expansion of gigantic dimensions[56] was getting a free ride militarily because of the security treaty. They also complained that while Japanese goods, ranging from automobiles to toys, were flooding American markets, Japan had built tariff walls so high against foreign industrial products that American manufactured goods were virtually excluded from Japanese markets. In some sectors of American industries grumbling voices were increasingly heard against Japanese "invasion" of their markets, demanding higher tariffs by the United States. In an effort to mitigate the situation the Japanese government, under strong pressure from Washington, had set "voluntary controls" on its exports to the United States. But it remained only a palliative.

These dilemmas, inherent cause for American-Japanese frictions, were carried over into the following decade of the 1970s. In addition, there was another unresolved, continuing source of strain between the two countries. The Japanese felt that their desire to pursue their own independent foreign policy as they saw fit to promote their national interests was constantly constrained by the United States. Japan believed, for example, it would be a good policy to improve relations with mainland China, even to recognize the Peking regime, so as to increase trade and to broaden contacts in various fields, but such policies would be invariably construed by Washington as basically unfriendly to the United States. Worrying about potential American trade reaction, Japan tolerated its political peonage in exchange for economic rewards.

Such was the atmosphere in which Japan was hit by two successive waves of what became known as the "Nixon shocks." The first shock came on July 15, 1971, when President Nixon revealed that he would make an official visit to the People's Republic of China in early 1972. From a realistic and pragmatic standpoint, the Nixon *demarche* was a wise and welcome policy which Japan would readily endorse and accept, but what shocked Japan into a "trauma" was the manner in which the Nixon administration had conducted itself. It had failed to consult in advance with Japan— America's closest friend in Asia—and it had neglected the simple courtesy of informing Japan of its intentions. Washington had been telling Tokyo that Peking was a "forbidden fruit" and now President Nixon was about to pick it for himself. The severity of the shock stemmed primarily from Japanese sensitivity toward the American insensitivity with which the United States had undertaken the unilateral initiative to a point of betrayal of a faithful ally.

Scarcely had the Japanese recovered from the trauma when they were hit again by the second wave of the "Nixon shocks." On August 15, 1971, President Nixon announced the imposition of a 10 percent surcharge on all imports and suspended convertibility of the dollar into gold and other reserve assets. Although these measures were designed to deal with a worldwide economic problem, especially America's balance of payments crisis, Washington could not hide the fact that it was aiming at reversing an unfavorable balance of trade with Japan. President Nixon admitted afterwards: "We knew that the impact would be particularly strong in Japan, because of the dimensions of our commerce with each other and because of Japan's strong dependence on foreign trade."[57] The Japanese government and business community resented the fact that the United States was trying to solve its economic difficulties by exporting them, especially to Japan. Yet Japanese trade depended so heavily on the United States that the Sato government had no choice but to fall in line with American policy and it carried out a revaluation of the yen and the liberalization of restrictions on imports and foreign capital inflows. Premier Sato became the chief casualty of the "Nixon shocks." He resigned in July 1972 and was succeeded by Tanaka Kakuei.

The "Nixon shocks," like *tsunami,* swept the nation in force, but as they subsided they left little permanent damage either to Japan's economy or to its international position. The endurance and the adaptability of the Japanese people were too profound and resilient to succumb to them. The favorable Japanese trade balance continued to grow and Sino-Japanese relations began to turn from good to better. Following the path of the Nixon visit to Peking, Prime Minister Tanaka also journeyed there at the invitation of Premier Chou En-lai and established diplomatic relations with the People's Republic of China on September 29, 1972. This was not a formal peace treaty to end the state of hostilities from World War II. It was yet to be negotiated in the subsequent years.

Tanaka leadership, especially its apparent self-assertive foreign policy, helped rejuvenate Japan's self-confidence and self-respect in coping with complex external relations. This self-confidence was once again shattered by the oil crisis of 1973–1974. The Arab oil embargo exposed to the world the basic fragility of "Japan, Inc." Ninety-nine percent dependent on foreign sources for oil, Japan could not easily diversify either into other sources of energy or away from heavy dependence on Middle Eastern oil. The Japanese were rudely awakened to the fact that the foundations of "Japan, Inc." were rather shaky and unstable, lacking in self-supporting essential materials. They began to compare their country to a luxury liner equipped with modern technology, lavishly furnished, carrying passengers beyond capacity—verily a luxurious S.S. *Japan*.

This ship, however, is not self-sufficient either in food or in oil. All it needs is bought at the ship's ports of call. In spite of the ship's colossal size, the steel plate of its hull is thin, and it is not of very sturdy construction. No one can predict what would happen if it ran into a big typhoon or hurricane. And what would it do if attacked by a pirate ship? Having no weapons, it would be unable to put up a resistance. The only consolation is that it has a contract according to the terms of which a battleship would come to its aid from somewhere if it sent out an SOS. Is there not a danger, however, that before this can happen, some elements in collusion with the pirates try to hijack the ship, or that great confusion or even riots occur as a result of the fear induced by the impending attack? Once we started entertaining such fears, an uneasy feeling creeps up on us that the luxury liner S.S. *Japan* may be a surprisingly frail craft.[58]

Nevertheless, in 1974, the S.S. *Japan* continued its turbulent voyage through the "trilemma" of inflation, recession, and a balance of payments deficit. Inflation reached 25 percent, industrial output dropped 18 percent, and the balance of payments ran a deficit of $3.4 billion due, primarily, to the increase in oil prices. Then it ran into what the Japanese described as the "Lockheed swirl," in which key governmental officials and business leaders were implicated in the multimillion-dollar payoff scandal involving Lockheed briberies in connection with the sale of its Tristar airbuses to Japan. Prime Minister Tanaka, under suspicion of being implicated in the scandal (subsequently he was indicted and convicted), stepped down from the premiership in late 1972 and was succeeded by Miki Takeo of the liberal wing of the LDP.

With Premier Miki at the helm, Japan made a slow recovery. Inflation was down to 14 percent, the balance of payments was again favorable, and economic growth reached about 4 percent. The reappearance of the growing gap in bilateral United States-Japanese trade balances became again a matter of concern. Japanese exports to the United States for 1976 ended in a surplus of $5.3 billion. The Miki cabinet, however, resigned *en masse* to take responsibility for the LDP's poor showing in a general election held on December 5, 1976. Fukuda Takeo of the same party became the new prime minister and formed his cabinet on December 24.

Under the Fukuda administration the Japanese economy continued to expand and at the same time Japan became increasingly active on the international scene. Premier Fukuda visited President Carter in Washington in March 1977 and explored the possibility for further entry of Japanese firms into the United States.[59] In May he attended the London summit conference where he assured the Western leaders that Japan would play the role of an "engine" to pull the world economy out of the recession. In August Premier Fukuda, who also attended both the ASEAN summit meeting in Kuala Lumpur and the ensuing conference of eight Pacific nations, pledged $1 billion aid for industrial development projects for the Southeast Asian nations with which Japan would cooperate as an equal partner.[60] Premier Fukuda was steering the S.S. *Japan* toward a trilateral system of the "free world" economy and simultaneously toward the center of Southeast Asia.

Premier Fukuda's crowning achievement was the historic signing of the Sino-Japanese peace treaty on October 23, 1978. The treaty negotiations had been stalled for a number of years by a dispute over Peking's insistence on an "anti-hegemony" clause, a euphemism for Soviet dominance. Although agreeable in principle to such a clause, Japan was mindful of the fact that the Soviet Union had indicated that such language in the treaty would be considered an unfriendly act. The treaty received the blessing of the United States but was sharply opposed by the Soviet Union because it contained the anti-hegemony clause. Prime Minister Fukuda extolled the treaty in a ceremonial speech: "The conclusion of the treaty added a new, brilliant page to the history of Japan-China relations." In response, Vice-Premier Deng Xiaoping of the People's Republic of China stated: "It was the common desire of one billion peoples of the two countries to unite on friendly terms and cooperate with each other . . . [toward] a bright future in Sino-Japanese relations and for the sake of peace in Asia and the world."

In late December 1978, in an LDP election, the party dropped Fukuda and turned to Ohira Masayoshi for leadership. As Ohira took the office of prime minister, he had to cope with the two most familiar and serious issues: U.S.-Japanese relations on trade and defense. Japan's trade surplus with the United States in 1977 exceeded $7.5 billion and in 1978 $11.5 billion. Premier Ohira seemed powerless to change promptly Japanese trade realities. Japan was dominated by cartel-prone industries and allied trading houses. To lessen the iron grips of the cartels on Japanese business would require a sweeping change in antitrust legislation which the LDP, the party of big business, would not consider. The LDP leaders were insisting that Japan had done everything possible to facilitate imports: sending purchase missions to the United States, removing nearly all import quotas, and reducing tariffs below Western levels as agreed during recent "Tokyo Round" tariff cuts.

As to the defense issue, the United States disengagement from Vietnam and President Carter's troop reduction plan in Korea had made Japan restive. The low profile of the United States in the Pacific and, conversely, the heightened presence of the Soviet Far Eastern Fleet, including the construction of military facilities on the disputed islands of Etorofu and Kunashiri, raised some doubts about the efficacy of the American commitment to Japan under the joint security treaty. Japan was pressed to consider the need for strengthening its self-defense capabilities. But Japan's constitution inhibited any rapid adoption of a strategic armament law. The United States, meanwhile, put pressure on the Japanese government to increase substantially its contributions to local American military expenditures, but Premier Ohira could see little hope of satisfying American demands.

On May 2, 1979, Prime Minister Ohira visited Washington to confer with President Carter in an effort to resolve these outstanding issues and to chart future courses of action between the two countries. The Carter-Ohira summit was a low-keyed affair and no specific decisions were made. Only in general terms did the two leaders agree to persevere and cooperate into the 1980s for mutual benefits in all bilateral relations and to place more responsibility for maintaining world trade and peace on Japan. Two months later Premier Ohira sponsored the seven-nation economic summit conference in Tokyo attended by President Carter, Chancellor Helmut Schmidt of West Germany, Prime Minister Margaret Thatcher of Great Britain, President Giscard d'Estaing of France, Premier Giulio Andreotti of Italy, and Premier Joe Clark of Canada. They discussed the growing problem of worldwide inflation and the menacing spectre of global economic recession caused largely by the rising cost of energy—oil. The Tokyo summit coincided with the thirteen-nation OPEC (Organization of the Petroleum Exporting Countries) Ministers Conference in Geneva, where they raised oil prices to a new ceiling of $23.50 a barrel— nearly a tenfold jump in six years. The Tokyo summit nations assailed the oil price increase and drew up stiff conservation programs to curb oil consumption through 1985. Such a conservation policy was expected to make it difficult for Japan, whose industries depended heavily on imported oil, to maintain economic growth at the same pace it had achieved.

Prime Minister Ohira suffered a slight political setback in October 1979 because of his party's poor showing in the elections, which he had called a year earlier than was constitutionally required in the hope of increasing LDP representation. Intraparty rivals contended that Ohira committed an inexcusable blunder in calling the elections prematurely, but he successfully defended his position and remained a party leader and prime minister.

In the area of Ohira's foreign policy, the central issue continued to be U.S.-Japan relations. Specifically, he had to find satisfactory means to cope with dual American pressures: (1) for an accelerated Japanese armament and (2) for a reduction in Japanese automobile exports to the United States. The complexity of these issues and strong domestic opposition to them constituted a source of strain between the two countries. Iran further contributed to the strain. When Iranian militants, on November 4, 1979, seized the U.S. embassy in Teheran and held fifty-three embassy personnel hostage, Washington looked for strong support from Tokyo, including participation in an economic boycott. Instead, Japanese companies rushed in to purchase all available Iranian oil at inflated prices. Washington's bitter protest of Japanese insensitivity caused Japan to back off temporarily, but eventually Japan bought the oil at a lower price. The Japanese claimed that they understood the American position but the United States failed to understand the Japanese position—Japan's total dependency on foreign oil for her energy needs.

The Iranian crisis was followed by another international crisis in December when the Soviet Union invaded Afghanistan. In this event, Japan was readily inclined to please the United States by siding with Washington in condemning Soviet action, boycotting the scheduled Olympic games in Moscow, and urging the Soviets to withdraw troops from Afghanistan. Yet, Japan was also cautious not to offend the Soviets so unnecessarily as to make Tokyo-Moscow relations overly antagonistic.

In spite of the growing demand among the Japanese for more "independent" foreign policy, Prime Minister Ohira was committed to continue close ties with the United States so long as Washington would regard Japan as a "partner" rather than a "client." In April 1980, he visited Washington to confer with President Carter in an effort to iron out policy differences and to enhance mutual trust. The result of their meeting was inconsequential. Two months later on June 12 Prime Minister Ohira died of a heart attack. The ruling LDP elected Suzuki Zenko to succeed Ohira.

Détente with the People's Republic of China

The establishment of the People's Republic of China on October 1, 1949, by the Communists in the wake of their victory in the civil war over the Kuomintang's Nationalist government under Chiang Kai-shek marked the end of the latest interdynastic transitional period. Chinese history has shown a unique pattern known as "dynastic cycle" in that there was invariably an intermediate period of political instability between the fall of an old dynasty and the rise of a new one. The demise of the Ching Dynasty (1644–1911) signaled the beginning of one of those periods, which ended with the rise of the People's Republic of China. In the view of cyclical historians, the People's Republic of China was but a new dynasty, perhaps expediently called the "Communist Dynasty."

Be that as it may, the People's Republic of China from its inception continued its march toward internal and external greatness. It embarked at home upon construction of socialism and "new democracy" based on the principles of Maoism and strove to achieve great world power status abroad. But the road to these goals was replete with hopes and frustrations, successes and failures, agony and glory. The new leaders in China were especially concerned with American hostility and antagonism toward them and they reciprocated in kind.

Sino-American antagonism was heightened during the Korean War, and it was also the major factor responsible for the United States' refusal to endorse the Geneva agreements of 1954, as discussed earlier in this book. The Peking leaders were especially frustrated and angered by the U.S. policy to protect the Chiang Kai-shek regime on Taiwan (Formosa). The United States concluded a mutual defense treaty with Taiwan and, in addition, Congress passed a joint resolution authorizing the president to employ United States armed forces "for the specific purpose of securing and protecting Formosa and the Pescadores against armed attack." Viewed from Washington, the advent of a hostile Communist regime in China forced the United States to retreat from mainland China and to establish America's frontier defense line from the southern half of Korea to the beachhead of Vietnam through Taiwan. The United States was determined to hold this line at any cost in the face of a Chinese Communist threat which loomed as an ogre in the American mind.

The United States not only refused to recognize the Peking regime but also to accept the possibility of a Sino-Soviet rift. In August 1958, the United States government issued a policy declaration, which read in part:

The Alliance between Moscow and Peking is one of long standing; it traces its origin to the very founding of the Chinese Communist Party in 1921. . . . It is based on a common ideology and on mutually held objectives with respect to the non-Communist world. All recent evidence points to the closeness of the tie between the Chinese Communists and the

U.S.S.R. rather than in the other direction. . . . It is scarcely credible that they [the Chinese Communists] would dare risk any course of action which could lead to loss of their source of military supplies.[61]

The United States at this time was either unable to detect or was willing to ignore the genesis of the Sino-Soviet conflict which began to surface. There were irrefutable symptoms of fundamental differences between Peking and Moscow. For instance, China's complaint of the slow pace of Soviet economic aid as provided for by the Sino-Soviet agreement of 1954, China's criticism of Khrushchev's de-Stalinization policy which opened a Pandora's box of dissent and disunity within the Communist bloc, and China's dissatisfaction with Soviet handling of the Polish revolt and the Hungarian revolution of 1956. Soviet leaders, on the other hand, ridiculed Mao's economic program, the "Great Leap Forward," scorned the Chinese commune system, and charged Peking leadership with being old-fashioned and reactionary.

To Peking leaders, the Kremlin's "sin" was bearable for the time being at least, while Washington's "crime" was intolerable. They were convinced that the United States stood in the way of their goal of liberating Taiwan and of destroying completely the remnants of the Kuomintang regime under Chiang Kai-shek who was hiding behind an American shield. They branded the United States as a malevolent, reactionary, imperialistic nation so incapable of understanding changed political realities in China as to support a corrupt, fugitive, illegal government which represented China's infamous past. The Chinese Communists felt it mandatory to "liberate" Taiwan because without its liberation the Communist revolution would be incomplete and American imperialism would remain on Chinese soil.

In August 1958, the Chinese Communists carried out their heaviest artillery attack on the two offshore islands: Quemoy, barely six miles from the port of Amoy, and Matsu, less than ten miles from the Foochow coast. The bombardment gave the impression that it could be a prelude to an invasion of Taiwan. The United States, therefore, made it immediately clear that a Communist attempt to take these islands would not be a limited operation and that the Formosa Resolution of 1955 would include Quemoy and Matsu in "such related positions and territories" as necessary for the defense of Taiwan. Secretary of State Dulles hinted at a bombing of mainland China if the Communists launched an attack on these islands and President Eisenhower declared that he would consider such an attack as a Communist design to "liquidate all of the free world positions in the Western Pacific." The president then ordered naval escorts of Nationalist convoys to Quemoy and a portion of the Pacific Fleet was sent to the China Sea. This crisis over the Taiwan Strait gradually subsided in the midst of puzzlement and consternation of the European allies who could not perceive or tolerate the notion that the United States was ready to risk a major war with Communist China over these "insignificant" islands. Two years later Quemoy and Matsu resurfaced to attract national and international attention by the televised Kennedy-Nixon debate on the issue during the 1960 presidential election campaign, in which Richard Nixon declared: "Now what do the Chinese Communists want? They don't want just Quemoy and Matsu. They don't want just Formosa. They want the world."

By the time President Kennedy took office, the United States was deeply involved in Vietnam and Laos, the southern flank of Communist China. President Kennedy believed that the state of Washington-Peking relations was "irrational" but he could do little to rectify the situation because he had inherited the anti-Communist-oriented Washington bureaucracy, still tinged with the legacy of the McCarthy era. The Bureau of Far Eastern Affairs of the Department of State, for example, had been "purged of its best China experts, and of farsighted, dispassionate men, as a result of McCarthyism."[62] Those who remained were committed, by choice or by fear, to the policy of containment and isolation of Communist China. Above all, President Kennedy was well-tuned to the domestic mood or the "national psyche" toward Communist China. The American public viewed Communist China as an outlaw nation which should be incarcerated and kept from such world organizations as the United Nations. President Kennedy "had no doubt in 1961 that the international gains (if any) of admission [of Communist China to the United Nations] would be far outweighed by the uproar it could cause at home." Even Eisenhower had told Kennedy before the inauguration that he hoped to support his successor on all foreign policy issues except Peking's admission to the United Nations. "With his slim majority, Kennedy felt that he could not take on the China problem this year."[63] Kennedy's assessment of the situation proved astonishingly correct as the Senate adopted in July a resolution by a 76–0 vote to support the Nationalist government on Taiwan as the lawful representative in the United Nations and, therefore, to "oppose the seating of the Chinese Communist regime in the United Nations" and to support "the President in not according diplomatic recognition" to it. The House unanimously passed this resolution the following month.

Meanwhile, the Sino-Soviet "quarrel" grew with added vehemence. Soviet Premier Khrushchev chastised Albania's "dogmatism" as an attack in disguise on the Chinese Communists, who in turn assailed Yugoslavia's "revisionism" as a veil for an attack on the Kremlin leaders. Soviet economic and technical assistance programs to Communist China came to an abrupt halt as Soviet technicians and experts were recalled to Moscow with their blueprints. Peking accused Khrushchev of "defeatism" and "adventurism" in the Cuban missile crisis, condemned Soviet delivery of MIG fighters to the Indian Air Force, protested against the expulsion of three Chinese embassy officials, denounced the partial nuclear test ban treaty initialed in Moscow on July 25, 1963, and rejected Soviet proposals for a conference to cease polemics. The range of their conflicts, revealed in their polemics, covered, in addition to those specifics noted above, a variety of issues: war and nuclear weapons, peace and disarmament, dogmatism and revisionism, revolution and world communism, social development and economic relations, the cult of personality and the dictatorship of the proletariat, and racism.[64]

China's persistent pursuit of great world power status gained momentum in October 1964, when Peking made a terse announcement: "China exploded an atomic bomb at 1500 hours on October 16, 1964, and thereby conducted successfully its first nuclear test." The test had taken place near Lake Lop Nor in the Takla Makan desert in the Province of Sinkiang. It was reported to be a low-yield device—equivalent to twenty thousand tons of TNT —about the size of the atomic bomb dropped on Hiroshima on

August 6, 1945. The Chinese Communist leaders had literally blasted into the exclusive "atomic club." The psychological repercussions of the China bomb were greater throughout the world than its immediate military significance. The developing nations of the Third World now tended to look more to Peking for leadership than to Moscow. Hence, it became more difficult for the Soviet Union to insist on its claim to undisputed guardianship of the national liberation movement.

The intensification of the Sino-Soviet conflict, the emergence of a "tricentric" (Washington-Moscow-Peking) balance of power, and America's ever-deepening involvements in Vietnam compelled the United States to revamp its China policy with candor so as to approximate it with existing realities. In March 1966, the Senate Foreign Relations Committee held hearings in the form of a forum to which a number of scholars and experts on China were invited to present their views on China and American attitudes. The central issue was how to open a reasonable and meaningful dialogue between Washington and Peking. The immediate impact of such a forum upon the American public was not clear, but the fact that it took place at all to "educate" them was itself in striking contrast to the McCarthy hearings in the early 1950s. Professor John K. Fairbank of Harvard University summed up the theme as he elucidated: "Containment alone is a blind alley unless we add policies of constructive competition and international contact. . . . Peking's rulers shout aggressively out of manifold frustrations. . . . Isolation intensifies their ailment and makes it self-perpetuating, and we need to encourage international contact with China on many fronts."[65] At the administration level, two small, inconspicuous steps were taken in 1966 toward relaxation of Sino-American tensions: (1) the United States government eased restrictions on the travel of scholars to Communist countries, (2) President Johnson in a televised speech expressed his view on the necessity of eventual reconciliation with Communist China.

These steps were obscured by both America's escalation of the war in Vietnam and China's domestic turmoil in the Great Proletarian Cultural Revolution. Chairman Mao Tse-tung and his close followers, in their desire to rekindle patriotic fervor by stressing absolute social equality and to prevent reemergence of new classes in the party and in the government, sought to consolidate their power and to establish a solid foundation for a monolithic, egalitarian society under their leadership.[66] It was a classic example of a power struggle between Maoist radicals and the moderate faction within the Chinese Communist party. The radicals mobilized millions of young revolutionaries, called "Red Guards," to stage mass meetings and parades in praise of Chairman Mao and in denunciation of "capitalist roaders" in the party. Many high-ranking party officials, including Deng Xiaoping, were humiliated in public. For nearly three years, 1966–1969, schools were shut down, industrial production crippled, communication and transportation disrupted, and social order disorganized. By early 1969 the Cultural Revolution had run its course and China began to return to "normalcy," with emphasis on economic stability and growth. In foreign relations China also resumed normal diplomacy by sending out scores of ambassadors to foreign capitals. Peking received a parade of visiting foreign dignitaries and signed a number of trade agreements. Premier Chou En-lai himself made an extensive tour of Europe, the Middle East, and Africa.

The changing political climate in China was equaled by a similar change in political atmosphere in the United States. After President Nixon took office, he became convinced more than ever that even if he ended the war in Vietnam with "honor," his "generation of peace" could not be guaranteed without China's participation and cooperation. Nixon for some time had felt the need for a new China policy attuned to the changed situation in Asia. During his 1968 campaign for the presidency, he had declared, "We simply cannot afford to leave China forever outside the family of nations, there to nurture its fantasies, cherish its hates and threaten its neighbor. There is no place on this small planet for a billion of its potentially most able people to live in angry isolation."

Believing that China's continued isolation would pose more danger to peace than its positive participation in world affairs, President Nixon in his first year in office took three carefully worked out steps to improve Washington-Peking relations: (1) in July the administration eased travel and trade restrictions on mainland China, (2) in November the president ordered the termination of U.S. Navy patrol in the Taiwan Strait, and (3) in

December the United States government permitted American firms abroad to sell nonstrategic goods to Communist China and to buy its products for resale in foreign markets. The president, meanwhile, found that one of the formidable obstacles to an American-Chinese accommodation was the Taiwan issue. Both Peking and Taipei maintained that Taiwan was an integral part of China, each firmly rejecting any suggestion of a "two-China" solution and each claiming to be the genuinely legitimate representative government of the Chinese people. There was no difficulty for the Nixon administration to rule out any "two-China" policy, but as to the question of legitimacy it had to refrain from taking sides, except for reaffirming its commitment to Taiwan's autonomy.

At this stage the Peking leaders were not fully convinced of the Nixon overtures. They believed that the United States was pro-Soviet in China's ideological rift with the Soviets and in the frequent military skirmishes along their common border. They attacked what they believed to be an American-Soviet "collusion" in arms control and feared a Soviet preemptive nuclear attack on China with America's acquiescence. Curiously, the Soviets on their part suspected Washington-Peking "collusion" to squeeze them out of East Asia. This trilateral diplomacy of suspicion led the then under-secretary of state Elliot Richardson to clarify the American position: "We are not going to let Communist Chinese invective deter us from seeking agreements with the Soviet Union where those are in our interest. Conversely, we are not going to let Soviet apprehensions prevent us from attempting to bring Communist China out of its angry, alienated shell."

President Nixon's continued, unilateral measures—the reduction of United States forces in the Taiwan area, the continued relaxation of trade and travel restrictions toward Peking, and his policy of withdrawing U.S. troops from Vietnam—made the leaders in Peking receptive and convinced of Nixon's sincerity to the extent that Chairman Mao was reportedly ready to greet Nixon whether as a tourist or as president of the United States.[67] A dramatic demonstration of change in the United States' China policy toward a serious dialogue appeared in a presidential report to Congress on February 25, 1971, when President Nixon stated:

The twenty-two-year-old hostility between ourselves and the People's Republic of China is another unresolved problem, serious indeed in view of the fact it determines our relationship with 750 million talented and energetic people. It is a truism that an international order cannot be secure if one of the major powers remains largely outside it and hostile toward it. In this decade, therefore, there will be no more important challenge than that of drawing the People's Republic of China into a constructive relationship with the world community, and particularly with the rest of Asia.[68]

A decade earlier, in 1961, President Kennedy had committed the U.S. to achieving the goal, before that decade was out, of landing a man on the moon and bringing him safely back to the earth. The moon was Kennedy's frontier, and his goal was achieved in 1969 during the Nixon administration. Now in 1971, President Nixon committed the U.S. to achieving the goal in this decade of normalizing relations with the People's Republic of China and bringing it into the family of nations. Mainland China was Nixon's frontier and his goal was achieved in 1979 during the Carter administration. Indeed, before the Nixon initiative, Peking might as well have been as far away and strange to the American people as the moon had been.

In any case, for the first time the president of the United States referred to Communist China or "Red China" by its official name, the *People's Republic of China.* He continued:

For the United States the development of a relationship with Peking embodies precisely the challenges of this decade: to deal with and resolve the vestiges of the postwar period that continue to influence our relationship, and to create a balanced international structure in which all nations will have a stake. We believe that such a structure should provide *full scope* for the influence to which China's achievements entitle it.[69]

President Nixon's words were further translated into deeds. He terminated all restrictions on travel to China and lifted the twenty-one-year-old embargo on trade with the People's Republic of China. These measures were followed by what was called a "ping-pong diplomacy." On April 6, 1971, Peking invited the U.S. table tennis team to visit mainland China. The team, upon its arrival at Peking, was greeted with a warm, friendly reception. It travelled extensively in China and was received on April 14 by Premier Chou En-lai, who told them: "With your acceptance of our invitation, you have opened a new page in the relations of the Chinese and American people." It was China's most positive response to American signals.

The Nixon announcement, sudden and dramatic, of July 15, 1971, was an astonishing public revelation of events and negotiations which had taken place behind the scenes. In a televised address to the nation, President Nixon disclosed that his national security advisor, Henry Kissinger, had met with Premier Chou En-lai in Peking July 9–11 and that the Chinese leader had invited the president "to visit China at an appropriate date before May 1972," adding that he had accepted the invitation.

What considerations had shaped the Nixon administration's approach to the People's Republic of China? Four major assumptions could be examined. First, the world of 1971 was no longer the bipolar world made up neatly of "free" and "Communist" blocs dominated by Washington and Moscow respectively. There ceased to be a monolithic Communist world any more than there existed a unified "free" world. Vietnam proved beyond doubt that the kind of foreign policy based on the rationale of anticommunism was contrary to vital national interests of the United States in both short and long terms. If the United States failed, as it did, in containing communism in Vietnam, how could it contain communism in China? The growing prestige and power of the People's Republic of China convinced the United States that peaceful co-existence was the only sane alternative to the perpetual hostility and that it was not China which lived in angry isolation but it was American anger which attempted to isolate China. The true reality was, in the words of President Nixon, "in this era we could not afford to be cut off from a quarter of the world's population."

Second, one of the classic Chinese strategies was *i-i-chih-i*, "control barbarians with barbarians." Throughout the history of China's dynastic struggles, *i-i-chih-i* remained an honored military and diplomatic maxim. In the ever-shifting tides of contemporary international relations, especially in the Sino-Soviet conflict, the United States saw an opportunity to play China's game of *i-i-chih-i*. Through adroit diplomacy, the Nixon-Kissinger team hoped to create a stable, tricentric balance of power by using Peking, Moscow's bitter rival, as a counterweight against the Soviet Union. Fearful of Sino-American collusion, the Soviets would, it was hoped, act with restraint and cooperate willingly with the United States in major outstanding issues.[69] Notwithstanding the claim that the United States' policy was not aimed against Moscow, America's various negotiations with the Soviets, for example, Berlin and SALT, made major progress subsequent to the July 15 announcement.

Third, for far too long, over twenty years, the United States shared Chiang Kai-shek's daydream of a reconquest of the mainland. The United States continued to believe in the Acheson thesis of 1949 that "however tragic may be the immediate future of China and however ruthlessly a major portion of this great people may be exploited by a party in the interest of a foreign imperialism, ultimately the profound civilization and the democratic individualism of China will reassert themselves and she will overthrow the foreign yoke." For over two decades the United States had hoped to witness this prophecy materialize under the Nationalist leadership. The Nixon administration, however, came to perceive that the prophecy had been realized under Communist leadership, and it simply accepted that reality. As a congressman, Nixon had accused President Truman of the "loss" of China; as president, Nixon wanted to "regain" China. He believed, "it is in America's interest, and world's interest, that the People's Republic of China play its appropriate role in shaping international arrangements that affect its concerns."

Fourth and finally, American businessmen were traditionally enchanted and obsessed by China's tremendous commercial potentials as sources of raw materials and as markets for manufactured products. There was growing pressure from the American business community to tap mainland China—its territories larger than the

United States and its population of over 800 million—for American commercial interests. It was argued that China trade would help alleviate America's chronic deficit in balance of payments. The United States was trading with the Soviet Union and other European Communist countries; then why not with Communist China? The United States should adopt "the separation of politics and economics" formula, as the Japanese and the British did, to carry on reciprocal trade for mutual benefit. That the commercial consideration had been a pivotal aspect of the Nixon approach to China became evident in the Nixon-Chou joint communiqué of February 28, 1972:

> Both sides view bilateral trade as another area from which mutual benefit can be derived and agreed that economic relations based on equality and mutual benefit are in the interest of the peoples of the two countries. They agreed to facilitate the progressive development of trade between their two countries.[70]

President Nixon's China policy won widespread approval from congressional members of both parties and from the American people as well. Democrats were nearly unanimous in praising presidential leadership for closer relations with the People's Republic of China. There was no "national uproar" that President Kennedy had feared a decade earlier. Only a few anti-Communist die-hards voiced their opposition to the Nixon initiative. But, who could dare pin the label of "soft on communism" on Richard M. Nixon, whose political career had been built on an anti-Communist platform and on the image of an arch "Cold Warrior." The new Nixon policy on China was, in all fairness, rational, prudent, wise, and in the best interests of the United States.

On October 25, 1971, the UN General Assembly passed a resolution by a vote of 76–35 (17 abstentions) to admit the People's Republic of China to the United Nations and to expel Nationalist China. The United States voted against the resolution because it objected to the expulsion of Nationalist China; it was not opposed to the seating of the People's Republic of China but rather welcomed it. Thus, the Chinese Communists accomplished the second "Long March" from Peking to Manhattan in twenty-two long, turbulent years.

President Nixon's China visit, February 21–28, 1972, proved to be a monumental success. The American people were thoroughly informed, by television and other mass media, of their president's activities in a strange, mysterious land of inscrutable people, all invariably looking alike, with such unfamiliar names as Mao Tse-tung, Chou En-lai, Deng Xiaoping, and Hua Guofeng. To many Americans it appeared as though their president stepped into new, remote frontiers to make peace with Communist chief Mao, just as in their country's earlier history a lone western frontier-town marshal single-handedly rode into Indian territories to make peace with the Indian chief.

At the conclusion of President Nixon's visit, at Shanghai, a joint communiqué was issued, stating that the United States and the People's Republic of China should not "seek hegemony in the Asia-Pacific region and each is opposed to efforts by any other country or group of countries to establish such hegemony." The Chinese side reaffirmed its position that Taiwan was "the critical question obstructing the normalization" of Sino-American relations and that "the liberation of Taiwan is China's internal affair in which no country has the right to interfere." The United States side declared that "there is but one China and that Taiwan is a part of China." The United States would ultimately withdraw "all U.S. forces and military installations from Taiwan" and would expect "a peaceful settlement of the Taiwan question by the Chinese themselves." Subsequently, the two countries opened in each other's capital "liaison offices" headed by officials of ambassadorial rank. President Nixon's resignation did not derail the Sino-American relations which he had put on the right track. His successor, President Gerald Ford, visited Peking on December 1–5, 1975, to confer with the Chinese leaders, and they reaffirmed their continued efforts toward rapprochement. President Ford, however, was hesitant to normalize relations with Peking because he feared possible "adverse" impact of such a step on his prospects for nomination and election in the 1976 presidential election. He had no desire to rock unnecessarily his ship of state which had nervously sailed through the collapse of Saigon and the deterioration of détente with Moscow.

When President Carter took office in January 1977, the issue of normalizing relations with the People's Republic of China was considered of less importance than the issue of concluding a new SALT agreement with the Soviet Union. Hence, the Carter administration's foreign policy priority was directed toward Moscow. In late March Secretary of State Cyrus Vance visited Moscow and proposed sweeping, major arms reductions far below the level which had been agreed upon at Vladivostok in 1974 between President Ford and General Secretary Brezhnev. The Soviets not only rejected the proposal outright without even offering a counter-proposal but also demonstrated visible ire toward the United States. Their displeasure was further compounded by Carter's outspoken human rights policy, aimed clearly at the Soviet Union as evidenced by his personal letter to prominent Soviet dissident Andrei Sakharov.

The deterioration of Soviet-American détente brought the China issue to the forefront in U.S. foreign policy, and in August 1977, Secretary of State Vance visited Peking to discuss the problem of normalization of Sino-American relations. Despite Vance's insistence that U.S.-China relations would be dealt with in a *bilateral* rather than in a *tricentric* context, the Carter administration was clearly adopting the strategy of *i-i-chih-i* in order to gain leverage over the Soviet Union.

Refusing to ease tensions with the Soviet Union, the Peking government, for its part, as an old hand in *i-i-chih-i,* sent friendly signals to Washington in the hope that President Carter would vigorously pursue the hard line toward Moscow. Against this background, Zbigniew Brzezinski, national security advisor to the president, visited Peking on May 20–23, 1978. Pointing to the importance of "parallel interest" between the United States and the People's Republic of China, Brzezinski stated to his hosts: "We approach our relations with three fundamental beliefs: that friendship between the United States and the People's Republic of China is vital and beneficial to world peace; that a secure and strong China is in America's interest; that a powerful, confident and globally engaged United States is in China's interest." He added that the United States appreciated "China's resolve to resist the efforts of any nation which seeks to establish global or regional hegemony"—the idea which had been incorporated in the 1972 Shanghai communiqué. In June Soviet president Brezhnev charged that the United States was playing "the China card against the USSR."

While Soviet-American relations continued to deteriorate to what Brezhnev termed "cold peace," the pace of friendly relations between Peking and Washington continued to accelerate. Peking received a parade of high-ranking U.S. governmental dignitaries: the president's science advisor, Frank Press, Secretary of Energy James Schlesinger, and Secretary of Agriculture Robert Bergland. Their trips were designed to establish the basis for growing commercial and industrial relations.

The process set in motion by the Carter administration in the summer of 1978 culminated in the presidential announcement on December 15, 1978, that the United States and the People's Republic of China would formally establish diplomatic relations on January 1, 1979, and that Vice-Premier Deng Xiaoping would visit Washington. In an effort not to leave the impression of overplaying *i-i-chih-i,* Secretary Vance reiterated that U.S. policy toward Peking and Moscow would be "balanced" and there would be "no tilts" one way or the other, and "this is an absolutely fundamental principle." President Carter further assured that the United States would "be cautious in not trying to have an unbalanced relationship between China and the Soviet Union."

Deng's visit to the United States from January 29 to February 5, 1979, was an unqualified, dramatic success. At the end of his stay in Washington, a U.S.-China joint communiqué was issued, reaffirming their opposition to any hegemonic policy by any country. The two countries then signed agreements on cooperation in science, technology, space, and cultural exchanges. Among other things, China agreed to purchase a high-energy particle accelerator for its atomic industry and a communications satellite system, including ground stations, both at a cost of several hundred million dollars. They also agreed that China would open consulates in San Francisco and Houston in return for American consulates in Canton and Shanghai.

To the Soviets the Sino-American normalization seemed to indicate that the United States and the People's Republic of China, along with Japan and Western European nations, were forming an informal global "capitalist encirclement" of the Soviet Union. They were especially incensed by Deng's remark in Washington that "the main hotbed of war" was Moscow, and they requested a "clarification" from Washington on what had been said and agreed upon. The United States simply denied that its recognition of Peking was aimed at the Soviet Union. Nevertheless, there was some apprehension that the normalization might jeopardize SALT II under negotiation. But the fear was not substantiated when, on June 18, 1979, in Vienna, Austria, Presidents Carter and Brezhnev signed the SALT II agreements. The Chinese response to the SALT II accord was as anticipated. On June 20, addressing the National People's Congress, Chairman Hua Guofeng stated that the agreement could in no way check the arms race or solve the fundamental question of safeguarding peace due largely to the increasingly adventuristic policies of "social imperialism"— China's euphemistic designation of the Soviet Union.

After thirty years of mutual isolation and recrimination, the United States and the People's Republic of China rediscovered each other. The history of Sino-American relations in the twentieth century, beginning with America's Open Door policy, was indeed filled with bittersweet experiences. There were many fundamental differences between the two countries in cultural backgrounds, politico-ideological orientations, and socio-economic systems. But they had never been at war with each other in formal hostilities; they had quarrels, including the Korean conflict. Now that the oldest (China) and the mightiest (United States) in the world were "reunited" in goodwill and friendship, the relationship was hoped to last into the twenty-first century. Deng Xiaoping might well have been right when he said: "I see no danger that the honeymoon will not continue."

The "honeymoon" diplomacy led to Vice-President Walter Mondale's visit to China in August 1979. In a speech at Peking University, Mr. Mondale stated that "any nation which seeks to weaken or isolate you in world affairs assumes a stance counter to American interests"—an obvious reference to Soviet involvement in Vietnam to isolate and encircle China. The Mondale mission paved the way for the signing of two agreements: (1) cultural exchange in 1980 and 1981 in the areas of arts, education, sports, books, and broadcasting, and (2) cooperation in technological fields such as hydroelectric power and water resource management, including joint research and exchange of specialists.

Peking carried its pro-American foreign policy to U.S. allies in Western Europe. This was the natural sequel to China's strategy of *i-i-chih-i.* In October and November 1979, Chairman Hua Guofeng embarked upon an unprecedented twenty-two-day trip through the Western European nations, primarily France, West Germany, Great Britain, and Italy. His message to his various hosts was that world peace would require "a united and strong Europe and a prosperous and strong China" and that resistance to "the hegemonists" would be the only way to maintain peace. China's heightened presence on the international scene created a subtle new constraint on the Soviets in their attitude toward Western Europe.

In July 1980, Chairman Hua travelled to Tokyo to attend the memorial service for the late Premier Ohira. His decision was made only after he had learned of President Carter's plan to visit Japan for the same purpose. The contents of the meeting between the two leaders were not immediately known, but the Sino-American summit was a logical response to the Soviet invasion of Afghanistan and underscored the growing Sino-American-Japanese de facto alliance. The Carter administration had announced that it would allow Peking to purchase C-130 military cargo planes, air defense radar, trucks, transport helicopters, and computer equipment. Furthermore, American companies were permitted to build factories in China to manufacture U.S.-designed helicopters and computer parts. In a trade agreement concluded earlier between the two countries the United States had granted China most-favored-nation treatment, which was denied to the Soviet Union.

The big question remains how far the United States would go to form a partnership with the People's Republic of China in the global strategy of *i-i-chih-i* to blunt Soviet adventurism.

CHAPTER TWELVE

Summary
and Conclusion

Frederick Jackson Turner wrote: "Up to our own day [1893] American history has been in a large degree the history of the colonization of the Great West. The existence of an area of free land, its continuous recession, and the advance of settlement westward, explain American development." He argued that the frontier had contributed to "a composite nationality for the American people," had made the growth of democracy possible, had strengthened the spirit of independence and individualism, and had fostered materialism and pragmatism. Although the Turner Thesis, as it is called, was in some instances challenged by other historians, it left enduring influence upon American thinking, in combination with the theory of "American destiny." The United States was, it was argued, destined to rank among the great powers of the world.

The combined forces of "frontier" and "destiny" in American ideas and actions propelled the United States across the Pacific into the rimland of Asia by the turn of this century. The United States had become a bona fide Far Eastern power by virtue of the acquisition of the Philippines after the Spanish-American War of 1898. Not only did the United States gain great-power status but, in doing so, joined the imperialist club. In the great debate over the question of whether or not the United States should acquire the Philippines, the imperialists prevailed. The first concrete exercise

353

of this new status was the pronouncement of the Open Door policy, which was designed to keep open the door for trade and commerce and American investment in China. The major obstacles to America's free, open, frontier trade in China were not only the Chinese themselves, who wanted to be left alone, but also the preferential system, the sphere of influence, that had been established in China by the early imperialist powers—Great Britain, France, Germany, Russia, and Japan. American leaders acted at this time upon an industrial conception of the economy and its needs—business opportunities for trade and commerce.

Economic expansionism could not be separated from political and military foundations of national power. In the age of social Darwinism, national greatness depended on political will and military forces—the instrument of coercion—capable of successfully carrying out the struggle for power and of imposing national will upon others. President Theodore Roosevelt, a disciple of Admiral Mahan, declared:

> The twentieth century looms before us big with the fate of many nations. . . . It is only through strife, through hard and dangerous endeavor, that we shall ultimately win the goal of true national greatness.

As the new century dawned, United States involvement in Asia increased. For the first time American fighting men were sent to China to join international expeditionary forces against the Boxer rebels. In the ensuing negotiations for the Boxer settlement, the United States played a key role. A few years later President Theodore Roosevelt effectively mediated the Russo-Japanese War to a successful finish with the Portsmouth peace treaty, although not without a degree of dissatisfaction expressed by the Japanese public. President Roosevelt recognized the growing power of Japan and accepted its suzerainty over Korea. The Taft-Katsura Agreement (1905) and the Root-Takahira Agreement (1908) signified the acceptance by the United States of the new balance of power in Asia. Fearing, however, that Japan would become a formidable foe in the Pacific and in East Asia, Roosevelt felt the need for a show of force. He sent the American fleet on a round-the-world tour, making sure that it would visit Tokyo. It was a subtle exercise of coercion.

The builders of American greatness and protectors of America's Asian frontier were men like William McKinley, John Hay, Theodore Roosevelt, Elihu Root, Henry Stimson, and Philander Knox. Secretary of State Knox in the Taft administration substituted dollars for bullets and proposed to effectuate "the complete commercial neutrality of Manchuria." Although the scheme failed to materialize, it indicated the direction, intent, and means of America's Asian policy.

Wilson's presidency did little to change the basic direction of the United States' course of action in Asia. He withdrew his country from the international consortium in China on the grounds that it would infringe upon the sovereignty of China. It should be noted, however, that conducting business in an unstable country like China involved far greater risks than a normal commercial transaction in the United States. His inclination toward a moral-idealistic approach to international problems proved inconsequential. When World War I broke out, Japan captured the German holdings in China and continued to exploit Chinese political and social instability, imposing the Twenty-One Demands upon China. The United States, thereupon, reminded Japan of the Open Door and urged it to respect China's territorial and administrative integrity. But in the end President Wilson was able neither to blunt Japanese imperialism nor protect China's integrity. At Versailles, in an effort to save the peace conference, President Wilson sacrificed China's territorial integrity by allowing Japan to assume former German possessions in Shantung. Ultimately, due to the senatorial rejection, President Wilson lost the entire Versailles system, especially the League of Nations, which he had salvaged at the expense of his moral principles. Versailles was the lowest point in American influence in Asia. Wilson's difficulties with Japan did not end at Versailles but continued even into Siberia in what was known as the "Siberian Intervention." For the second time American troops were sent to the Asian continent for a limited exercise of military power. This action was a dismal failure in terms of its professed objectives and its results.

With the coming of another Republican administration under

Harding, the United States attempted to reassert its power. Cognizant of and uneasy with the growing power of Japan with its vastly expanded empire from Manchuria to the Marianas and from Sakhalin to the Solomons, Secretary of State Charles Hughes came to believe in the need for "containment" of Japan's naval power in the Pacific. In addition, he was troubled by the Anglo-Japanese Alliance which could theoretically be invoked against the United States in the event of American-Japanese hostilities. The Washington Naval Conference of 1921–1922 resulted from these considerations. The conference produced a number of resolutions and treaties: the Four-Power Treaty terminating the Anglo-Japanese Alliance, the Five-Power Treaty establishing capital ship ratios, and the Nine-Power Treaty affirming the Open Door policy. The Washington Conference was hailed as a diplomatic success for all concerned, having demonstrated the spirit of cooperation, compromise, cordiality, and goodwill under the most difficult circumstances. The "spirit of Washington" between the United States and Japan was shattered in 1924 when the U.S. Congress passed the Japanese exclusion act. The relations between the two countries deteriorated.

The Japanese were taking the road to militarism which they considered not only in their proud tradition but also as the indispensable instrument of imperial policy in *weltpolitik*. They were determined to challenge the notion of "white man's supremacy" and to destroy the myth of "white man's invincibility." Japan, therefore, embarked upon the construction of territorial and economic foundations of its national power. In 1931 the Japanese invaded and systematically occupied Manchuria—the land which Secretary Knox had once coveted as an American frontier. The Japanese scornfully ignored the Kellogg-Briand Pact, willfully violated the Nine-Power Treaty, and openly challenged the League of Nations, in the making of which American leadership had been so pivotal and instrumental. In response to the Japanese action in Manchuria, Secretary of State Henry Stimson, who had held the post of secretary of war when Knox was secretary of state in the Taft cabinet, declared that the United States would not recognize any change in status quo in Asia brought about by illegal means. This policy pronouncement became known quite appropriately as the Stimson Doctrine. It should be emphasized that the Stimson Doctrine was a restatement of the Open Door policy, reaffirmation of both the Bryan and the Lansing notes, and the reassertion of the Nine-Power Treaty. It should also be noted that there was a remarkable continuity in America's Asian policy from Hay through Root, Knox, Bryan, Lansing, Hughes, to Stimson. The baton of U.S.-Asian policy was to be relayed further—from Stimson, through Hull, Marshall, Acheson, Dulles, Rusk, Kissinger, to Vance; none of them deviated from the basic frontier policy in Asia.

Lacking in military means to coerce Japan to desist its aggression, Secretary Stimson depended heavily on moral and legal principles in admonishing Japan.

The decade of the 1930s was characterized by the rise of totalitarianism and the retreat of democracies. In Europe, Hitler's Nazism, Mussolini's fascism, and Stalin's communism were on a steady ascent; in Asia, Japanese militarism was in full swing. The Anglo-French appeasement of Hitler at Munich symbolized the pusillanimity of Western democracies, and Japan's full-scale invasion of China demonstrated the uselessness of paper promises (treaties). The United States, meanwhile, was smarting from the lingering pains of the Great Depression, while the American public was slumbering in the shadow of isolationism. Yet, in the latter part of the 1930s the United States was steadily drawn into the Sino-Japanese conflict. Finally, by design or destiny, Pearl Harbor catapulted the United States into total involvement in Asia. The United States now had power, capability, and will to defend its Asian frontier with overwhelming military force. For the third time American fighting men were sent to Asia. After four years of struggle with "blood, toil, sweat, and tears," the United States emerged unscathed as the greatest military and industrial power that mankind has ever known. The American vision of a "brave new world" was in its grasp, the world "free" from trade restrictions and "free" for American investment. The United States became the world's largest manufacturer, the world's banker; the dollar became the international currency.

But the forces of communism were also on the rise. The Grand Alliance between the Western democracies and the Soviet Union against Hitler's Third Reich disintegrated as soon as the guns of

World War II were silenced, and the Eastern European nations rolled into the Soviet orbit. In Asia the United States occupied Japan and began the task of remaking the vanquished in its own image. The American troops also occupied the southern half of Korea, and the thirty-eighth parallel became America's farthest frontier line. In China, where lay America's greatest real and potential commercial interests, a titanic civil war between the Communists and the Nationalists raged for four years. United States mediation efforts in that struggle resulted in failure, clearly evidencing the fact that there were limits to United States capability and influence. But anti-Communist crusaders, in government and in public, refused to accept this premise and engaged in political recrimination in placing blame for the "loss of China." To them what had happened in China could happen anywhere in the "free" world. Therefore, they were determined to contain, resist, and repress communism wherever it could be found. Their fear and assessment of the Communist threat seemed substantiated by the North Korean attack on South Korea. The United States immediately took up arms and defended its frontier posts. For the fourth time American troops were sent to Asia and here, in Korea, United States military might was directly challenged by the armed forces of North Korea and Communist China. However, since the heart of communism was not in Pyungyang or in Peking but in Moscow, the United States decided that the war in Korea was a wrong war with wrong enemies and agreed to an armistice to terminate the hostilities.

The Korean War was a bitter, unpleasant experience for the United States, and American bellicosity and hatred toward the People's Republic of China became intensified. The United States adopted the policy of "containment" and "isolation" of the People's Republic and attempted to strengthen South Vietnam as a bastion against Peking. When France was defeated in Vietnam by the Vietminh forces and the subsequent Geneva agreements were signed, the United States refused to accept the settlement. Instead, it began to bear the burden of defeating communism in China's southern flank. For the fifth time in this century United States fighting troops were sent to Asia and for twelve long years the United States waged what turned out to be a tragic war. The Vietnam tragedy resulted primarily from America's ignorance of the Vietnamese people, their history, their culture, their society, and their nationalism.

United States policy in Vietnam was postulated on the false premise that Vietnamese Communists were Chinese vassals and that Peking exercised suzerainty over Hanoi. Ironically, to a degree, that premise brought Nixon to Peking in his search for "enduring peace" in Indochina. The Nixon trip to the People's Republic of China was the harbinger of a new era of Sino-American rapprochement. After thirty years of *closed door policy,* the two nations finally normalized their relations, making it possible to resume commercial and cultural activities in each other's domain.

In conclusion, American frontier activities in this century in Asia have shown a distinctive pendulum-like pattern: repetitive cycles of active, positive, aggressive involvement (A period) followed by passive, negative, regressive adjustment (B period). Specifically, the period beginning with the acquisition of the Philippines through the Open Door policy and the Portsmouth mediation (A) was followed by the period of Versailles and Siberian disillusionment (B). It was then followed by the occasion of the Washington Naval Conference (A), moving gradually into the era of the Stimson Doctrine (B). World War II forced the United States into maximum involvements in Asia (A), but the postwar American failure in the mediation of the Chinese civil war compelled the United States to keep a low posture (B). The United States, however, militarily resisted the Communist expansion in the Korean War (A) only to retreat from it by accepting the Armistice at Panmunjom (B). Then, the United States' all-out commitment, no matter how erroneous it might have been, to defend South Vietnam from a Communist takeover (A) led the nation through the path of national anguish to the Paris peace talks (B).

Today, the United States, recovering from the Vietnam trauma, has set fresh objectives in rapprochement with the People's Republic of China (A) for increased contact and commerce. Commerce has been a long-established objective of American activities in Asia. To protect and promote it, the United States often resorted to the use of military power (coercion) especially during the (A) period, while characteristically pursuing a legal-moralistic approach to Asian problems and difficulties during the (B) period. There is no doubt that American frontier activities in Asia will continue for many decades to come, perhaps following the same cyclical pattern.

Notes

Chapter 1

1. Charles S. Olcott, *The Life of William McKinley* (Boston and New York: Houghton Mifflin, 1916), vol. 2, pp. 110–11.
2. Allan Nevins, *Henry White: Thirty Years of American Diplomacy* (New York and London: Harper & Row, 1930), p. 136.
3. A. Whitney Griswold, *The Far Eastern Policy of the United States*, 4th ed. (New Haven and London: Yale University Press, 1964), pp. 15–16.
4. Foster Rhea Dulles, *America in the Pacific* (Boston: Houghton Mifflin, 1932), pp. 227–28.
5. Chauncey M. Depew, ed., *The Library of Oratory* (New York: Globe Publishing Co., 1902), vol. 14, p. 439.
6. Julius W. Pratt, "The Origin of 'Manifest Destiny,'" *American Historical Review*, vol. 32 (July 1927), pp. 795–96.
7. W. G. Sumner, *War and Other Essays* (New Haven: Yale University Press, 1919), pp. 303–5.
8. G. D. E. Hall, *A History of Southeast Asia* (New York: St. Martin's Press, 1968), p. 767.
9. Funston had previously boasted that he would "rawhide these bullet-headed Asians until they yell for mercy" so they would not "get in the way of the bandwagon of Anglo-Saxon progress and decency."
10. William F. Mayers, ed.., *Treaties Between the Empire of China and Foreign Powers* (Shanghai: North-China Herald, 1902), pp. 280–81.

361

11. Three years earlier, Japan had been warned by Russo-Franco-German "advice" (the Triple Intervention) not to take the Liaotung Peninsula.
12. Chinese Maritime Customs, *Treaties, Conventions, etc., Between China and Foreign States,* 2nd ed., 2 vols. (Shanghai, 1917), vol. 1, p. 541.
13. Department of State, *Papers Relating to the Foreign Relations of the United States, 1898* (Washington: Government Printing Office, 1901), p. xxii. Italics added. Cited hereafter throughout this book as *Foreign Relations of the United States.*
14. It should be recalled that the Chinese customs service was supervised by the British, a privilege ultimately sanctioned by a treaty in 1898 for so long as Britain's share of China's foreign trade should exceed that of any other nation.
15. W. M. Malloy, ed., *Treaties, Conventions, International Acts, Protocols and Agreements Between the United States of America and Other Powers, 1776–1909,* 2 vols. (Washington: Government Printing Office, 1910), pp. 246–47.
16. Literally the "Righteous Harmony Band" with their clenched fists as the symbol of their determination and unity.
17. John W. Foster, *American Diplomacy in the Orient* (New York: Houghton Mifflin, 1903), p. 416.
18. *Foreign Relations of the United States, 1900–1901,* p. 299. Italics added.
19. William R. Thayer, *The Life and Letters of John Hay,* 2 vols. (New York: Houghton Mifflin, 1915), vol. 2, pp. 247–48.
20. Griswold, Far Eastern Policy, p. 83.
21. *Foreign Relations of the United States, 1915,* p. 113.
22. Ibid., p. 115.

Chapter 2

1. Alfred L. P. Dennis, *Adventures in American Diplomacy, 1896–1906* (New York: E. P. Dutton & Co., 1928), p. 242.
2. Andrew M. Pooley, *The Secret Memoirs of Count Tadasu Hayashi* (New York: G. P. Putnam's Sons, 1915), pp. 87–88.
3. *Foreign Relations of the United States, 1902–1903,* pp. 514–15.
4. Asakawas Kanichi, *The Russo-Japanese Conflict: Its Causes and Issues* (Boston and New York: Houghton Mifflin, 1904), pp. 206–7.
5. *Foreign Relations of the United States, 1903,* p. 930.
6. Ibid., p. 931.
7. Ibid., pp. 610–20.
8. The Sino-Japanese War ended in a Japanese victory and the signing of the Shimonoseki Treaty on April 17, 1895. One of the treaty provisions stipulated that: "China cedes to Japan in per-

petuity ... the southern portion of the Provinces of Feng-tien [the Liaotung Peninsula]." Less than a week later, on August 23, Russia, France, and Germany sent to the Japanese government identic notes stating: "[Each government] ... in examining the conditions of peace which Japan has imposed on China, finds that the possession of the Peninsula of Liaotung, claimed by Japan, would be a menace to the Capital of China, would at the same time render illusory the independence of Korea and would henceforth be a perpetual obstacle to the peace of the Far East." Thus, the triple powers advised Japan to renounce the possession of the peninsula. Japan was in no position to oppose the implicit threat of a joint military action by three of the great powers of Europe. On May 5, 1895, the Japanese government complied with their "advice" and renounced the peninsula in the midst of public indignation toward the three-power intervention.

9. *Foreign Relations of the United States, 1904,* p. 301.
10. Dennis, *Adventures in American Diplomacy,* p. 390.
11. President Roosevelt's intimacy with both Kaiser Wilhelm II and Baron Speck von Sternburg, the German ambassador to Washington and a long-time personal friend whom the president called "Specky," was a significant factor in the success of this diplomatic undertaking. In addition, the kaiser and Czar Nicholas II of Russia were cousins: the kaiser being the grandson of Queen Victoria of England and the czar being the son of a sister of Queen Victoria's daughter-in-law (King Edward VII's wife). Through the famous "Willie-Nickie" correspondence, on June 3, 1905, the kaiser urged his cousin to accept President Roosevelt's mediation and the following day he notified the president of his action. On June 6, the czar agreed to a peace conference.
12. Tyler Dennett, *Roosevelt and the Russo-Japanese War* (New York: Doubleday, 1925), pp. 178–80.
13. J. V. A. MacMurray, *Treaties and Agreements with and Concerning China,* 2 vols. (New York: Oxford University Press, 1921), vol. 1, pp. 522–28.
14. Payson J. Treat, *Diplomatic Relations Between the United States and Japan, 1895–1905* (Stanford: Stanford University Press, 1938), p. 254.
15. *Foreign Relations of the United States, 1905,* p. 613.
16. Thomas A. Bailey, *Theodore Roosevelt and the Japanese-American Crisis* (Stanford: Stanford University Press, 1934), p. 14.
17. Elting E. Morison, ed., *The Letters of Theodore Roosevelt,* 8 vols. (Cambridge, Mass.: Harvard University Press, 1951–1954), vol. 4, pp. 1205–6.
18. At this time there were only ninety-three Japanese pupils in all of San Francisco's public schools. Among them: 25 were American citizens, 28 girls, 33 over 15 years old, and two 20 years old.

19. Bailey, *Theodore Roosevelt*, p. 64.
20. Ibid., p. 50.
21. Griswold, *Far Eastern Policy*, p. 140, citing *Memorandum of Assistant Secretary of State William Phillips*, May 10, 1909.
22. Ibid., p. 140.
23. Annual Message to Congress, December 3, 1912, in *Foreign Relations of the United States, 1912*, x.
24. Ibid., *1910*, pp. 234–35.
25. Ibid., pp. 235–36.
26. Ibid., *1909*, p. 178.
27. Ibid., p. 179.
28. Frederick V. Field, *American Participation in the China Consortium* (Chicago: University of Chicago Press, 1931), p. 93.

Chapter 3

1. The bill passed the state Senate by a vote of 25 to 2 and the Assembly by 73 to 3.
2. Arthur S. Link, *Wilson: The New Freedom* (Princeton: Princeton University Press, 1956), p. 296. There were about 50,000 Japanese in California in 1913, out of a total population of 2.5 million. Of California's 27 million acres of agricultural land, 12,726 acres were owned by Japanese. See Thomas A. Bailey, "California, Japan, and the Alien Land Legislation of 1913," *Pacific Historical Review* (March 1932), p. 38.
3. Yamamoto Ichihashi, *Japanese in the United States* (Stanford: Stanford University Press, 1932), p. 275.
4. *Foreign Relations of the United States, 1914*, p. 426.
5. Ibid., *Supplement*, p. 162.
6. Ibid., pp. 164–70.
7. Ibid., pp. 172–74.
8. Ibid., 189–90.
9. The territorial limits within which belligerent operations had been allowed. Japan seized and retained the Tsingtao-Tsinanfu Railroad and reached 240 miles inland from the German leasehold.
10. For the complete text of the Demands, see *Foreign Relations of the United States, 1915*, pp. 99–103.
11. Hanyehping Company was one of the larger, better-known Japanese-dominated (since 1902) mining and manufacturing ironwork in Central China. In an exchange of notes with Japan, the Chinese Minister of Foreign Affairs wrote: "I have the honor to state that if in the future the Hanyehping Company and the Japanese capitalists agree upon cooperation, the Chinese Government, in view of the intimate relations subsisting between the Japanese capitalists and the said Company, will forthwith give its permission. The Chinese Government further agree not to confiscate the said Company, nor, without the consent of the Japanese

capitalists, to convert it into a state enterprise, nor cause it to borrow and use foreign capital other than Japanese."

12. On March 13, 1915, in a diplomatic note to the Japanese ambassador, Secretary of State Bryan had stated that "the United States has ground on which to base objections to the Japanese 'demands' relative to Shantung, South Manchuria, and East Mongolia, nevertheless the United States frankly recognizes that territorial contiguity creates special relations between Japan and these districts." *Foreign Relations of the United States, 1915,* pp. 105–11.

13. Robert Lansing, *War Memoirs* (Indianapolis: Bobbs-Merrill, 1935), p. 284.

14. *Foreign Relations of the United States, 1914–1920,* vol. 2, p. 450.

15. Ibid., *1917,* pp. 264–65.

16. MacMurray, *Treaties and Agreements,* vol. 2, No. 1917/12, pp. 1396–97.

17. *Foreign Relations of the United States, 1917,* pp. 48–49.

18. Ibid., pp. 71–72.

19. Ibid., *1918, Russia,* p. 297.

20. General Graves recalled that the Japanese Commanding General with whom he had had a number of wrangles "sent a band to the dock to furnish music . . . and as the boat backed away from the dock the Japanese band began playing the good old American tune, Hard Times Come Again No More." Some looked upon this tune as amusing, others as indicative of past official relations. William S. Graves, *America's Siberian Adventure* (New York: J. Cape and H. Smith, 1931), p. 328.

21. *Foreign Relations of the United States, 1918, Russia,* vol. 2, pp. 289–90.

22. David H. Miller, *The Drafting of the Covenant,* 2 vols. (New York: G. P. Putnam's Sons, 1928), vol. 1, p. 183.

23. MacMurray, *Treaties and Agreements,* vol. 2, No. 1917/7, pp. 1361–62.

24. *Foreign Relations of the United States, 1919,* vol. 1, p. 719.

25. China, however, became a member of the League of Nations by signing the Treaty of St. Germain with Austria, September 10, 1919.

26. Blanche E. C. Dugdale, *Arthur James Balfour* (New York: G. P. Putnam's Sons, 1937), p. 245.

27. David Hunter Miller, *My Diary at the Conference of Paris* (New York: Appeal Printing Co., 1924), vol. 16, p. 458.

28. Ray S. Baker, *Woodrow Wilson and World Settlement* (Garden City: Doubleday, 1922), vol. 2, p. 266.

29. Griswold, *Far Eastern Policy,* p. 258, citing Lansing date book, April 30, 1919.

30. MacMurray, *Treaties and Agreements,* vol. 2, No. 1919/1, pp. 1500–1504.

31. *Foreign Relations of the United States, 1919,* vol. 1, p. 705.

32. Ibid., pp. 694–99.
33. Ibid., p. 703.
34. Ibid., pp. 713–14.
35. Ibid., p. 718.
36. Versailles Treaty, Part IV, Section VIII, Article 156. Germany renounces, in favor of Japan, all her rights, title and privileges—particularly those concerning the territory of Kiaochow, railways, mines and submarine cables—which she acquired in virtue of the Treaty concluded by her with China on March 6, 1898, and of all other arrangements relative to the Province of Shantung.

All German rights in the Tsingtao-Tsinanfu Railway, including its branch lines, together with its subsidiary property of all kinds, stations, shops, fixed and rolling stock, mines, plant and material for the exploitation of the mines, are and remain acquired by Japan, together with all rights and privileges attaching thereto. The German State submarine cables from Tsingtao to Shanghai and from Tsingtao to Chefoo, with all the rights, privileges and properties attaching thereto, are similarly acquired by Japan, free and clear of all charges and encumbrances.

Article 157: The movable and immovable property owned by the German State in the territory of Kiaochow, as well as all the rights which Germany might claim in consequence of the works or improvements made or of the expenses incurred by her, directly or indirectly, in connection with this territory, are and remain acquired by Japan, free and clear of all charges and encumbrances.

Article 158: Germany shall hand over to Japan within three months from the coming into force of the present Treaty the archives, registers, plans, title-deed and documents of every kind, wherever they may be, relating to the administration, whether civil, military, financial, judicial or other, of the territory of Kiaochow. Within the same period Germany shall give particulars to Japan of all treaties, arrangements or agreements relating to the rights, title or privileges referred to in the two preceding Articles.

Chapter 4

1. A proponent of isolationism would say, "Let us stay away from their affairs," while an advocate of the Monroe Doctrine would say, "Let them stay away from our affairs."
2. Griswold, *Far Eastern Policy*, p. 273.
3. *Inaugural Addresses of the Presidents of the United States from George Washington 1789 to Richard M. Nixon 1969* (Washington, D.C.: Government Printing Office, 1969), pp. 208–9.
4. *Foreign Relations of the United States, 1920*, vol. 2, pp. 680–81.

5. Participants in the disarmament conference were limited to the United States, Great Britain, Japan, France and Italy. In addition to these powers, China, Belgium, the Netherlands, and Portugal were invited to confer on the Pacific and the Far East. The last three felt that they were entitled to participate in such a conference because of their interests and possessions in the Far East, i.e. international consortium, Indonesia, Macao and Timor respectively.

6. It was originally intended to be tripartite—the United States, Great Britain, and Japan—invited to join by Secretary Hughes for three reasons: (1) not to leave the United States in a minority, (2) to soothe France's somewhat ruffled pride, and (3) to corral France within the Pacific treaty system. Italy's request for inclusion was rejected on the ground that it had no territorial possessions in the Far East or in the Pacific.

7. The general terms used in this treaty such as "insular possessions" and "insular dominions" bred uncertainty and ambiguity. Immediately after the signing of the treaty a number of questions arose; e.g. "Were the Japanese home islands and the mandate territories covered by the treaty?" It was agreed to exclude Japanese homelands; and an amendment to the Four-Power Treaty, signed on February 6, specified that the insular possessions of Japan were Formosa, Pescadores, the mandate territories, and the southern half of Sakhalin. *Foreign Relations of the United States, 1922,* vol. 1, pp. 46–47.

8. Ibid., pp. 271–72.

9. Ibid., pp. 272–74.

10. Ibid., pp. 276–81.

11. This was precisely what happened in 1937 when Japan launched the undeclared war on China. The treaty powers met in Brussels and "discussed" the situation. That was as far as they went; no countermeasure was taken.

12. MacMurray, *Treaties and Agreements,* vol. 2, pp. 853–62.

13. Thomas A. Bailey, *The American Spirit* (Boston: D. C. Heath, 1963), pp. 747–48, citing *Selections from the Writings and Speeches of William Randolph Hearst* (1948), pp. 193–94.

14. Ibid., pp. 748–49, citing Tokyo *Kokumin,* quoted in *Literary Digest,* vol. 72, no. 18 (January 28, 1922).

15. Specifically, the cases involved were *Ozawa* vs. *United States* (1913), *Terrace* vs. *Thompson* (1913), and *O'Brien* vs. *Webb* (1913).

16. U.S. Congress, House Committee on Immigration and Naturalization, *Restriction of Immigration, House Report No. 350,* 68th Congress, 1st session (Washington, D.C.: Government Printing Office, 1924), p. 27.

17. *United States Public Documents, July 1923–June 1924* (Wash-

ington, D.C.: Government Printing Office, 1924), vol. 24, pp. 358–62.

18. Raymond L. Buell, "Japanese Immigration," *World Peace Foundation Pamphlets* (Boston: World Peace Foundation, 1924), vol. 7, p. 310.

19. Ibid., p. 375.

20. Henry L. Stimson, *The Far Eastern Crisis: Recollections and Observations* (New York: Harper and Row, 1935), p. 3.

21. Jane Degras, ed., *Soviet Documents on Foreign Policy* (London: Oxford University Press, 1951), vol. 1, pp. 159–60.

22. Ibid., pp. 370–71.

23. The United States, Japan, and France protested at this agreement because they had advanced money and materials to the Chinese Eastern Railway (CER) during World War I.

24. One of his personal aides was a young Vietnamese revolutionary by the name of Le Thuy, alias Nguyen Ai Qoc, better known in later years as Ho Chi Minh.

25. The head of the Political Education Department, in charge of political indoctrination of the cadets, was Chou En-lai.

26. Following the Portsmouth Peace Treaty of 1905, the Russian leasehold in the Liaotung Peninsula, the South Manchurian Railway, and other economic rights were transferred to Japan. Tokyo appointed the acting army general as a governor-general to be in charge of Japan's interests in Manchuria. In 1919 a civilian administrator was appointed the governor-general, while a separate Kwantung Army Command assumed the duty of guarding the leased territory and the railway zone. In due time the Kwantung Army became so powerful as to enjoy a semiautonomous status and to spearhead Japanese imperialism on the Asian continent. See Satako N. Ogata, *Defiance in Manchuria: The Making of Japanese Foreign Policy, 1931–1932* (Berkeley: University of California Press, 1964).

27. The other being French foreign minister Aristide Briand, hence it was also known as the Kellogg-Briand Pact.

28. John W. Wheeler-Bennett, ed., *Documents on International Affairs, 1929* (London: Oxford University Press, 1930), pp. 278–80.

29. Ishii Kikujiro, *Diplomatic Commentaries,* trans. by W. R. Langdon (Baltimore: Johns Hopkins University Press, 1936), pp. 134–35.

30. League of Nations, *Report of the Commission of Enquiry,* League Publications Series VII, Political 1932, vol. 7, pp. 40–41.

31. The treaty was signed April 22, 1930, by the United States, Great Britain, and Japan. It established a 5:3 ratio (United States and Great Britain 5 each and Japan 3) in heavy cruisers, with slightly higher ratios in light cruisers and destroyers and parity in submarines. The treaty was to remain in force until the end of 1936. The Japanese Imperial Navy strongly opposed its ratification.

32. *Report of the Commission of Enquiry,* p. 67.
33. *Foreign Relations of the United States, Japan, 1931–1941,* vol. 1, p. 3.
34. See W. W. Willoughby, *The Sino-Japanese Controversy and the League of Nations* (Baltimore: Johns Hopkins University, 1935), Chapter 3.
35. Stimson, *Far Eastern Crisis,* p. 56.
36. The commission subsequently formed was chaired by the Earl of Lytton (Britain). Other members were: Henri Claude (France), Count Aldrovandi (Italy), Heinrich Schnee (Germany), and Frank Ross McCoy (United States). McCoy served on the commission, with Secretary Stimson's approval, as an official representative of the League and not of the United States.

Chapter 5

1. Stimson, *Far Eastern Crisis,* pp. 88–90. Italics added.
2. U.S., Department of State, *United States Relations with China, with Special Reference to the Period 1944–1949* (Washington, D.C.: Government Printing Office, 1949), pp. 446–47. Cited hereafter as *China White Paper.*
3. Italics were added to show the identical words used in both the Bryan and the Stimson notes. Cf. pp. 192–93.
4. Briefly, it called for (1) an immediate ceasefire, (2) no further reparations for hostilities, (3) mutual troop withdrawals, (4) an establishment of neutral zones, and (5) an adherence to the provisions of the Pact of Paris.
5. *Foreign Relations of the United States, Japan, 1931–1941,* vol. 1, pp. 103–4.
6. Ibid., pp. 104–5.
7. Joseph C. Grew, *The Turbulent Era* (New York: Houghton Mifflin, 1952), vol. 2, pp. 928–30.
8. Akira Iriye, *Across the Pacific: An Inner History of American-East Asian Relations* (New York: Harcourt, Brace and World, 1967), pp. 173–74.
9. The committee had been created for the purpose of coordinating actions and attitudes among the members of the League and with the nonmember states.
10. Dorothy Borg, *The United States and the Far Eastern Crisis of 1933–1938* (Cambridge, Mass.: Harvard University Press, 1964), p. 522.
11. J. Stalin, *The Result of the First Five Year Plan* (New York: Workers Library, 1933), pp. 24–25.
12. Gregory Z. Bessedovsky, *Revelations of a Soviet Diplomat* (London: Williams and Nogate, Ltd., 1931), p. 176.
13. Stimson, *Far Eastern Crisis,* p. 138.

14. *Foreign Relations of the United States, Japan, 1931–1941*, vol. 1, pp. 224–25.
15. Akira Iriye, *Across the Pacific*, p. 189.
16. W. H. Shepardson and W. O. Scroggs, *The United States in World Affairs, 1934–1935* (New York and London, Harper and Brothers, 1936), pp. 164–70.
17. Borg, *United States and Far Eastern Crisis*, p. 522.
18. Assassinated were former premier Admiral Saito, finance minister Takahashi, and inspector general of military education, General Watanabe. Grand Chamberlain Admiral Suzuki was critically wounded. Prime Minister Okada, former Lord Keeper of the Privy Seal Count Makino, and Genro Saionji managed to escape the assassin's attack.
19. Yukuna Kiyosachi, comp., *Seito Seiji Hyakunenshi* (A Centennial History of Party Politics) (Tokyo: Political Research Association, 1964), p. 121.
20. See James P. Harrison, *The Long March to Power: History of the Chinese Communist Party, 1921–1972* (New York: Praeger, 1972), chapter 11, pp. 238–59.
21. A special military court sentenced him to ten years' imprisonment, but it was commuted by Chiang and instead he was put under house arrest.
22. Japanese troops were stationed in Hopei Province under the Boxer protocol of 1900 for the purpose of guarding the Peking-Tientsin railway. The maneuvers were held beyond the confines of the authorized localities.
23. T. A. Bisson, *Japan in China* (New York: Macmillan, 1938), p. 39.
24. They were Hopei, Chahar, Suiyuan, Shansi, and Shantung.
25. Bolivia, Denmark, Mexico, Norway, and Sweden had joined the original members of the Nine-Power Treaty.
26. See *The Conference of Brussels, November 3–24, 1937, Convened in Virtue of Article 7 of the Nine-Power Treaty of Washington of 1922*, Department of State Conference Series 37 (Washington, D.C.: Government Printing Office, 1938).
27. *Foreign Relations of the United States, Japan, 1931–1941*, vol. 1, pp. 313–14.
28. The Soviet Union and Germany signed a nonaggression pact on August 23, 1939.
29. *Foreign Relations of the United States, Japan, 1931–1941*, vol. 1, p. 478.
30. Ibid., p. 800.
31. U.S., Department of State, *Peace and War: United States Foreign Policy, 1931–1941* (Washington, D.C.: Government Printing Office, 1943), p. 447.
32. Grew, *Turbulent Era*, pp. 1219–20.

"But they will, they must, listen to you," said Joseph Smith eagerly.

"They *won't*, but I must *make* them," replied Cosmo Versál. "Anyhow, I must make a few of the best of them hear me. The fate of a whole race is at stake. If we can save a handful of the best blood and brain of mankind, the world will have a new chance, and perhaps a better and higher race will be the result. Since I can't save them all, I'll pick and choose. I'll have the flower of humanity in my ark. I'll at least snatch that much from the jaws of destruction."

The little man was growing very earnest and his eyes were aglow with the fire of enthusiastic purpose. As he dropped his head on one side, it looked too heavy for the stemlike neck, but it conveyed an impression of immense intellectual power. Its imposing contour lent force to his words.

"The flower of humanity," he continued after a slight pause. "Who composes it? I must decide that question. Is it the billionaires? Is it the kings and rulers? Is it the men of science? Is it the society leaders? Bah! I'll have to think on that. I can't take them all, but I'll give them all a chance to save themselves—though I know they won't act on the advice."

Here he paused.

"Won't the existing ships do—especially if more

are built?" Joseph Smith suddenly asked, interrupting Cosmo's train of thought.

"Not at all," was the reply. "They're not suited to the kind of navigation that will be demanded. They're not buoyant enough, nor manageable enough, and they haven't enough carrying capacity for power and provisions. They'll be swamped at the wharves, or if they should get away they'd be sent to the bottom inside a few hours. Nothing but specially constructed arks will serve. And *there's* more trouble for me—I must devise a new form of vessel. Heavens, how short the time is! Why couldn't I have found this out ten years ago? It's only to-day that I have myself learned the full truth, though I have worked on it so long."

"How many will you be able to carry in your ark?" asked Smith.

"I can't tell yet. That's another question to be carefully considered. I shall build the vessel of this new metal, levium, half as heavy as aluminum and twice as strong as steel. I ought to find room without the slightest difficulty for a round thousand in it."

"Surely many more than that!" exclaimed Joseph Smith. "Why, there are ocean-liners that carry several times as many."

"You forget," replied Cosmo Versál, "that we must have provisions enough to last for a long time, because we cannot count on the immediate re-emergence of any land, even the most mountainous, and the most compressed food takes space when a great quantity is needed. It won't do to overcrowd the vessel, and invite sickness. Then, too, I must take many animals along."

"Animals," returned Smith. "I hadn't thought of that. But is it necessary?"

"Absolutely. Would you have less foresight than Noah? I shall not imitate him by taking male and female of every species, but I must at least provide for restocking such land as eventually appears above the waters with the animals most useful to man. Then, too, animals are essential to the life of the earth. Any agricultural chemist would tell you that. They play an indispensable part in the vital cycle of the soil. I must also take certain species of insects and birds. I'll telephone Professor Hergeschmitberger at Berlin to learn precisely what are the capitally important species of the animal kingdom."

"And when will you begin the construction of the ark?"

"Instantly. There's not a moment to lose. And it's equally important to send out warnings broadcast immediately. There you can help me. You know what I want to say. Write it out at once; put it as strong as you can; send it everywhere; put it in the shape of posters; hurry it to the newspaper offices. Telephone, in my name, to the Carnegie Institution, to the Smithsonian Institution, to the Royal Society, to the French, Russian, Italian, German, and all the other Academies and Associations of Science to be found anywhere on earth.

"Don't neglect the slightest means of publicity. Thank Heaven, the money to pay for all this is not lacking. If my good father, when he piled up his fortune from the profits of the Transcontinental Aerian Company, could have foreseen the use to which his son would put it for the benefit—what do I say, for the benefit? nay, for the *salvation*—of mankind, he would have rejoiced in his work."

"Ah, that reminds me," exclaimed Joseph Smith. "I was about to ask, a few minutes ago, why airships would not do for this business. Couldn't people save themselves from the flood by taking refuge in the atmosphere?"

Cosmo Versál looked at his questioner with an ironical smile.

"Do you know," he asked, "how long a dirigible can be kept afloat? Do you know for how long a voyage the best aeroplane types can be provisioned with power? There's not an air-ship of any kind that can go more than two weeks at the very uttermost without touching solid earth, and then it must be mighty sparing of its power. If we can save mankind now, and give it another chance, perhaps the time will come when power can be drawn out of the ether of space, and men can float in the air as long as they choose.

"But as things are now, we must go back to Noah's

33. The Japanese division commander committed suicide for the humiliating defeat and the head of the Kwantung Army was forced to resign.
34. Yukuna, *Seito Seiji Hyakunenshi*, p. 136.
35. *Foreign Relations of the United States, Japan, 1931-1941*, vol. 2, p. 219.
36. Ibid., pp. 293-94.
37. Ibid., p. 297.
38. In December 1938, the Export-Import Bank had authorized $25 million credits to a Chinese-owned American corporation.

Chapter 6

1. For the complete text of this pact, see Office of United States Chief of Counsel for Prosecution of Axis Criminality, *Nazi Conspiracy and Aggression*, 8 vols. (Washington, D.C.: Government Printing Office, 1946-1948), vol. 5, pp. 356-57.
2. *Foreign Relations of the United States, Japan, 1931-1941*, vol. 2, p. 169.
3. Ibid., p. 167.
4. Ibid., pp. 172-73.
5. *Department of State Bulletin*, January 4, 1941, pp. 3-8.
6. Ibid., p. 8.
7. *Foreign Relations of the United States, Japan, 1931-1941*, vol. 2, p. 132.
8. H.R. 1776, approved March 11, 1941; 55 Stat. 31.
9. The code name for the Nazi plan of military invasion into the Soviet Union. Early in 1941 the United States government had acquired the information "from reliable and confidential sources that Germany had decided to attack Russia" and had "communicated this information confidentially to the Soviet Ambassador." See *Foreign Relations of the United States, Japan, 1931-1941*, vol. 2, p. 328.
10. For the contents, see Ibid., pp. 398-402. See also John H. Boyle, "The Drought-Walsh Mission to Japan." *Pacific Historical Review*, vol. 36 (May 1965), pp. 141-61.
11. Ibid., p. 407.
12. The "Konoye Principles" included: (1) neighborly friendship, (2) joint defense against communism, and (3) economic cooperation.
13. *Foreign Relations of the United States, Japan, 1931-1941*, vol. 2, p. 504.
14. The United States intelligence community had broken the Japanese codes in the cryptographic operation known as "Magic" and was regularly intercepting and translating Japanese code messages to diplomatic agents abroad. See Roberta Wohlstetter, *Pearl Har-*

bor: Warning and Decision (Stanford: Stanford University Press, 1962).

15. *Foreign Relations of the United States, Japan, 1931–1941*, vol. 2, p. 518.
16. Ibid., p. 555.
17. It would be a pointless conjecture to dwell on what might have happened had the two leaders held the proposed summit conference. It could have produced a compromise agreement acceptable to both sides and might well have succeeded in averting Pearl Harbor, as Ambassador Joseph Grew had believed then and later. On the other hand, a summit impasse might have so exacerbated their relations as to hasten the clash of arms. Konoye's memoirs seemed to indicate that he had been rather optimistic about reaching a reasonable agreement with Roosevelt. Many historians have questioned the American refusal: What harm or risk would such a meeting have brought upon the United States?
18. *Foreign Relations*, pp. 556–57.
19. Yakuna, *Seito Seiji Hyakunenshi*, p. 144.
20. *Foreign Relations of the United States, Japan, 1931–1941*, p. 355.
21. Ibid., pp. 755–56.
22. Cordell Hull, *The Memoirs of Cordell Hull* (New York: Macmillan, 1948), vol. 2, p. 1070.
23. U.S., Congress, *Pearl Harbor Attack: Hearings Before the Joint Committee on the Investigation of the Pearl Harbor Attack*, 79th Congress (Washington, D.C.: Government Printing Office, 1946), part 14, pp. 113–15.
24. See Ike Nobutaka, *Japan's Decision for War: Records of the 1941 Policy Conference* (Stanford: Stanford University Press, 1967).
25. *Foreign Relations of the United States, Japan, 1931–1941*, vol. 2, pp. 377–78.
26. Stimson diary in *Pearl Harbor Attack*, part 2, p. 5433.
27. *Foreign Relations of the United States, Japan, 1931–1941*, vol. 2, pp. 784–86.
28. The attack took place on December 7, 1941, at 1:20 P.M. Washington time (7:50 A.M. Honolulu time), which was December 8, 3:20 A.M. Tokyo time.
29. *Foreign Relations*, p. 787.
30. Ibid., pp. 787–92.
31. See Charles C. Tansill, *Back Door to War: The Roosevelt Foreign Policy* (Chicago: Henry Regnery, 1952); W. H. Chamberlin, *America's Second Crusade* (Chicago: Henry Regnery, 1950); and H. E. Barnes, ed., *Perpetual War for Perpetual Peace* (Idaho: Caxton Printers, 1953).
32. U.S. Congress, *Pearl Harbor Attack*, part 10, pp. 4662–63.

Chapter 7

1. Winston Churchill, *The Grand Alliance* (Boston: Houghton Mifflin, 1950), p. 641.
2. George C. Marshall, H. H. Arnold, and Ernest J. King, *The War Reports . . .* (New York: Lippincott, 1947), pp. 80–81.
3. The Battle of Midway was conceived and planned by Admiral Yamamoto Isoroku, commander-in-chief of the Japanese Imperial Navy, and executed by Admiral Nagumo, the very admiral who had led the Pearl Harbor attack. It should be noted that "Magic" was still in full operation and consequently the United States Navy knew of the Midway plan a month in advance and was well prepared to meet the enemy. In April 1943, "Magic" intercepted Admiral Yamamoto's plan to visit his troops in the Solomons. Knowing his exact flight schedule, a number of American "ace" pilots took off on an aerial ambush and shot him down over Bougainville Island on April 18. See Mikiso Hane, *Japan: A Historical Survey* (New York: Scribner, 1972), p. 534 and p. 538.
4. For the complete text of the Declaration, see Department of State *Bulletin* (November 6, 1943), pp. 308–9.
5. Ibid., December 4, 1943, p. 393.
6. This invasion was code named "Overlord."
7. The famed Admiral Nagumo committed hara-kiri as the Americans were about to capture Saipan, "the naval and military heart and brain of Japanese defense strategy."

   During the battle of Tinian, the United States first used napalm.
8. Kishi became prime minister of Japan, 1957–1960. His brother, Sato Eisaku, held the premiership 1964–1972.
9. Hane, *Japan*, p. 547.
10. Department of State, *Occupation of Japan: Policy and Progress*, Publication 2671 (Washington, D.C.: Government Printing Office, n.d.), pp. 52–53. Cited hereafter as *Occupation of Japan*.
11. The Mongolian People's Republic achieved its formal independence from China in 1946 as a result of a plebiscite to which China had agreed in the Sino-Soviet treaty of 1945. The republic was admitted to the United Nations in 1961.
12. Akira Iriye, *Across the Pacific*, p. 243.
13. He was the American ambassador to Moscow, who accompanied the president at Yalta. Ambassador Averell Harriman and Soviet Foreign Minister V. M. Molotov were the two key architects of the Yalta Agreement.
14. President Roosevelt had died on April 12, 1945, of a massive cerebral hemorrhage at Warm Springs, Georgia, and was succeeded by his vice president Harry S Truman. Incidentally, May 8, 1945, was President Truman's sixty-first birthday.

15. In the summer of 1281, the Mongols dispatched about 140,000 men in an attempt to conquer Japan. Shortly after they reached the coast of North Kyushu, they were struck by a typhoon, which destroyed much of the invading Mongol fleet. Less than half of the Mongols managed to return home in disastrous defeat. The Japanese have attributed their victory to the *Kamikaze* (divine wind) that helped destroy the enemy.

16. The Labor party won the 1945 general elections and its leader, Clement Attlee, became the prime minister who replaced Winston Churchill at the closing session of the conference.

17. Hane, *Japan*, p. 556.

18. Since the Soviet Union was still at peace with Japan, it did not officially become a party to it.

19. Robert J. C. Butow, *Japan's Decision to Surrender* (Stanford: Stanford University Press, 1954), p. 148.

20. *Public Papers of the Presidents, Harry S Truman, 1945* (Washington, D.C.: Government Printing Office, 1961), pp. 197–200.

21. The use of the atomic bomb has become a never-ending controversy. The advocates maintain that it was a military necessity. The atomic bombs made Japan surrender; otherwise the Allies would have been compelled to make a direct invasion into the Japanese mainland, which not only would have prolonged the war but also would have caused an infinitely greater loss of lives, both American and Japanese, than the number of casualties at Hiroshima and Nagasaki by the bombs. In short, the atomic bomb shortened the war and saved lives. The critics, on the other hand, argue that it was an unnecessary, inhumane megaviolence inflicted upon a hopelessly exhausted nation, especially in view of the fact that the United States had known all about the Japanese decision to surrender. The United States, they say, should have let the Japanese know of the invention of the atomic bomb and its horrendous destructive power by means, perhaps, of a demonstrative explosion near Japan. Another theory is that the use of the atomic bomb was designed to overawe the Soviets. See Gar Alperovitz, *Atomic Diplomacy: Hiroshima and Potsdam* (New York: Simon and Schuster, 1965).

22. This provision was eventually incorporated in the Instrument of Japanese Surrender signed on September 2, 1945

23. Wohlstetter, *Pearl Harbor*, p. 350.

24. Thakin Nu, *Burma Under the Japanese* (New York: St. Martin's Press, 1954), p. 84.

25. For the complex and controversial issue of Filipino collaboration with the Japanese, see David Steinberg, "Jose Laurel: A 'Collaborator' Misunderstood," *Journal of Asian Studies*, 24 (1965), pp. 651–65.